The Reformation of the Heart

The Reformation of the Heart

Gender and Radical Theology in the English Revolution

SARAH APETREI

Great Clarendon Street, Oxford, OX2 6DP,
United Kingdom

Oxford University Press is a department of the University of Oxford.
It furthers the University's objective of excellence in research, scholarship,
and education by publishing worldwide. Oxford is a registered trade mark of
Oxford University Press in the UK and in certain other countries

© Sarah Apetrei 2024

The moral rights of the author have been asserted

All rights reserved. No part of this publication may be reproduced, stored in
a retrieval system, or transmitted, in any form or by any means, without the
prior permission in writing of Oxford University Press, or as expressly permitted
by law, by licence or under terms agreed with the appropriate reprographics
rights organization. Enquiries concerning reproduction outside the scope of the
above should be sent to the Rights Department, Oxford University Press, at the
address above

You must not circulate this work in any other form
and you must impose this same condition on any acquirer

Published in the United States of America by Oxford University Press
198 Madison Avenue, New York, NY 10016, United States of America

British Library Cataloguing in Publication Data
Data available

Library of Congress Control Number: 2023943384

ISBN 978–0–19–883600–1

DOI: 10.1093/oso/9780198836001.001.0001

Printed and bound in the UK by
Clays Ltd, Elcograf S.p.A.

Links to third party websites are provided by Oxford in good faith and
for information only. Oxford disclaims any responsibility for the materials
contained in any third party website referenced in this work.

For Daniel

Acknowledgements

My thanks go first to my son Daniel, who was my constant, lovely, patient companion throughout intense writing sessions in the autumn of 2022. On a related note, my debt to the makers of all fourteen films in *The land before time* series, and the National Geographic solar system videos, is not inconsiderable.

This book happened gradually, and then suddenly. It would not have been written without past periods of research funded by the British Academy and the Panacea Society with Goldsmiths College, and leave granted by Keble College.

Conversations and collaborations with each of the following have inspired and shaped the book in different ways: Daphne Hampson, Hilary Hinds, Ariel Hessayon, Philip Lockley, Diarmaid MacCulloch, Charlotte Methuen, Paul Monod, Sarah Mortimer, George Pattison, Christopher Rowland, Alec Ryrie, Jane Shaw, Hannah Smith, Nigel Smith, Johannes Zachhuber, and Simeon Zahl. I remain indebted to teachers and advisors from an earlier time in my life: Wolfgang Behringer, John Bossy, Ian Cawood, Judith Maltby, David McKinnon-Bell, and Lyndal Roper.

For their encouragement and support at different times, I am sincerely grateful to Anna Sapir Abulafia, Markus Bockmuehl, Kylie Crabbe, Nathan Eubank, Sarah Foot, Carol Harrison, Christine Joynes, Mary Marshall, Alister McGrath, Sarah Mortimer, Joel Rasmussen, Jenn Strawbridge, William Wood, and Mark Wynn. A number of brilliant graduate students have greatly enriched my research, among them Elliott Cramer, Colin Donnelly, James Hooks, Madeleine Pennington, Naomi Richman, Lucy Walton, Paul Williams, and Rick Yoder (who provided first-rate research assistance for a brief period).

For sharing this life and for always providing a horizon, I thank Marian Davidson, Lis Jardine, Catherine Kennedy, and Richard Trethewey. For sustaining friendship, I thank Sophie Cartwright, Nick Fowler, Michael Hawcroft, Dominic Keech, Sam Kiss, Elliott Ing, Daniel Inman, Fran Roach, Iain Trethewey, Ruth Trethewey, Jude Verjee, Hannah Vickery, Jonathan Vickery, Alan Waters, Alison Waters, and my wider family.

My final, heartfelt thanks are offered to Marius, who taught me so much about the mystical tradition, and to my parents, Fred and Margaret Trethewey, who taught me everything that matters. Between them, they have been to me the enduring love by which I know something of the great love that is all in all.

Contents

List of Illustrations — xi
    Introduction — 1
1. Incarnation — 26
2. Salvation — 55
3. Revelation — 79
4. Grace and Sin — 113
5. Song — 138
6. Church — 165
    Conclusion — 193

Bibliography — 199
Index — 217

List of Illustrations

Cover image. Title page to John Saltmarsh, *Holy discoveries and flames* (London, 1640), sig. A2v. By permission of the Bodleian Libraries, University of Oxford, shelfmark Vet. A2 f.241.

1. Title page to anon. *A discoverie of six women preachers* (London, 1641), sig. A1r. By permission of the Bodleian Libraries, University of Oxford, shelfmark Wood 654a (5). — 9

2. The opening of the spiritual eye, in John Pordage, *Theologia mystica* (London, 1683), adj. p. 29. By permission of the Bodleian Libraries, University of Oxford, shelfmark Lawn f. 479. — 47

3. The vision of God, in Giles Randall, *Ophthalmos aplois, or the single eye* (London, 1646), sig. A1v. By permission of the British Library Board, shelfmark E. 1212. — 90

4. Detail of title page to Anon., *The Quakers dream* (London, 1655). By permission of the British Library Board, shelfmark E.833 (14). — 151

5. 'Debora', in Pierre Le Moyne, *The gallery of heroick women* (London, 1652), adj. p. 1. By permission of the Taylor Institution Library, Bodleian Libraries, University of Oxford, shelfmark 86.I.10.A. — 158

6. God and man, in Hendrik Niclaes, *A figure of the true and spiritual tabernacle* (London, 1655), p. 109. By permission of the Bodleian Libraries, University of Oxford, shelfmark S. 23 (1) Th. BS. — 171

7. The cosmos, in Robert Fludd, *Utriusque cosmi maioris scilicet et minoris metaphysica* (London, 1617), p. 141. By permission of the Bodleian Libraries, University of Oxford, shelfmark Ashm. 1699. — 182

Introduction

Historians have long been fascinated by two related aspects of the English Revolution in the 1640s and 1650s: the unprecedented prominence of women as preachers, prophets, and pamphleteers; and the emergence of radical religious ideas. In both cases, the enthusiasm of an earlier generation of historians in discovering the precocity or 'modernity' of these phenomena has been tempered by scholarship questioning the extent (and even the existence) of genuine radicalism in this period. There remains, however, a growing body of literature on radical religious movements and their ideas, as well as on the women of the Revolution. It is hard to dismiss their importance altogether as points of discontinuity, fresh horizons, in the febrile climate of civil war and political disturbance. It is striking that the intellectual history of radical religion and the study of female participation have proceeded more or less along separate tracks, despite the fact that women prophets and preachers came to public attention first in connection with a radical milieu or network linking elements in the New Model Army with certain Baptist and Independent congregations across England. This study seeks to offer a fresh assessment of the theological radicalism of this milieu, using gender as a primary lens. I hope to contribute to the understanding both of female participation in the religious reform movements of the Revolution, and of the intellectual formation of religious radicalism. The involvement of women does not appear to me a secondary or incidental feature of the religious challenge: radicalism on gender was integral. On the other hand, using gender as an analytical tool helps to isolate the distinctiveness of key themes and doctrines in radical thought, and to identify more precisely the nature of its sources and origins: whether Reformation spiritualism or the English separatist tradition.

The 'reformation of the heart' is the designation I am using in this book for the phase of the Revolution under consideration, spanning roughly the years between 1646 and 1654. It was a phrase used controversially by the army chaplain William Dell in a sermon before the House of Commons on 25 November 1646, following the systematic dismantling of the established episcopal church by the Long Parliament. By 'heart reformation', Dell did not mean simply the renewal of piety, the conversion of life, which all early modern church leaders (whether episcopal, Presbyterian, or Catholic) intended as an outworking of ecclesiastical reform. He preached vehemently that the reformation of the heart was not allied, but *opposed*, to the movements of church reform which had characterized the foregoing century. 'True Gospel Reformation', he wrote, 'is a cleer different thing from Civil-Ecclesiasticall Reformation'. The reformation of liturgy, doctrine, the clergy, and church government was 'but a carnall Reformation, wrought by the power of flesh and blood, and stands in outward and fleshly things'. True reformation wrought by God was 'an inward Reformation', it 'layes hold upon the heart, and soul, and inner man, and changes, and alters, and renews, and reforms that; and when the heart is reformed, all is reformed'.[1] It was a sermon that would make Dell notorious. The printed version, *Right reformation*, was classified as an 'Objectionable Publication', and Dell and his printer (Giles Calvert) were summoned by the House of Commons to answer for its contents.[2] The sermon also provoked a backlash in print. Samuel Rutherford, a Presbyterian commentator, identified Dell with a Familistical, Antinomian, Anabaptist strain in English religion, as he 'onely mindes the reformation of the heart', and taught that 'All Ordinances, hearing, preaching, Scripture, scripture-learning, Baptisme, the Lords Supper, all confession of Christ before men, all externalls in religion are things of no worth, indifferent, free, triviall'.[3] Christopher Love, the Welsh Presbyterian divine, also wrote in reaction to Dell's sermon, noting that 'Master Del knowes no other Gospell Reformation besides heart Reformation'. He showed his colours as 'a grosse Antinomian' by his conclusion that all 'Laws and Ordinances devised by men... are therefore all to be at an end when this time of Reformation comes'.[4]

William Dell's proclamation of a spiritual revolution, to nullify all previous reformations focused on the external trappings of religion, fell in the midst of escalating antagonism between army and parliament, following the end of the first civil war and fierce debates over the role of the magistrate in determining a religious settlement. A good deal of contentious energy arose from bitter disputes on this question between Independents and Presbyterians in the Westminster Assembly. Dell's sermon formed part of what David Como has recently called a 'war on ordinances', or what J.C. Davis characterized as an 'anti-formalist' movement, which emerged as a force in the mid-1640s and was profoundly disruptive to the orthodox Reformed agenda in parliament.[5] As Anthony Milton has observed, Dell's challenge was anticipated 'right at the beginning of the parliamentarian Reformation' in a debate between the royalist churchman Thomas Fuller and the parliamentarian John Saltmarsh in 1643. Saltmarsh criticized

---

[1] William Dell, *Right reformation: or, the reformation of the church of the New Testament, represented in Gospell-Light* (London, 1646), p. 6.
[2] 'House of Commons Journal Volume 5: 12 December 1646', *Journal of the House of Commons*, vol. 5: *1646–1648* (London, 1802), pp. 10–11.
[3] Samuel Rutherford, *A survey of the spirituall Antichrist opening the secrets of familisme and antinomianisme in the antichristian doctrine of John Saltmarsh and Will. Del* (London, 1648), p. 60.
[4] Christopher Love, *Short and plaine animadversions on some passages in Mr Dels sermon* (London, 1647), pp. 4, 7. Love had been converted by another radical army preacher, William Erbery—his 'spirituall Father'—but came to reject his 'dangerous opinions'. See Christopher Love, *A cleare and necessay vindication of the principles and practices of me Christopher Love* (London, 1651), p. 36.
[5] David Como, *Radical parliamentarians and the English Civil War* (Oxford: Oxford University Press, 2021), pp. 384–408.

those who made of church reformation 'a work of Policy, not of Piety, of Reason not Divinity', and saw true Reformation as something 'extraordinary', wrought by the 'inward call' of God in the hearts of the people.[6] Dell and Saltmarsh, along with other army chaplains, came to be central to a radical network, expectant of the dawning of a spiritual dispensation which would supersede the foregoing covenants of Law and Gospel. This is what I regard as 'mystical radicalism': radical in the sense that, following J.C. Davis's broad definition, it challenged the very foundations of existing structures, envisaging a new order of things, and did not simply seek to return to those foundations.[7] It was mystical both in that it heralded the revelation of mysteries long concealed; and in that it drew deeply from and paralleled wider early modern mystical and visionary currents (Paracelsian, Behmenist, Familist, even Catholic).[8] The essence of these radicals' vision was *discontinuity* with a discredited and lifeless religion; not merely a critique of its degeneracy from primitive roots.

This book examines the relationship between theological radicalism and gender radicalism in the 'reformation of the heart'. The study is focused mainly on the period 1646 to 1654, an interval which opens with the challenge of the radical mystics (or 'sectaries', or 'enthusiasts', or 'seekers') erupting in the public sphere, not least as the career of the radical publisher Giles Calvert gathered momentum. This was in the context of bitter disputes over the nature of England's religious settlement, as the episcopal church and its liturgy had been legally abolished. The main period under consideration concludes following the dissolution of the Nominated Assembly in December 1653, and abandonment of radical hopes in a godly parliament to bring about the government of the saints. It stops short of the emergence of Quakerism as a major movement, which harnessed so many of the energies of the early mystical radicals, and brought to fruition earlier trends towards female participation in preaching and prophetic vocations. The heart reformation represented the quest for the mystical New Jerusalem of a network of spiritual revolutionaries active in the period after 1645, centred on the army

---

[6] See Anthony Milton, *England's second Reformation: the battle for the Church of England* (Cambridge: Cambridge University Press, 2021), pp. 219, 260; John Saltmarsh, *Examinations, or a discovery of some dangerous positions* (London, 1643), pp. 4, 5.

[7] J.C. Davis, *Alternative worlds imagined, 1500–1700: essays on radicalism, utopianism and reality* (London: Palgrave Macmillan, 2017), p. 26.

[8] It may be significant, in terms of locating a network of interests in mystical anthropology in the revolutionary period, that other calls for a 'reformation of the heart' included the famous sermon before the Commons by the Platonist Ralph Cudworth, preached just a few months after the Dell controversy, in Mar. 1647: *A sermon preached before the Honourable House of Commons at Westminster, March 31, 1647* (London, 1647), pp. 81–2. Cudworth, like Dell, had been at Emmanuel College, Cambridge, in the 1630s. Another Cambridge fellow of the 1630s with interests in mystical and Platonist theology but also alleged Familist connections, Robert Gell, was minister at St Mary Aldermary from 1641, and in an undated sermon (published posthumously) taught there that true reformation was not the business of purifying ordinances, or psalm singing, or Bible reading or any other such 'outward Sanctimony, all palpable and visible', but the 'Reformation of the heart, and affections'. See Robert Gell, 'Notes and observations upon Matthew v.22', in R. Bacon, ed., *Gell's remaines, or, select several Scriptures of the New Testament opened and explained* (London, 1676), pp. 61–2.

preachers, but also linking radical congregations in the city of London with communities in the provinces and beyond. These radical mystics came to see the Revolution in terms of an inward apocalypse, or the rising of Christ in the hearts of the saints. It was, I argue, a movement both more radical in its theology and more united in its promotion of female activists than has been fully recognized. Variously evolving as Fifth Monarchist resistance or Quaker spiritualism in the 1650s, these groups inspired women and men to advocate openly for female and lay preachers and prophets, as part of a comprehensive programme of renewal and levelling. In particular sections of the book, evidence will be examined from a later period, but this is taken from communities and movements with their origins in the revolutionary years, with a view to illuminating those origins as well as tracking legacies and development. My primary aim is to contribute to the historical understanding of women's religious activism in the Revolution, by taking a fresh look at the challenging and often remarkable world of ideas in the radical mystical milieu in which female participation was fostered, within this closely defined scope. A secondary aim is to build on recent research into English radicalism to illuminate further the wider European context for the lay visionary culture of the Revolution, and the gender imagery and themes which emerged therein.

The disruption to gender conventions cannot simply be attributed to an apocalyptic sensibility, whereby conventional Protestants were authorized by Scripture (Joel 2.28 and Acts 2.17) to accept the prophetic gifting of 'sons and daughters' alike. Neither was women's preaching merely an expedient in a time of crisis. Mystical revolutionaries not only challenged the 'formality' of the churches, and the Reformed doctrine of grace (both of which are well established as radical concerns), but showed a remarkable radicalism on core Christian doctrines: on concepts of God, the singularity of the incarnation, the scope of salvation, and revelation in Scripture. At the same moment as patriarchal institutions were being shaken, the words of female prophets, preachers, and pamphleteers were embraced by the most visionary reformers as instantiations of the living Word, authenticated by their distance from institutional power. What was at stake in both the most profound theological iconoclasm of the period and the radicals' opening up to women's prophetic voices was the rejection of an objectified God. Inspired by the collapse of so many received institutions, radical theologians (lay and ordained, female and male) also reassessed what they saw as the conception of a God external to oneself, fixed in time by the single historical reference point of the incarnation, bound up in a closed canon of revealed texts. Instead, they taught what might be called a 'subjectivized' doctrine of God, exceeding the mystical union with Christ mediated by Scripture knowledge, preaching, and sacraments in the magisterial Reformation churches. Divine love and knowledge were rising in women and men, in a second birth of Christ bearing fresh revelations. This rising would overtake not only the external institution of the church, but also the partial discoveries of God under the retreating Gospel dispensation.

The gender radicalism of this heart reformation is perhaps surprising, considering its prominence within a military context. There is a vital connection between reformism on women's status and the Leveller movement within the army, with its assertion of universal human dignity and rights, and repudiation of traditional hierarchies. John Saltmarsh, who acted as chaplain to Sir Thomas Fairfax from May 1646, was a vehement supporter of Leveller politics and reputedly radical on female ministry before his military career began. It was said by Thomas Edwards that he allowed women to 'break bread', or preside, at the Lord's Supper, while rector of Brasted in Kent from 1645-6.[9] Saltmarsh was undoubtedly one of the most original and powerful of the New Model Army preachers, and others may have developed as radicals under his influence. To varying extents and in distinctive ways, other army chaplains—William Dell, William Erbery, Henry Pinnell, Abiezer Coppe, William Sedgwick, John Webster—were theologically radical on gender and women's ministry, as well as being politically radical, either defending women's preaching explicitly or openly supporting female prophets. The army chaplains formed the core of a network perhaps best conceptualized as a 'radical milieu', to borrow Christopher Hill's designation.[10] In the period under consideration, it does not work to think in terms of hard denominational boundaries between the various groups and doctrines which interacted, with communities sharing itinerant preachers and exchanging ideas.[11] Lawrence Clarkson's report of his own peregrinations among radical religious groups in the mid-1640s, leading him from mainstream churches to Baptist, Seeker, and Ranter groups has been famously questioned as a reliable source, but it perhaps illustrates something of the volatility of commitments and fluidity of identities amid the turmoil.[12] It is possible to identify specific instances in which radical reforming groups collaborated or converged: the audience attracted by the Baptist prophetess Sarah Wight in 1647, for instance, included fellow Baptists but also prominent Independent ministers such as Thomas Goodwin and Walter Cradock (See below, pp. 118-20). The gathered church founded and hosted by Dorothy Hassard in Bristol eventually became established as a Particular Baptist congregation, but in the

---

[9] Thomas Edwards, *Gangraena* (London, 1646). p. 89. Saltmarsh dismissed this in print as 'a meere untruth', but in other writings, he expressly supported the principle of women's preaching. See John Saltmarsh, 'Groanes for liberty', *Some drops of the viall, powred out in a season, when it is neither night nor day* (London, 1646), p. 91.

[10] Christopher Hill, *Milton and English Revolution* (London: Verso, 2020), p. 100.

[11] On the 'dangers and potential anachronism of denominational labelling', see Davis, *Alternative worlds imagined*, p. 142; also Matthew Bingham, *Orthodox radicals: Baptist identity in the English Revolution* (Oxford: Oxford University Press, 2019), pp. 3-6.

[12] Lawrence Clarkson, *The lost sheep found* (London, 1660). The reliability of Clarkson's account has been most notoriously challenged in J.C. Davis, *Fear, myth and history: the Ranters and the historians* (Cambridge: Cambridge University Press, 1986), especially pp. 64-74.

1640s various itinerants were associated with the church: among them Henry Pinnell, and, again, Cradock, alongside other Welsh preachers.

There remain unanswerable questions about the numerical significance, and the extent of the influence, of the mystical radicals. The great historian of the New Model Army, Mark Kishlansky, concluded that the roles of the radical army chaplains 'have certainly been overplayed'; radical doctrines, he noted, 'existed in far greater profusion in London'.[13] Anne Laurence's subsequent study of parliamentary army chaplains indicated that there was no hegemony of the radicals over the religious ideology of the army itself, or independence from metropolitan radicalism.[14] More recent historiography has linked religious radicalism in the army more firmly not only to elements in London and to the patronage of army grandees, but also to the provincial towns and cities, where women and men were electrified and galvanized by the preaching of an Erbery or a Sedgwick.[15] Ian Gentles has also, however, restored to central view the undoubted charisma and popularity of the radical chaplains within the New Model Army. He reminds us of narratives of soldiers climbing trees to hear Dell, Sedgwick, or Saltmarsh preach, even though their sermons could last up to two hours. Gentles has also observed that the 'spiritual egalitarianism preached by Dell, Saltmarsh and Peters' was a serious force within the army: a powerfully unitive message of solidarity, fellowship, and equality.[16] It was a message with realized implications for gender relations, as well as for a brotherhood at arms. The 'mystical radicals' under consideration in this study include many, especially women, who were outside the army, but the chaplains and lay preachers to the army—immortalized by William Prynne as 'prodigious new wandring-blasing-stars'—feature centrally.[17] The affinities between them on gender but also on key, distinctive points of doctrine—notably apocalyptic ideas about the 'heavenly flesh' of Christ and the saints (see Chapter 1)—points to a coherent culture of radical theology, springing up within and beyond the army.

Instances of women's prominence, and gender radicalism, in the period of crisis in the 1640s seem to reflect the progression of existing ideas and trends among radical separatists. In his seminal article on 'Women and the civil war sects', Keith Thomas noted that the English separatist congregations in the Netherlands had debated the participation of women as prophets and as full voting members, in the

---

[13] Mark Kishlansky, *The rise of the New Model Army* (Cambridge: Cambridge University Press, 1979), pp. 71–2.

[14] Anne Laurence, *Parliamentary army chaplains, 1642-1651*, Royal Historical Society Studies in History (Woodbridge: Boydell Press, 1992), pp. 76–87.

[15] See, for instance, Como, *Radical parliamentarians*.

[16] Ian Gentles, *The New Model Army: agent of revolution* (New Haven and London: Yale University Press, 2022), pp. 49–50, 53–5.

[17] William Prynne, *A fresh discovery of some prodigious new wandring-blasing-stars & Firebrands* (London, 1645).

early Stuart period.[18] There are indications that women were assuming roles of spiritual authority in certain groups and networks in England before 1640. A Northumberland gentlewoman, Anne Fenwick (or 'Phoenix') gained some reputation in Puritan circles in the 1620s and 1630s for her gifting as a prophetess, and her biblical commentary.[19] Her published *Collection of certain promises out of the word of God* (1629; with a new edition in 1631) set out a fairly conventional Calvinist anthropology, though it hinted at more radical promises of direct relevation, mystical union, and liberation from ecclesiastical tyranny, which would become so central to discussions of women's participation in the 'reformation of the heart'. God would 'work in the hearts of his people, even to make them partakers of the divine nature'; the Holy Spirit would be the inward teacher, planting knowledge of God in the hearts of the least as well as the greatest; the saints would be strengthened under the 'feare of wicked sheepheards'.[20] Most notably, of course, in the context of the Boston settlement in New England, the Lincolnshire woman Anne Hutchinson became a leading actor in an 'antinomian' or 'free-grace' movement in the mid-1630s. At the heart of this controversy lay claims about union with Christ and the immediate inspiration of the Holy Spirit. It was suggested by Henry Church that women were foremost in English antinomian circles: 'their forces consist first of women, their front is ranked with them'.[21] It is undoubtedly the case that a number of English women, isolated from each other but with shared grievances and aspirations, became radicalized during the early Stuart period, especially at the time of the Laudian reforms. Katherine Chidley, who would become a proponent of religious toleration and leader in the Leveller movement, was conventicling in Shrewsbury in the 1620s, and refusing to be churched following childbirth.[22] Grace Cary, the widow of a Bristol brewer living in rural Monmouthshire, was granted an audience with Charles I in 1639, aided by the Marquess of Hamilton, to present her 'revelations and visions'. These included highly inflammatory references to a 'cruel queen' and to the 'loud and lamentable cries of God's people persecuted'.[23] In Lichfield in 1636–7, the aristocratic prophetess Eleanor Davies, together with her friends Susan Walker and

---

[18] Keith Thomas, 'Women and the civil war sects', *Past and Present* 13 (1958), p. 46. See also Elaine Hobby, *Virtue of necessity: English women's writing 1649–1688* (London: Virago, 1988), p. 36.

[19] See David Como, 'Women, prophecy and authority in Early Stuart Puritanism', *Huntingdon Library Quarterly* 61:2 (1998), pp. 203–22.

[20] Anne Phoenix, *The saints legacies or, a collection of certain promises out of the Holy Scripture* (London, 1629), §. I5r, pp. 62–7, 130–1.

[21] Henry Church, *Divine and Christian letters to relieve the oppressed* (London, 1636), pp. 27–8; see also David Como, *Blown by the Spirit: Puritanism and the emergence of an antinomian underground in pre-Civil-War England* (Stanford: Stanford University Press, 2004), p. 52.

[22] See Ian Gentles, 'Katherine Chidley (fl. 1616–1653)', in David Cannadine, ed., *The Oxford dictionary of national biography* (Oxford: Oxford University Press, 2004).

[23] See David Cressy, *Charles I and the people of England* (Oxford: Oxford University Press, 2015), pp. 200–1; also 'Visions and Revelations to Grace Carye', in Cambridge University Library, Additional MS 32.

Marie Noble, made a series of provocative gestures challenging the clerical hierarchy at the cathedral (see p. 64), and claiming episcopal authority over all England. This was in direct defiance of Laud's personal authority, but also the ecclesiastical order he represented.

The involvement of women in the resistance movement against the Babylonian church of bishops and Prayer Book was not, however, universally welcomed by those seeking to perfect England's Reformation. Women's preaching and ministry were among the great scandals of the revolutionary period, and panic about social disorder and inversions of authority early on in the crisis found a focus in the figure of the female preacher. Famously, in 1641, a pamphlet 'discovered' to the world the sensational activities of six women preachers in Middlesex, Kent, Cambridgeshire, and Salisbury (Figure 1). They were said by the (unsympathetic) author to have asserted themselves because of 'a deficiency of good men'; the male ministers could offer nothing 'but to make their texts good by expounding the language of the Beast'. The women, by contrast, 'would preach nothing, but such things as the spirit should move them'.[24] Anne Hempstall from the parish of St Andrew's Holborn was the 'first and chief of this female and Sacerdoticall function', bringing together an assembly of women to whom she described a prophetic dream in which she was visited by the biblical prophetess, Anna. The report suggests that Hempstall interpreted this as the passing on of the prophetic mantle, which she herself then bestowed upon her female audience: she 'cryed out, Now doth the Holy Ghost descend downe upon you'.[25] She inspired, it is suggested, a number of other 'female Teachers' in the locality. Several other publications from the period 1640–2 cited women preachers as a sign of the growing breakdown in social relations and the established order: women were said to 'catechize and preach' in a Brownist congregation; or freely to 'vent their opinions' on religious matters in the sects.[26] While the evidence for female preaching is sparse for the earlier 1640s, it is clear that women were mobilized and engaged by the wars in unprecedented and highly visible ways: news pamphlets reported on the 'many hundreds of women who crie for peace' in what amounted to a mass protest at Westminster in the summer of 1643.[27]

Anxieties about women's preaching were not, it seems, entirely baseless, and they continued to beset the opponents of the sects, especially the leaders of the Presbyterian faction desperate to rein in the most radical forces unleashed by the crisis. In 1645, William Prynne accused Independents of 'admitting Women, not

---

[24] Anon., *A discoverie of six women preachers, in Middlesex, Kent, Cambridgeshire, and Salisbury* (London, 1641), p. 1.
[25] Anon., *A discoverie of six women preachers*, p. 2.
[26] Quoted in David Cressy, *England on edge: crisis and revolution, 1640–1642* (Oxford: Oxford University Press, 2006), p. 242.
[27] Anon., *Parliament scout communicating his intelligence to the kingdome* (London, 10 Aug. 1643), p. 55.

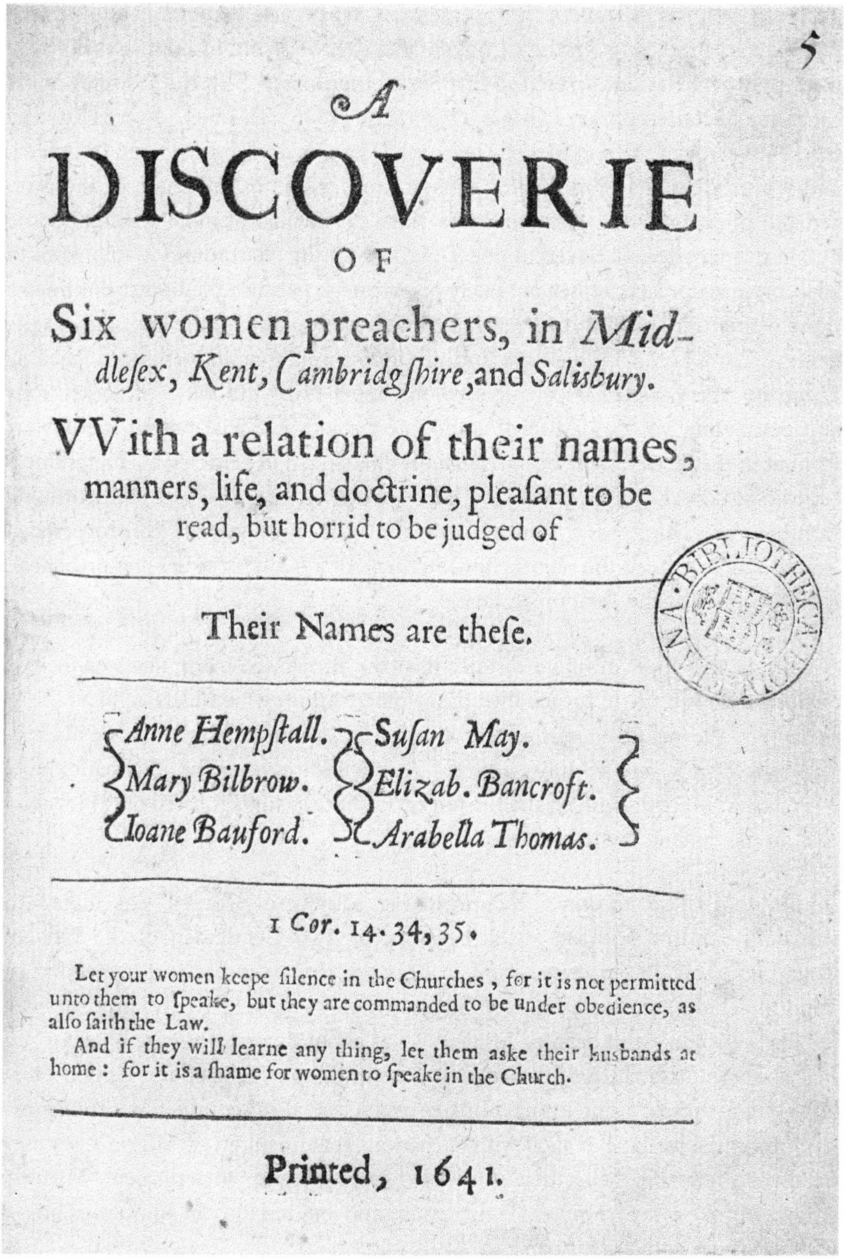

A DISCOVERIE OF

Six women preachers, in *Middlesex*, *Kent*, *Cambridgshire*, and *Salisbury*.

VVith a relation of their names, manners, life, and doctrine, pleasant to be read, but horrid to be judged of

---

Their Names are these.

Anne Hempstall. Susan May.
Mary Bilbrow. Elizab. Bancroft.
Ioane Bauford. Arabella Thomas.

---

1 *Cor.* 14. 34, 35.

Let your women keepe silence in the Churches, for it is not permitted unto them to speake, but they are commanded to be under obedience, as also saith the Law.

And if they will learne any thing, let them aske their husbands at home: for it is a shame for women to speake in the Church.

Printed, 1641.

Figure 1 Title page to anon. *A discoverie of six women preachers* (London, 1641), sig. A1r.

onely to vote as members, but sometimes to preach, expound, and speake publikely as Predicants, in their Conventicles'. He was convinced that this was 'a meer politick invention to engage that Sex to their party'.[28] In the first part of his catalogue of contemporary heresies, *Gangraena* (1646), Thomas Edwards listed as the 124th error of the sectaries the teaching 'That 'tis lawfull fo women to preach, and why should they not, having gifts as well as men? And some of them do actually preach, having great resort to them'. A further scandal was that some heroic women, 'ten or eleven in one Town or vicinity', had found it 'unlawfull to hear any man preach, either publikely or privately, because they must not be like those women in Timothy, ever learning, and never coming to the knowledg of the truth, 2 Tim. 3.6.7'.[29] (There are, indeed, indications that some women, such as Elizabeth Avery, were boycotting sermons, repelled by the Babel of contentious and competing voices.) Edwards undoubtedly had a special hatred for upstart women in the sects, having been repeatedly challenged in print for his hierarchical ecclesiology by Katherine Chidley. He was not alone, however, in identifying women's preaching as a growing menace. The Presbyterian controversialist Robert Baillie echoed the reports in *Gangraena* of a network of women preachers, in his account of the London sectaries:

> Only in this they are more distinct then the Brownists, many more of their women do venture to preach then of the other; *Attaway* the Mistresse of all the She-preachers in *Colemanstreet* was a disciple in *Lambs* Congregation, and made Antipaedobaptism oftentimes a part of her publick exercises: the other feminine Preachers in *Kent, Norfolk,* and the rest of the Shires had their breeding, as I take it, in the same or the like school.[30]

In some of these accounts, the preaching activity of women was linked to sexual libertinism. Edwards tells the story of 'two Gentlemen of the Inns of Court' who, out of curiosity, 'went to hear the women preach' at a meeting in London. These men were engaged in discussion by the elusive 'Mistris Attaway the Lace-woman', who debated Milton's ideas about divorce with them (reporting that she was dissatisfied with her own husband's spirituality), and denied everlasting damnation.[31] The implied link between sexual misconduct and transgressive preaching is made explicit with allegations that, inspired by Milton's writings on divorce and her belief that she was called to preach in Jerusalem, Mistress Attaway broke away from her lawful spouse and entered into an adulterous union with 'another womans husband'.[32]

---

[28] Anon., *Parliament scout*, p. 47.   [29] Edwards, *Gangraena*, p. 26.
[30] Robert Baillie, *Anabaptism, the true fountaine of Independency, Brownisme, Antinomy, Familisme* (London, 1647), p. 53.
[31] Thomas Edwards, *The second part of Gangraena* (London, 1646), p. 9.
[32] Edwards, *The second part of Gangraena*, p. 9; Thomas Edwards, *The third part of Gangraena* (London, 1646), pp. 26–7.

Reports of the activity of women preachers reached the heart of government. A delegation of the aldermen and Common Council of the City of London came before the House of Commons on 15th January 1646, to 'acquaint the House with some Instances of private Meetings of Women-Preachers of new and strange Doctrines and Blasphemies that are vented; and of great Rents and Divisions in divers and sundry Families in and about the City'. The House referred the matter to the Committee of Examinations.[33] An intelligence letter dated October 1647 told

> of a Sect of woemen (they are at Southworke) come from beyond the Sea, called Quakers, and these swell, shiver, and shake, and when they come to themselves (for in all this fitt Mahomett's holy-ghost hath bin conversing with them) preache what hath bin delivered to them by the Spiritt.[34]

The reference to the inspiration of 'Mahomett's holy-ghost' is not to be taken as a suggestion that these were converts to Islam, or travellers from the Muslim world, but rather it illustrates the tendency of hostile commentators to portray female preachers and prophets as exotic, and un-Christian. The association with Islam also stemmed from that religion's stereotyped reputation for 'enthusiasm', and ecstatic or visionary experience.[35] Popular hostility towards women preaching was in evidence in London on a Sunday in July 1653, when 'a woman preached in the pulpit at Somerset-house, but was carried away by the soldiers, or else the people would have stoned her'.[36] Another royalist letter, intercepted by John Thurloe's agents in the summer of 1653, reported growing disorder under the Nominated Assembly, the temporary parliament of the saints: they 'pretend their immediate power from the Lord', meanwhile the 'soldiers begin to be unruly, the women begin to preach'.[37]

Clearly, many of these reports were politically charged, and the threat was exaggerated. Nonetheless, it seems clear that, at least from 1645–6 and probably earlier, women's preaching was seriously countenanced, practised in places, and elsewhere debated, especially among Independent and Baptist congregations, and indeed within the army, where so many 'settled' questions were up for discussion. In his *Certain scruples from the army* dated June 1647, the pro-army printer John

---

[33] 'House of Commons Journal Volume 4: 15 January 1646', *Journal of the House of Commons*, vol. 4: *1644–1646* (London, 1802), p. 407.
[34] Letter from Secretary Nicholas, 14 Oct. 1647, in Bodleian Library, Clarendon MS 30, letter no. 2624, fol. 140.
[35] In 1642, for instance, a report from the English ambassador of a vision of a celestial woman was published, with its 'Propheticall interpretation made by a Mahumetan Priest'. Anon., *Strange and miraculous newes from Turkie* (London, 1642).
[36] 'For Raph, July 21 [1653]', in 'State Papers, 1653: July (4 of 5)', in Thomas Birch, ed., *A Collection of the State Papers of John Thurloe*, vol. 1: *1638–1653* (London, 1742), p. 368.
[37] 'An intercepted letter. London 11/1 August, 1653', in Birch, *A Collection*, p. 393.

Pounset published as a dialogue the outlines of debate between a Presbyterian minister and a soldier on this issue. Following a discussion of Acts 8, and the soldier's argument that laymen were authorized to preach by the apostle, the Presbyterian seeks to catch out his disputant: 'I thought where I should have you, then it seemes women and all may preach, by your grounds?' The soldier replies: 'Yes, for it is warranted by Scriptures; for I know no difference betwee preaching, and prophecying... and it is cleare that women may prophesie'. He then lists examples of gifted women in the New Testament:

> The woman of Samaria brought many of her City to beleeve in Christ, by her testify what shee had heard, and learned of Christ, Joh. 4.39. Priscilla did preach the way of God more perfectly, to him that was a Preacher of it before, Act. 18.26. Paul intreateth his true yoke fellow, to help those women, which laboured with him in the Gospel, Phil. 4.3 we see Paul was a man of a gallant, free, self-denying spirit he did rejoyce if Christ was preached, either by men or women; he did not feare the eclipsing of his own glory (he stood more upon the glory of God) notwithstanding he knew some did preach to that end, Phil. 1.16.[38]

Whether or not it is plausible to see Paul as a 'gallant, free, self-denying spirit', it is striking that these manly qualities were invoked in defence of women's preaching: the nobility of Paul lies in his fearlessness about the risk to his own dignity of a gifted female. Pounset's soldier goes on to qualify his advocacy of women preachers, agreeing with the Presbyterian that Paul excludes women's preaching 'in the Church', but 'out of the Church he leaves them to their liberty'.[39] This chimes with a similar argument put forward by the Baptist itinerant Thomas Collier, a lay preacher to the army, who acknowledged that the apostle prohibited women from preaching publicly in the church, but was rather ambiguous as to whether or not the prohibition still pertained in a new age of prophecy in which 'this silly distinction of publike, private, &c' rang hollow.[40] Ultimately, Collier concluded that 'God is free... and worketh by whom and how he pleaseth'.[41] Parallel debates were held in individual gathered churches. In January 1654, Anne Harriman refused to attend meetings at a Baptist congregation in London because one Brother Naudin 'said he would not walk with such as gave libertie to woemen to speak in the Church'. Harriman herself concluded that she 'could not walk where she had not libertie to speak'. The congregation then debated women's speaking, and determined that 'a Woeman (Mayd, Wife,

---

[38] John Pounset, *Certaine scruples from the army: presented in a dialogue between a minister of the new moulded Presbytery, and a souldier of his Excellencies (formerly new-moulded, but now despised) army* (London, 1647), p. 9.
[39] Pounset, *Certaine scruples*, p. 9.
[40] Thomas Collier, *The pulpit-guard routed, in its twenty strong-holds* (London, 1651), p. 93.
[41] Collier, *The pulpit-guard routed*, p. 102.

or Widdow) being a Prophetess 1. Cor:11 may speake, Prophesie, Pray, with a Vayl. Others may not'.[42]

In other congregations, while women may not have preached, they were so integral to the community that their leadership roles were unquestioned. Dorothy Hassard (née Kelly) pioneered the founding of a separatist congregation in Bristol, which later developed as the Broadmead Baptist Church. Her story has long been familiar to those interested in the role played by women in the Puritan reaction of the 1640s, and has recently been important in the reconstruction of the radical milieu in Bristol.[43] There are many points of connection with army radicalism: Hassard influenced the spiritual development of the army chaplain Henry Pinnell, discussed at various points in this book; Hassard's son Abel Kelly served in the parliamentarian army; and the Bristol godly network was associated with Levellers like Nicholas Cowling.[44] Edward Terrill's late-seventeenth-century record of the Broadmead church's founding includes an extraordinarily celebratory account of Hassard's religious activism, as a woman both economically and spiritually independent. As the widow Dorothy Kelly, she ran her late husband Anthony Kelly's grocers shop on the high street, and became renowned throughout the city for her zealous Puritanism. She had shared her religious commitments with Anthony, described by Como as the 'lay leader' of a godly conference associated with St Philip's, Bristol, in the 1620s and 1630s.[45] Following the deaths in the early 1630s of her husband and the Puritan minister at St Philip's, she became 'like a hee-goat before ye flock...well knowne to all, bearing a liveing testimony against ye Superstitions and traditions of those days, and she would not observe their invented times and feasts, called Holy days'.[46] The metaphor of the he-goat leading the flock is startling; it seems to echo a well-known sermon preached in 1643 by the Congregationalist Jeremiah Burroughs, which contains the following comment on Proverbs 30.31:

> the going of the he-goat is said to be very comely...because the he-goat useth to go before the flock. Those that out of love to the cause of God are willing (if they be called to it) to goe before the flock, they goe comely in the eyes of God.[47]

---

[42] Champlin Burrage, 'A True and Short Declaration, both of the Gathering and Joining Together of Certain Persons [with John More, Dr Theodore Naudin, and Dr Peter Chamberlen]: and also of the lamentable breach and division which fell amongst them', *Transactions of the Baptist Historical Society* 2.3 (1911), pp. 145–6.

[43] See, for instance, Claire Cross, '"He-goats before the flocks": a note on the part played by women in the founding of some civil war churches', in G.J. Cuming and Derek Baker eds., *Popular belief and practice*, Studies in church history (Cambridge: Cambridge University Press 1972), pp. 195–202; also Como, *Radical parliamentarians*, pp. 39–42.

[44] See Como, *Radical parliamentarians*, pp. 41–5.   [45] Como, *Radical parliamentarians*, p. 39.

[46] Roger Hayden ed., *The records of a church of Christ in Bristol, 1640–1687* (Bristol: Bristol Record Society, 1974), p. 85.

[47] Jeremiah Burroughs, *An exposition of the prophesie of Hosea* (London, 1652), p. 93.

Hassard was certainly willing to make herself conspicuous as a reformer. She kept her shop open on Christmas day, and sat sewing ostentatiously in full view. At the peak of Laudian ceremonialism,

> this gracious woman (afterwards called Mrs. Hazzard), like a Deborah she arose, with strength and holy Resolution in her soul from God, even a Mother in Israell. And soe she proved, because she was ye first woman in this Citty of Bristoll that practised that truth of ye Lord (which was then hated and Odious), namely, Separation.[48]

She brought together an informal association of those 'awakened' by the Spirit, mostly local women, who gained a reputation as 'women Preachers' for their habit of speaking 'very Heavenly' in 'their buying or selling' around the city.[49] This group survived mob attacks on their meeting place, as well as pressure from the bishops. At some point before 1640, Dorothy married again, taking as her husband Matthew Hassard, a zealous young minister at St Ewen's.[50] Even while he was still conforming and presiding at Prayer Book services, however, she continued to act as the host of a growing separatist assembly, resolving 'to lead ye way out of Babilon', and take a stand against 'Corrupt Worship'.[51]

Mrs Hassard was the very engine of this new resistance movement, building networks, convincing women and men (including ordained ministers) to secede from the established church, and, in a remarkable display of courage, organizing a godly, all-female human shield at the Frome gate in Bristol during the royalist siege in 1643.[52] Eventually, Dorothy Hassard's gathered church attracted 160 people, from all over the city of Bristol and the surrounding areas. The Broadmead congregation continued to be a seedbed of radicalism, with a significant party (including Hassard's son, Abel Kelly), breaking away to join the Quaker movement in 1654.[53] The congregation included a servant named Francis, a 'Blackymore maide', a person 'somewhat rare in our dayes and Nation'. Her conversion and public testimony led Terrill to reflect 'experimentally' on Acts 10.34–5 (a text frequently referenced by those supportive of women's inspirations and ministry), 'God is no respecter of persons: But in every nation he that feareth him, and worketh righteousness, is accepted with him'.[54] The levelling principle

---

[48] Hayden, *Records of a church of Christ*, p. 85.
[49] Hayden, *Records of a church of Christ*, p. 86.
[50] See Jonathan Harlow with Jonathan Barry, *Religious ministry in Bristol 1603–1689: uniformity to dissent* (Bristol: Bristol Record Society, 2017), pp. 3–7.
[51] Hayden, *Records of a church of Christ*, p. 88.
[52] See Ann Hughes, *Gender and the English Revolution*, (Abingdon: Routledge, 2012), p. 75.
[53] See T.L. Underwood, *Primitivism, radicalism, and the Lamb's war* (Oxford: Oxford University Press, 1997), p. 17; Kelly is listed as one of those fined for dissent in Anon., *The distressed case of the people called Quakers in the city of Bristol* (London, 1682), p. 24.
[54] Hayden, *Records of a church of Christ*, pp. 101–2.

encompassed not only female participation but the public contributions of those of other ethnicities, and even (in the most radical reformism) toleration of other faiths. One of the major protagonists of this study, the preacher William Erbery, made representation to parliament to grant full 'libertie to the Jewes and others' in 'the exercise of their religion', in the course of his contributions to the discussion of readmission of the Jews.[55]

Female prophets and reformers increasingly engaged in public activity after 1646. One of the earliest women pamphleteers, Elizabeth Warren, was not a radical but an educated Suffolk Puritan, and her first published work in 1646 was a treatise defending the learned ministry against radical challenges to the clerical elite. Despite her protestation of her 'Mentall and Sex-deficiencie', Warren was Latin literate and in possession of deep knowledge of the Scriptures, skills which she rather ostentatiously displayed in support of her clericalist argument.[56] Challenging interventions by women with less orthodox ideas were, however, starting to enter the public sphere by 1647. Leveller women, derided in the newsbooks as 'a holy brood of free-borne Babes', or the 'gifted Sisterhood of new Babilon', were petitioning parliament and exploiting the presses.[57] In April 1649, hundreds of women appealed to the House of Commons under the leadership of Elizabeth Lilburne and Katherine Chidley, many of them, according to a parliamentary newsbook, mobilized through London's 'Congregationall Meetings'.[58] Elizabeth Poole took her visions to the council of officers, and may have been an unsuccessful instrument of mediation between the council and the Levellers; subsequently, she was a critic of the regicide, using the metaphor of husband and wife in her exhortation to the army to subordinate itself to the kingly spouse of the people.[59] Lady Eleanor Davies, who was 50 in 1640, had more than sixty prophetic works printed during the 1640s, chiefly by the radical printer Thomas Paine (but unlicensed), many of them advancing her theological case for universal salvation. Sarah Wight, who refrained from publishing in her own right, was nonetheless gaining celebrity as a spiritual advisor, attended by leading preachers in the radical network, as well as women seeking her counsel.

Other women were supported by that most infamous of radical printers already named, Giles Calvert, who published—along with Leveller tracts—works by Elizabeth Avery, Mary Cary, and Anne Yemans, before becoming the favoured printer of the early Quakers. Calvert's press was at the hub of the network of mystical radicals in the city of London and in the army. Avery, a mother in her 30s

---

[55] 8 Jan. 1649, in C.H. Firth, ed., *Selections from the papers of William Clarke*, vol. 2 (London: Camden Society, 1894), p. 172.
[56] Elizabeth Warren, *The good and old way vindicated* (London, 1646), §A3r.
[57] *Mercurius Militaris or times only truth teller*, 22–29 May 1649 (London), §A3r.
[58] See Patricia Higgins, 'The reactions of women, with special reference to women petitioners', in Brian Manning, ed., *Politics, religion and the English Civil War* (London: Edward Arnold, 1973), p. 217.
[59] Elizabeth Poole, *An alarum of war given to the army and to their high court of justice* (London, 1649), §A3r–A4r.

or possibly 40s when she first published, was no plebeian prophetess. She was the daughter of the early separatist theologian Robert Parker, a leading Puritan scholar who raised his family in Amsterdam, and would later be considered a founding father of Congregationalism. Avery was nothing if not independent minded, however, and she did not acknowledge any debt to her father's erudition or to his ideas about church government. She showed signs of engagement with some of the most radical theological ideas of the moment, and was in 1648 blacklisted by a group of Puritan ministers in London as a heretic, the only woman in a list of substantial heterodox thinkers which included John Biddle, Lawrence Clarkson, John Milton, and John Saltmarsh.[60] Mary Cary was in her late 20s when she first published in 1647; like Avery, she was a woman of some means, but uncompromising in her views on social justice and toleration. Anne Yemans' background is obscure, but she certainly shared radical themes and priorities with Giles Calvert's other female theologians. It is possible that she was the Anne Yeamans of Bristol, widow of one William Yeamans, whose will was proved in December 1668.[61] Yeamans named as an executor her son-in-law Thomas Speed, a Bristol merchant and lay preacher who had become a prominent Quaker in the 1650s, and who had himself published several times with Calvert in the 1650s. In his first Calvert pamphlet of 1651, Speed attacked the clergy and rejected the 'external duties' which were the 'carcase' of religion; celebrating in terms strongly redolent of Leveller rhetoric the delivery of the English people 'from that yoke, which was likely to have continued upon our necks, through that inevitable ruine that was coming upon our LAWS, and LIBERTIES, our BIRTH-RIGHTS'.[62]

It is not, of course, as though the anomalous prominence of women in the radical 'sects' of the Revolution has gone unnoticed, or as though there has been a lack of serious attention to particular women's contributions, or to female-affirming groups. Early interest in women's religious activity in the Revolution identified a cyclical pattern of women's extraordinary roles in early reform or revivalist movements. Ronald Knox famously noted, with reference to the female prophets of this period, among others: 'the history of enthusiasm is largely a history of female emancipation, and it is not a reassuring one'.[63] ('Not reassuring

---

[60] T.C., *A glasse for the times by which according to the Scriptures, you may clearly behold the true ministers of Christ, how farre differing from false teachers* (London, 1648), pp. 1–2. See Crawford Gribben, *God's Irishmen: theological debates in Cromwellian Ireland* (Oxford: Oxford University Press, 2007), p. 166.

[61] Will of Anne Yeamans, National Archives, PROB 11/328/403. It seems likely that this William Yeamans was connected to the William Yeamans of Bristol whose Puritan circle once gathered in the parish of St Philip's, including Dorothy Hassard and many nonconformists who later became both Baptists and Quakers. See David Harris Sacks, *The widening gate: Bristol and the Atlantic economy, 1450–1700* (Berkeley: University of California Press, 1992), p. 234.

[62] Thomas Speed, *Ton sesosmenon umnon, or, the song of the delevered* (London, 1651), pp. 16, 21.

[63] Ronald A. Knox, *Enthusiasm: a chapter in the history of religion* (New York: Oxford University Press, 1950), p. 20.

to whom?', riposted one feminist scholar in 1988.)[64] The landmark 1958 article on women and the sects by Keith Thomas has already been mentioned. Though occasionally dismissive towards ecstatic females—describing one or another woman as 'extravagant', or 'delirious'—Thomas established many of the themes which would preoccupy later scholarship.[65] The appeal to the freedom of the Spirit was 'an extremely powerful solvent of the established order'.[66] The sects proved 'more attractive' to women because they offered more opportunities for female self-expression and participation.[67] Nonetheless, he concluded, 'Appeal to divine inspiration was of very questionable value as a means of female emancipation. The whole emphasis was placed upon the omnipotence of God and the helplessness of his chosen handmaid should she be thrown upon her own resources'.[68] Patricia Crawford noted that Thomas focused more on the contemporary reaction than on the women themselves. She called for historians to take more seriously religion as a driving motivation for the female prophets and activists, to weigh duly 'the intensity of their search for individual salvation, and the sense that their own experiences were all that they had to guide them'. This was not a feminist quest for sexual or political liberation, and Crawford questioned Dorothy Ludlow's claim that the sects were 'emancipatory' for women, indeed that they were responsible for 'shaking patriarchy's foundations'.[69] Crawford concluded that attitudes to women's roles in the sects were marked by 'contradiction and ambiguity', as sectarian groups found themselves beset by external as well as internal pressures on account of women's activity, and that 'patriarchal authority' continued to hold sway.[70]

Historians have generally acknowledged the distinctiveness of the Quaker movement of the 1650s in promoting spiritual equality among women and men. Since the 1980s, however, this affirmation of Quakerism's egalitarian impulse has been increasingly qualified and restrained. Barry Reay observed that equality was not fully realized in social terms.[71] Influentially, Phyllis Mack's 1992 study of prophecy in the Quaker movement examined forensically the limited value of feminist concepts of 'agency', as well as of psychoanalytical and Marxist perspectives, for an understanding of seventeenth-century women's religious activity.

---

[64] Patricia Crawford, 'Historians, women and the civil war sects, 1640–1660', *Parergon* 6 (1988), p. 19; see also her *Women and religion in England, 1500–1700* (London and New York: Routledge, 1993), p. 119.
[65] Thomas, 'Women and the civil war sects', p. 48.
[66] Thomas, 'Women and the civil war sects', p. 48.
[67] Thomas, 'Women and the civil war sects', pp. 50–1.
[68] Thomas, 'Women and the civil war sects', p. 56.
[69] Crawford, 'Historians, women and the civil war sects', pp. 22, 24; see Dorothy Ludlow, 'Shaking patriarchy's foundations: sectarian women in England, 1641–1700', in Richard L. Greaves, ed., *Triumph over silence: women in Protestant history* (Westport, CN: Greenwood Press, 1985), pp. 95–108.
[70] Crawford, 'Historians, women and the civil war sects', p. 32.
[71] Barry Reay, *The Quakers and the English Revolution* (New York: St Martin's Press, 1985), p. 28.

Mack argued persuasively that the notion that 'visionary women were pursuing a covert strategy of self-assertion' overlooked the complexity of religious ideas of selfhood. The aim of such women was ultimately 'self-transcendence', or even erasure of self, rather than self-fulfilment or self-expression.[72] Literary scholars, among them rewardingly Hilary Hinds, have discussed the problematic concept of 'authorship' and authority in connection with visionary texts, framed as they so frequently were by self-abnegating rhetoric.[73] Such has been the scholarly consensus on the limits of gender radicalism in Quaker thought and practice that Christopher Marsh made the somewhat definitive remark in 2006 that 'historians are now aware that even Quakerism did not truly challenge patriarchy'.[74] Scholarly interest in the female prophets active in the revolutionary decades of the seventeenth century shows no sign of abating, nonetheless, as new generations of scholars encounter the disruptiveness and strangeness of visionary texts, not least by women.[75] Following the pioneering insights of the 1990s, feminist criticism and historiography more widely have developed an increasingly nuanced account of prophetic discourse, as equally 'subversive and conservative', arising as much from an apprehension of the passive instrumentality of the human agent— or 'silenced subjectivity'—as from female efforts at self-assertion.[76] Women's expressions of prophetic revelation have sometimes come to be seen as a kind of ventriloquism, the production of texts imitative of Scripture prophecy, finding an audience and authority only through gestures of self-renunciation.[77] In particular cases (such as those of Elinor Channel, Sarah Wight, or Anna Trapnel), men were the authoritative 'exegetes' of this prophetic revelation, or Spirit ventriloquism.[78]

---

[72] Phyllis Mack, *Visionary women: ecstatic prophecy in seventeenth-century England* (Berkeley: University of Berkeley Press, 1992), p. 5.

[73] Hilary Hinds, *God's Englishwomen: seventeenth-century radical sectarian writing and feminist criticism* (Manchester: Manchester University Press, 1996).

[74] Christopher Marsh, '"Godlie matrons" and "loose-bodied dames": heresy and gender in the Family of Love', in David Loewenstein and John Marshall, eds., *Heresy, literature and politics in early modern English culture* (Cambridge: Cambridge University Press, 2006), p. 69.

[75] Recent studies include Carme Font, *Women's prophetic writings in seventeenth-century Britain* (New York and London: Routledge, 2019); Elizabeth Bouldin, *Women prophets and radical Protestantism in the British Atlantic World, 1640–1730* (Cambridge: Cambridge University Press, 2015); Rachel Adcock, *Baptist women's writings in revolutionary culture* (Abingdon: Routledge, 2016).

[76] The phrase is taken from the Finnish scholar Tuija Hovi's work on gender and agency in the neo-charismatic movement, but for a similar idea in the secondary literature on early modern women's prophecy, see, for instance, Hind, *God's Englishwomen*, p. 49; Diane Purkiss, 'Producing the voice, consuming the body: women prophets of the seventeenth century', in Isobel Grundy and Susan Wiseman, eds., *Women, writing, history 1640–1740* (Athens, GA: University of Georgia Press, 1993), pp. 139–58.

[77] On prophecy as ventriloquism, see Helen Ostovich and Elizabeth Sauer, eds., 'Religion, prophecy, and persecution', *Reading early modern women: an anthology of texts in manuscript and print* (New York and London: Routledge), p. 134.

[78] Carme Font Paz, 'The case for prophecy: politics, gender and self-representation in seventeenth-century prophetic discourses', *Revista Alicantina de Estudios Ingleses* 22 (2009), p. 70.

This book aims to question the rather sweeping assumption, which sometimes now prevails, that women's religious interventions in the Revolution did not represent even the slightest disruption to patriarchal thinking. It examines female radical writers as active theologians, as active *interpreters*, and not merely passive paraphrasers of Scripture, offering evidence that visionary writing could be a dynamic form of engagement with live theological controversies. I argue that both mystical theology and post-Reformation prophecy as a genre opened up possibilities for fresh appraisals of key points of doctrine and interpretation of the Bible, rather than acting as a discursive strait-jacket, stifling subjective or creative thought. Revolutionary prophecy could indeed be a liberative genre, challenging the authority of received interpretations, and admitting experiential knowledge as a source for theological understanding. As the prophet Elizabeth Avery wrote in her own explorations of biblical prophecy, in interpreting the Scriptures 'we must look for new discoveries, such as have not been yet'.[79] Visionary discourse is certainly taken more seriously now than at points in the mid-twentieth century by literary and political historians, sometimes as 'semiotic irruption', sometimes as serious polemic, sometimes as a form of poetics, or a distinct cultural form in its own right.[80] It has, however, tended to be sidelined in intellectual history or historical theology, despite the evidence of original thought in prophetic works. In the chapters which follow, I examine significant shifts in gendered religious symbolism, and challenges to received doctrines, in the radical theology of the milieu in which women were most prominent as preachers and prophets.

It is now a commonplace observation that 'petticoat preachers' and their presumptuous inspirations became a potent symbol of the disorder ensuing from religious deviance and political disobedience. Gender politics was central to the construction and alienation of the subversive category of 'enthusiasm'. What seems to admit of further reflection and explanation, despite the attention to female prophets and preachers of the Revolution, is the *positive* significance and status attached to female mouthpieces. In his haunting study of seventeenth-century mystics in Catholic France, Michel de Certeau offered a powerful account of the significance of the inspired 'maids, cowherds, villagers' who in their simplicity humbled the learned clerics, and became sites of pilgrimage, the sacred places where God dwelt. In a church stripped by religious crisis of its traditional certainties, in which the old shared symbolic system was crumbling, the clergy 'became exegetes of female bodies, speaking bodies, living Bibles spread here and there in the countryside or in the little shops, ephemeral outbursts of the "Word"

---

[79] Elizabeth Avery, *Scripture-prophecies opened: which are to be accomplished in these last times, which do attend the second coming of Christ* (London, 1647), p. 11.
[80] See, for instance, James Holstun's advocacy of engagement with prophetic literature in *Ehud's dagger: class struggle in the English Revolution* (London and New York: Verso, 2000), p. 265.

erstwhile uttered by a whole world'.[81] Something like this quest for witnesses can be discerned in the appeal of women and lay preachers—bricklayers, carters, button-makers, cobblers—who were welcomed by radical ministers, those with Oxford degrees and biblical languages, as authentic mouthpieces. This is discussed more fully in Chapter 3, 'Revelation', but the Welsh Independent Walter Cradock (a magnetic preacher, admired by many women) helps to illustrate this appeal. In preaching exercises held at All Hallows the Great by Cradock in the 1640s, he reminded his audiences that

> the Lord chose simple people to go, and preach [the Gospel], he chose generally fisher men, and such poor men, and women sometimes. Rude men, in a manner without learning; these were to go and tell a simple story of Iesus Christ, and him crucified, &c. And so we finde by experience, that the Lord sends the Gospel to poor silly people: the simplest people most commonly understand the Gospel of Jesus Christ best.[82]

Men and women should not be hindered from preaching, if they 'have no degrees in the University, or it may be have not the knowledge of the tongues':

> And let us not think so hardly in these dayes, of those men that God hath raised to preach the Gospel. It is strange you shall have your Pulpits ring, calling them Tub-preachers, and Tinkers, and Coblers. We should think better of them; Why? they are filled with good newes, and they go and tell it to others.[83]

Such a man (or woman), suggested Cradock, may have 'more of God in him than I, and a hundred that have all this' (i.e. university learning).[84] In an exhortation to his listeners to share the good news in 'the poor Countries in the North, and West of England, in many places, in Townes, [where] they have not so much as a Service-booke', regardless of their status, the example he gave of the preaching commission was Mary Magdalen: 'when Christ was risen Mary runs to tell the newes to the Disciples'.[85]

De Certeau's account helps to make sense of the motives of the male ministers and disciples who promoted women as simple unlettered mouthpieces of the Spirit. It does not, however, fully elucidate the motivations and self-understanding of the dozens of women moved to prophesy and challenge amid religious turmoil,

---

[81] Michel de Certeau, *The mystic fable*, vol. 1: *The sixteenth and seventeenth centuries*, trans. Michael B. Smith (Chicago: University of Chicago Press, 1992), pp. 25–6.

[82] Walter Cradock, *Divine drops distilled from the fountain of Holy Scripture* (London, 1649), pp. 224–5.

[83] Cradock, *Divine drops distilled*, pp. 224–5. See also Walter Cradock, *Gospel-libertie in the extensions limitations of it* (London, 1648), pp. 49–51.

[84] Walter Cradock, *Glad tydings from Heaven to the worst of sinners* (London 1648), p. 51.

[85] Cradock, *Glad tydings from Heaven*, p. 49.

against the cultural grain. These were women who believed themselves authorized to confront more than just the contingent, local arrangements and principles of the reformed English Church. They challenged historic doctrines and structures of Western Christianity, on the authority of the true teacher: namely, an inward union with divine love, which grounded knowledge of God neither in the Word preached nor in the encounter with Scripture, but in the heart alone. While this study at points illustrates how English radicalism drank deeply from the wells of European mysticism and radical Reformation, there is also something of the logic of Puritan iconoclasm in radical theology, brought to its ultimate conclusion. John Saltmarsh, one of the most eloquent of the mystical iconoclasts, aimed his critique at those who tried to 'fix' God in outward forms, 'whether as to Religion, or to natural, civil and moral things'. The setting up of outward ordinances of worship and practice was 'an immediate way of fixing God, and his Spirit upon it, which indeed is a finer kinde of Idolatry'.[86] Divine truths were not to be discovered through the outward letter of Scripture—'not as they are meerly in their grammaticall constuction and sense or common reading, which any that understand the Hebrew or Greek may receive'—but rather 'as the spirit of God reveals them to be that very truth and minde of God in those who receive them'.[87]

The child prophet Sarah Wight, who gained a wide and influential following in 1647 (including John Saltmarsh), provides a striking example of the transformation in perspective undergone by a woman in the revolutionary context; as well as of the aspirations projected onto 'innocent', uneducated prophets by those seeking uncompromised witnesses of the eternal Word amid the turmoil. She has been aptly described by Katherine Gillespie as the 'girl-king', for her assertion—so politically charged against the backdrop of the conflict between parliament and monarch—that the throne of God is located not only in the highest heavens, but also 'in the poorest contemptible hearts'.[88] At the height of her popularity Wight was a child of 16, recovering from a suicide attempt and characterized by herself and her leading disciple, the leading Independent (and Baptist) minister Henry Jessey, as an 'Empty Nothing'.[89] She was 'well trained up in the Scriptures', importantly by her mother and grandmother, but 'understood not aright', and was tormented by horror at the prospect of damnation.[90] She described her spiritual disorientation before her knowledge of grace: she was 'a wandering bird', who 'sought to every Idol which I made an Idol below the true God for

---

[86] John Saltmarsh, *Sparkles of glory, or, some beams of the morning-star* (London, 1647), p. 14.
[87] Saltmarsh, *Sparkles of glory*, pp. 268–9.
[88] See Katharine Gillespie, *Domesticity and dissent in the seventeenth century: English women writers and the public sphere* (Cambridge: Cambridge University Press, 2004), p. 191.
[89] Henry Jessey, *The exceeding riches of grace advanced by the Spirit of grace, in an empty nothing creature, viz. Mistress Sarah Wight* (London, 1647); Sarah Wight, *A wonderful pleasant and profitable letter written by Mris Sarah Wight, to a friend* (London, 1656), p. 80.
[90] Jessey, *The exceeding riches of grace*, pp. 5–6.

soul-rest, peace of conscience and joy in the Holy Ghost: but like Noahs dove, found this not in any thing to refresh my weary soul'.[91] The discovery of God, beyond all usurping idols, came when she 'found and enjoyed Christ in the inmost Holy Places of its new heart'. Wight's experience of 'this indwelling presence in the hearts of his sanctified ones' was a dramatic reorientation of her relation to God, brought close: 'happy are they whom God is thus nigh unto in all things'.[92] Her account of God revealed as an intimate divine presence rather than a remote and harsh judge is echoed throughout the writings of the mystical radicals, not least in Gerrard Winstanley's insistence that 'Jesus Christ at a distance from thee, will not save thee'.[93]

This study situates itself as both gender history and women's history, based on the observation that gender ideology interacts dynamically with both women's and men's experience. I share Ann Hughes's reluctance to see women's and gender history as separate, even opposed. Her questions—'how gendered understandings are implicated in political crisis; how political divisions might be seen in gendered terms, and how political crisis might transform these gendered cultural frameworks'—are not dissimilar from my own, though my questions specifically pertain to the radical religious response to the revolutionary crisis.[94] Like Hughes, however, I am also interested in the active participation and contributions of women. The cultural category of 'woman' was multiply differentiated, but it also seemed self-evident who was a woman and who was not. The studies examining and complicating this cultural category are many and various, and I will not attempt an all-encompassing definition of the seventeenth-century 'weaker vessel'. Associating intellectual positions with a female subject perspective need not entail a crude essentialism. I acknowledge that specific shared features of female experience—whether biologically, socially, or culturally determined—led to shared perspectives on certain issues. This claim is particularly relevant to Chapter 2, 'Salvation', in which I argue that women were disproportionately represented among those defending the doctrine of universal salvation in seventeenth-century England. Indeed, I suggest, a female theologian was among the very first to advocate for universalism. There is evidence to suggest that the appeal of this doctrine was related to a distinctively *maternal* sensibility, namely, a concern for the souls of lost infants. Men, of course, grieved for deceased children no less bitterly than women, but the gendered imperative (both cultural and biological at some level) to show unconditional compassion to the helpless infant seems to have been a factor in the development and reception of universalist soteriology among women.

---

[91] Wight, *A wonderful pleasant and profitable letter*, pp. 55–6.
[92] Wight, *A wonderful pleasant and profitable letter*, p. 60.
[93] Gerrard Winstanley, *Truth lifting up its head above scandals* (London, 1649), p. 10.
[94] Hughes, *Gender and the English Revolution*, p. 3.

Another distinctive contribution made by female prophets in the English Revolution (notably Anna Trapnel and Mary Cary; see Chapter 4) was the conceptualization of Jesus as a maternal figure, a move not unlike that made by Julian of Norwich, the fourteenth-century mystic, though it also had parallels in the earlier devotional works of Bernard of Clairvaux and Anselm. This metaphorical shift, attaching to Christ the image of a mother—rather than the more conventional masculine imagery of king, judge, priest, or bridegroom which dominated Reformed christology—was linked to a reappraisal of the doctrine of grace, and an emotional release from the fear of judgement and rejection. Male metaphors for Christ are of course more prominent in the New Testament as well as in Protestant thought, though there is the famous exception in Matthew 23.37 and Luke 13.34, the words used by Jesus to Jerusalem: 'how often would I have gathered thy childen together, even as a hen gathereth her chickens under her wings'. The image used by Anna Trapnel for divine love in Christ was that of a nursing mother, more redolent of Hebrew scriptural poetry and prophecy (Isaiah 49.15; Psalm 131).

The importance, for gender relations in the lived world, of gendered symbolism for God has been asserted emphatically in feminist philosophy and theology since the 1970s. In various essays, Luce Irigaray offered an influential, Feuerbachian analysis of the way in which relation to an ideal object is a necessary aspect of self-realization, and the formation of communal as well as individual identities. Irigaray has suggested that the gods of the Abrahamic religions have been projections of dominant masculine qualities. Women lack a divine feminine, a spiritual mother, which will provide a 'horizon', a prospect for women to emerge and flourish as women.[95] Carol Christ, inspired by the anthropologist Clifford Geertz, has argued that a radical reform of religious symbols is an essential task of modern feminism. Religion, understood as a symbolic order, shapes psychologies and political ideologies, creating the 'inner conditions' which establish the status of women. For Carol Christ, a spirituality empowering for women must be rooted in an understanding of divinity as 'goddess': not an external masculine authority, but an inwardly experienced creative force, an inner power imaged as female.[96] The major American feminist theologians—especially Elisabeth Schüssler Fiorenza and Elizabeth Johnson—have sought to recover traditions in Christianity which allow for a female principle in the Godhead.[97] This includes the tradition which associates Jesus with divine Wisdom, or

---

[95] See especially Luce Irigaray, 'Divine Women', in *Sexes and Genealogies* (New York: Columbia University Press, 1993), pp. 55–72.

[96] Carol Christ, 'Why women need the Goddess', in Carol P. Christ and Judith Plaskow, eds., *Womanspirit rising: a feminist reader on religion* (San Francisco: Harper & Row, 1979), pp. 273–87.

[97] Elisabeth Schüssler Fiorenza, *Jesus, Miriam's child, Sophia's prophet: critical issues in feminist christology* (New York: Continuum, 1995); Elizabeth Johnson, *She who is: the mystery of God in feminist theological discourse* (New York: Crossroad, 1992). See also Janet Soskice, *The kindness of God: metaphor, gender and religions language* (Oxford: Oxford University Press, 2007), pp. 100–56.

Sophia; a tradition notably prominent among the readers of the German mystic Jacob Boehme during and after the English Revolution. It is also striking to find in that context the extraordinary idea, first put forward by Paracelsus, of the Virgin Mary as goddess or female principle in the Godhead (see Chapter 1, pp. 31, 37–8). I wish to show how transformation at the level of symbols and metaphors provided a renewed framework for the affective dimensions of religious experience, which were so important for radical women's identities and commitments. To explore early modern religious thought through symbols and metaphors need not imply that the whole of religion is reduced, conceptually, to culture. Early modern religion is rightly approached as multi-faceted: as existential faith; as applied ethics; as ecclesiastical politics; as apocalyptic hope; as theology; as spirituality; but also as symbolic structures and metaphorical references which provided frameworks for all of the above.

Although informed by historical research, this study is also unashamedly inspired by the arguments of feminist epistemology and liberation theology: put crudely, the claim that involving women in religious discourse makes a difference. A female subject perspective in knowledge production will not only give different weighting to marginalized categories of knowledge (such as experiential, personal, or practical, rather than abstract or theoretical), but will alter—and has altered—the content and formation of thought.[98] Concomitantly, the analysis draws upon the assertion by feminist theologians, philosophers, and psychologists that the ways in which God is conceptualized has significance for women's sense of self. What is striking about most of these challenges, including original insights offered by women themselves, is that they anticipate criticisms of orthodox doctrines made by feminist theologians in a much later period. On the singularity of the incarnation, on the autonomy and self-sufficiency of the divine being, on the doctrine of salvation, on the divine feminine, the radicals took distinctive positions with implications for gender ideals and relations. That is not to say that they provide heritage or a point of origin for feminist theology, but to observe that the opening up of an environment hospitable to female perspectives involved, then as now, disruption to received ideas and symbols. It was a moment at which discontinuity seemed freshly possible as well as desirable, and a fundamentally different world was imagined.

The English Revolution can be seen as a profound disruption to a symbolic order. It was, indeed, a tectonic disturbance as deep and as intellectually, culturally, spiritually convulsive as the sixteenth-century reformations in religion; not merely their aftershock. This book considers the relationship between radical theology and gender radicalism as an interplay. The quest for transformation,

---

[98] See for instance Elizabeth Anderson, 'Feminist epistemology: an interpretation and a defense', *Hypatia* 10:3 (1995), 50–84; Kathleen Lennon and Margaret Whitford, eds., *Knowing the difference: feminist perspectives in epistemology* (London and New York: Routledge, 1994).

for a vision of God which would transcend bitter theological disputes, overturn Babylonian oppression, and bring about revolution in the heart brought an openness to the insights of marginalized witnesses: women, workers, the unlearned. This openness, in turn, brought fresh theological insights and emphases. Some of the most creative and active female visionaries, among them Sarah Wight, wrote movingly of a kind of homecoming in their spirit, and this was linked to a fresh understanding of divine love not only as a thing more generous and unlimited in scope than they had been taught, but also as something intimately experienced, united to their own purest and tenderest passions. God was no more an alien, distant object, but a living presence rising within them; they no longer sought to derive understanding or loving aspirations towards God from external sources, whether texts or preachers, but drew breath (as they saw it) with the same Spirit of God which animated the ancient writers. I want to suggest that this shift in lenses—from the objectified, or externally mediated, to the indwelling God—provided part of the impetus for widespread female participation in the radical religious movements of the English Revolution. Of course, this was not a modern feminist conception of agency. There was in it, however, an apprehension of the realization of a true self, not its negation; and the recovery of a primal communion with the true God. The visionaries sometimes wrote of self-annihilation, but what was meant by this was the destruction of the illusory self, the false self, the inner 'antichrist' that tended towards spiritual tyranny and idolatry. The Spirit was experienced not as an alien intruder, nor a possessing masculine force, but as divinity (sometimes imaged as feminine) manifested in one's own flesh.

1
Incarnation

This chapter examines two closely related and distinctive christological doctrines: that of spiritual or heavenly flesh, and that of spiritual senses, which gained currency among the radical theologians of the 1640s. The doctrines provided part of the intellectual framework for the openness to women's ministry and preaching among the radicals. Both doctrines assumed an intimate identification between the saints and the person of Christ, in his incarnate, resurrected, and ascended state. Several women preachers and prophets confidently adopted the identity of Christ's new flesh. In his 1997 novel, *An instance of the fingerpost*, Iain Pears gave a central plotline to a female prophet in the period just after the Restoration, the maidservant Sarah Blundy, ultimately revealed to be an instantiation of the incarnate Deity. Those who embraced her as a new manifestation of Christ held that divinity condescends to take flesh in every generation: 'a beggar, a cripple, a child, a madman, a criminal or a woman is born Lord of us all in entire obscurity, and is spurned and ignored and killed by us to expiate our sins'.[1] Pears's prophetess was an imagined one, and the idea of a particular reincarnation of Christ in each successive generation is nowhere to be found in seventeenth-century radicalism. Pears was, however, justly praised for his meticulous research and profound understanding of the religious and political context for his story. He was also, I would suggest, onto something in connecting the promotion of gifted lay visionaries (female and male) with a radical doctrine of the incarnation. Some of the proponents of heavenly flesh christology also developed ideas about a female principle in the Deity; the reunion or reintegration of male and female genders in restored human nature; and divine love as a maternal quality. The implications of the radicals' christology led to a vision of rebirth, and participation in Christ, which was strikingly non-dualistic, or at least not dualistic in conventional ways, and obscured the distinction between literal and metaphorical accounts of regeneration and mystical union.

Heavenly Flesh

Among the female prophets, preachers, and pamphleteers active across England in the 1650s, Dorcas Erbery had a notably eventful period of public activism. Dorcas

[1] Iain Pears, *An instance of the fingerpost* (London: Jonathan Cape Ltd., 1997), p. 691.

became a Quaker at some point in the mid-1650s, and spent much of the following period in and out of prison, mostly in the West Country. Together with her mother Mary and some twenty other early Quaker itinerants (including the soon-to-be-notorious prophet James Nayler), she was imprisoned at Exeter in July 1656 in squalid conditions. After the men were fined, the women were returned to prison, where they languished on foul straw alongside ordinary felons. One of Dorcas's fellow prisoners and preachers, Jane Ingram, became sick and died. Dorcas would later famously claim that she herself also died at Exeter, and, like her namesake Dorcas in the narrative of Acts 9, was raised from the dead two days later by James Nayler (a new Peter). Nayler denied that the resurrection was literal or carnal, but her testimony suggested that she understood the event as a supernatural miracle, witnessed by her mother. This story, and Dorcas Erbery's name, became infamous following James Nayler's supposed prophetic reenactment of Christ's triumphal entry into Jerusalem, on horseback into Bristol in October 1656, for which he was charged and punished under the Blasphemy Act. Dorcas was one of his companions on that day, and was examined at the blasphemy trial, hardly helping Nayler's cause by refusing to deny that she had been raised by him from the dead after two days, or that she had fallen upon him in the manner of Mary of Bethany anointing Jesus, kissing his feet, and referring to him as 'the holy one of Israel'.[2] She was imprisoned again at least twice in the later 1650s, for 'preaching and declaring the Truth to the People in the publick Places of Report and Concourse'.[3]

Dorcas was the daughter of the great Welsh preacher William Erbery, who had been a New Model Army chaplain, and was an avid petitioner on behalf of 'the poare of the nation' until his death in 1654, long after the Leveller challenge had been suppressed. In letters and representations to Parliament and Cromwell, Erbery linked the rooting out of 'the pr[e]lates and their clergicall cathedrall Company' to a wider movement to 'break in peices the Oppressor': including the exploitations of lawyers, and other 'covetous' rich men. Erbery wanted to see the 'raisinge a publique stocke out of the estates of the unrighteous Rich ones', a 'publique Treasury... that there be noe begger in Israell'.[4] William Erbery was also, it seems, practically a supporter of women's ministry. His widow Mary preached and prophesied alongside their daughter in the 1650s. One of William's more distinctive theological teachings, centred on the apocalyptic appearance of Christ in the renewed flesh of the saints, appears to have influenced Dorcas's response to Nayler. It is implicit in her reported testimony that Nayler

---

[2] Anon., *A true narrative of the examination, tryall and sufferings of James Nayler* (London, 1657), pp. 7–8, 15.

[3] Joseph Besse, *A collection of the sufferings of the people called Quakers* (London, 1753), vol. 1, pp. 149, 365.

[4] Letter from William 'Erberry' to Lord General Cromwell, dated July 29, 1652, London Society of Antiquaries, MSS/0138, fol. 158r–v.

was 'the onely begotten son of God', and that he had 'shoke off his carnal body' and taken on a spiritual body.[5] The doctrine may also lie behind the story of her miraculous restoration to life in Exeter prison. At the time of Nayler's trial, it was suggested by Colonel Sydenham that Dorcas Erbery and Martha Simmonds were 'greater offenders than Nayler, inasmuch as they actually committed idolatry'.[6] Dorcas was all but neglected in later Quaker martyrologies and memorials, an obscure figure after Nayler's leadership in the early Quaker movement was overshadowed by that of George Fox. William Erbery, meanwhile, would be remembered favourably as an ancestor of the movement. In 1658, a pamphlet of writings by William was published by the radical printer Giles Calvert, including a short essay entitled 'The woman preacher: or, the man of war. That is, the strength of weakness, and the strong man made weak by God'.[7] Erbery had been a remarkable and independent-minded thinker, radicalized in his army days, and influenced deeply by engagement with spiritualist and heterodox writings rooted in the radical reformation: Socinian, Familist, perhaps also Paracelsian ideas all flowed into his distinctive spiritualist synthesis.[8] For Erbery, during the apocalyptic days through which he lived in the 1640s and early 1650s, Christ was becoming manifest in the flesh of the poor and oppressed saints: a new incarnation. According to his adversaries, he was defending some version of 'heavenly flesh' teaching (oddly attributed to Socinian influences) from at least 1646 when preaching at Oxford. At a public disputation with the Presbyterian Francis Cheynell, he was said to have preached 'That all the fulnesse of the Godhead, the same fulnesse of the Godhead which is in Christ, dwells in the Saints in the same measure, though not in the same manifestation as it doth in Christ'; and that indeed the saints 'have a more glorious power then Christ'.[9] Erbery was accused of appealing to 'very many, especially women' with his 'strange mysterious Expositions of Scripture'.[10]

In 'The woman preacher', Erbery meditated on Psalm 68, a martial hymn commemorating the Exodus, in which God shatters his enemies and leads his people by his holy presence, ultimately to settle at the high place of the temple in Jerusalem. Erbery's epigraph, Psalm 68.11, followed Henry Ainsworth's reading of the Hebrew in attributing to women the task of preaching God's goodness to the poor: 'God gave the word, and great was the company (or Army) of Preachers

---

[5] Anon., *The Quakers quaking: or, the most just and deserved punishment inflicted on the person of James Naylor for his most horrid blasphemies* (London, 1656), p. 11.

[6] '18 December 1656', in John Towill Rutt, ed., *Diary of Thomas Burton Esq*, vol. 1: *July 1653–April 1657* (London, 1828), p. 174.

[7] William Erbery, 'The woman preacher', *The testimony of William Erbery, left upon record for the saints of suceeding ages* (London, 1658), pp. 146–51.

[8] On Erbery's reception of Socinian thought, see Sarah Mortimer, *Reason and religion in the English Revolution: the challenge of Socinianism* (Cambridge: Cambridge University Press, 2010), pp. 169–70. On Erbery's early reputation for antinomianism, in 1643, see also David Como, *Radical parliamentarians and the English Civil War* (Oxford: Oxford University Press, 2021), p. 246.

[9] James Cranford, *Truth triumphing over errour and heresie* (London, 1647), p. 5.

[10] Cranford, *Truth triumphing*, p. 7.

(according to the old Translation) or of the she-preachers, as the Hebrew reads'.[11] Since Ainsworth, in his *Annotations* on the Psalms printed in 1617, had pointed out that the Hebrew referred to a *female* company of preachers, a number of women, including the civil war prophetess Sarah Jones, had looked for a new ministry of 'shee preachers...exercising the power of Christ'.[12] 'The woman preacher' is not, at first sight, all that the title promises: it contains little by way of advocacy for 'shee preachers'. We might expect such an apologetic to resonate especially in the late 1650s, when several Quaker voices were defending women's preaching. Setting out his broader vision of the empowerment of the saints, Erbery interpreted Psalm 68 figuratively as referring to the crisis of church and state in England: the 'she-preachers' in the Hebrew signified all the 'common creatures and obscure fellows there are abroad, who are not taken notice of nor respected by men, but by God they are, who will lead them forth out of their holes, and hidden retirements into publick view at last, with power and glory'.[13] For Erbery, however, the literal and the metaphorical were all one. The 'she-preachers' signified all the weak and despised of the world, including men, but the prophecy applied in a particular way to women themselves. His wife and daughter, as we have seen, would become prominent Quaker preachers, and Dorcas at least continued William's prophetic teaching about the manifestation of Christ in the flesh of the saints. Their sufferings for their confrontational activity were far from 'merely' spiritual; they were subject to imprisonment and persecution. Erbery's own short discussion suggested that he saw the 'woman preacher' in more than metaphorical terms. The Gospels provided concrete, historical precedent for women's apostolic ministry:

> For though the Apostles first preached the Gospel to the world, yet the women first preached the Gospel (Christ risen) to the Apostles; yea, when all the Apostles forsook Christ, the women followed him to his cross, waited for him at the grave, and were the first who both saw him risen, and preached his resurrection. The Apostles would not believe the Message nor Ministry of the women, but thought it no better than an old wives tale.[14]

The she-preachers heralding the new rising of Christ in the saints, whether female or male, were akin to those early female apostles, speaking not in their own voices with 'the speech of men', but rather with 'the language of God' and of angels.[15]

---

[11] See Henry Ainsworth, *Annotations upon the book of Psalmes* (Amsterdam, 1617), Psalm LXVIII:11.

[12] Sarah Jones, *To Sion's lovers being a golden egge to avoide enfection* (London, 1644), §A4r. On the appeal to this translation as the basis for defending women's preaching throughout the later seventeenth century, see also my *Women, feminism and religion in early Enlightenment England* (Cambridge: Cambridge University Press, 2010), pp. 240–2.

[13] Erbery, 'The woman preacher', p. 147. [14] Erbery, 'The woman preacher', p. 151.

[15] Erbery, 'The woman preacher', p. 151.

The texts and narrative of the Erbery family in the 1650s illustrate well the open boundary between literal and metaphorical expression in the radical writing of the Revolution, especially the tangle of gendered imagery, radical doctrine, and radical practice.[16] William's 'woman preacher' was shorthand for humble saints taught by experience; but it also refers to literal women inspired to preach. Dorcas's 'resurrection' was ambiguously spiritualized by Nayler, but given significance as the living sign of a new age of miracles by the woman herself. Nayler's renewed body was spiritual and not carnal, but no less truly the site of the new birth of Christ. The very concept of 'spiritual bodies' or 'heavenly flesh' appears oxymoronic, and implies a complication of traditional distinctions between types of substance. The penetration of these ideas in England, in the work of revolutionary apocalyptic theologians, has been rather understudied, but they were remarkably prevalent and seem to have taken various forms, reflecting complex provenance and engagement with Familist, Anabaptist, and Paracelsian sources of the radical reformation. They were especially prevalent in the New Model Army, among chaplains and laymen alike. In 1647, Robert Wastfield of Brislington, an army officer, announced that 'God is about to make known to this Generation, or to many of this Generation, the Mysterie in Christ or God manifest in the flesh': a radical statement of the expectation that 'the fulnesse of the Godhead shall dwell in us, bodily'.[17] Another 'member of the Army', John Lewin, published the suggestively titled *Manchild brought forth in us: or God manifest in flesh*, with Giles Calvert in 1648. Lewin envisioned 'a bringing forth of Christ in us...Christ in our flesh, God in our flesh, in every Saint, in the least Saint'.[18] Lewin interestingly reflected on the appearance of Christ in 'woman', ambiguously to weakness in human nature but also possibly to the female saint: 'a woman, the weaker vessel, that is the weakest Saint, yet there God, and his greate power will appeare'.[19] Wastfield became a Quaker, and as Ariel Hessayon has shown, the works of Lewin, Wastfield, together with works by Richard Coppin and others ended up in the library of Benjamin Furly, a notable Quaker intellectual of a later generation.[20] Similar teachings about the 'celestial inhabitation' of the substance of Christ in the flesh of his saints were, as Richard Bailey has argued, characteristic of early Quakerism; more recently Madeleine Pennington has tracked the development of this

---

[16] See Nigel Smith, *Perfection proclaimed: language and literature in English radical religion, 1640–60* (Oxford: Oxford University Press, 1989).

[17] Robert Wastfield, *Christ coming in the cloudes* (London, 1647), pp. 1, 17. I am grateful to David Como for this reference. Wastfield was deputy in the first civil war to the Brislington radical Nicholas Cowling, alongside one Abel Kelly, son of Dorothy Hassard.

[18] John Lewin, *The man-child brought forth in us, or, God manifest in flesh* (London, 1648), p. 13.

[19] Lewin, *The man-child*, p. 21.

[20] Ariel Hessayon, 'Fabricating radical traditions', in M. Caricchio and G. Tarantino, eds., *Cromohs virtual seminars: recent historiographical trends of the British studies (17th–18th centuries)* (Cromohs: Cyber Review of Modern Historiography, 2006), pp. 1–6.

distinctive Quaker christology in the notion of the 'Vehiculum Dei', prominent in Robert Barclay's thought.[21]

The ambiguous conception of 'spiritual flesh', of renewed humanity participating in the celestial flesh of Christ, drew deeply from sixteenth-century theological radicalism. In a recent article, the historical theologian Anselm Schubert has shared his discovery that the doctrine of heavenly flesh, as it emerged in the sixteenth-century radical reformation, had likely origins in the writings of Paracelsus on the Trinity.[22] In a distinctive fusion of alchemical ideas, Galenic medicine, and Aristotelian natural philosophy, Paracelsus developed the theory of a heavenly body of the Trinity analogous to human bodies. Building on late medieval alchemical traditions about the high status of the Virgin Mary's body, according to which Mary herself was begotten from within the Godhead and divine in nature, Paracelsus in his 1524 treatise *Liber de Sancte Trinitate* suggested that Mary was the earthly incarnation of a goddess figure: a 'heavenly queen' brought forth by the celestial flesh of the Trinity.[23] Christ in his earthly incarnation brought the heavenly body into the human sphere, and the believer's participation in Christ involves communion with this celestial flesh. As Schubert explains, 'for Paracelsus also the redemption of human beings consists in overcoming earthly corporality in such a way as to bond with the heavenly corporality of the resurrected Christ'.[24] While the Mariological dimensions of Paracelsus' doctrine were discarded by most radical reformers, the notion of Christ's celestial flesh and a participatory exchange of natures by mystical communion endured in various forms. Heavenly flesh christology was adapted by Caspar Schwenckfeld, and influentially by the Anabaptist leaders Melchior Hoffmann and Menno Simons. It is therefore not surprising to find it surfacing in both Baptist and Behmenist circles in England in the 1640s and 1650s. It is worth noting that both Schwenckfeld and Hoffman had a significant following among women, and championed female prophets. Ruth Gouldbourne has explicitly linked Schwenckfeld's christology to his ability to attract and encourage female disciples.[25] This doctrine of a general incarnation has something in common with an idea attributed to Familism by the Presbyterian Robert Baillie, 'that Jesus Christ had not a particular soul and body that was created in the womb of the Virgin, but the flesh and bloud of the whole world'.[26] Certainly, the dissemination

---

[21] See Richard Bailey, *New light on George Fox and early Quakerism: the making and unmaking of a God* (San Francisco: Edwin Mellen Press, 1992), pp. 77–80; Madeleine Pennington, *Quakers, Christ, and the Enlightenment* (Oxford: Oxford University Press, 2021), pp. 135–59.

[22] Anselm Schubert, 'Celestial sex: Paracelsus and the teaching of the "heavenly flesh" of Christ' (trans. James Stayer), *Church History and Religious Culture* 101 (2021), pp. 194–213.

[23] Schubert, 'Celestial sex, p. 204.   [24] Schubert, 'Celestial sex, p. 206.

[25] Ruth Gouldbourne, *The flesh and the feminine: gender and theology in the writings of Caspar Schwenckfeld* (Milton Keynes: Paternoster, 2006), p. 33.

[26] Robert Baillie, *Anabaptism, the true fountaine of Independency, Brownisme, Antinomy, Familisme* (London, 1647), p. 103.

of celestial flesh christology owes much to spiritual Anabaptism, and Familism may have been one vehicle for its entry into English thought.

The Paracelsian tradition remained, however, a primary influence, through its interpretation by Jacob Boehme and Valentin Weigel – at least from 1647 onwards. The reception of Paracelsian ideas about Christ's flesh from an earlier date can be discerned in a highly heterodox manuscript treatise entitled 'Resolutions of misticall theologie grounded upon the creation & God's disposing of the creature as discribed by Moses' dated January 1644, apparently authored by one 'P.W.'. Although there is no clear evidence of a link to army radicalism, the 'Resolutions' suggestively contain distinctive themes which would find their fullest expression among the army chaplains. The treatise sets forth an account of the historical incarnation as the 'first externall begetting of the Son of God', which was a 'prefiguration of ye manner of Christ's second comeing' whereby 'we art members of his body of his flesh, and of his bones, in his second generation'.[27] In the elect, God 'begetts his Sonn againe in them by his manifested shining in their hearts'; and just as Christ conceives and brings forth his saints as 'Sons of God', 'soe may the Elect be said to bring forth Christ'.[28] By an alchemical transmutation, God transforms human nature, making 'the thin thick, the subtile gross, the Spirit body'.[29] Some contemporaries were aware that teachings about the transformation of human flesh into Christ's heavenly substance owed much to the Paracelsian heritage. In 1635 Samuel Hartlib, in his *Ephemerides*, remarked censoriously on the 'errors' of the 'spirituall divinity' taught by the Lutheran Paracelsian Paul Felgenhauer, concerning the celestial flesh of Christ.[30] Richard Baxter, writing to the Behmenist mystic Thomas Bromley in 1654, listed Boehme's errors (which he attributed ultimately to Paracelsus) as including the idea 'yt God hath a body of flesh', as well as the 'Astrologye of Xts Celestiall flesh'.[31]

Along with John Pordage and his circle, William Erbery would at least by 1653 certainly be familiar with works of German spiritualism, among them the 'Teutonicke Theosopher', Jacob Boehme.[32] Boehme had introduced his own themes, and these found their way into English renderings of the doctrine by the 1650s. In particular, he suggested that the original human creation, Adam, had possessed an angelic body of heavenly flesh, not a bestial, mortal body.[33]

---

[27] P.W., 'Resolutions of misticall theologie grounded upon the creation & God's disposing of the creature as discribed by Moses', British Library, Harley MS 1296, fol. 142. I am grateful for the excellent assistance of Rick Yoder in transcribing parts of this manuscript.

[28] P.W., 'Resolutions', fol. 152.   [29] P.W., 'Resolutions', fol. 159.

[30] 'Phelgehawer author est sublimioris illius Auroræ habet horrendum Errorem de Carne Christi', in Samuel Hartlib, *Ephemerides*, Sheffield University Library, Hartlib Papers, 29/3/31B.

[31] Quoted in Ariel Hessayon, *'Gold tried in the fire': the prophet Theauraujohn Tany and the English Revolution* (Aldershot: Ashgate, 2007), p. 306.

[32] 'An Answer to the Articles & Charges exhibited agt Mr William Erbery before ye Honble Comitte for plundred Ministers March ye 9th 1652' (i.e. 1653), Royal Society, Boyle Papers, MS 1/40/11, fol. 56v.

[33] Jacob Boehme, *The fifth book of the author, in three parts, the first, Of the becoming man or incarnation of Jesus Christ* (London, 1659), p. 13.

The incarnation of Christ, in 'heavenly flesh... in which the Holy Trinity dwelleth undivided' was ultimately a means by which humanity could be restored to its original state in divine bodies.[34] The translations of Boehme's writings published in the 1650s contained numerous references to the 'heavenly flesh' that was in Adam at his first creation, the 'inward Spiritual Body of Man', which 'in Christs Spirit buddeth and springeth up in Man, again'.[35] Interestingly, Boehme made Christ's heavenly flesh virtually synonymous with the work of grace, or the 'Love-fire' in the human which quenches the 'Anger-fire' of the Father in the souls. It was the active agent by which 'Sinne in the Adamicall flesh was destroyed'; through 'the sweet heavenly flesh: viz: through the Substantiall Word of Love, through JESUS, viz: Gods greatest Sweetnesse'.[36] By faith we 'conceive or receive the Spirit of Christ out of the Regeneration, which draweth heavenly substance into our soules, viz: Christs heavenly flesh and Blood'.[37]

Heavenly flesh doctrine in its various forms found a significant reception among the mystical radicals, and may have something to do with the fact that, according to Lawrence Clarkson, the 'ranting' circle around the publisher Giles Calvert (which included Abiezer Coppe and a number of women preachers) called itself 'My one flesh'.[38] It almost certainly stands behind the scandal of William Franklin and Mary Gadbury, a collar-maker and a lace-seller (both married, but not to each other) tried at Winchester in 1650 for blasphemously claiming that Franklin had taken on the spiritual body of Christ.[39] The couple felt called out of London to Andover in Hampshire, where in 1649 they became the centre of a small visionary circle. Under examination, the wife of a local minister, Margaret Woodward, acknowledged Franklin as 'her Lord, and her King, and that she is saved by his Death and Passion':

> Farther she saith, That the man, her Saviour, was nothing but dry bones; his flesh was clean scrap't away, and his skin and bone hanged together: and his skin likewise very suddenly fell off from him, and that he had nothing left but the hair of his head, and of that one hair was not diminished; and afterwards new flesh came again as a young childe.[40]

---

[34] Boehme, *The fifth book*, p. 119.
[35] Jacob Boehme, *Concerning the election of grace* (London, 1655), §Ggr-v. This was published by Giles Calvert.
[36] Jacob Boehme, *Of Christs testaments, viz: baptisme and the Supper* (1652), p. 48.
[37] Boehme, *The fifth book*, p. 163.
[38] Lawrence Clarkson, *The lost sheep found* (London, 1660), pp. 24–5.
[39] The trial is described by Humphrey Ellis, in *Pseudochristus: or, a true and faithful relation of the grand impostures, horrid blasphemies, abominable practises, gross deceits; lately spread abroad in the county of Southampton* (London, 1650). An independent report of the case is given in a private contemporary letter between a son and his father, dated 'March 16 1649' (i.e. 1650), in the Clarke papers at Worcester College, Oxford, Clarke MS 18. See also Hessayon, 'Gold tried in the fire', pp. 164–7.
[40] Ellis, *Pseudochristus*, p. 39.

Franklin did not identify this new flesh with the body of the historical Christ; the body 'that suffered, and was layed down at the Sepulchre at Jerusalem' was an 'old body, but that which he now hath is a new body'.[41] This was a 'glorious glorified body', of an uncreated nature like the substance of divinity, rather than the wounded human body of Christ with 'ye printes of nailes' or 'wounds of ye speares in his side'.[42] Gadbury, who professed to be a devotee of Henry Jessey (Sarah Wight's principal disciple) and the army preacher William Sedgwick, took on an exalted status as 'ye bride & ye Spouse ye lambes wife' or indeed 'ye Virgin Mary yt bore Christ': she was designated 'the Mother of Christ that bears him, the woman clothed with the Sun'.[43] It was reported by their associates that she 'brought forth a spiritual birth', a 'fiery flyeing Serp[en]t' or 'old dragon': the Justices suspected this was a real child, born illegitimately and 'destroyed' by the couple.[44] Whatever the truth of the 'spiritual birth', the couple's claims chime with contemporary heavenly flesh teachings. Gadbury was in some ways a more charismatic figure than Franklin himself, reporting 'Visions, Revelations, Voyces', and powerful ecstatic experiences, which included spontaneous singing and bodily shaking for hours through the night. She had such a 'fresh and beautiful' appearance at her examination that the Justices could not believe it was natural, and they checked for cosmetic enhancement; she attributed the glow of her complexion to 'the glory of God' shining through her face.[45] Her inglorious fate, however, was committal to Bridewell. Mrs Woodward was reportedly indicted as a bawd for playing hostess to the adulterous couple.[46]

More tangibly, heavenly flesh christology was explicitly adopted and taught by the radical network of spiritualists across Oxfordshire and Berkshire, certainly influenced by Familism as well as Paracelsus and Boehme, in which women were prominent. John Pordage, tried for heresy in 1654, had apparently heard William Erbery preach publicly on the 'imperfections' of the historical Christ, at Somerset House; several of Pordage's associates were also described as 'Erberists'.[47] The sermon at Somerset House, given at some point in the early 1650s, was apparently highly controversial, and Erbery was later compelled to defend himself in print.[48] What Pordage appears to have heard in Erbery's sermon was that Christ was

---

[41] Worcester College, Oxford, Clarke MS 18, fol. 27f; Ellis, *Pseudochristus*, p. 11.
[42] Worcester College, Oxford, Clarke MS 18, fol. 28v.   [43] Ellis, *Pseudochristus*, pp. 8, 53.
[44] Ellis, *Pseudochristus*, pp. 39–40; Worcester College, Oxford, Clarke MS 18 fols. 27f–28r.
[45] Ellis, *Pseudochristus*, p. 42.   [46] Worcester College, Oxford, Clarke MS 18, fol. 30r.
[47] See Manfred Brod, 'The seeker culture of the Thames Valley', in M. Caricchio and G. Tarantino, eds., *Cromohs virtual seminars: recent historiographical trends of the British Studies (17th–18th Centuries)* (Cromohs: Cyber Review of Modern Historiography, 2006), pp. 1–10; Christopher Cheesman, *Berk-shires agents humble address to the honourable commissioners for compounding* (London, 1651), pp. 37–9; Christopher Fowler, *Daemonium meridianum: Sathan at noon* (London, 1656), p. 31; John Pordage, *Innocencie appearing through the dark mists of pretended guilt* (London, 1655), p. 62.
[48] See 'An Answer to the Articles and Charge, exhibited against Mr William Erbery, before the Honourable Committee for Plundered Ministers', in Erbery, *The testimony of William Erbery*, p. 314.

merely a 'Type', and not a perfect being.[49] A weaver of Bradfield, one of Pordage's disaffected parishioners, deposed against him that he taught 'that it was a vain thing to trust in the Blood of him that died at Jerusalem 1600 Years since, or more, unless it were acted in me or in thee, for that was but in the Type, the Substance must be fulfill'd in us'.[50] Like Erbery, Pordage regarded the idea of a 'particular' or singular incarnation in history as the anticipation, rather than the fulfilment, of salvation history. At the second incarnation, there would be a plenary manifestation of divinity in human nature. His interest in the doctrine of 'spiritual flesh' developed principally, however, under the influence of Jacob Boehme, whose alchemical mysticism provided a major source of inspiration for Pordage and his circle. Boehme described the regeneration of the soul in union with the incarnate Christ in terms of casting off 'rude drossy Earthly flesh' to allow 'the virgin-like spiritual flesh' in restored humanity to be manifest. This was not a conventionally dualistic idea; Boehme insisted that the 'New-Man is not onely a Spirit: He is even Flesh and Blood'; the human creature has 'a true real Heavenly divine Body in flesh and blood' which could, like Christ's dynamic resurrection body, pass through stone and wood, or 'subsist in the Fire'.[51]

An intriguing episode, akin to the miraculous experiences of both Mary Gadbury and Dorcas Erbery, is that of Mrs Flavel, an associate of John Pordage and the predominantly female circle which met to share prophetic revelations and spiritual experiences at his rectory at Bradfield in Berkshire. It has been suggested that Flavel was Pordage's mistress. According to his maidservant, she slept in his room, and also allegedly gave birth to their daughter Hannah in 1645, described to those outside the inner circle as the child of a dear friend.[52] On a separate occasion, a deponent against Pordage (whose testimony was one of the factors leading to his later ejection from Bradfield) reported hearing her cries of 'extreme' pain from a room in the Rectory. In a striking echo of the Gadbury case, other eyewitnesses claimed that they had seen her 'in travell of a man-child'. Pordage denied this, claiming instead that the 'travell of a man-child was not any naturall birth of a child out of the womb, But the cry that was then made was nothing else but the groaning and intercession of the spirit in her prayer'. The birth was a spiritual incarnation: 'the birth, death, and resurrection of Christ in the nature of Ms Flavell'.[53] Whatever the true nature of Pordage's relationship to the unfortunate Mrs Flavel, the Bradfield group certainly held to a doctrine of the incarnation which may have supported Pordage's mystical interpretation, though the distinction between spiritual and corporeal experience was deeply ambiguous. The Pordage community, not least its female members (among them Mrs Flavel and

---

[49] See *Tryals for high-treason and other crimes* (London, 1720), part II, pp. 641, 649–50.
[50] *Tryals for high-treason*, p. 657.   [51] Boehme, *The fifth book*, pp. 116–17, see also 165.
[52] *Tryals for high-treason*, p. 646; Pordage, *Innocencie appearing*, p. 70.
[53] Fowler, *Daemonium meridianum*, pp. 96–7.

a visionary named Mary Pocock, as well as Pordage's own wife), were strongly influenced by Renaissance alchemical ideas about the union of divine and human natures in Mary and Christ (designated the 'philosopher's stone'), and a dissolution in that union of gender difference.[54] It was one of the articles brought against Pordage that he taught: 'That by Male and Female, *Gen.* 1. we are to understand by Male, the Deity, by the Female, the humanity, and that these two became one flesh'.[55] Mrs Flavel allegedly reported a vision 'the Philosophers stone, which she knew to be the Divinity in the Humanity' (though she and other witnesses denied this).[56] This site of renewed incarnation, with all its implications for the transformation of human nature, was the true meaning of 'the philosopher's stone'.

Marks of gender were marks of fallen nature, and as such would be eliminated or transcended in the new angelical state of restored humanity, in which human and divine natures were united. An undated manuscript in the Rawlinson collection at the Bodleian Library contains 'A Tract of Christ's Birth & Incarnation', originally written by John Pordage, though the manuscript seems to be a fair copy by one interested in investigating the blasphemous content of Pordage's thought, with critical asides in marginal comments.[57] In it, Pordage affirmed that the incarnation in Jesus of Nazareth was 'true, historical', but that in Jesus there was no complete union of divine and human natures: 'his Godhead & his Manhood are however notwithstanding this close Union, distinct in themselves from each other'.[58] This might seem a statement of Chalcedonian christology and the principle that the two natures, while undivided, remain distinct and unconfused; but there Pordage did not stop. He described the incarnation as 'Dreadful' in the violence it did to Christ's being, transforming him 'in an instant from an heavnly to an Earthly Creature; from an Angelical to a Bestial Form; from a Virgin Body to such as had brutal Marks of Distinction, the signatures of Male & Female'.[59] Similarly, Adam shared in this angelical form in his primitive, prelapsarian state: 'man was not originally created in the same Bestial form, we are now born in after the Fall'.[60] The resurrection of Jesus, for Pordage, involved his restoration to a virgin body, a restoration in which humanity participates. In musing on the possibility of this transformation into a 'New Angelical Creation' (such as Adam and Eve were in their innocence), Pordage made a declaration in the voice of the

---

[54] Brod, 'The seeker culture of the Thames Valley'; see also Urszula Szulakowska, *The alchemical Virgin Mary in the religious and political context of the Renaissance* (Newcastle: Cambridge Scholars Publishing, 2017), pp. 73, 88.

[55] Pordage, *Innocencie appearing*, p. 2.   [56] Pordage, *Innocencie appearing*, pp. 83–4.

[57] Internal evidence suggests that the earliest possible date would be the late 1650s, as it contains references to christological disputes between the Quakers and the Baptists. John Pordage, 'A tract of Christ's birth & incarnation', Bodleian Library, Rawlinson MS A. 354, p. 19.

[58] Pordage, 'A tract of Christ's birth', p. 6.   [59] Pordage, 'A tract of Christ's birth', pp. 46–7.

[60] Pordage, 'A tract of Christ's birth', p. 37. This chimes with the deposition at Pordage's trial by the commissioners, in which Pordage was accused of teaching one Mr Lewin that 'Adam was Male and Female in himself', Pordage, *Innocencie appearing*, p. 56.

Devil, who also longs for the restoration of his diabolical kind to a state of original glory. Certainly, Pordage and some of his disciples shared Origen's view that the Devil and his demonic agents would ultimately be restored to their original angelical state. The annotator comments that the speech is 'too Blasphemous to be publish'd, tho Milton in his Paradise Lost & Beaumont in his Psyche are Precedents for doing so in Verse'.[61]

Some of the most extraordinary passages in the tract relate not to the Devil, however, but to the role of the Virgin Mary in the incarnation. This is where Pordage, who was a physician (made MD at Leiden in 1639) before he was a minister in Reading and Berkshire, showed his Paracelsian colours, more than he betrayed the influence of Jacob Boehme. He set out a remarkably high Mariology, linking, as Paracelsus did, the Virgin Mother with Virgin Wisdom.[62] Pordage granted to Mary a highly exalted state in heaven, in which she is dignified for eternity as a 'Masculine Virgin', as was Adam in his androgynous state. Although the Romish language of Mary as 'Queen of Heaven' is not used, she is said to be 'in a higher state of Glory & Dignity' than any other creature, by virtue of her virgin motherhood by which 'All Marks of Distinction between Male & Female' are 'swallow'd up; for in Christ they are all one'.[63] This led Pordage into a discussion of Mary's own 'spiritual Mother', the eternal Wisdom of God: divine Sophia, who held such a significant place in the thought of the English followers of Jacob Boehme.[64] In Sophia, Pordage envisioned a divine mother, whose spiritual maternity played a vital role in the generation of the new angelical birth both of Christ and humanity in general. Sophia is the spiritual mother of the virginal Mary, as Mary is mother of Jesus: 'so that here we have a Mother within a Mother; as a wheele within a wheele'. He elaborates:

> For as Eve is the universal Mother of all living, under the state of the Fall, or Apostacy: so too is the Divine Wisdom, the Universal Mother of the Church of the First-born; & therefore too of all newborn Babes in general. But not to Digress too far; There is some Foundation in the first place for our notion of the Divine Wisdom; That she is a Female, & a Mother; wch is a pretty fair stop towards her being Mother to the Virgin-Mary in the spiritual sense of the new Birth. I shal here only add, before I proceed any further; That tho God indeed be in himself

---

[61] Pordage, 'A tract of Christ's birth', p. 27.
[62] See Szulakowska, 'Mary as Sophia, the Holy Virgin, in Paracelsian theosophy', in *The alchemical Virgin Mary*, pp. 131–148.
[63] Szulakowska, *The alchemical Virgin Mary*, p. 63.
[64] For feminist explorations of Sophia as a feminine divine principle, see Elizabeth Johnson, *She who is: the mystery of God in feminist theological discourse* (New York: Crossroads, 1994; Elisabeth Schüssler Fiorenza, *Jesus, Miriam's child, Sophia's prophet: critical issues in feminist christology* (New York: Continuum, 1995).

neither Male nor Female (& therefore is equally capable of either Denomination, that is not at all:) yet if He pleases to take either upon Him, as in the Letter of the Scripture he undeniably does Both; we are not easily to recede from any such Denomination.[65]

Pordage pointed out, in the concluding remark of this passage, that God has no gender, though he can assume feminine properties; he went on to argue for the application of female pronouns—'(Her) & (She)'—to Divine Wisdom, incorporated into the Trinity.[66] Like Paracelsus, Pordage embedded a female principle, mother of the incarnation, in the Godhead. The fact that he associated this principle so closely with the Virgin Mary brought him much closer to Paracelsus than to Boehme, who explicitly rejected the Paracelsian account of Mary's heavenly flesh and divine status in his writings.[67]

It appears from other writings that an essential quality of this feminine principle was, for Pordage, passivity. Whereas the Trinity 'is all Act, all acting power', she by contrast 'is perfectly passive, and moves not her self, but as the Eye [the Father] is moved'; she is 'an Eternal stillness in herself'.[68] Importantly, however, Sophia was also the agent of regeneration. Thomas Bromley, a leading member of the Bradfield circle, described how the perfectly resigned soul, 'being freed from the principle of Selfness', returns to a prelapsarian infancy through its 'Conception [and rebirth] in the Womb of Wisdom'.[69] The motifs of regeneration were ubiquitous in 'Erberist' writings, and closely linked to his doctrine of general incarnation. In 1653, Erbery published a series of letters among the 'saints' in England, Scotland, Ireland, and Wales, entitled *The babe of glory: breaking forth in the broken flesh of the saints*. In it, he elaborated on his theme of 'the Mystery of the Gospel... Christ in us the hope of glory; the glory, is God in mans flesh'. Christians were 'waiting... as a woman with child, to bring forth the Babe, the first born of glory in themselves; that is, to bring forth Christ fully in their flesh'.[70] In a fascinating anticipation of Pordage's concept of 'masculine virgins', Erbery included an anagram at the end of his preface, referring prophetically to Christina Queen of Sweden:

---

[65] Pordage, 'A tract of Christ's birth', pp. 70, 72–3.

[66] Pordage, 'A tract of Christ's birth', p. 73.

[67] See, for instance, *The fifth book*, in which Boehme commented (p. 61) that 'Many have attempted to write of the Virgin Mary; and *supposed* that she was *not* an Earthly Maid: to them indeed hath been presented a *Glimpse* of the Eternal virginity; but the right Mark they have hitherto failed of'. He explicitly denied 'that she is a Goddess' (p. 64).

[68] John Pordage, *Theologia mystica, or, the mystic divinitie of the aeternal invisibles* (London, 1683), p. 68.

[69] Thomas Bromley, *The way to the Sabbath of rest, or, the souls progresse in the work of regeneration* (London, 1654), p. 41.

[70] William Erbery, *The babe of glory: breaking forth in the broken flesh of the saints* (London, 1654), reprinted in Erbery, *The testimony of William Erbery*, p. 95.

> *Christina Regina Suecia,*
> A word in season   Anagram   By a Swedish Scholar
> *Hic est in viragine Cæsar.*
> Here's Cæsar in a manly woman.[71]

What did this signify, for Erbery, in the context of his discussion of the resurrected flesh of the saints in the new dispensation? Christina of Sweden, who famously defied gender stereotypes, was at the time of the publication of the tract, still queen of a Sweden dominant in the Baltic and North Sea. Christina's interests in Paracelsian alchemy are well established, and she was, by 1652, interacting with Boehme.[72] Her imperial reign seems to have been regarded by Erbery as a sign of the times, a breaking out of the third dispensation in which saints reborn in heavenly flesh, transcending gender distinctions, were in the ascendancy.

The Pordage circle took up this theme of glorified flesh within a more explicitly Paracelsian and Behmenist framework, sharing Erbery's emphasis on the communion of saints in the new resurrection. Boehme had written of the regeneration of the whole person, flesh and soul, but also introduced the idea of spiritual communion between lovers of Christ in a celestial body. Union with God in Christ involved a union of all the faithful: like lovers they 'transmute themselves into one body' and have 'an invisible commerce and Communion with all'.[73] Thomas Bromley wrote that 'they that are in this near Union, feel a mutual in-dwelling in the pure Tincture and Life of each other; and so, the further we come out of the animal Nature, the more universal we are, and nearer both to Heaven, and to one another in the Internal'.[74] For the Pordage circle, the sign that a transmutation of the brute body was underway was the experience of 'holy Commerce in pure Love' with fellow saints.[75] Elsewhere, in a retrospective manuscript account of the visions he received at Bradfield in 1649, Pordage reflected on the distinction between his doctrine of the new incarnation, and the 'sharp fire' doctrines taught by the Quakers in the first generation. Pordage felt that the Quakers were too high-flown in their assertion that

> they are all borne the Sons of god, as well as [Jesus Christ], sons as he was borne both God and man, both divine and human, so are they truly divine human, and that as the eternall was incarnated in that man and prefect, of Jesus of Nazareth, so the same eternall word, was incarnated in them.[76]

---

[71] Erbery, *The testimony of William Erbery*, p. 95.
[72] Szulakowska, *The alchemical Virgin Mary*, p. 181.
[73] Jacob Boehme, *Aurora, that is, the day-spring, or dawning of the day in the Orient* (London, 1656), p. 168; Jacob Boehme, *A consolatory treatise of the four complexions* (London, 1654), §C4r.
[74] Bromley, *The way to the Sabbath of rest*, p. 31.
[75] Bromley, *The way to the Sabbath of rest*, p. 47. On this theme, see Arthur Versluis, *Wisdom's children: a Christian esoteric tradition* (New York: SUNY, 1999), p. 199.
[76] John Pordage, 'Experimentall experiences concerning what God is in himselfe out of nature', Edinburgh University, MS DC.4.1, p. 82.

Although the differences (as he and his group acknowledged) between early Quaker theology and his own ideas about the 'new birth' were slight, the emphasis in Pordage's thought was not full identification with Christ, but on mystical participation and communion in Christ. This communion was not only with Christ and other Christians, but also extended to 'frequent and familiar converse with Angels'.[77] Reports of interactions with the angelical world are intelligible in light of Pordage's claim that the consummating union with Christ would involve transformation into a genderless, celestial form. This cosmic perspective recedes from view when one reads the witness statements describing stories of spirits hovering around Pordage's window; or angels appearing in 'clothes, band and cuffs', and coming into bedchambers and drawing the curtains.[78] The boundary between the spiritual, heavenly world and the visible, mundane world appears to have collapsed.

Rather than simply being a 'flesh-affirming' idea (which can only be argued with many qualifications), an important implication of spiritual flesh theology for conceptions of gender was that it expanded the idea of incarnation, far beyond a unique historical point and person. Feminist theologians in the twentieth and twenty-first centuries have wrestled continually with the problem of the singularity of the incarnation, and the assumption by God of a male body by which humanity is redeemed. For Daphne Hampson, the problem lies not so much in the maleness of Christ as in a more general philosophical difficulty with the particularity of incarnation, Deity rooted in a specific human life and time.[79] For theologians influenced by gender and queer theory, the incarnate body has sometimes been conceived as androgynous, or having feminine aspects.[80] The exclusionary tradition around Christ's sex, making maleness normative for humanity, remains a vexed aspect of incarnational theology. It is striking that radical preachers who seem to have sponsored and encouraged female ministry during the English Revolution, among them William Erbery and John Saltmarsh, developed such a distinctive doctrine of the incarnation. The incarnation narrated in the Gospels was, according to them, merely a shadow and glimpse of a greater manifestation of the Spirit of Christ in an age to come. Saltmarsh wrote that 'all that God did in this single and particular manifestation in flesh, as in one man' was a 'figure of the whole nature into which God enters, or is born into the world'.[81] The popular Baptist preacher Thomas Collier, similarly, wrote of

---

[77] Pordage, 'Experimentall experiences', p. 14. See Joad Raymond, 'Conversations with angels: the Pordages and their angelical world', *Milton's angels: the early modern imagination* (Oxford: Oxford University Press, 2010), pp. 125–61.

[78] Pordage, 'Experimentall experiences', pp. 68–9.

[79] Daphne Hampson, *Theology and feminism* (Oxford: Blackwell, 1990), p. 51.

[80] See, for instance, Graham Ward, *Christ and culture* (Oxford: Blackwell, 2005), pp. 129–58; Susannah Cornwall, 'The kenosis of unambiguous sex in the body of Christ: intersex, theology and existing for the other', *Theology and Sexuality* 14:2 (2008), pp. 181–99.

[81] John Saltmarsh, *Sparkles of glory* (London, 1647), pp. 203, 205.

Christ as an anticipatory figure of the plenary incarnation. At a disputation at Axbridge in Somerset in 1651, Collier was accused of teaching (among other heterodox ideas) that the saints would, in union with Christ, assume a 'spiritual body' and that the saints were sons of God 'in the same manner of Christ'.[82] Christians are 'Christed' (a suggestively Familist term), he wrote,

> and indeed Christ and Christians make but one Christ, one annoynted, one God fills them both: so that Christ was not only a Glorious dispensation of the Father, to sinners, and a figure in his death,... but likewise he was a paterne of our perfection, of our Glory in every particular, wherein Saints Union with God appears.[83]

It was orthodox christology by early modern standards to say that Christ was the instrument whereby 'the Lord takes our [human] nature or this whole Creation into union with himself'. On the other hand, to describe the singular incarnate Christ as a 'one man, the figure of the whole mystery' of God in all his saints was clearly a step beyond mainstream Reformed doctrine.[84]

William Erbery's departure from orthodoxy was clearer. He envisioned the passing away or vanishing of 'the old heaven and old earth (both Legal and Gospel-dispensation)'. Under the former Gospel dispensation, Christ was a 'Minister of the Circumcision' (this picks up the language used by Paul for Jesus' Jewish identity in Romans 15.8), and the true revelation of God's presence in the world was kept a mystery.[85] The second dispensation of the Gospel 'went no further than death': the saints were baptized into Christ's suffering and death, and participated in the breaking of his body at the eucharist, but underwent no resurrection.[86] A new dispensation was approaching (and indeed had come to some of the highest saints already), in which the new flesh of the resurrected Christ would break forth in the saints: 'This I call the third dispensation, or last discovery of God unto and in men, differing from Law and Gospel-order; yet comprehending both, and above both, yea above all: for here all men and things are nothing, but God is all and alone, yea God is All in all'.[87] This mystical union of 'all in all', without distinction or particularity, is what Erbery called the 'Mystery of Incarnation'. It was not so much this account of mystical union

---

[82] Anon., *The heads and substance of a discourse; first private, and afterwards publike; held in Axbridge, in the county of Somerset, about the 6th of March, 1650. Between Iohn Smith of Badgworth, and Charls Carlile of Bitsham, &c. on the one part; and Thomas Collier of Westbury on the other* (London, 1651), pp. 12–14.

[83] Thomas Collier, *A general epistle to the universal church of the first born* (London, 1649), p. 16.

[84] Saltmarsh, *Sparkles of glory*, pp. 203–4, 206.

[85] William Erbery, *A call to the churches; or, a packet of letters to the Pastors of Wales, presented to the baptized teachers there* (London, 1652), pp. 25–6.

[86] Erbery, *The babe of glory*, reprinted in Erbery, *The testimony of William Erbery*, p. 94.

[87] Erbery, *A call to the churches*, pp. 25–6.

(especially as it is set out in *The great mystery of godlinesse*, published in 1639 after his removal from Cardiff) which distinguished Erbery from other Protestant thinkers, as the dispensational thought which developed later in his army career, dividing the approaching time from the age of the Gospel. Nonetheless, the mystical doctrine of a general incarnation minimized the role of a particular, male Saviour.[88] Erbery wrote of the saints that 'tho they be never so many millions of men in multiplyed flesh, yet they make but One perfect Man in whom the Godhead is embodyed fully, or One spirit, that is, God manifest in flesh'.[89] The incarnation was subjectivized, in such a way that a woman could experience or discover the divine nature united to herself. It was a bilateral exchange: 'as [Christ] tooke my flesh and made it his, so I take his flesh and make it mine'.[90]

Ideas about spiritual incarnation appeared, indeed, in a number of women's writings in the 1640s and 1650s, and shaped their understanding of their prophetic vocation and identity. This version of 'heavenly flesh' was not always recognizably Paracelsian or Melchiorite, and seems to have developed as something quite distinctive in the apocalyptic, dispensational theology of the English sects. Nonetheless, the English radicals shared concepts of corporate participation and transformation which were strongly indicative of radical reformation origins. Mary Cary showed clear signs of having been influenced by celestial flesh doctrine. She wrote about the transformation of the bodies of the saints on earth, by which 'they shall be raised spiritual bodies', having 'laid down their mortal bodies'. Their life on earth would be a manifestation of the life of heaven: 'the actings and walkings, of the raised Saints here on earth, may be much like the actings of the Angels of God'.[91] Anne Yemans quite openly suggested, as Erbery had done, that the manifestation of Christ in the saints would be superior as a manifestation or revelation of the divine nature to that of the historical Christ in flesh. She compared the coming dispensation to the coming of Christ following John the Baptist:

> when Christ did come in the flesh, and revealed himselfe in a great deale more clearer and excellenter manner than he did by John; yet Christ came to prepare a way for a further manifestation of his owne glory to them in a clearer and great deale more fuller and glorious manner.[92]

---

[88] The notion of a general and living 'incarnation' has something in common with the process theology of Monica Coleman and the feminist theology of Anna Mercedes. See Anna Mercedes, *Power for: feminism and Christ's self-giving* (London and New York: T & T Clark, 2011), p. 137.
[89] William Erbery, *The armies defence, or, God guarding the camp of the Saints and the beloved city* (London, 1648), pp. 22–3.
[90] William Erbery, *The great mystery of godlinesse* (London, 1639), p. 9.
[91] Mary Cary, *The little horns doom & downfall* (London, 1651), p. 311.
[92] Anne Yemans, *Crooked pathes made straight: or, the wayes of God made knowne to lost sinnes, or bewildered saints* (London, 1648), pp. 108–9.

The fuller more glorious manifestation was 'the glory of Jesus being revealed more and more in his Saints', which 'outshines' the previous dispensations, and causes them to 'decrease' in significance.[93] Although she did not seem to have a well-developed notion of celestial flesh, she did have an Erberist sense of the corporate dimension of the new incarnation, in which distinctions would be dissolved. It was certainly an enduring theme in certain streams of Quakerism, shaped by the Nayler circle, the 'church of the first-born'. Susanna Bateman, writing in 1656, referred to the light within as the 'New-born babe' of Christ 'manifest in flesh'; Sarah Blackborow also touched on Erberist themes: the 'immortal birth' and the enjoyment of 'the Babe of Glory', by which women and men 'come to possess the power of God'.[94]

One of the earliest female exponents of the apocalyptic doctrine of Christ's new manifestation in the flesh, and certainly one of the most interesting, was Elizabeth Avery. Avery was identified in a Presbyterian anti-heresy polemic as a deviant theologian teaching the fourth-century Euchite or Messalian heresy that 'man was made after the likeness of God, that therefore God had a body in shape like mans body'.[95] She published with the favoured printer of the radicals, Giles Calvert, and like so many of the women whose works were printed in this period, made a virtue out of her perceived 'weaknesse and contemptiblenesse' as an instrument of God's power and communication to the saints.[96] By her foolishness, she wrote in her preface to the reader, 'he doth bring to nought the wisdom of the wise'. Having dispensed with the conventional rhetoric of female prophets, she took a bolder tone: she would pay for the truth she was setting forth with her blood, if required, and feared no reproach or reprisal. Her preface concludes with the following words:

> And so I shall leave thee (good Reader) to the manifestation of Christ in thy flesh which doth begin to appear in some, and we do likewise expect it in general unto all the Saints, when God shall bring them out of darknesse into his marvellous light; which is begun, and shall increase until it be pefect day.[97]

This new 'manifestation of Christ in flesh', the second incarnation to prevail over the reign of Antichrist in the world, was central to the message of the prophetic letters which Avery addressed to a general readership in 1647. Antichrist would

---

[93] Yemans, *Crooked pathes*, p. 108.
[94] Susanna Bateman, 'I matter not how I appear to man' (London, 1657), pp. 3, 8; Sarah Blackborow, *Herein is held forth the gift and good-will of God to the world* (London, 1659), p. 2.
[95] Richard Allen, *An antidote against heresy* (London, 1648), p. 27. See David Loewenstein, *Treacherous faith: the specter of heresy in early modern English literature and culture* (Oxford: Oxford University Press, 2013), p. 426.
[96] Elizabeth Avery, *Scripture-prophecies opened: which are to be accomplished in these last times, which do attend the second coming of Christ* (London, 1647), §A3r.
[97] Avery, *Scripture-prophecies opened*, §A3r.

rule in Babylon (the nation governed by arbitrary rule, and the national church which comprehends all people) 'till God is manifested in the flesh of the Saints, as he was in the Humanity of Christ'.[98]

Like Erbery, Avery could see this manifestation already underway, as the signs of the times indicated Babylon was falling. As she later reflected, her own experience of grace in the period of the wars in the three kingdoms was that of an inward incarnation:

> I found Christ in me, ruling and reigning, and taking all power to himself, and he hath caught the man-childe up to God, which I brought forth. i.e. The flesh, (by his incarnation) and I have found in me (and do yet) his judgement-seat, to judge and sentence sin, and lust, and corruption, and his throne is there for himself to sit, and to rule by his own Laws: And thus it continues with me at this day, and the Lord leads me on, higher and higher in himself; and for that I see so much of him here in the midst of this Church, I desire to be one also with you.[99]

Christ 'is come into his temple in many of the Saints', and there would be 'no more sin, nor hell, nor death'. This was not a distant and objectified God or remote prospect of the afterlife, but 'a heaven within us, even God manifested in the flesh of his Saints, as in the humanity of Christ'.[100] Avery was at her most radical when she began to reflect on the status of the saints in this new condition of glorified flesh. She appeared not merely to claim that this incarnation had equal status with that of Jesus Christ of Nazareth, but at points, to suggest that the general incarnation was superior to the original manifestation of God in human nature. Certainly, this new appearance of God transcended theological 'Truth' as it was taught by the 'ministry of man in Babylon'. The saints, she wrote, 'are more excellent then the Truth: they are the temples of the living God, the sons and daughters of God Almighty, who do partake of the same nature, union, love and glory as Christ our Saviour, our Head and Elder Brother'.[101] Although Avery did not develop the theme of the new dispensation exceeding the first, as Erbery did, she did emphasize the 'fullness' of this fresh revelation of God, dissolving all particularity, all distinctions between persons. As she put it, 'the spiritual bodies of the Saints are not distinct one from another, but they make up the fulnesse of God, and so this full God shall be manifested in the flesh of those Saints who shall live to the state of perfection'.[102]

---

[98] Avery, *Scripture-prophecies opened*, pp. 1–2.
[99] See John Rogers, 'A fuller testimony as it was taken from Elizabeth Avery', *Ohel or Beth-shemesh: a tabernacle of the sun* (London, 1653), p. 406.
[100] Avery, *Scripture-prophecies opened*, pp. 5, 21.
[101] Avery, *Scripture-prophecies opened*, p. 11.
[102] Avery, *Scripture-prophecies opened*, p. 37.

Spiritual Senses

A further incarnational framework for the radicals' thought, their revival of the patristic doctrine of 'spiritual senses', helps to interpret the visionary dimension of the experiences reported in these testimonies. The notion of revelation by 'spiritual senses' had particular resonances in the apocalyptic climate of the mid-seventeenth century and was, in several of its expressions, closely related to spiritual flesh christology. The doctrine had early Christian origins, first expounded by Origen and subsequently taken up by a variety of Western theologians, among them Augustine, Aquinas, and Nicholas of Cusa. In its earliest articulation in Origen's homilies on the Song of Songs, the acquisition by sanctified Christians of spiritual senses—inward faculties exactly parallel to the five external or corporeal senses—is described as one of the implications of the incarnation. According to Origen, Christ entered into human flesh and bodily experience, and now 'looks out' through the windows of the body, the five senses. Union with Christ allows the soul to share in the sensibility of the incarnate God.[103] Classical statements in the Origenist tradition of spiritual sensation were available only to a limited extent in English translation, and mostly mediated by authors schooled in patristic theology, in commentaries on the Song of Songs or other Hebrew texts.[104] There was, however, an important radical context for the reception of the theme in the seventeenth century, which has been largely overlooked in influential recent scholarship on 'spiritual senses'.[105] The patristic idea of spiritual sensation had numerous attractions and applications among the radicals. It provided a framework for a vital and immediate access to the divine in which direct sense perception rather than any external pedagogue—whether textual or human—was Teacher. The concept supplied a language for talking about interactions with the divine at the level of visions and intuitions.

Samuel Rutherford identified the doctrine as a distinctively Familist or Antinomian teaching that was circulating among the army preachers in the late 1640s, referring derisively to 'the spirituall senses, that *Antinomians* and *Familists*

---

[103] Origen, 'Second homily on the Song of Songs', 2.12, in R.P. Lawson, ed. and trans., *Origen: the Song of Songs commentary and homilies* (New York: Newman Press, 1956), pp. 301–2; see also the discussion in Benjamin Myers, 'Exegetical mysticism: Scripture, *Paideia*, and the spiritual senses', in Janice McRandal, ed., *Sarah Coakley and the future of systematic theology* (Minneapolis, MN: Fortress, 2018), pp. 12–13.

[104] See, for instance, John Trapp's *Commentary or exposition upon these following books of holy Scripture: Proverbs of Solomon, Ecclesiastes, the Song of Songs, Isaiah, Jeremiah, Lamentations, Ezekiel & Daniel* (London, 1660), pp. 320–3, dense with references to patristic and contemporary exegesis; or Hanserd Knollys, *An exposition of the first chapter of the Song of Solomon* (London, 1656).

[105] Sarah Coakley and Paul Gavrilyuk, eds., *The spiritual senses: perceiving God in Western Christianity* (Cambridge: Cambridge University Press, 2011). Derek Michaud has recently written on the Cambridge Platonist John Smith's engagement with the spiritual senses tradition, but the wider context for the reception of the doctrine in this period remains largely unexamined. See Derek Michaud, *Reason turned into sense: John Smith on spiritual sensation*, Studies in Philosophical Theology (Leuven: Peeters, 2017), vol. 62.

boast off'.[106] An example of the visionary exercise of spiritual senses among the spiritualist radicals is mentioned in a letter printed in Thomas Edwards' *Gangraena*, dated 14 October 1645, concerning a group in Poole which included the radical chaplain Henry Pinnell. Pinnell was at that time devoted to an unnamed prophetess who had just given birth, and whose spiritual experiences included olfactory sensations. Edwards' correspondent, the Presbyterian minister Simon Ford, recalled that 'she told us Christ did appear to her gloriously, & perfumed her, (and she would ask those about her, whether they smelt not those perfumes)'.[107] A modern clinical assessment might conclude that this new mother was experiencing hyperosmia due to recent hormonal changes. Within the framework of antinomian mysticism, her heightened receptivity to sense impressions was a spiritual gift. Some of the fullest explorations of the spiritual senses were undertaken by the circle around John Pordage, and the manuscript remains of this mystical network indicate that the idea of spiritual perception drew inspiration from visionary writing of the Thirty Years' War, and not only that of Jacob Boehme. A vision of an itinerant lay prophet in Lutheran Brunswick, the 'German Lazarus' Hans Engelbrecht (who was visited by Paul Felgenhauer in the 1620s and 1630s, and notably claimed to have experienced a resurrection from the dead in 1622), was translated into English by the group at some point before 1660.[108] Engelbrecht recorded in 1634 a terrible 'anguish of spirit' in which he experienced the 'abominable stink and bitter savour' of hell. In his torment, Engelbrecht cried a prayer of faith, and the 'loathsome scent disappeared', giving way to a miraculous angelic visitation in which he was given 'the understanding of ye whole Bible in a moment'. His spiritual senses were opened to celestial music, which made him break forth in singing, and a vision of 'a transparent Earth...adorned with all sorts of most beautifull flowers, which were sparkling and shining, and their colours farr more lively than those here below'. The climax of this vision was the sight of Jesus Christ, alone on the earth, 'in his glorified body...his Body was transparent', with his wounds shining like stars, in which Engelbrecht saw his own face, as well as that of another young man: 'wee look'd upon one another through ye Body of Christ'. In this revelation of the new earth, the prophet hears, tastes, sees, and smells in Christ and through Christ.[109]

---

[106] Samuel Rutherford, *A survey of the spirituall Antichrist opening the secrets of familisme and antinomianisme in the antichristian doctrine of John Saltmarsh and Will. Del* (London, 1648), p. 311.

[107] Thomas Edwards, *Gangraena* (London, 1646), p. 84.

[108] On Engelbrecht's writings and career, see Jürgen Beyer, *Lay prophets in Lutheran Europe, 1550–1700* (Leiden: Brill, 2017), pp. 158–60; 208–27.

[109] 'A short account of ye wonderfull life and visions of Hans Engelbrecht, taken out of a large Treatise writ by himselfe in ye German tongue', in Bodleian Library, Rawlinson MS C. 266, §§2v–3v, 4v–5r, 7r–v. Another manuscript translation of Engelbrecht, or 'John Angelbright of Brunswick', can be found in British Library, Sloane MS 2569, 'Theological Treatises', fols. 91r–125v: it contains his 1641 'Divine vision'. This manuscript collection also contains later visions of Jane Lead.

Figure 2 The opening of the spiritual eye, in John Pordage, *Theologia mystica* (London, 1683), adj. p. 29.

It was reported that in August 1649, John Pordage and his household started to enjoy in a similar fashion the 'wonderful exercise' of 'opening their inward or spirituall senses sometyme to se heaven, and its inhabitants, and sometyme to se hell, and its inhabitants'; senses which would never be shut again unless they were to forsake 'the pure life of virginity' (Figure 2).[110] At first sight, this appears to refer simply to the onset of the season of visionary experience at the Bradfield rectory. Pordage's followers, however, developed and expanded explicitly the Origenist doctrine of the spiritual senses in intentional ways. One of the more comprehensive accounts of the doctrine comes in an undated 'A letter concerning the nature

[110] Preface to Pordage, 'Experimentall experiences', p. 70; Pordage, *Innocencie appearing*, p. 77.

of the opening of the spiritual senses' which circulated later in the clandestine group around Pordage and Jane Lead, and was perhaps written by Lead herself.[111] The continuity between physical and spiritual senses is made explicit in this letter, so that the spiritual sense is actually situated in the physical sensory organ: 'the Superiour are situated in the Inferior, each in their proper corresponding part, the spiritual Eye and Eare in the Outward Eye and Eare: and so the rest'.[112] This correspondence gives spiritual significance to every physical component of the organ, including nerves and connecting tissue: since the 'Spirituall Eye is seated in the outward', for instance, this means that 'the pupill the Retina the optick nerve &c. have in their manner their spirituall power'.[113] In a preface to his manuscript works, one of Pordage's disciples, the Aberdeen physician James Keith, also wrote extensively on the spiritual senses, describing a 'perfect analogy between the spiritual and the corporeal'.[114]

Origen's theme supported the emphasis on the *proximity* of God and intimacy of union with the divine, in mystical and prophetic writings proclaiming a dawning age of spiritual renewal. Sarah Wight (or at least, the letter published in her name in 1656) wrote suggestively, though not extensively, about the exercise of her 'spiritual senses'. Her quest for Christ led her not to any external creaturely idol, but inward, to 'Christ in the inmost places' of her own heart.[115] Gerrard Winstanley contrasted the old regime of religious tyranny, under which man 'exercised outward senses to follow creatures', with a new way of knowing opened up to all people, so that 'now he lives in the exercise of his spirituall senses, and hee doth rightly, and he knowes wherefore; for his soul now sees, feels, tasts, smells and hears the Father spiritually in all things, and so doth all things in love'.[116] This vital experience of divine life through the inward senses is the only way to God, and cannot be accessed through objectified or theological knowledge: 'Jesus Christ at a distance from thee, will not save thee'.[117] Another figure of considerable significance in the radical politics of the 1640s and 1650s, Sir Henry Vane, was also an exponent of this doctrine. According to Vane, Christ was the first in human form perfectly to exercise his spiritual senses, and by his incarnation, his followers might share in this deeper sensual experience. As a sign of 'the last administration of Christs kingdom', those who enter into union with him,

---

[111] The letter contains a cross-reference to her *Revelation of Revelations*, which suggests a date after its publication in 1683. 'A letter concerning the nature of the opening of the spiritual senses', Bodleian Library, Rawlinson MS C. 266, fol. 52v.

[112] 'A letter concerning', fol. 40r.   [113] 'A letter concerning the nature', fol. 42r.

[114] James Keith, 'A preliminary treatise which may serve for an introduction to the following work of Dr John Pordage', Bodleian Library, Rawlinson MS A. 404, pp. 16, 32–36.

[115] Sarah Wight, *A wonderful pleasant and profitable letter written by Mris Sarah Wight, to a friend* (London, 1656), pp. 54, 58.

[116] Gerrard Winstanley, *Truth lifting up its head above scandals* (London, 1649), p. 10.

[117] Winstanley, *Truth lifting up its head*, p. 10.

have the use of spiritual senses set up in them, enabling them to hear and obey what the spirit saith unto the Churches: and so are worshippers of God in spirit, rejoycing in Christ Jesus, & having no confidence in the flesh; enjoying within themselves the witness of a better and more enduring substance then what is experienced under the first-covenant-ministry.[118]

Mystical union with Christ would unlock these powers of perception, a superior witness to God than (it is implied) the external Scriptures. Vane's Restoration biographer, George Sikes, likewise affirmed that

> where the Principle of new-creature Life, or Life of Faith, is sown by Christ in any man... it will spring up into such a prevailing exercise of its spiritual senses, over all fleshly, first-creation Life and principles in him, that his whole person may thence be called a spiritual man.[119]

Vane's account of spiritual sensation as an aspect of regeneration influenced a number of preachers active in the 1650s. It finds a strong echo in the teachings of one Gloucestershire minister, Anthony Palmer, who proclaimed that 'the Gospel-new-creature is a living new creature, and doth exercise Spiritual Life, and hath new spiritual senses'.[120]

Peter Sterry, a close associate of Vane and Republican chaplain to Cromwell, also developed an imaginative and lively account of the spiritual senses, embedded in a narrative of regeneration and union with Christ (what he called the 'Love-Birth').[121] In a letter to Cromwell himself in September 1650, Sterry wished upon the Lord General 'a spirituall sight' of Christ, and the blessings of Christ 'by which a peculiar presence and appearance of God is made manifest, drawing the eyes of his people by that which they see, to that of him which is invisible'.[122] Sterry was much admired by female followers, among them the prominent visionary Jane Lead, and enjoyed an intense spiritual relationship with his wife and daughter.[123] He urged his daughter, for instance, 'to bee a Priest to God, sanctifying all things', enjoining her to treat her relations 'as Divinity coming downe from above in a

---

[118] Henry Vane, *The retired mans meditations, or, the mysterie and power of godlines* (London, 1655), p. 137.
[119] George Sikes, *The life and death of Sir Henry Vane, Kt.* (London, 1662), p. 26.
[120] Anthony Palmer, *The Gospel new-creature; wherein the work of the spirit is opened, in awakening the soul* (London, 1658), p. 217.
[121] Peter Sterry, *The rise, race, and royalty of the kingdom of God in the soul of man* (London, 1683), p. 370.
[122] 'Mr Peter Sterry to the Lord General Cromwell' (dated 19 Sept. 1650), in John Nickolls, *Original letters and papers of State* (London, 1747), p. 18.
[123] Francis Lee, in an unpublished letter reporting Jane Lead's death, mentions that she praised the late Sterry's preaching in her dying words, as she recalled the funeral sermon given by Sterry's colleague Jeremiah White (whom she remembered as an 'old Friend') on the occasion of the death of a fellow female visionary, Ann Bathurst. 'Letters of Francis Lee', Lambeth Palace Library, MS 1559, p. 24.

Cloud of fflesh, here offer them up, and Return them to Heaven, & your-selfe ascend with them'.[124] In the summer of 1652, Sterry briefly found himself in the spotlight for his interactions with prophetic women when he was preaching at Whitehall on the Resurrection, and a woman in his congregation created a sensation by stripping until she was 'bare to the middle of her back'. Sterry was publicly criticized for keeping silence in the face of this disturbance, to which he responded briefly with a politician's answer, that the true nature of the scandalous behaviour was 'hid from my sight in the throng'.[125] Although his ministerial career took him to high places, Sterry was a somewhat obscure figure, who, like Vane, failed to publish widely in his lifetime, and seemed wary of committing his writing to print (his only two published works appeared after his death). His diffidence led one Richard Baxter, who could never be accused of holding back from public interventions, to note scornfully that 'he hath not opened himself in writing', and to associate him as a spiritual sectarian with the 'Vanists' with the memorable pun: 'Vanity and Sterility were never more happily conjoined'.[126] Sterry, nonetheless, left a wealth of unpublished writings, now held at Emmanuel College in Cambridge, his alma mater. These are extraordinarily rich and luminous spiritual letters and meditations, literary in their quality, full of sensual imagery evocative of the mystical tradition. Sterry's poetic mysticism continually illustrates the exercise of the spiritual senses.

A distinctive characteristic of Sterry's mystical writing is the prominence of female language for God, drawn from scriptural imagery but also evidently inspired by his neo-platonic learning. In one of his letters to Scipio, the literary name he gave to a close friend (with its evocations of the classic neo-platonist text, Macrobius's Commentary on the *Dream of Scipio*), he noted that 'The Antients say of ye Gods, yt every God is Male, & ffemale, because every God, every Angell, every Spirit is an Unity comprehending in itselfe ye full variety, wch is as ye female to that male, ye Unity'.[127] He went on to suggest that Christ, as a divine birth, also comprehends both male and female nature in himself. In his unpublished christological treatise, 'The palace of the sun', Sterry wrote of a 'Divine Mother' that is a female principle in the Godhead, endlessly generating the variety of forms, images, and creatures which reflect the beauty of the supreme unity.[128] Christ is the image of unity, containing within himself both male and female principles, in 'the Divine Love marriage of a twofold fforme'.[129] In a spiritual letter to his son Peter, Sterry

---

[124] Peter Sterry, letter dated 10 Dec. 1662 and undated letter, in Emmanuel College, Cambridge, MS 289, pp. 26, 43.
[125] David Brown, *The naked woman, or a rare epistle sent to Mr Peter Sterry minister at Whitehall* (London, 1652), p. 16.
[126] Richard Baxter, *Reliquiæ Baxterianæ* (London, 1696), p. 75.
[127] Peter Sterry, 'Letter to Scipio' (undated), in Emmanuel College, Cambridge, MS 289, p. 134.
[128] Peter Sterry, 'The palace of the sun', in Emmanuel College, Cambridge, MS 294, p. 173. I am grateful to Edward Youasamouth for alerting me to the existence of this treatise.
[129] Sterry, 'The palace of the sun', p. 147.

wrote in figurative terms drawn from 1 Peter 2.2, of Christ the Word as a nursing mother, evoking the savour of spiritual milk: 'O Son', he urged: 'thirst continually for, continually suck in this sweet milk of ye immortall Word in ye bosome of yt Word'.[130] Elsewhere, to Scipio, Sterry characterized God as the platonic ideal of motherhood—as well as fatherhood, and spousal love—and played on the maternal metaphor in Isaiah 49.15 ('Can a woman forget her sucking child, that she should have compassion on the son of her womb? Yea they may forget, yet will I not forget thee'.): 'The Mother may forget ye Son of her wombe: but he is a ffather, a Mother, an Husband all in one, where ye most perfect loves of all Relations in their highest truth, & sweetnesse meet in one'.[131] Sterry also used powerful maternal imagery, the imagery of one who has closely observed a woman's care for her infant, in relation to his own spiritual state. To Scipio, he wrote yearningly:

> As a mother with a lovely child in her lap, and a full breast, but a sore niple, grieves that she cannot milk forth into ye sweete streams which is her cheifest work, and delight: so hath ye spirit truly lovely, and beloved in the beauties, and tendernesses of ye heavenly birth in our Jesus, been ever in the embraces of my Spirit before my eyes; so have I grieved yt the weaknesse of my body hath not suffered me to pour forth these loves in the spirit, which my soul is filled with for you.[132]

The striking image with which Sterry expressed his longing for an encounter with his friend, that of a mother desperate to nurse her beautiful child, but too sore to do so, was the preface to a longer discourse on what he called the 'spiritual body' of the saints resurrected in union with Christ.

As other recent commentators on the tradition of 'spiritual senses' in Eastern and Western Christianity have observed, proponents of the doctrine did not conceive of a hard dichotomy between physical and spiritual sensation, but rather understood the relation in terms of integration and continuity, within the framework of the incarnation. Natalie Carnes put it well in her study of Gregory of Nyssa: 'the physicality of the Incarnation affirms the importance of the physical senses in opening the spiritual senses'.[133] In his unpublished writings, Sterry struck 'Erberist' as well as Origenist notes in describing the opening of the spiritual senses, in relation to the glorification of the body of the saints in union with Christ's body. He distinguished between gross material flesh (bodily substances, which decompose), and the human body understood as the site of both

---

[130] Emmanuel College, Cambridge, MS 289, p. 131.
[131] Emmanuel College, Cambridge, MS 289, p. 134.
[132] Emmanuel College MS 289, p. 109.
[133] Natalie Carnes, *Beauty: a theological engagement with Gregory of Nyssa* (Eugene, OR: Wipf & Stock, 2014), p. 224.

physical and spiritual sense perception. In this, however, he was not implying that the material and spiritual body were radically divided, as he was careful to specify that the sinful or worldly 'flesh' to which the New Testament writers so frequently refer is a lower state which is part of a continuum with the higher, spiritual nature. The material body was not to be opposed to spirit; it was a 'an Image, in which some spirit, some principle, some power of life makes it self manifest, and visible to ye fleshly, and spirituall senses'. This was something like human personhood; the body as *imago Dei*, 'adequate to ye Godhead'. He concluded:

> Can this body be any other than one essence, one substance, one eternall Spirit, with God? This is one Jesus ye divine body in ye first place, as he is ye 2d person in ye Trinity, ye Essentiall image of God, in his humane nature, in his humane body glorified, doth all ye fullnesse of ye Godhead dwell bodily, as ye humane body is taken up into one person, into one Spirit one glory with ye Essentiall Image. Soe is ye humane body of Christ soe is ye glorified body of every saint, a Spirit an eternall Spirit in its own proper forme, in its own Essentiall, substantiall and compleat likenesse.[134]

For Henry Vane, the perfection of 'Christs heavenly manhood' lay not only in 'the compleat exercise of his spiritual senses' but also his

> retaining withal, in perfect use, the exercise of his natural senses, powers and faculties of soul and body, in a glorified state, as being in one and the same person, the fulness of Jew and Gentile; the perfection of the spiritual and of the natural man; joyning them both together in one sheepfold, whereof himself is the one great shepheard and overseer.[135]

Sterry likewise wrote of the spiritual senses in christological terms. In his account, Christ presents himself to the disciples after the Resurrection 'with his whole Man-hood, Soul and Body', and it is this vision of 'Jesus Christ united in his own Person' which, 'by these Signs to the outward senses, at once opened, fortified, heightned, enlarged the Understanding, and the spiritual senses of the Apostles'.[136] Thus, according to Vane, 'the putting on of the new man' by the Christian would entail

> the exercising as well their spiritual senses (in likeness and conformity to Christs actings and life in that unity wherein he and his Father are one, whereby he crucified and kept under his natural man) as to the exercising of their

---

[134] Sterry, 'Letter to Scipio' (dated July 1669), pp. 111–12.
[135] Vane, *The retired mans meditations*, p. 116.
[136] Peter Sterry, *A discourse of the freedom of the will* (London, 1675), pp. 243–4.

natural powers and faculties in likeness and conformity to the actings of Christs natural man.[137]

Throughout his private meditations, Sterry evoked scenes of natural beauty, 'ravishing Musick', sweet flavours of fruit and honey, the scent of divine perfume, in the quest for a lively account of mystical union.[138] All of this sensual imagery could be equally readily summoned, of course, by any Puritan devotional writer versed in the Song of Songs and the Psalms. Sterry, rather like his contemporary Thomas Traherne, intended his engagement of the senses to reflect his understanding of the continuous relationship between the visual, material world, and the heavenly sphere, of which all earthly enjoyments are a representation and anticipation. The correspondence between sensual delights and celestial glory had its exact counterpart in the relationship between the bodily and spiritual senses. A bright spring would put Sterry in mind of 'a new heaven & a new earth, in wch at once all things sing, shine, send forth their sweet ardours together, flowers, Birds, ye Sun, ye holy Angells, our Beautifull Jesus, ye ever glorious God, ye supream love'.[139] On one occasion, he recorded for his daughter a dialogue with his wife, which took place while they walked alongside the Thames river on a winter's day, from their home at West Sheen in Richmond. It was a 'very lovely ffrost' that day, so that 'ye sky, & ye earth seeme to shine, & sparkle, & smile one upon another; like Christ, & His Spouse from Heaven above'.[140] At one point, Sterry's wife Frances commented that 'The plaine on ye other side ye Thames looks like a tart with sugar upon it, finely iced over'. This observation led her husband to reflect on a rabbinic interpretation of one of the Psalms, that 'there shall be a Cake on ye tops of ye Mountaines, and interpret it of the Messias, who shal be in every Creature, as a Cake ready prepared inviting us to eate of it'.[141] The fact that Sterry recorded this conversation suggests that he was somewhat pleased with his apt and learned reference, adding a third layer of meaning to his wife's homely simile. For this spiritually sympathetic couple, the sensual world was full of cues: even a field in frost with the appearance of a sugared tart could be a signpost to the indwelling Christ.

As they appeared in the radical theology of revolutionary England, both the doctrines of heavenly flesh and spiritual senses continued traditions reassessing the incarnation and human participation in Christ. They formed part of a much wider early modern probing of Chalcedonian christology (the classical account of

---

[137] Emmanuel College, Cambridge, MS 289, p. 124.
[138] Emmanuel College, Cambridge, MS 289, pp. 70, 95.
[139] Emmanuel College, Cambridge, MS 289, p. 136.
[140] Emmanuel College, Cambridge, MS 289, p. 58.
[141] Emmanuel College, Cambridge, MS 289, p. 59. Sterry was apparently referring to rabbinic interpretations of Psalm 72.16, which some Catholic writers (among them Petrus Galatinus) adopted as a reference to transubstantiation or the 'wafer-cake' of the mass. See G. Lloyd Jones, *The discovery of Hebrew in Tudor England: a third language* (Manchester: Manchester University Press, 1983), p. 134.

Christ's two natures), and in several instances clearly developed christological speculations from antiquity. More immediately, English radicalism on the incarnation drew inspiration from the thought of Paracelsus and his followers among the apocalyptic theologians of the Thirty Years' War. Central to their vision was an account of progression to an ultimate mystical union with Christ, and the complete transformation of the full human person, body and soul, as the final outworking of the incarnation. It was in the context of the English Revolution, however, that the implications of this vision for gender were most fully realized. Heavenly flesh dissolved the gendered distinction between matter and spirit, as well as between persons; female as well as male bodies were imagined as transmuted into a glorified, corporate body. The concept of spiritual senses made more tangible the mystical interaction between the sensual and the spiritual worlds, a distinction which was, ultimately, largely collapsed by the radicals.

2
Salvation

This chapter focuses on the doctrine of universal salvation in women's prophetic writings of the 1640s, and the interplay between gendered experience and Scripture interpretation which gave rise to an expansive account of divine love.[1] Women were pioneers of this doctrine in an inhospitable intellectual climate, to an extent which has been overlooked by historians and theologians alike. The debate among Christian theologians over the afterlife can hardly be said to be closed, and the historical provenance and development of universalist doctrines remain as central to the controversy as biblical interpretation. Michael McClymond's two-volume *Devil's redemption: a new history and interpretation of Christian universalism* (2018) seeks to discredit the tradition by identifying it with esoteric and kabbalistic currents in Christian history; while David Bentley Hart's impassioned recent essay repudiating the doctrine of eternal damnation takes on centuries of Christian (especially Western Christian) 'infernalism'.[2] In historical-theological surveys of Christian universalism—the doctrine of the ultimate restoration of all things to loving communion with God—the female theologians of the seventeenth century are anonymous, almost certainly unknown to the surveyors. Exceptionally among twentieth-century commentators, D.P. Walker's classic account of *The decline of hell* (1964), acknowledged the contributions of Lady Anne Conway and Jane Lead, whose works were published in the 1680s and 1690s; but he was unaware of an earlier generation of women universalists.[3] Richard Bauckham's 1978 article summarizing the history of the doctrine mentioned a number of male 'radical religious thinkers' of the English Revolution (among them, Gerrard Winstanley) who were also theorists of universalism, as part of a 'reaction to the particularism of high Calvinism'.[4] A recent survey traces universalist thought back to Origen and takes its title from the works of

---

[1] I am grateful to Charlotte Methuen for granting permission to reproduce parts of the chapter 'Women prophets and universalist interpretations of Scripture in revolutionary England', in Charlotte Methuen, ed., *Protestant Reformation and Catholic reforms in northern and central Europe*, part of the Society of Biblical Literature's *The Bible and women, an encyclopedia of exegesis and cultural history* edited by Mary Ann Beavis, Irmtraud Fischer, Mercedes Navarro, and Adriana Valerio (Leiden: Brill, 2023).
[2] Michael J. McClymond, *The Devil's redemption: a new history and interpretation of Christian universalism* (Grand Rapids, MI: Baker, 2018); David Bentley Hart, *That all shall be saved: heaven, hell and universal salvation* (Yale, CN: Yale University Press, 2019).
[3] D.P. Walker, *The decline of hell: seventeenth-century discussions of eternal torment* (Chicago: University of Chicago Press, 1964), pp. 137–45, 218–30.
[4] Richard Bauckham, 'Universalism: a historical survey', *Themelios* 4:2 (1978), p. 49.

Julian of Norwich, but offers three men of the eighteenth century as examples of those who, in the early modern period, arrived at 'universalist convictions without having been taught them by anyone else' (there is a chapter in the same volume on two male seventeenth-century Origenists, Peter Sterry and Jeremiah White).[5]

Universalism in the English Revolution

It has long been established that there were proponents of universal salvation among the revolutionary preachers of free grace. A.L. Morton identified the doctrine of universal salvation with 'the more advanced sects', namely the mystical Ranters and Seekers.[6] Christopher Hill noted that Richard Coppin and Lawrence Clarkson, mystical radicals in the circle of Abiezer Coppe, preached universal salvation. He also observed that contemporaries linked universalist ideas with the prophetic notion of the 'Everlasting Gospel': the opening of a new spiritual dispensation, in which mysteries which had been kept hidden throughout history would be revealed.[7] Nigel Smith has suggested that Coppin was 'one of the first in England to preach universal salvation; the Digger Gerrard Winstanley may have preceded him in this but only just'.[8] Coppin first published his *Divine teachings* in 1649, though his preaching activity undoubtedly predates this. It is certainly true that Coppin offered one of the fullest reasoned accounts of 'general redemption', as it was known among its proponents. He argued that hell was an inward condition: 'in the persons of wicked men, there may be chambers of hell', but not an eternal state of alienation.[9] He depersonalized Satan, and distinguished between the sinful nature and the sinful man, suggesting that it was the inward principle of sin, not the person, that would be destroyed at the last.[10] The force of the logic of universalism, so apparent to some modern commentators, impressed itself on Coppin: 'the whole designe of Gods wrath is to take away our sins... this love of God to his poore creatures cannot be seen more in any one thing, then in this his thus taking away their sins'. He asked,

---

[5] Louise Hickman, 'Love is all and God is love: Universalism in Peter Sterry (1613–1672) and Jeremiah White (1630–1707)', in Gregory MacDonald, ed., *All shall be well: explorations in universal salvation and Christian theology, from Origen to Moltmann* (Eugene, OR: Wipf & Stock, 2011), ch. 5.

[6] A.L. Morton, *The world of the Ranters: religious radicalism in the English Revolution* (London: Lawrence and Wishart, 1970), p. 117.

[7] Christopher Hill, *The world turned upside down: radical ideas during the English Revolution* (London: Penguin, 2019), pp. 140–3, 160–70, 354.

[8] Nigel Smith, 'Richard Coppin (fl. c 1645–1659)', in David Cannadine, ed., *Oxford dictionary of national biography* (Oxford: Oxford University Press, 2004).

[9] Richard Coppin, *The exaltation of all things in Christ, and of Christ in all things* (London, 1649), third part, p. 29.

[10] Coppin, *The exaltation of all things*, pp. 44–5.

shall God now leave the creature, because he is thus fallen? and be angrie with him because he is thus filthy? No, but as soon as the creature was fallen, God was ready to make him clean; no soone do we sin against him, but he is ready to pardon.[11]

As he sought to characterize the limitless love of God, Coppin reached for a maternal metaphor from Isaiah 49, 'Can a woman forget her suckling child, that shee should not have compassion on the Sonne of her wombe? Yea, they may forget, yet will I not forget, saith God'.[12] As Bernard Capp has wryly observed, Coppin's 'doctrine of universal love aroused bitter hatred'; he was repeatedly arrested and indicted for blasphemy during the 1650s.[13]

It seems evident, however, that neither Coppin nor Winstanley was the first of the preachers of universal restoration in the 1640s. It is possible to argue that it was a woman, Lady Eleanor Davies, who first publicly affirmed the doctrine in her own name, in a series of explicitly Origenist tracts dating from 1644. Increasingly, hers was not an isolated voice, and universalism gained currency in reaction to a hyper-Calvinist mood, itself a reaction to the Laudian reforms. An early indication of the circulation of universalist thought may be detected in the teachings of the London preacher John Everard, whose mystical translations and sermons would later be influential among the army preachers. Everard was called upon in 1638 by Laud's High Commission to account for privately communicating that 'he did not beleeve ye fires of Hell to be eternall'. He was also forced to retract his opinion 'that after the end of the world & day of Judgement all things shal be turned into God againe & yt God shal be all things as before the creacon'.[14] A controversial work by an Anabaptist cloth factor, Lawrence Sanders, was printed anonymously in 1643 as *The fulnesse of Gods love manifested*, and in it Sanders came extremely close to asserting that all humanity would be saved, condemning the 'dark and dismall doctrines' of the Puritans which suggested that 'God did from eternity decree the ruine, and damnation of the most part of men'.[15] He was imprisoned by the parliamentary Committee of Examinations for a breach of the Licensing Ordinance, and the book was later mentioned in a Leveller petition, as an early victim of parliamentarian oppression.[16] Sanders' clandestine critique of Calvinist soteriology was mild in comparison with the public radicalism of the period after 1645. One of the 'errors' of the sects

---

[11] Coppin, *The exaltation of all things*, pp. 38–9.
[12] Coppin, *The exaltation of all things*, pp. 38–9.
[13] See Bernard Capp, *England's culture wars: Puritan Reformation and its enemies in the Interregnum, 1649-1660* (Oxford: Oxford University Press, 2012), pp. 91–2.
[14] 'An order of submission or Retracton of certaine hereticall, pernitious, & Atheisticall opinions vented & published by John Everard Dr in Divinitye', Bodleian Library, Tanner MS 67, fols. 144r, 187v.
[15] Anon., *The fulnesse of Gods love manifested* (London, 1643), p. 154.
[16] See David Como, *Radical parliamentarians and the English Civil War* (Oxford: Oxford University Press, 2021), pp. 197–201.

catalogued by Thomas Edwards in 1646 was the doctrine of 'generall Redemption', the teaching that 'there shall be a generall restauration, wherein all men shall be reconciled to God and saved, only those who now beleeve and are Saints before this restauration shall be in a higher condition then those that do not beleeve'.[17] In *The third part of Gangraena*, Edwards reported that the general restitution preached by sectaries would include not only fallen humanity, but 'all shall be saved at last, both all men and devils: Christ by suffering hath merited for the transgressions of his Creation, Angels and Mankind, and all immortall Spirits, paying the price of our transgressions, and the transgressions of all Angels, Spirits, and Mankind'.[18] Another hostile commentator, Thomas Bakewell, observed that Anabaptists in London were teaching that 'if Christ died for the universall world, then he died for divels, and for Angels that never sinned, and for the creatures in the whole world', including all beasts.[19]

Versions of universalism or 'general redemption', according to Edwards, were being debated in several gathered congregations in the city of London in 1645–6, including the congregation of John Goodwin on Coleman Street, and Edward Barber's meeting at Bishopsgate Street.[20] Above all, the General Baptist congregation of the soapboiler (or 'oilman') Thomas Lambe, in Bell Alley off Coleman Street, was a notorious seedbed of radical universalist doctrine. It was also, as we shall see, a church in which women reportedly preached and taught freely in the 1640s. One of its notable members in the mid-1640s was one Henry Denne, who had been curate at Pirton in Hertfordshire in the 1630s. Pirton was home to the estate of Eleanor Davies, her jointure from her first marriage, and it would be to this estate that Gerrard Winstanley and other Digger companions would travel to work the land in the autumn of 1650. In that year, it was claimed that Davies had 'time out of minde mainteyned a preachinge minister' at Pirton: presumably including Henry Denne.[21] Following his association with Lambe's church in 1643, Denne went on to be a leading General Baptist minister, founding churches in Cambridgeshire and Lincolnshire. He subsequently joined the parliamentary army as a captain in 1647, and was also, significantly, a radical on social and political ethics, participating in the Leveller mutiny in January 1649.[22] David Como has described his position, linked to his antinomian preaching, as 'egalitarian redistributionism', or a levelling doctrine of community of goods

---

[17] Thomas Edwards, *The first and second part of Gangraena* (London, 1646), p. 30.
[18] Thomas Edwards, *The third part of Gangraena* (London, 1646), p. 10.
[19] Thomas Bakewell, *An answer, or confutation of divers errors broached, and maintained by the seven churches of Anabaptists* (London, 1646), p. 19.
[20] On this universalist milieu, see Ariel Hessayon, 'Winstanley and Baptist Thought', *Prose Studies Special Issue: Gerrard Winstanley: Theology, Rhetoric, Politics* 36 (2014), p. 22.
[21] See Esther Cope, *Handmaid of the Holy Spirit: Dame Eleanor Davies, never soe mad a ladie* (Minnesota: University of Michigan Press, 1992), p. 156.
[22] See T.L. Underwood, 'Denne, Henry (1605/6?–1660)', in Cannadine, *Oxford dictionary of national biography*.

(with possible Familist origins).[23] Also connected to his vision of self-giving love for one's poor brethren, and radically free grace, was a tendency towards an inclusive soteriology, which emerged in his pamphlet entitled *Grace, mercy, and peace*, printed in 1645. In this work, he emphasized strongly the love of God for his enemies, for the sinful and unconverted. He ventured to ask, 'Whether this great love wherewith God loved sinners, be not his infinite love like himself?'[24] Denne emphatically described the image of 'an angry God' as an idol. 'How often have we thought God to be like unto ourselves?', he asked.

How many times have we imagined an angry God, a wrathfull Majesty? And sought to appease his indignation by fasting, by praying, by almes, by teares, and such like things? O foolish man![25]

Instead of the idol of an authoritarian and angry king to be appeased by grovelling tributes, Denne emphasized the biblical image of Christ as lover or husband of the soul; in a relationship in which he gave dignity to a wholly unlovely, destitute spouse.

Denne's network among the General Baptists was one in which classical Calvinist teachings about the double decree, the predestination from eternity of the elect and the reprobate, were already broadly rejected. Instead, they generally held to the 'hypothetical universalism' usually associated with Arminianism or Amyraldianism: that is, the notion that Christ died for all, but that the benefits of grace are only received by the faithful. The role of human free will in the reception of grace continued to be a vexed question, and absolute rather than conditional universalism may well have appeared to some to be a doctrine more compatible with Reformed ideas about divine sovereignty than the Arminian account. Tracking the reception of genuinely universalist (rather than hypothetically universalist) teachings is complicated by the fact that 'universalism', like 'atheism', could be used as a slur, imprecisely.[26] Moreover, the language of 'universall redemption' could be used by universalists and Arminians alike.[27] Thomas Edwards, however, accused 'Mr Den and his followers', along with others in Lambe's congregation, of subscribing to 'far greater Errors than Arminianism' in his teachings on free grace.[28] However widely the most radical ideas were circulating, they contributed to the Presbyterian panic over the spread of blasphemy and heresy, and maintaining that 'all men shall be saved' was listed among the errors made punishable under the

---

[23] Como, *Radical parliamentarians*, pp. 189–90.
[24] Henry Denne, *Grace, mercy and peace* (London, 1645), p. 23.
[25] Denne, *Grace, mercy and peace*, p. 59.
[26] See, for instance, Obadiah Howe, *The Universalist examined and convicted* (London, 1648).
[27] As in the debate between Vavasor Powell and John Goodwin, see John Weekes, *Truths conflict with error. Or, Universall redemption controverted* (London, 1650).
[28] Edwards, *The first and second part of Gangraena*, p. 76.

Ordinance for the punishing of Blasphemies and Heresies in 1648. Despite its increasing number of adherents, the doctrine never made much headway in the Reformed congregations, even among the Independents: William Erbery noted in 1652 that 'both Presbyters and Independants abhorre as Paganisme' the doctrine of the 'universal Redemption of mankind', though in his estimation, it was 'nearest the Gospel indeed'.[29]

Among those preaching 'the Gospel of Generall Redemption' at the time Edwards was writing was an unknown prophetic author, whose manuscripts were published by another member of the Lambe congregation, Richard Overton, in 1645 and 1646.[30] This fascinating discourse on the love of God narrates the soul's liberation 'from sinne and curse, to blessednesse', as a progression from feminine weakness or subjection to virility: 'from effeminacy and bondage, to strength and Freedome in blessednesses'.[31] The author also makes statements suggesting that women and men were commissioned to witness to the doctrine of universal restoration, such as the following:

Oh Infinite is the blessedness of such a People, such Sonnes and Daughters of God, who are made Instrumentall meanes of God through Christ only by beleeving, and declaring his Goodness...they are made Instruments of Blessing unto the whole Creation.[32]

The liberation envisaged by the author was not just a spiritual, individual emancipation from tyrannizing sin and judgement; it was the liberation of the gospel of love itself from its imprisonment in false doctrines. Perhaps reflecting the accuracy of Edwards' report about the 'higher condition' some universalists gave the saints within the generality of restored humanity, the author of *Divine light* argued that it was not the case that there was no special favour shown to 'these sonnes and Daughters of God, who should manifest the Glory of Gods love in Christ'. They were the 'First-fruits' of the work of general redemption, and God's love 'unto his Elect Sonnes and Daughters, is great in such Particularity, making them so blessed'.[33] In the final analysis, however, 'Our God is LOVE', and that love extends to all creatures, 'even the whole Creation, specially the Poore and needy in Reprobate Condition, who being a long time out of Grace, were grinded with the Curse, and Confusion, unto horrour and torment'.[34]

This same essential doctrine, this account of the universal and radically inclusionary scope of divine love, was developed in certain women's writings and

---

[29] William Erbery, *The grand oppressor, or the terror of tithes* (London, 1652), pp. 33–4.
[30] On this author and the publication of his manuscripts, see Como, *Radical parliamentarians*, pp. 400–3.
[31] Anon., *Divine light, manifesting the love of God unto the whole world* (London, 1646), p. 15.
[32] Anon., *Divine light*, pp. 10, 14.   [33] Anon., *Divine light*, p. 3.
[34] Anon., *Divine light*, p. 3.

teachings in the 1640s. It seems of considerable interest that several of the earliest, and most original, defenders of the doctrine of universal salvation in England in the seventeenth century were women, exploring for themselves the full extent of divine mercy, through a reading of Scriptures animated by their experience and sense of inspired calling.[35] Universalism was not universal even among the most radical theologians. John Saltmarsh stopped short of conceiving of a comprehensive restoration, and Vavasor Powell vehemently opposed the softer version of hypothetical universalism (or, the general offer of salvation, accepted only by the faithful) in a debate with John Goodwin in 1650.[36] For many of the Fifth Monarchists, a vision of the vindication of the elect saints under Christ's kingdom was essential to a sense of corporate identity and mission.[37] Within a Reformed mindset more widely, universalist doctrine was an almost unthinkable departure from received orthodoxy. The fact that some women were willing to nail their hard universalist colours to the mast is striking; it speaks of the power and resonance of the idea for them. As mentioned above, the earliest and most prolific universalist female prophet of the English Revolution was Lady Eleanor Davies (also known by her birth name of Touchet, or her father's baronial title of Audley, or her second married name, Douglas), notorious for printing political prophecies from 1625 through to the early 1650s. Her universalist doctrine had much in common with the most contentious views held among General Baptists, as reported by Edwards, and was unequivocally radical. Her precocious ideas developed in distinctive ways, informed by study not only of the apocalyptic Scriptures but also by some knowledge of patristic theology, and by her own experiences of alienation and denunciation in the 1630s.

The remarkable story of Eleanor Davies has been told, most comprehensively and authoritatively, in Esther Cope's 1992 biography, and she is a staple ingredient in anthologies of early modern women's writing.[38] As a theologian of universal salvation, she has been given sensitive treatment by Diane Watt, who places her in a gendered tradition of compassionate soteriology, linking her to Julian of Norwich and Margery Kempe.[39] She remains, however, a somewhat marginal

---

[35] I have written elsewhere about two such female theologians active in the later seventeenth century, Elizabeth Bathurst and M. Marsin, in '"The universal principle of grace": feminism and anti-Calvinism in two seventeenth-century women writers', *Gender and History* 21:1 (2009), pp. 130–46. See also *Women, feminism, and religion in early Enlightenment England* (Cambridge: Cambridge University Press, 2010), pp. 208–42, on Jane Lead and the Philadelphians.

[36] See Weekes, *Truths conflict with error*; see also John Saltmarsh, *Sparkles of glory* (London, 1647), pp. 198–9, and 219–20, which deals with the 'generall Redemptionist'; see also Nicholas McDowell, 'The beauty of holiness and the poetics of antinomianism', in David Finnegan and Ariel Hessayon, eds., *Varieties of seventeenth- and early eighteenth-century English radicalism* (Farnham: Ashgate, 2011), pp. 35–6.

[37] Elizabeth Avery, *Scripture-prophecies opened: which are to be accomplished in these last times, which do attend the second coming of Christ* (London, 1647), pp. 41–2.

[38] Cope, *Handmaid of the Holy Spirit*.

[39] Diane Watt, *Secretaries of God: women prophets in late medieval and early modern England* (Cambridge: Brewer, 1997), pp. 137–54.

figure in studies of the English Revolution. Her densely allusive, self-referential, and often tangled prose resists easy analysis. More significantly, her anomalous status among female prophets as a litigious aristocrat with connections in high places (among them Elizabeth Stuart, Princess of Bohemia), and an inventory of personal grievances related to dynastic pride and prestige, perhaps make her a less appealing figure than some of her female contemporaries. The opaque expressions of Lady Eleanor's prophetic thought, her enigmatic anagramming and crude numerology, have arguably resulted in a lack of attention to or appreciation for her originality as a theologian. She has sometimes been characterized as an idiosyncratic soothsayer, rather than a significant protagonist in the story of revolutionary prophecy or theology.[40] It was first of all as an overreaching female interpreter of Scripture that she was condemned by the Laudian courts, and she had by the 1640s undoubtedly acquired knowledge and skill, if not lucidity, in this work. Her insights could be penetrating, particularly on the biblical mandate for the doctrine of 'general redemption', or the restoration of all creatures. Davies' provocative interpretations of the prophetic and apocalyptic books triangulated between the biblical text, contemporary political events, and her own personal history. Informed and invigorated though she was by scholarly controversies and philological analysis of particular texts, and engaged as she was with political developments, she also allowed her experiences of maternal loss and emotion to provide a frame of reference when seeking meaning and theological truth in Scripture.

Eleanor Davies' prophetic career began some years into an abusive marriage, and followed the premature loss of two sons while she was resident in Ireland with her much older husband, Sir John Davies, the attorney-general. In an account written much later in 1646, Eleanor recalled that shortly before James I died in 1625, she was moved to take into her home a mute Scottish boy named George Carr. At the age of 13, Carr had attracted attention in London as a 'Fortuneteller', becoming known for his prophetic gifts, such as using signs and gestures to represent the content of a biblical text opened at random by a visitor, 'though [he] saw not a letter of the Book'.[41] Eleanor was indignant at first at the exploitation of the boy's gifts for vulgar gain by neighbours and 'Learned Divines', and then further enraged by the rumours that 'he was a Vagrant, a Counterfeit, or a Witch'. It was at this point, with Carr in her care, that she experienced the 'Spirit of Prophesie falling likewise upon me'.[42] It is telling that Davies discovered her own vocation as the 'prophetess of the Most High' who would reveal the hidden mysteries of the prophetic Scriptures, through her encounter with a deaf, mute

---

[40] See Nigel Smith, *Perfection proclaimed: language and literature in English radical religion, 1640–60* (Oxford: Oxford University Press, 1989), p. 32.

[41] Eleanor Davies, *The Lady Eleanor her appeal present this to Mr Mace the prophet of the most High, his messenger* (London, 1646), pp. 4–7.

[42] Davies, *The Lady Eleanor her appeal*, p. 7.

child capable of miraculous insight into the Bible, both vilified and venerated for his supernatural gifts. As Teresa Feroli observes, the misuse and humiliation of this innocent child visionary by the clergy became a key point of reference and identification for Eleanor Davies, in her own struggles with ecclesiastical authority.[43] In the same year of 1625, Davies began to identify herself with the prophet Daniel, in whose visions she found anticipations of contemporary events and disruption: she famously made the anagram 'REVEALE O DANIEL' of her name, ELEANOR AVDELIE.[44] Her complex interaction with the Bible—upon which she stood as an authority, but alongside which she also claimed independently a spirit of inspiration—is neatly illustrated by this verbal tangle. Whether or not she 'phancied the Spirit of the Prophet Daniel to have been infused into her Body', as Laud's biographer Peter Heylyn sneeringly suggested, is not entirely clear from her own writings; though she considered herself a divine 'handmaid', and a 'Prophetess of the Most High'.[45] There were few signs of her later universalism in her first published anti-popish jeremiad of 1625, which was littered with references to 'everlasting fire' and 'everlasting Damnation'.[46] From the beginning, however, Eleanor conceived of her vocation both in terms of 'the true interpretation of the Scripture', and in terms of a prophetic mission to sing 'a new Song' in the last days, in which God 'powreth out his Spirit upon his hand-maidens'.[47]

There were good reasons to take pride in her prophetic gifts: she accurately predicted the death not only of her own husband in 1626, but also that of the duke of Buckingham in 1628, which, according to Heylyn, 'raised her to the Reputation of a Cunning Woman amongst the ignorant people'.[48] This hints at the possibility of a following, or at least local celebrity; evidence of which is otherwise elusive. Ominously, in the 1630s, Davies began to predict apocalyptic events that would cleanse the 'howse of God poluted', in which the English episcopate figured as the Beast of Revelation, and Archbishop Laud in particular was doomed.[49] She was fined heavily, and imprisoned at the Gatehouse, a

---

[43] Teresa Feroli, *Political speaking justified: women prophets and the English Revolution* (Newark: University of Delaware Press, 2006), pp. 62–3.

[44] Eleanor Davies, *A warning to the dragon and all his angels* (London, 1625), p. 1.

[45] Peter Heylyn, *Cyprianus anglicanus, or, The history of the life and death of the Most Reverend and renowned prelate William, by divine providence Archbishop of Canterbury* (London, 1668), p. 266; Eleanor Davies, *The new Jerusalem at hand* (London, 1649).

[46] Davies, *A warning*, pp. 27, 87. Indeed, her earlier, more clearly Reformed prophecies have led some commentators to contrast her, perhaps misleadingly, with a later female proponent of *apokatastasis*, Jane Lead. Amanda Capern, 'Jane Lead and the tradition of Puritan pastoral theology', in Ariel Hessayon, ed., *Jane Lead and her transnational legacy* (London: Palgrave Macmillan, 2016), pp. 91–117. In fact, their developed critiques of the doctrine of hell had much in common.

[47] Davies, *A warning*, §A4r–v, p. 52.

[48] Heylyn, *Cyprianus anglicanus*, p. 266. See also Phyllis Mack, *Visionary women: ecstatic prophecy in seventeenth-century England* (Berkeley: University of Berkeley Press, 1992), pp. 15–17.

[49] 'Lines by Lady Eleanor Touchet, or Davies, entitled "A Spiritual Anthem"' (1637), National Archives, SP 16/345 fol. 200; Lines intended to reflect on Archbishop Laud (1633), National Archives, SP 16/248 fol. 212.

humiliation which she later documented vengefully in a 1649 pamphlet entitled *The blasphemous charge against her*, in which she announced to Charles Stuart in prison that 'you are hereby required to make a publique acknowledgement of such your capital Trespass and high Offence; and first to Ask me forgiveness, if so be you expect to finde Mercy in this world or the other'.[50] This 'high offence' against God himself was the condemnation of Lady Eleanor's prophecies, and interpretations of Scripture prophecy. *The blasphemous charge* included the full text of the court of High Commission's judgement, which set out clearly that the grounds for prosecution included first her transgression in assuming authority to interpret the Bible.

> [Lady Eleanor] took upon her (which much unbeseemed her Sex) not only to interpret the Scriptures, and withal the most intricate and hard places of the Prophet Daniel, but also to be a Prophetess, falsly pretending to have received certain Revelations from God; and had compiled certain Books of such her fictions and false Prophesies or Revelations.[51]

Following her release, Davies went on to generate more sensation, performing a series of anti-Laudian prophetic gestures at Lichfield Cathedral. On one occasion, it was reported that she 'went into the bishop's throne and sat there, and said she was primate and metropolitan', and subsequently 'most profanely defiled the hangings at the altar of the cathedral' with 'a pot of water, tar, and other filthy things'.[52] Her dramatized annexation of episcopal power reflected her growing radicalism on the validity of the institutional Church, not just its popish ceremonies, and also on the role of women as spiritual authorities in the day of judgement.

Amid the escalating conflicts of the 1640s, in which hyper-Calvinist theology and ecclesiology regained a dominant voice, the primary focus of Eleanor Davies' biblical interpretation shifted from anti-Laudian polemic and personal grievance (though these aspects of her prophetic challenge continued to feature), increasingly to the question of universal restoration. The expansion of a more generous soteriological vision became most explicit first in her treatise *The restitution of reprobates*, printed in 1644. Davies declared herself to be a messenger of 'A Generall Pardon for Reprobate Rebels, all of them', announcing that her revelation

> Shall cansell that oppinion of old, of Hell to be a place or prison without redemption, as it stands not in truth well with Equitie, where mercy is so unmeasurable for the offence of our first deceived parents; Who knew not

---

[50] Eleanor Davies, *The blasphemous charge against her* (London, 1649), p. 2.
[51] Davies, *The blasphemous charge*, pp. 9–11.
[52] 'Articles objected by the Commissioners for causes ecclesiastical against Marie Noble, wife of Michael Noble, town clerk of Lichfield' (1638), National Archives, SP 16/380 fol. 138.

what they did: That for their cause, so many without compassion, and commiseration, utterly should be undon & cast away, whereas SODOM for so few, their sakes had been spar'd when prest, shall not the Judge of all the world doe right?[53]

Her prophetic knowledge of the afterlife was the opening of 'a Mistery folded up', which had been kept hidden during the time of the Roman Church, and obscured by the false doctrine of purgatory. Davies proceeded to provide various evidences from Scripture in support of her understanding of the 'unlimited plentifull Redemption' offered in Christ, culminating in the breaking loose of Hell and the 'generall delivery of the damned at last'.[54] Importantly, the preaching of universal redemption was, according to Lady Eleanor, 'most proper to be done by that [female] Sex: a Woman being the occasion of the worlds woe and undoeing: Therefore this PLASTER, or PARDON by a Womans hand; shewing after condigne punishment, the reward of sin, He the propitiation of the whole world, and not the Elects only'.[55] Eve's instrumental role in the Fall is turned on its head; women would reveal the cancellation of all the Fall's effects. Divine forgiveness 'extends to pardoning all Adams proginie: Whose ignorance or Errour not imputed to the utter ruine of the whole World'.[56] The illustration with which Davies concludes her (typically amorphous and rambling) defence of the doctrine seems to be that of the Syrophenician (or Canaanite) woman's daughter, who was healed by Jesus of demon possession despite the fact that she was not one of the 'lost sheep of the house of Israel' (Matthew 15.24). Davies comments, 'that dispossessed Woman whereby forbids any to murmur and grudge at his goodnesse, HEE giving to the first and last both, Even forgivenesse'.[57] In this early publication, Davies shows an acquaintance with and support for Origen's ideas about the afterlife, remarking that his doctrine of *apokatastasis*, or the restoration of all things after a finite period of sufferings in hell, caused him to be 'cast out of the Churches favour for his paines'.[58]

Davies was clearly affected by the unfolding crisis in church and state. While she naturally perceived the breakdown into civil war as part of the foretold divine judgement, and enjoyed some sense of vindication as a result (some of her earlier prophecies were reprinted in 1650), she also expressed horror at the violence. Her *Prayer or petition for peace*, published in 1644, was self-consciously the prayer of a woman in despair, but a woman assuming the intercessory authority of Mary the mother of Jesus and of Mary Magdalen, apostle to the apostles:

---

[53] Eleanor Davies, *The restitution of reprobates* (London, 1644), pp. 3–5.
[54] Davies, *The restitution*, p. 14.   [55] Davies, *The restitution*, p. 18.
[56] Davies, *The restitution*, p. 25.   [57] Davies, *The restitution*, pp. 33–4.
[58] Davies, *The restitution*, p. 26.

To conclude (O forsake us not! thou of unspeakable Mercy) cause thy face to shine upon us, for the Lords sake, our alone Savior Jesus Christ, made of the womans seed according to the flesh: A woman making her first witness of the resurrection... Let thy mighty voyce be heard, that speakest sometime to the Fish, the Fig-tree, the Deaf, the Dead, and very Devils subjects... say the word and it is DONE, that henceforth let there be no more DEATH, no more Killing and Slaying, stay thy Hand she beseeches thee.[59]

There followed a torrent of publications in the period 1646–7, following the transformation of the national church. The 'unspeakable' mercy of God, and the finitude of death and torment were consistent themes in this later period of Lady Eleanor's writing. One of her tracts on 'the general restitution' (published in 1646) was dedicated to a flat denial of the claim that 'out of Hell is no redemption', countering the 'envious', Puritan vision of hell with an assertion of God's 'abundant love to all', of 'Mercy and Goodnes so immeasurable'.[60] Her visions were profoundly rooted in gendered biblical imagery. In *Sions lamentation* (1649), a 'funeral blessing' (elsewhere called a 'sermon') for Henry Hastings, the adult son of her surviving daughter Lucy, Lady Eleanor again laments not only as grandmother but as a kind of archetypal mother. Here she identifies not with the Virgin Mary (though this identification was of great significance to her), but with 'the mother of all', Sion, depicted in 2 Esdras as a grieving widow who has lost her sons.[61] Significantly, Davies joined a European tradition of radical dissent and millenarian prophecy in her appeal to 'Esdras testimony, termed Apocrypha, or miscalled'.[62] In response to radical theological uses of the apocryphal books, the Protestant canon was reaffirmed in the heresy ordinance of 1648; Lady Eleanor was beyond troubling herself with imposed definitions of orthodoxy or authority. The black sorrow for the lost grandson is cosmic in scale and scope (with powerful apocalyptic imagery taken from Matthew 24.29): 'The Sun [has] become as sackcloth of hair, The Moon as blood, The Stars falling'. The whole of creation and history participates in the anguish of the 'mourning mother'; not least the nation, and Church of England, whose sons are also lost. She paraphrased Zechariah 12.11:

And in that day there shall be a great mourning in Ierusalem, as the mourning in Hadadrimmon, in the valley of Megiddon, the house of Huntingdon of which participates: Also in London, every family apart mourning and their wives, &c.[63]

---

[59] Eleanor Davies, *A prayer or petition for peace November 22, 1644* (n.l., 1644), pp. 6–7.
[60] Eleanor Davies, *Je le tiens, or, the general restitution* (London, 1646), pp. 5, 40.
[61] Eleanor Davies, *Sions lamentation, Lord Henry Hastings, his funerals blessing, by his grandmother, the Lady Eleanor* (London, 1649), p. 6.
[62] Davies, *Sions lamentation*, p. 5. On the reception of 2 Esdras among early modern prophecy movements, see Alastair Hamilton, *The apocryphal apocalypse: the reception of the second book of Esdras (4 Ezra) from the Renaissance to the Enlightenment* (Oxford: Clarendon Press, 1999).
[63] Davies, *Sions lamentation*, p. 3.

Yet the mourning is pregnant with expectation and hope; the name of 'Hastings' signifies the 'hastning' not only of judgement, but of the final restoration, when the 'Spirit of Grace' will fall and the new Jerusalem—'all Light and Lustre'—will recover her sons.[64]

It must be acknowledged that Lady Eleanor was not isolated as a universalist theologian, and it has already been indicated that previously heterodox ideas about hell and salvation were being preached and discussed from at least the mid-1640s, especially in London, and especially in Baptist circles. The doctrine of 'general redemption', or a general 'pardon' issued not only hypothetically, and not only to humankind but to the fallen angels, at the end of all things, nonetheless remained a step taken by only the most radical. To a thinker as creative as Eleanor Davies, this unthinkable doctrine not only made sense of the broad testimony of the Scriptures, but also upheld the principle of equity so valued by Reformation theologians, and overcame the harshly dualistic vision of the afterlife which ensued from the abandonment of purgatory. For one reason in particular, for the sake of children, Davies embraced a warm belief in a 'general redemption'. It cancelled the unbearable implications of Augustinian original sin: namely, that innocent children suffered everlasting damnation because of the received sins of their parents. She noted that the Roman doctrines of purgatory and limbo had been developed as humane responses to the same problem, to mitigate the implications of original sin.[65] Concomitantly, Davies also rejected infant baptism, though the Reformed defence of infant baptism did not of course retain any claim for the sacramental remission of original sin: instead, it was argued that the infants of believing parents were included in the salvation covenant.[66] This conception of grace as limited to a particular category of infants had been rejected by Anabaptists, who insisted that no infant was accountable for sin; children were held innocent by God until the age of moral maturity. Stephen Marshall, a Presbyterian defender of infant baptism, observed that the Anabaptist view 'puts all the Infants of *all Beleevers* into the self-same condition, with the Infants of *Turkes* and *Indians*'. Such a doctrine implied either that 'all of them are damned who die in their infancy, being without the Covenant of grace'; or that 'All of them are saved, as having no originall sinne' (in other words, bringing in 'Universall grace'); or that 'Christ doth *pro beneplacito*, save some of the infants of Indians and Turkes, dying in their infancy, as well as some of the infants of Christians; and so carry salvation by Christ out of the Church, beyond the Covenant of grace, where God never made any promise'.[67] The second and third of these implications were far less offensive than the first to the several women with Baptist associations

---

[64] Davies, *Sions lamentation*, p. 8.
[65] Eleanor Davies, *The writ of restitution* (London, 1648), §A2r.
[66] Eleanor Davies, *The mystery of general redemption* (London, 1647), p. 20.
[67] Stephen Marshall, *A sermon of the baptizing of infants preached in the Abbey-Church at Westminster* (London, 1644), p. 7.

68   THE REFORMATION OF THE HEART

(we may include among them Lady Eleanor Davies) who found the logic of the universalist position compelling because of the vexed question of the salvation of infants.

One of Davies' most rewarding readings of Scripture in support of the doctrine of general redemption is her meditation on the Book of Jonah, interpreted by some modern biblical scholars as an expression of Jewish universalism.[68] Lady Eleanor was struck by the triumph of divine mercy over judgement in the narrative, and God's relenting not only in response to the repentance of the people, but also to the presence of 'more than sixscore thousand persons that cannot discern between their right hand and their left hand': often thought to be a reference to infants (Jonah 4.11, KJV).[69] Lady Eleanor concluded, echoing Deuteronomy 24.16 and Ezekiel 18.20, that it was God's will that 'children ought not for the Parents to suffer', and argued that the whole world was figured in Nineveh, in this 'tender consideration of a world of Infants pardon all'.[70]

At a time when Origenist ideas about the afterlife were still rarely discussed outside the universities, Lady Eleanor was clearly aware that Origen shared her vision of finite judgement and ultimate restitution. She was a sincere admirer of Origen, and regarded the other Fathers who dissented from him on this point as heretical:

> Of which general deliverance well understood to be an Article of the Christian faith, famous *Origen*, from whose judgment other fathers erring, forced were to erect a Purgatory for Saints, that *Babel* edifice of theirs; of whom the aforesaid ancient father, the worst they could say of him was, *As he did worst of any when he wrote ill, so exceeded all men when he did well.*[71]

Elsewhere, she frequently appealed to 'Origin that Father',[72] and to 'the Ancients Origin, Tertullian and others' in support of her denial of the doctrine of eternal damnation.[73] Nonetheless, the appeal to ancient authority was secondary both to her appeal to compassionate and humane sensibilities, and to the sustained and systematic interrogation of Scripture, in which she advanced in skill. As an example of her efforts to engage in philological analysis, Lady Eleanor's starting point in her essay on *The mystery of general redemption* (1647) was the

---

[68] For a summary of this trend in modern interpretation, see R.B. Salters, *Jonah and Lamentations* (Sheffield: Sheffield Academic Press, 1994), pp. 53–62.
[69] See, for instance, Nicholas Gibbens, *Questions and disputations concerning the Holy Scripture* (London, 1601), p. 68.
[70] Davies, *The writ of restitution*, §A2r.
[71] Davies, *The mystery of general redemption*, p. 26; Eleanor Davies, *Tobits book a lesson appointed for Lent* (s.l., 1652), p. 14.
[72] Davies, *The restitution*, p. 26.
[73] Davies, *The mystery of general redemption*, p. 26; Davies, *The writ of restitution*, §A2r; Davies, *Tobits book*, p. 14.

observation that there was no distinction in either Hebrew or Greek between 'the Grave and Hell, one and the same word serving for both in the Native Tongue or Language'.[74] This was a point made in contemporary commentaries, and as part of debates over Christ's descent into hell, but the doctrinal implications perceived by Eleanor Davies were never drawn.[75] Rather, it was typically emphasized that the original words had 'divers significations'.[76] Davies' conclusion, by contrast, was that the 'penalties and forfeitures' of sin would not be everlasting, and that 'not some, but All, the whole degenerate mass of Angels and Men' would be pardoned.[77] The translation of the Hebrew 'Sheol' as 'grave' has been significant for subsequent critiques of the traditional doctrine of hell, up to the present day.[78]

Baptist Women and General Redemption

It would be fair to characterize Lady Eleanor Davies as exceptionally privileged and learned among the female prophets of the 1640s, and she was convinced above all of her individual prophetic vocation. Nonetheless, she did see a distinctive place for women in general in disseminating the true word of universal divine love in the last days: as second Eves to proclaim the good news of a general healing from the curse of the Fall, or as Magdalen-like prophets of renewal and compassion in a violent world. There is some evidence to suggest that Davies might indeed have formed part of a network of likeminded female preachers of restoration. She appears to have held much in common with a woman at the other end of the social scale, one Elizabeth Attaway ('Mistris Attaway'), another member of and indeed preacher in the congregation of Thomas Lambe. Attaway is one of the most tantalizingly elusive and interesting protagonists in Thomas Edwards' famous catalogue of heresies and sects in 1640s England, the bestselling *Gangraena* (1646). A dominant theme in the first edition of *Gangraena* was the prevalence of female teachers in the sects; like the women preachers in Hertfordshire who took it upon themselves 'to expound the Scriptures in Houses, and preach upon Texts'. Attaway, described by Edwards as a seller of lace or 'Lace-woman' (a common euphemism for a bawd or prostitute), was a choice example of this new disorderly

---

[74] Davies, *The mystery of general redemption*, p. 3.
[75] On the significance of the translational issue in the 'Descensus' controversy, see also Peter Marshall, 'Catholic and Protestant Hells in Later Reformation England', in Margaret Toscano and Isabel Moreira, eds., *Hell and Its Afterlife: Historical and Contemporary Perspectives* (Farnham and Burlington, VT: Ashgate, 2010), pp. 98–9.
[76] See, for instance, William Slatyer, *The compleat Christian, and compleat armour and armoury of a Christian* (London, 1643), p. 134.
[77] Davies, *The mystery of general redemption*, p. 5.
[78] In his recent book *Heaven and hell: a history of the afterlife* (New York: Simon & Schuster, 2020), the provocative scholar of early Christianity Bart Ehrman argues for the translation of the Hebrew 'Sheol' as 'the grave', in denying that the Christian account of hell as eternal punishment had a Hebrew provenance. See pp. 85–6.

conduct among women, expounding biblical texts to crowds 'every Tuesday about four of the clock'.[79] The implied link between sexual misconduct and transgressive preaching is made explicit in later editions of *Gangraena*, with allegations that, inspired by Milton's writings on divorce and her belief that she was called to preach in Jerusalem, Mistress Attaway broke away from her lawful spouse and entered into an adulterous union with 'another womans husband'.[80]

It has been persuasively argued that Attaway was not in fact merely a maverick member of the congregation, but one of the pioneers of a new practice of public lecturing by women at the church, from 1645 onwards.[81] It was reported to Edwards by a 'godly minister' of London that Attaway presided over a meeting in Bell Alley to expound the Scriptures:

> Three...women came with *Bibles* in their hands, and went to a Table;...Then the Lace-woman began with making a speech to this purpose, That now those dayes were come, and that was fulfilled which was spoken of in the Scriptures, That God would poure out of his Spirit upon the handmaidens, and they should prophecy, and after this speech shee made a prayer for almost halfe an hour, and after her Prayer took that Text, *If ye love me, keep my Commandements*; when she had read the Text, shee laboured to Analyze the Chapter as well as she could, and then spake upon the Text drawing her Doctrines, opening them, and making two uses, for the space of some three quarters of an houre.[82]

According to Edwards's informant, the meeting proceeded with an attempt by a wealthy gentlewoman, the mayor's wife, to preach on 1 John 4 on the discernment of spirits, but she became 'disturbed and confounded in her discourse...jumbling together some things against those who despised the ordinances of God, and the Ministery of the Word'.[83] Throughout the meeting, it is said that Attaway insistently encouraged other women to speak and give their own insights communicated by the Spirit, freely and not only to their own sex, as: 'the glory of God was manifested in Babes and Sucklings'.[84] It is heavily implied that Attaway, the 'Lace-woman', was keen to flatter the wealthy women who attended her sermons, by exhorting them to preach. It seems clear that, quite apart from other sensational rumours, Attaway had a reputation as a champion of women's preaching and prophetic interpretation of the Bible. The Presbyterian controversialist Robert Baillie described her as 'the Mistresse of all the She-Preachers' in her district, and

---

[79] Edwards, *Gangraena*, p. 84.
[80] Edwards, *The first and second part of Gangraena*, p. 9; Edwards, *The third part of Gangraena*, pp. 26–7.
[81] See Jason A. Kerr, 'Elizabeth Attaway, London preacher and theologian, 1645–1646', *The Seventeenth Century* 36:5 (2021), pp. 734–5.
[82] Edwards, *Gangraena*, p. 85.   [83] Edwards, *Gangraena*, p. 86.
[84] Edwards, *Gangraena*, p. 88.

an example of a new species of 'feminine Preacher' emerging not only in London, but also in the provinces. In comparing the new Baptist congregations to a previous generation of separatists, Baillie remarked:

> Only in this they are more distinct then the Brownists, many more of their women do venture to preach then of the other; *Attaway* the Mistresse of all the She-preachers in *Colemanstreet* was a disciple in *Lambs* Congregation, and made Antipaedobaptism oftentimes a part of her publick exercises: the other feminine Preachers in *Kent*, *Norfolk*, and the rest of the Shires had their breeding, as I take it, in the same or the like school.[85]

In fact, Attaway is said to have expressed some doubt that 'any in the world this day living, had any Commission to Preach'; but there is a strong suggestion that she considered women—those innocent 'Babes and Sucklings'—to be more suited to interpreting divine revelation than the learned ministry.[86] She reportedly described women preachers as 'Ambassadors' as well as ministers, a distinctive designation which would later be used by George Fox in connection with female ministers, and the Philadelphian Society in London, to describe its prominent female leaders.[87]

For all her enthusiasm for unlettered ministers of the Gospel, it seems that, like Eleanor Davies, Attaway had some rather well-developed interests in apocalyptic interpretation of the Bible, including the apocryphal books. Edwards reported that 'Mistris Attaway held that the Book of Esdras and some other Apocryphall Books were Canonicall Scriptures'.[88] Jason Kerr has recently connected Attaway's interest in the books of Esdras to the anonymous author of *Divine light*, promoted by the Lambe congregation.[89] *Divine light* proclaimed a message of salvation for 'the whole world, and every immortall Creature therein contained'. The prophet heralds an epochal change, anticipated in 2 Esdras 6. 7–10, from the old 'Esaus world' in which the Christian understanding of divine love was limited, to 'Jacobs world', in which God's promise 'to restitute all things' would be fully realized.[90] It was reported by Edwards that Attaway was the spokeswoman for an imprisoned prophet, and together, inspired by reading the Books of Esdras, they 'held no hell but what was in the conscience' and taught, among other things:

---

[85] Robert Baillie, *Anabaptism, the true fountaine of Independency, Brownisme, Antinomy, Familisme* (London, 1647), p. 53.
[86] Baillie, *Anabaptism, the true fountaine*, p. 88.
[87] See George Fox, *A New-England-fire-brand quenched* (London, 1678), p. 156: 'And then thou fall'st a scoffing at Women-Ambassadors, &c. Thou might'st as well scoff at those Woman, that carried the Message and glad Tidings of the Resurrection of Christ'. On the idea of the 'female embassy' in Philadelphian thought, see B.J. Gibbons, *Gender in mystical and occult thought: Behmenism and its development in England* (Cambridge: Cambridge University Press, 1997), pp. 143–62.
[88] Edwards, *The third part of Gangraena*, p. 26.   [89] Kerr, 'Elizabeth Attaway', pp. 736-7.
[90] Anon., *Divine light*, p. 23.

that there was *Esaus* world and *Jacobs* world; this was *Esaus* world, but *Jacobs* world was comming shortly, wherein all creatures shall be saved; And this Prophet who was shut up, was to come forth to preach this new Doctrine of generall Restauration and Salvation of all; and though all should be saved, yet there should be degrees of glory between those that have been Saints (they should be more glorious) and those who were the wicked, though now restored.[91]

This doctrine of universal salvation was not just for humanity: elsewhere, Edwards reported that Attaway had adopted the radical Origenist position that 'all the Devils should be saved'.[92] It is significant that in her Origenist exposition of the book of Jonah, *The mystery of general redemption* (1647), Eleanor Davies also referred to 'Esaus world', in connection with a 'spirit of Envie' and anger among those who thought of themselves as righteous or elect, and who, like the brother of the prodigal son, could not bear to see mercy extend to all.[93] As Ariel Hessayon has pointed out, the apocalyptic typology of Mistress Attaway also anticipated a similar scheme in Gerrard Winstanley's writings from 1648: the coming triumph of an age of Jacob, in which Christ would rise spiritually in the saints and all things would be held in common, over the current world of Esau, dominated by the rule of the first Adam, the selfish will and corrupt flesh.[94] Winstanley is also often celebrated as one of the most distinguished revolutionary proponents of a doctrine of universal salvation. In this, he was certainly in good female company. It is noteworthy that in 1650, Winstanley with a group of Diggers worked on the estate of Lady Eleanor Davies, although this short-lived arrangement was not entirely successful, and Winstanley eventually concluded that Lady Eleanor (who failed to pay her workers) was one of the citizens of Esau's world, full of 'a proud loftie spirit advanceing it self above all, [which] is Satan the divell'.[95]

Several other female prophets of the Revolution offered accounts of salvation, or of heaven and hell, which implied a comprehensive vision of divine mercy, even if it was not explicitly universalist. In her lengthy spiritualist treatise, *Crooked pathes made straight* (1648), Anne Yemans's doctrine of grace was all-embracing. Christ is 'the author of eternall salvation unto all'; or 'a common salvation to all', though he offered a 'speciall salvation' to his beloved saints.[96] At points in her free-grace discourse she affirmed the predestination of an elect people, and suggested

---

[91] Edwards, *The third part of Gangraena*, pp. 26–7.
[92] Edwards, *The second part of Gangraena*, p. 9.
[93] Davies, *The mystery of general redemption*, pp. 26–7.
[94] Hessayon, 'Winstanley and Baptist thought', p. 22.
[95] Thomas Corns, '"I have writ, I have acted, I have peace": the personal and the political in the writing of Winstanley and some contemporaries', *Prose Studies Special Issue: Gerrard Winstanley: Theology, Rhetoric, Politics* 36 (2014), pp. 47–8; see also Thomas Corns, Ann Hughes, and David Loewenstein, eds., *The complete works of Gerrard Winstanley* (Oxford: Oxford University Press, 2009), vol. II, p. 425.
[96] Anne Yemans, *Crooked pathes made straight: or, the wayes of God made knowne to lost sinners, or bewildered saints* (London, 1648), p. 131.

that the unfaithful condemned themselves by their unbelief, but at other moments salvation is described in radically inclusive terms. 'Here is the free mercie of God,' she wrote,

> and his love belonging to all man-kinde, that ever was, is, or shall be; there is not any one excluded from his love; for there is nothing can keep us from God but our sins, and that Christ hath dyed for... and hath obtained of his Father a full pardon for the sinne of all man-kinde.[97]

This complete and perfect satisfaction for the sins of all was, for Yemans, linked to her justification for her publishing and theological writing as a woman. God is 'no respecter of persons', either in appointing females as his agents, or in bestowing on sinners his grace: 'let not us undervalue any thing that is God, whosoever it be spoken by; for God is no respecter of persons... let not this my labour seeme odious to you, nor cause you to slight it, because it is written by a weak woman'.[98] Her appreciation of divine impartiality also underpinned an irenical outlook—her insistence that Presbyterians, Independents, and others should not disregard each other's lights—and an ethical commitment to valuing the least distinguished, the weakest, and the poorest.

Anna Trapnel, like other Fifth Monarchist prophets, retained the language of election and judgement in her writings. She looked forward to the vindication of the 'remnant' of the saints, 'his little number', and anticipated the 'confounding and destroying of Antichrist root and branch', when Christ 'will come forth... terrible as a Lyon. O who can abide the day of his coming? It will be very terrible to the deceitful in heart'.[99] At other times, however, Trapnel wrote about hell and damnation as inward states of torment, and seemed to envision something like a universal restoration: 'The time will come that the whole Creation shal have a Rest and Redemption which shall abide not for a day, but shall continue'.[100] She also frequently looked forward to the 'day of Redemption' as the time when Christ would become 'all in all'.[101] Her account of free grace, as discussed elsewhere (Chapter 4), was one which centred on divine compassion and mercy. God was unreal to her until she discovered him as boundless love: 'I could not find nor see God any where, nor in any thing as a God of love'; elsewhere, she insisted that 'you cannot out-sin mercy, your sins are finite, but grace is infinite; do not think that any sin can shut thee out of divine love'.[102] Although she did not explicitly set forth the doctrine of universal salvation, Trapnel's account of the boundlessness of

---

[97] Yemans, *Crooked pathes made straight*, pp. 52–3.
[98] Anne Yemans, 'To the Reader', *Crooked pathes made straight*, §A2v.
[99] Anna Trapnel, *Poetical discourses* (1657–8), Bodleian Library S. 1. 42. Th., pp. 804, 808.
[100] Anna Trapnel, *The cry of a stone* (London, 1654), p. 47.
[101] Anna Trapnel, *A legacy for saints* (London, 1654), p. 52.
[102] Trapnel, *A legacy for saints*, pp. 7, 51.

grace might well indicate an open door to the idea. Elizabeth Avery offered a somewhat ambiguous, spiritualizing account of the annihilation of the wicked, as an alternative eschatological solution to eternal torment, though still framed in traditional language. She spiritualized both heaven and hell: they 'cannot be apprehended in the carnal sense'; and elsewhere, 'we do not expect such a resurrection as formerly, yet we do expect a resurrection of the body mystical'.[103] Ultimately, she did not embrace universal salvation. In response to an anticipated question, 'If God be love to all, why are not all saved?', Avery responded 'Because God doth not manifest himself in his own nature to any but those who are ordained to life'.[104] She described the 'horrour of conscience and torment which shall be in the wicked' as something 'unspeakable':

For when a wicked man dies in respect of his natural death, that spirit of God which is in a wicked man, returns to God again; and so God and the wicked man is separated for ever and ever; and so God ceaseth to be Love as to them[.][105]

This alienation is very definitely spiritual rather than physical: 'these very bodies of flesh shall be annihilated and brought to nothing'. But the account also reflects equivocation on Avery's part about the judgement of the creature, as she explains that that which derives from God will return to God, and that which is infernal will join with the spirits of the devils: 'all the infernal spirits which have acted in the spirits of the children of disobedience from the beginning of the world, shall be comprehended in one body', a spiritual body or corporation. At the end of all things, this body would be 'cast into the lake of fire and brimstone, which is the second death'.[106]

There is compelling evidence, from a later period, of a Fifth Monarchist community of female universalists among the General Baptists. These were women of low social status, who espoused the radical doctrine of universal salvation on the basis of an assessment of divine love which drew upon their experience as women. This evidence comes in a previously unexamined narrative written by one James Warner, concerning his withdrawal from communion with John Belcher, a leading Fifth Monarchist who had been arrested for his activism in 1658. Belcher was excommunicated by the Particular Baptists in Abingdon by 1660 (he formed part of the Thames Valley milieu of radical theology), and became the head of a seventh-day Baptist congregation in Bell Lane in the city of London from 1666.[107] Bernard Capp describes him as 'one of the foremost'

---

[103] Avery, *Scripture-prophecies opened*, p. 36.
[104] Avery, *Scripture-prophecies opened*, pp. 41–2.
[105] Avery, *Scripture-prophecies opened*, pp. 44–5.
[106] Avery, *Scripture-prophecies opened*, p. 46.
[107] See Mark Bell, *Apocalypse how? Baptist movements during the English Revolution* (Mercer University Press, 2000), pp. 226, 231.

Fifth Monarchist agents under the scrutiny of the Restoration regime.[108] The account is undated, and although it is certainly post-Restoration (a date before November 1682, but possibly after February 1677 when Belcher signed a statement along with Francis Bampfield, vouching for 'Brother Warner'), it details debates which owe their provenance to the period of the Revolution.[109] Warner was deputized to examine one Mrs E., who was hoping to join with the Bell Lane congregation as a new convert. Under questioning about her beliefs, she expressed to Warner 'her faith that her Infants deceased were saved, & that the Heathens were not all damned & who never heard of Christ, That Christ dyed for all the Originall Sinn of all men & that there was none upon any'.[110] The priority given to her conviction 'that her infants deceased were saved', after which her other universalist beliefs seemed to follow, is telling. Certainly, it is presented in Warner's account as an essential (and possibly primary) reason for embracing the doctrine. Duly appalled, Warner reported back to Belcher and his wife 'to warn them of her', but Mrs Belcher wanted to know 'why I discoursed to Mrs E who was hope fully coming in to joyn with us for she owned only Generall Redemption which she also herselfe owned'. In fact, it was a belief she so zealously owned that she remarked playfully, 'Mr B could have no rest till he had preach'd this in publick'.[111]

The narrative goes on to set out the debate between Warner and Mrs Belcher on the doctrine of general redemption, which was evidently lively. Mrs Belcher 'said that all were put into a Capacity of being Saved by the death of Christ; that Christ layd down a price for every man'. As greatly as Warner was offended by her universalism, so was she affronted by his talk of reprobation: 'shee had much a doe to heare Reprobation Asserted & denyd that God did Reprobate any'. It was put to Mrs Belcher that another woman, one Sister 'K' (elsewhere identified as Katherine), had been excommunicated solely because of her espousal of general redemption, to which Mrs Belcher responded 'that the Church were too rash in ejecting K for nothing else then Generall Redemption wch she did owne'. When Warner involved John Belcher, and pressed him on his own beliefs, the husband was evasive, and gave an answer which might just satisfy an Arminian hypothetical universalist: 'That the Lord is peaceable pacifyable Reconsileable to all men'.[112] By contrast, Mrs Belcher doubled down on her radicalism, insisting that 'God would have all men to be saved & did

---

[108] Bernard Capp, *The Fifth Monarchy men: a study in seventeenth-century English millenarianism* (London: Faber, 1972), pp. 205-7.
[109] 'The little remnant walking with Mr. F. Bampfield, keeping the Lord's holy Sabbath, to any church of our Lord Jesus Christ to whom our brother Warner may come', National Archives, SP 29/30 f. 265.
[110] James Warner, 'A narrative of the manner, cause and occasion of my withdrawment from the society with Mr. B', National Archives, SP 29/421/2, p. 73.
[111] Warner, 'A narrative of the manner', pp. 73-4.
[112] Warner, 'A narrative of the manner', p. 74.

76   THE REFORMATION OF THE HEART

not offer it to all but did intend it really'; she also suggested rather obnoxiously that 'God should Reprobate any as was [of Warner's] opinion' (a comment which evidently embarrassed her husband: 'Mr B would not have had her so expressed it').[113] Eventually, frustrated at the direction of the discussion, Warner brought in two brethren as witnesses, and required Mrs Belcher to give a fuller account of her beliefs:

> she alleaged... that Christ did taste death for every man, & said she understood that every man to be all the ones that ever were & are in the world & we asking whether he dyed for all alike she liked not that word but said she knew no difference between one or another in his death Elect or Reprobate. Another Scripture she brought was as in Adam all dyed so in Christ shall all be made alive. She understood that Christ had put all men into a Capacity of life & Salvation by that text & as to Reprobation when she thought of it she had Blasphemous thoughts against God & she said it was a damnable doctrine & as to Pharaohs heart being hard she said it was God declared his heart hard. I said it was not so ye Translation was right. She said Mr B said it was so. I denyed that it was so, though I know he had said it was so.[114]

Warner manifested unease at gainsaying the woman's husband on the question of the translation of Exodus 9.12 ('the Lord hardened the heart of Pharaoh') and its interpretation in Romans 9; and both showed a certain deference to John Belcher's authority on this point. John Belcher was a bricklayer, the very image of the plebeian tub-preacher, and yet he had clearly developed some agility in biblical interpretation. (Most modern interpretations of Exodus 9.12 observe that the passive voice is used about Pharaoh's heart being hardened, though other parallel texts use the active voice; in particular, Paul in Romans 9.15 insists on a divine agent.) Among the other biblical passages discussed, Mrs Belcher quoted Jesus's words to Jerusalem in Matthew 23.37 (also Luke 13.34) 'I would have gathered you as a hen gathereth her Chickens & ye would not': a warmly maternal image of divine compassion.

The members of the congregation charged with holding universalist opinions were all women: Mrs Belcher, Mrs E, and Sister Katherine. No men, other than John Belcher himself, were accused or questioned by Warner. At the congregational debate over 'generall redemption' which followed Warner's questioning, the female universalists were publicly supported by another woman seeking to join the congregation and sharing their views, from 'Mr Lambs Society', as Warner reported:

---

[113] Warner, 'A narrative of the manner', p. 75.
[114] Warner, 'A narrative of the manner', pp. 75–6.

After some time a Lame Woman belonging to Mr Lambs Society propounded for Comunion wth us whom I asked whether she did own Generall Redemption, that Christ dyed alike for all men in the World She being at a Stand Answered Yes She believed that he dyed for all men in the world & that God had a Love for all men & when I said for all alike she Answered yes for none were saved any other way. & she had Answered Mr N that Christ had Satisfyed for all the Sins past present &...of all those for whom he dyed.[115]

The reference to 'Mr Lambs Society' may well be to Lambe the soapboiler who harboured Mistress Attaway and other female preachers and prophets. Lambe is said to have died by 1673, which may suggest the manuscript dates from before that date; or else that London Baptists still associated themselves with his name.[116] It was suggested that a representative should be sent from Belcher's church to the other congregation to 'Enquire about her'; Warner then wanted to know 'whether ye Church intended thereby to receive her if they should have satisfaction in all other points notwithstanding her holding of Generall Redemption', threatening to withdraw if they admitted her. Belcher, conscious of his wife's precarious standing, insisted that 'he would not be Enquired into about Generall Redemption'; another brother tried to cut off Warner, saying 'we have done Sir it is enough we are all one to have no more to do with it'.[117] When the congregation indicated, either by assent or by passive silence, that they would have communion with Mrs Belcher at the following Sabbath, Warner withdrew from communion with the Belcher congregation. He cited not only the Scriptural injunction to 'be not partakers of other mens sins', but also what seems to have been a just charge of 'partiallity' towards Mrs Belcher, given that 'Sister K' had been excommunicated for her views on general redemption.[118]

What this narrative seems to illustrate, apart from offering an insight into the internecine tensions in Baptist congregations and the dynamics of a dissenting minister's household, is the appeal to women of universalist doctrine in communities shaped by the radical theology of the English Revolution. The strength of this appeal is supported by other evidence from the period following the Restoration. Elizabeth Bathurst took pains to defend Quaker universalism in printed works. Jane Lead, a disciple and former associate of John Pordage, was influential among the German radical Pietists as a theologian of *apokatastasis*. The philosopher Lady Anne Conway, who had engaged seriously with mystical radicalism in the 1650s and famously converted to Quakerism late in life, was noted for her advocacy of universal salvation. It was not only true of the public sphere, in

---

[115] Warner, 'A narrative of the manner', p. 78.
[116] See Murray Tolmie, 'Thomas Lambe, Soapboiler, and Thomas Lambe, Merchant, General Baptists', *Baptist Quarterly* 27:1 (1977), 4–13.
[117] Warner, 'A narrative of the manner', p. 78.
[118] Warner, 'A narrative of the manner', pp. 79–80.

which a woman was perhaps the very earliest English theologian to defend Origenist universal salvation in print, but there are also indications of a proclivity toward that doctrine among women in certain constituencies in the sphere of private opinion. Mrs Belcher and Mrs E were not, it seems, preachers themselves, but openly 'owned' views about the limitless extent of divine love which were not dominant in their congregations, and held them as firmly and unequivocally as more conventional soteriology was upheld by their opponents. The case of Mrs E, like that of Lady Eleanor Davies, suggests that women's heightened sensitivity to questions about the fate of lost infants played a role. The doctrine of reprobation was not just repugnant, but nonsensical to those who identified divine compassion with a mother's unconditional love. This seems to be rather a successful example of 'affective reasoning', and the logic of their position was plain to Baptist women who had little or no exposure to high-level soteriological debates.

The disappearance of English female theologians of the seventeenth century from mainstream histories of universalist teaching is something to be lamented, and corrected. Amnesia set in early, and when universalist interpretations of Scripture started to gain wider currency in the context of early Enlightenment reappraisals of Christian doctrines, women's earlier advocacy of the same ideas was not something to be celebrated. In 1712, in a preface to the first printed edition of the Cambridge Platonist Jeremiah White's treatise, *The restoration of all things*, Richard Roach listed the 'Pious and Learned' men from antiquity to the contemporary age who had advocated for universalism. His aim was to show that 'this Opinion is not so strange and unusual ... as it is by the generality imagined to be', and was based 'only upon Scripture grounds'.[119] Gerrard Winstanley, Peter Sterry, and White himself, were included in this brief survey. Whether consciously or tactically, Roach omitted to mention the female theologians who had held and defended this 'Opinion': including his long-term associate, the visionary Jane Lead. As Roach's silence indicates, Lady Eleanor Davies and Mistress Attaway both faded from view following their brief celebrity in the 1640s: marginalized and discredited by heresiographers like Edwards (though it is also thanks to him that Attaway's teachings have been immortalized), and the propaganda of the post-Restoration Church of England. From the perspective of the learned readers in Augustan England to whom Roach was trying to appeal, the women's participation in universalist teaching would certainly have made it seem 'strange and unusual', a species of enthusiasm. In an environment less hostile both to universalism and to women's insights, their precocity and ambition in examining the received doctrine of salvation, based on fresh and insightful interpretations of key biblical passages and apocryphal texts, deserves to be acknowledged.

---

[119] Richard Roach (ed.), 'Preface', in Jeremiah White, *The restoration of all things: or, a vindication of the goodness and grace of God. To be manifested at last in the recovery of his whole creation out of their fall* (London, 1712).

3
Revelation

The radical writings of women in the English Revolution were not sermons, or overtly theological treatises: they were 'experiences', or 'discoveries', or 'prophecies', or 'openings'. This visionary idiom is often cited as an indication of their 'silent subjectivity' as women: they considered themselves merely passive instruments. It is certainly the case that several female prophets adopted a rhetoric of humility, presenting themselves as an 'empty, nothing creature' (Sarah Wight); or professing the 'weaknesse and contemtiblenesse of the instrument', 'most strong in God when I am weakest in myself' (Elizabeth Avery).[1] The connection made between women and the figure of the 'holy fool' in Christian tradition—the ignorant innocent raised up by God to confound worldly wisdom—does not seem terribly promising as the basis for accepting female agency. Women in visionary circles were often the objects of the projected hopes and ambitions of their 'exegetes' and supporters. Nonetheless, the surface rhetoric of passivity and self-effacement can blind the modern reader to the radical critique underlying the rhetoric, the far-reaching challenge to dominant systems of knowledge. Women became their own exegetes as well as interpreters of salvation history, given the opportunity, afforded by the mystical epistemology central to the radical theology in the Revolution under consideration in this book, to own and interpret their experience as a source of the Holy Spirit's revelation. The individual tragedies, dilemmas, and interactions of the quotidian human world took on significance as traces of divine immanence.

Mystical Theology and 'Silly Women'

This chapter considers the radical theology of the English Revolution in its confrontation with speculative knowledge, as a symptom of wider epistemological crisis which gave newly politicized meaning to mystical theology. Late-medieval and early modern mysticism have often been linked to modes of dissent from the hegemony of scholastic theology. Certain mystics articulated a protest against the presumption that the simple and unlettered were excluded from knowledge of divinity. Christ and his disciples were poor and unlettered;

---

[1] See Elizabeth Avery, *Scripture-prophecies opened: which are to be accomplished in these last times, which do attend the second coming of Christ* (London, 1647), §A3r, p. 17.

they spoke in provincial Aramaic, and in homely stories about shepherds, widows, and farmers, not in high-flown language about substances and essences. While this was not exclusively a gendered confrontation, the distinction, even antithesis, between learned theologian and holy fool could very easily lend itself to a gendered interpretation. The separation of spheres between a male intellectual culture that was Latinate and clerical, and a female, vernacular, mystical culture, somewhat subversive of the mainstream, has undoubtedly been overdrawn in some accounts of late-medieval mysticism.[2] Bonaventure, himself a scholastic theologian of some distinction, was said to have commented that 'an old woman can love God even more than a master of theology'.[3] Bernard McGinn's category of vernacular mysticism, defined as 'a third dimension or tradition of theology beginning in the thirteenth century', helps to make sense of the more prominent role played by women as visionaries and theorists of mystical union in the later Middle Ages, at the same time as the development of Latinate scholasticism. McGinn does not regard this strand as being in tension with the Latinate theology of scholars and monks, seeing the emergence of a 'third dimension' in positive terms as the extension of medieval theological discourse to 'a different and wider audience'.[4] But the historical fate of several of his vernacular mystics, including Meister Eckhard, Marguerite Porete, and the Beguines, all associated with the heresy of the Free Spirit, indicates that tensions existed, and that lay mysticism had the potential in some of its expressions to be subversive.

The perceived contrast between the sphere of the learned and luxurious cleric, and that of the holy pauper was conceptually powerful, and resonated in a different way in the post-Reformation world. Martin Luther famously played up his 'peasant' background in his polemic against the Roman Church's intellectual and spiritual corruption; his wealthy Wittenberg colleague, Andreas Bodenstein von Karlstadt, took performative poverty to an extreme and took to dressing in peasant's clothes.[5] Most famously, the mystical revolutionary Thomas Müntzer preached uncompromisingly that 'the spirit is only given to the poor in spirit'. He was emphatically clear by the time of the Peasants' War that by 'the poor', he had in mind above all the materially deprived, the man too flayed and exhausted by his

---

[2] This division has been critically examined by Sara Poor in 'Mechthild von Magdeburg, gender and the "unlearned tongue"', *Journal of Medieval and Early Modern Studies* 31:2 (2001), pp. 213–50, which offers a helpful corrective.

[3] See Kevin Hughes, 'Francis, Clare, and Bonaventure', in Julia Lamm, ed., *The Wiley-Blackwell companion to Christian mysticism* (Oxford: Blackwell, 2017), p. 291.

[4] See Bernard McGinn, 'Introduction: Meister Eckhart and the Beguines in the context of vernacular theology' in McGinn ed., *Meister Eckhart and the Beguine mystics: Hadewijch of Brabant, Mechthild of Magdeburg and Marguerite Porete* (New York: Bloomsbury, 1997), p. 8; also Bernard McGinn, *The varieties of vernacular mysticism (1350–1550)* (New York: Crossroad, 2012).

[5] See Ulinka Rublack, *Reformation Europe*, 2nd edn (Cambridge: Cambridge University Press, 2017), p. 41.

labours to read or study the Scriptures.[6] The mystic's increasingly uneasy relation to ecclesiastical institution and dogmatic theology contributed to the appeal of divine instruments distinguished by innocence rather than by power or education. This was not, however, an appeal restricted to Reformation radicals. It also resonated in Catholic circles, where mystical experiences were taken seriously as part of a continuous tradition of miraculous revelation. De Certeau has reflected eloquently on the figure of the 'enlightened illiterate' in seventeenth-century spirituality, particularly as it appeared in French spiritual writings. The figure of 'the wildman', the idiot, the pauper manifested something of the discrediting of institutions of knowledge and controversialist, speculative approaches to theology. For de Certeau, post-Reformation mystics subtly transformed interpretations of the traditional holy fool, or naïve savant, and linked saintly innocence to low economic status. In one exemplary case, the unschooled but saintly lay friend who effects Tauler's conversion is transformed into a wretched beggar in seventeenth-century accounts. Economic and institutional marginality are elided, and the traditional tension between mystical and scholastic theology has altered social significance. As he writes:

> Where there once was an opposition not only between the layman and the theologian-priest, but also between *mystic science* and *book learning*, the contrast now takes a social direction. Increasingly, poverty occupied the 'place' of *mystics*...Myriad accounts or legends accompany that reinterpretation of a spirituality henceforth marginalized and invested in one of the terms of a sociocultural conflict: religion is now on the side of the poor.[7]

Nonetheless, these innocent vessels were rather passive witnesses, as de Certeau observes: they were subject to the readings of the clergy, of the 'magi' seeking out guiding lights in a darkened landscape. It is the clerical 'readers' of the 'little ones', not the innocents themselves, who really 'testify to the disarray of their knowledge confronted with the misfortune that had stricken a system of reference'.[8] Economic and gender inequality are not, of course, of the same essence, but for the early modern mystics who challenged institutional theology, women and the unlearned poor were placed in a common category.

Before turning to the revolutionary mystics, it does not seem wholly digressive to pause momentarily with seventeenth-century Catholic spirituality, and consider the case of the Benedictine mystic Augustine Baker and his muse at the Cambrai convent where he was confessor, Gertrude More. Their spiritual writings

---

[6] See Tom Scott, *Thomas Müntzer: theology and revolution in the German Reformation* (New York: St Martin's Press, 1989), pp. 101–2.
[7] Michel de Certeau, *The mystic fable*, vol. 1: *The sixteenth and seventeenth centuries*, trans. Michael B. Smith (Chicago: University of Chicago Press, 1992), pp. 237–8.
[8] De Certeau, *The mystic fable*, p. 26.

were published in English in the 1650s by the convert Serenus Cressy, as part of an apologetic effort to appeal to vernacular readers through Baker's distinctive, Anglo-centric brand of spirituality. Baker and Cressy dedicated much energy to reviving the contemplative traditions which flourished in late-medieval England and the Netherlands (Hilton, Harphius, Julian of Norwich, the anonymous author of *The cloud of unknowing*). Later, at the Restoration of the episcopal church in England, Cressy's endeavour was caught up in the backlash against the enthusiasm of the sects. His advocacy of mystical theology and women's inspirations conveniently placed Catholics on the side of the enthusiasts. Historians of the early modern politics of religion are so used to seeing the conflation of radical religion and popery as an aspect of ecclesiastical polemic, especially after the Restoration, that it feels almost naïve to ask if there was any basis for the association. Ecclesiologically, Baker and Cressy on one side and the radical theologians on the other, were worlds apart. In terms of their religious epistemology, the relationship was more unstable. Radical Protestant and Catholic mysticism were utterly distinct in key respects, but they shared a critique and a cultural moment.

Augustine Baker's ambitions for the contemplative women at Cambrai, where he was spiritual director from 1624, undoubtedly drew inspiration from a notion of the sanctity of the marginalized. Baker himself was somewhat ambivalent about the office of spiritual director, describing his own spiritual progress as 'masterless, yet not without a master'. He had taken 'the spirit of God for his interior director'.[9] In the context of an exile community, and among women, the status of the oppressed innocent was defined by a double alienation. In Gertrude More (1606-33), Baker found his ultimate innocent vessel, though she was far from a pauper, More was linked by her name in religion to the ecstatic bride of Christ Gertrude of Helfta, and by her ancestry to the humiliated and martyred Catholic faith in England (her father was, as is well known, 'the lineall heire of the renowned Martyr Sir Thomas More').[10] In Baker's 'Life' of More, which is essentially a case study in his contemplative method, More's inner life veers from gentleness and docility, to stubbornness and wilfulness. Under Baker's guidance she discovered a method of contemplation 'which wrought in her Humilitie, and a total subjection to God, and obedience to man according to the Divin will'.[11] More's calling to the religious life is described as a passive response to an irresistible call—'she camme in as it were blindfolde'—guided by a 'privie Call'.[12] Her 'motto' or 'Poesie' was the rhyming couplet, 'Regarde your Call, that's all in all'.[13] More comes across as

---

[9] De Certeau, *The mystic fable*, p. 78.
[10] Baker in Ben Wekking, ed., *The life and death of Dame Gertrude More*, Analecta Cartusiana, 119/19 (Salzburg: Salzburg Institut für Anglistik und Americanistik, 2002), p. 10.
[11] Wekking, *The life and death*, pp. 3-4.   [12] Wekking, *The life and death*, p. 19.
[13] Wekking, *The life and death*, p. 26.

spirited, or 'Stoute-stomached'; initially she resisted Baker's direction of mental prayer at Cambrai, 'mocking and jesting (wherein she had a prettie gift of humor)' at him and his disciples.[14] It was a struggle for her to submit to the outward discipline of the cloister: she found 'obedience and other vertues' to be 'an intollerable burthen'.[15] Part of her attraction to Baker's direction seems to have been his unobtrusive approach, in that he did not prescribe a particular regime but encouraged her to find a way of mental prayer which suited her best. He admitted that 'all the spirituall men in the world were not able to teach her'; 'none but the divin spirit was able to guide or reforme her'.[16]

Gertrude More finally came to a suitable method of prayer: not by discursive meditations or the use of the imagination, which inspired a powerful reaction of 'Nausea or loathing' in her, but by 'seeking of God (as imagelesse) in her owne interior, and not in externall deeds nor by meanes of corporall images'.[17] The prayers which finally satisfied her inner rovings were inarticulate 'actuations' or 'aspirations' of the affections without any vocal or linguistic form. More's writings were published posthumously, with commentary by Baker, by Cressy at Paris in 1657 and 1658; her *Holy practises of a divine lover* carried the telling subtitle, *The sainctly ideots devotions*. Her devotions were those of an 'ideot':

> because they are for such as fervently and simply with all their affections, desire to *aspire* after *God* in the *Cloud of faith and feelings of Love* without troubleinge themselves with busye and impertinent operations of the understandinge, commonly called Meditations or discourses of the understandinge, to move & excite the will, which in the case of these devine & Seraphicke Ideots, are superfluous, they beinge alreadye sufficiently, yea aboundantly excited and bent to love *God*, and practise vertue, through their *light of Faith, which* telleth and assureth them, that all is vanitye of Vanities, *but Only to Love and serve God.*[18]

The 'ideot', who 'to others seemes ignorant, and foolish; to you is knowingly ignorant, and wisely unlearned', with 'more... satisfactorie knowledge then all the subtile Scholasticks, and suttle politicks put together could haue done'.[19] More's *Holy practises* consist of numbered 'ejaculations' or 'aspirations', which often imitate in content and style the versified Psalms, or Song of Songs. The aim of these spiritual exercises is to return to a 'state of innocencie', in total self-abnegation and passivity.[20] The 'ideot' systematically offers up all human dignity, comfort, pleasure, and status, diminishing to a point in order to become one with the cloud of unknown divinity. As well as accepting innumerable torments and

---

[14] Wekking, *The life and death*, pp. 35, 39. [15] Wekking, *The life and death*, p. 39.
[16] Wekking, *The life and death*, pp. 25, 78. [17] Wekking, *The life and death*, p. 41.
[18] Augustine Baker, 'Directions', in Gertrude More, *The holy practises of a devine lover, or, the sainctly ideots deuotions* (Paris, 1657), pp. 24–5.
[19] Baker, 'Directions', p. 168. [20] Baker, 'Directions', p. 8.

labours, she resigns herself to become esteemd 'abject, unworthy, base, ignorant, foolish, wittlesse, and most contemptible of all humayne creatures'.[21]

As de Certeau observed, none of this rhetoric, extolling the humility and resignation of the innocent or simple illiterate, was new to Christian thought in the seventeenth century. More and Baker clearly took their cue from the mystical doctrine of *Gelassenheit*—yielding, or resignation—and the affective, anti-scholastic tone of the Devotio Moderna and the late-medieval Rhineland and Flemish mystics. In Baker's translation of Hendrik Herp's preface to his 'Paradise of the Contemplatives', the ultimate end of mystical writing is that,

> all the wise ones of ye world may be confounded, & ye Humble may be comforted & rejoice, since y^t a simple old woman, or a country plouman or heardsman may with purity of soul & Elevation of spirit, be able, to raise themselves to this high & Divine knowledg, to wch none of al ye wise men of the world, swelling wth ye pride of their Learning are able by any industry of theirs, or by their Natural wils, though never so acute & subtill, in any sort to reach or attain unto.[22]

Baker quoted Jean Gerson, not himself an enemy to scholarship or theological erudition, to the effect that

> [e]ven as manie of those...who are tearmd or esteemed to be learned or wise, or Philosophers, or Divines, matters of Mistick divinitie are to be concealed and kept secret; so to verie many of them that be but simple (or of good wills and meanings) and unlearned may those matters be comunicated and imparted.[23]

There was an apocalyptic aspect to the hope that Baker placed in More, as a site of revelation, a plain glass through which one might see the light of the Spirit. In the digest of his writings produced by Serenus Cressy, *Sancta Sophia* (1657), Baker suggested that 'both History & fresher Experience', informed him that:

> in these latter times God hath as freely (and perhaps more commonly) communicated the Divine Lights and Graces proper to a Contemplative life to simple women, endued with lesser & more contemptible Gifts of Judgment, but yet enriched with stronger Wills and more fervent Affections unto him, then the ablest men.[24]

---

[21] Baker, 'Directions', p. 200.

[22] 'Out of Harphius: The same Author in the preface to his Book called the paradice of the contemplatives', in *An exposition of ye Book called ye Clowd*, Downside Abbey, Baker MS 12, fol. 2.

[23] *An exposition of ye Book*, p. 33.

[24] Augustine Baker, *Sancta Sophia, or, directions for the prayer of contemplation* (Douai, 1657), p. 156.

Mystical knowledge was the same as love of God, for Baker; true wisdom was to be found in union with divine love. Affective knowing therefore reached higher than speculative knowledge, and true holiness

> consists far more principally in the Operations of the will then of the understanding... And since women doe far more abound, and are more constant & fixed in Affections and other Operations of the will then Men, (though inferiour in those of the understanding) No mervayle if God doth oft find them fitter subjects for his Graces then Men.[25]

Baker and More both affirmed that the perfect wisdom of the mystic might be more accessible to women than to learned men. Gertrude More rejoiced that 'to shew thy power thou hast been pleased many times to bring a silly woman, loving thee, to that wisedom that no creature by wit or industry could attain to the same'.[26]

> For if we knew al, and could discourse with al the wit and eloquence of the Philosophers, Orators, and Divines of the causes and effects of al natural and supernatural things, yet if we did not know thee by endeavouring truly to love thee, we might truly be said to know nothing. For only by loving thee and knowing our selves is true Wisedom obtained.[27]

This feminine innocence could be a vehicle for a movement of pure divine love by which 'would the spirit of the *primitive Church* florish, and thy torne, and mangled members of thy Church be healed, and perfectly set together again'.[28]

A few examples from revolutionary prophetic texts will suffice to illustrate both the parallels between Catholic and radical Protestant conceptions of the 'holy fool', and some differences between them. Mary Cary appealed to a long tradition of gifted but unlearned prophets and preachers: Amos, 'a Heards-man'; the 'illiterate men' chosen by Jesus to be his disciples, and to whom he revealed spiritual truths. She warned those who would impose laws restricting the exercise of prophetic gifts that 'if you do prohibit any from Preaching Jesus Christ, you do quench the spirit, and oppose the freeness of the spirit, who is a free Agent'.[29] A time was coming in which Antichrist would finally be overthrown, and the Gospel would be preached throughout the world, 'and can any think that at that time the Lord will call forth none to this worke, but those that have taken such and such degrees in the Schooles?'[30] The Fifth Monarchist minister Christopher Feake, in his preface to Cary's *Little horns doom and downfall* (1651), observed that

---

[25] Baker, *Sancta Sophia*, p. 157.   [26] Gertrude More, *Spiritual exercises* (Paris, 1658), p. 189.
[27] More, *Spiritual exercises*, pp. 224–5.   [28] More, *Spiritual exercises*, p. 67.
[29] Mary Cary, *A word in season to the kingdom of England* (London, 1647), p. 5.
[30] Cary, *A word in season*, p. 6.

many wise men after the flesh have been (and now are) much offended, that a company of illiterate men, and silly women, should pretend to any skill in dark prophecies, and to a foresight of future events, which the most learned Rabbies, and the most knowing Politicians have not presumed to hope for.[31]

Feake had in mind not only his own generation, but the 'godly Nonconformists in Queen Elizabeths, and King James his days'; these were simple saints 'wiser than their enemies, wiser than their teachers, wiser then the Ancients'.[32] It was not the Bible scholars and learned ministers who possessed the knowledge of the mysteries in Scripture prophecy—the nature of the Beast, the new Jerusalem, the dominion of the saints—but the 'neglected, despised reproached Ones, both men and women'. These could 'clearly understand and perceive' such mysteries 'in the Visions of their own hearts who are the teachers of them'.[33] Anna Trapnel saw the empowerment of 'fools' to perceive and preach the hidden wisdom of the Scriptures as a judgement on a darkened and corrupt generation:

> Oh the height and depth, both of the wisdom and knowledge of God, his ways are past finding out! yet untrodden paths hath wisdom brought out, but to whom? even to fools, and low, base, vile nothings; and this the wise, learned, rich, knowing ones cannot bear. True Scripture language cannot be born in these days, the people of this generation vote it down, and the cry is amongst all sorts, especially the Clergy, and that of the refined sort too, that cryes, away with Christs raign and Subjects.[34]

Trapnel identified the 'wise and learned' with the rich and refined. She also considered the election of 'low, base, vile nothings' to be an illustration of divine love defying worldly hierarchies and status differences: 'Oh what manner of love is this! that makes no difference between fools and learned ones, preferring ideots before the wisdom of the world, making the ignorant and erring Spirit to have the greatest understanding?'[35]

Baker and More hinted at the contrast in quality between speculative and mystical theology but, in keeping with medieval Catholic tradition and unlike the radicals, did not imply that there was an actual opposition between scholarly knowledge and true divinity. For all his admiration for More, Baker retained a strongly gendered association of men and spirit, and woman and sensuality, and suggested that even though women's *love* was greater, men's *knowledge* was in some sense superior. He wrote, 'the Contemplations of Men are more noble, sublime & more exalted in Spirit, that is, lesse partaking of sensible effects, as Rapts, Extasies or Imaginative representations, as likewise melting tendernesses of

---

[31] Christopher Feake, in Mary Cary, *The little horns doom & downfall* (London, 1651), §a6r–a7r.
[32] Cary, *The little horns doom*, §a6r–a7r. [33] Cary, *The little horns doom*, §a6r–a7r.
[34] Anna Trapnel, *A legacy for saints* (London, 1654), p. 53.
[35] Trapnel, *A legacy for saints*, p. 16.

affections then those of women'.[36] Nonetheless, the defence of mystical divinity in Serenus Cressy's publications was roundly set upon by rationalist voices in the Restoration establishment, who characterized Baker and More as enthusiasts.[37] It was easy for Edward Stillingfleet, Edward Hyde, and others to conflate Cressy's account of 'experimentall knowledge' and immediate illuminations, with the 'mysticall familiarity with God' claimed by the spiritual sects. The scorn of the anti-Catholic polemicists was aimed squarely at Cressy's belief in holy fools: his insistence that women and persons of 'the meanest capacities' might attain to 'the perfection of contemplation'.[38] He aimed to show that the 'elevations' and 'exstasies' of the illuminated were 'neither dreams of ignorant souls, nor sublime extravagances of soaring *spirits*': they were reported equally by 'the greatest understandings that many of the last ages have brought forth (as S. Bernard, S. Thomas Aquinas, S. Bonaventure, and I. Picus Count of Mirandula &c)' and by 'S. Isidore a plain husband-man in Spain, S. Teresa, S. Catherine of Siena, and of Genoa, (silly ignorant women) & that unparallel'd young Heremite, Gregorio Lopez'.[39] It was of central importance to Cressy's apology that such ignorant souls as well as the highest intellects should be equally capable of achieving illumination. He was drawn to a church vindicated by the testimony of these pure souls, against a landscape of post-Reformation controversy and rationalism which he largely abhorred. The quality of *participatory* knowledge of the divine through union which he found in the practice of mystical theology was also unlike anything he had known in Protestant England, where 'contemplation' signified 'only the descanting upon any mystery of divinity, or passage of Scripture'.[40] Cressy explicitly distanced himself from sectarian claims to illumination, arguing that mystical knowledge did not derive from a 'private spirit', but must, by its nature, lead to communion with the institutional church.[41]

For all this perceived distance, the English radical spiritualists and Bakerite Catholics shared common sources. Sir Robert Cotton, whose library of manuscripts was a lively centre of antiquarian research in the 1620s, provided resources for Baker's enterprise of disseminating medieval mystical theology at the same time as Cotton was corresponding with an infamous anti-Laudian London preacher, John Everard (c.1584–1641).[42] Everard would be an important influence on the civil war radicals, not least through his anthology of mystical

---

[36] More, *Spiritual exercises*, 157–8.
[37] See my discussion of Cressy's role in provoking anti-enthusiast rhetoric in '"Between the rational and the mystical": the inner life and the early English Enlightenment', in Sara S. Poor and Nigel Smith eds., *Mysticism and reform, 1400–1750* (Notre Dame, IN: University of Notre Dame Press, 2015), pp. 198–219.
[38] More, *Spiritual exercises*, pp. 461–62.
[39] Serenus Cressy, *Exomologesis, or, a faithfull narration of the occaisiosn and motives of the conversion unto Catholick unity of Hugh-Paulin de Cressy* (Paris, 1653) p. 451.
[40] Cressy, *Exomologesis*, p. 446.   [41] Cressy, *Exomologesis*, p. 14.
[42] British Library, Cotton MS Julius C. III, fol. 171r. On Baker's use of the Cotton library, see Jennifer Summit, *Memory's library: medieval books in early modern England* (Chicago: University of Chicago Press, 2008), pp. 139–41.

and hermetic literature, almost certainly indebted to Cotton's library. Later sympathetic readers of Baker included the Quakers, especially in the second generation (notably, Robert Barclay), and irenic figures after the Restoration, such as John Worthington, master of Jesus College, Cambridge, from 1650 to 1660 and translator of a new edition of the *Imitatio Christi* by Thomas à Kempis in 1654.[43] The Cressy editions formed part of a body of eclectic mystical literature, discussed in the following section, and for all his efforts to distance them from sectarian spiritualism, they were received alongside radical theology.

The fertilization of English radicalism with mystical influences from the mainland, particularly from German and Dutch sources, gathered pace during the period of the Thirty Years' War. It is one of the arguments of this book that the radical theology of the English Revolution cannot be isolated from a wider environment of European radical religious reform and mystical theology. As in revolutionary England, prophets and mystics abounded amid the religious and political turmoil of the war in mainland Europe, including female visionaries. Some of the primary actors in the conflict, including Gustavus Adolphus and Albrecht von Wallenstein, took seriously the communications of prophetesses who sought an audience with them.[44] Samuel Hartlib and John Dury, in their quest for universal Reformation, identified a distinct stream of 'Mystical or Spiritual divinity' in around 1635, which might have potential as an engine of reform.[45] Initially, Hartlib and Dury compared notes on the works of Matthias Weyer (1521–60), a sixteenth-century prophet and exponent of mystical theology based in the confessionally ambiguous Rhineland city of Wesel.[46] Another mystical work that pleased Dury was the *Aurora sapientiae* of Paul Felgenhauer (1593–1661), a pro-Bohemian Lutheran prophet influenced by Jacob Boehme. Dury called this work 'one of the sublimest bookes that ever hee hase read, wherin is compacted a whole body of spiritual divinity in all their new-principles, so that all Men must admire it'. Dury evidently regarded the 'new' visionary mysticism as a fruitful source of inspiration for the project of healing Christendom. The German-born Hartlib himself seems to have been less enthusiastic than Dury about the 'new-principles' of his compatriots, and commented rather cautiously

---

[43] See Liam Peter Temple, *Mysticism in early modern England* (Woodbridge: Boydell Press, 2019), pp. 19–20.
[44] See Merry Wiesner, 'Women's response to the Reformation', in R. Po-chia Hsia, ed., *The German people and the Reformation* (New York: Cornell University Press, 1988), p. 162.
[45] On the *Ephemerides*, see Stephen Clucas, 'Samuel Hartlib's *Ephemerides*, 1635–59, and the pursuit of scientific and philosophical manuscripts: the religious ethos of an intelligencer', *The Seventeenth Century* 6:1 (1991), pp. 33–55.
[46] Matthias Weyer, *Theologiae mysticae triumque: illius viarum, purgativae, illuminativae atq; unitivae praxis viva*, trans. Johanne Spee (Amsterdam, 1658). Later, Weyer's writings would be published in an English edition by the Quakers, as Matthias Weyer, *The narrow path of divine truth described* (London, 1683).

on this new movement of spiritual divinity, which seemed the anti-rational mirror image of rationalizing, Socinian heresy, reserved for a kind of elite. Hartlib preferred 'English practical divinity', than the aggressive visionary mysticism 'elaborated by some in Germany'.[47]

The reception, and practice, of mystical theology in England was typically at the margins of orthodoxy. John Everard merits further attention as the pre-revolutionary Protestant who most successfully connected up experimental Puritanism and disaffection with the theology of the Caroline Church, with ancient and modern mystical influences. His translations of Hermes Trismigestus, Pseudo-Dionysius, Tauler, Sebastian Franck, and others enjoyed a scholarly audience among men like Elias Ashmole and Robert Boyle, but his readers were also some of the most imaginatively radical figures in the revolutionary period. Everard's work of disseminating mystical theology was continued by another London preacher, Giles Randall, who apparently gathered at Spitalfields in the 1640s 'as great a multitude of people as follows any sectary about the city'.[48] Randall had been in trouble with the Star Chamber in 1637 for preaching against ship-money; in 1645, he was among the London preachers identified by the heretic box-maker John Etherington as a leading Familist.[49] In a year of some significance for the reception of mystical theology in England, 1646, Randall printed two important mystical texts, expounding the 'hidden and deepe things of God',[50] editions of the third part of Benet of Canfield's *Rule of perfection* (published with the title *A bright starre*), and Nicholas of Cusa's *De visione dei*, apparently from a manuscript translation by John Everard. (Figure 3.) Shortly afterwards he translated the *Theologia germanica*.[51] His evaluation of this austere, anti-intellectual little book might apply to all his translations. It was:

---

[47] Sheffield University Library, Hartlib Papers 29/3/31A. Elsewhere, in unfinished notes, Hartlib divided all of theology into nineteen categories, apparently intending to attach a bibliography under each heading. They included 'Theologia scholastica', 'Theologia naturalis', and separate categories for 'Theologia practica' and 'Theologia mystica spiritualis'. See Sheffield University Library, Hartlib Papers, 22/21/1A-B.
[48] Robert Baillie, *Anabaptism, the true fountaine of independency, Brownisme, antinomy, familisme* (London, 1647), p. 102.
[49] See Peter Lake, *The box-maker's revenge: 'orthodoxy', 'heterodoxy' and the politics of the parish in early Stuart London* (Manchester: Manchester University Press, 2001).
[50] 'The Epistle to the Reader', in Benet of Canfield, *A bright starre* (London, 1646), §A7ʳ.
[51] According to his own account from Sebastian Castellio's Latin edition (reprinted in London in 1632), but possibly also drawing on the Grindleton minister Roger Brereley's version: another medieval mystical work filtered through the radical reformation *Theologia germanica* (London, 1632); Giles Randall, *Theologia germanica* (London, 1648). On the theory of Brereley's influence, see Nigel Smith, *Perfection proclaimed: language and literature in English radical religion, 1640–60* (Oxford: Oxford University Press, 1989), p. 117. See also Cambridge University Library, Additional MS 26, for a contemporary fair copy. Another manuscript edition (possibly late seventeenth or early eighteenth century in origin, bound in cheap vellum) sometimes erroneously associated with Randall is Bodleian Library, Rawlinson MS C. 610, a translation from Johann Arndt's 1597 reprint of Luther's edition, rather than from Sebastian Castellio.

90 THE REFORMATION OF THE HEART

Figure 3 The vision of God, in Giles Randall, *Ophthalmos aplois, or the single eye* (London, 1646), sig. A1v.

the extract or quintessence of other more thick and darkly composed Treatises of Theology; being much in little: thou shalt finde some kernels herein with their shell ready broken to thine hand; some Riddles in their plain sence unridled; some mysteries of Histories revealed: so, that in many things the Scripture

Parables are so explained, that thou shalt say, through the light of the truth herein; now know we that thou speakest plainly and not in parables; mysteries hidden from former ages, being now in measure more brought to light.[52]

The reference to 'mysteries of Histories' hints at Familist influences, as it was a characteristic phrase used by the Familist mystic 'Hiël' (whose works were circulating in English manuscript in the 1650s). Randall's English edition of the *Theologia germanica* became a staple of the libraries of religious radicals and nonconformists, among them the Sussex preacher Samuel Jeake and the Quaker intellectual Benjamin Furly. John Lambert, famously the author of the *Instrument of government* and a major-general of towering influence, read Randall's translation alongside the works of Juan de Valdés, the mystic associated with the Alumbrado and Spirituali movements in early sixteenth-century Spain and Italy, and his biographer suggests that this diet of mystical theology may have influenced his tolerant attitude towards Quakers in the 1650s (among them his former quartermaster, James Nayler).[53]

The translations were immediately condemned by several Presbyterian commentators as 'Popish Bookes...lately set forth by some Sectaries', showing an affinity between Catholic mystics and Protestant enthusiasts—or 'Monks and Familists', as Samuel Rutherford preferred to describe them.[54] They were, wrote Thomas Edwards, 'against the Perfection, Sufficiency, Perspicuity of the Scriptures, being for...Toleration and a Dispensation for want of an Infallible Judge, as the Papists are for the Pope upon that ground'.[55] It was thought, perhaps with some justice, that these mystical works contributed to the antinomian and anti-formalist thought of army preachers such as William Dell and John Saltmarsh, who taught that experience was the only teacher; that Christ could only be known through experimental knowledge of his love, and that the saints were only alienated from Christ by the law or ordinances.[56] Commentators anathematized the spiritualizing trend embodied in Randall's translations as the 'mysticall Antichrist' or the 'spiritual antichrist', rejecting such 'mysticall Divinity, that none can understand but themselves'.[57] From the Presbyterian perspective, the contentious elements of these works included chiefly the antinomian

---

[52] 'To the reader', in Randall, *Theologia germanica*, §A3r–v.

[53] See David Farr, *John Lambert, parliamentary soldier and Cromwellian major-general, 1619–1684* (Woodbridge: Boydell and Brewer, 2003), pp. 174–5; Michael Hunter, Giles Mandelbrote, Richard Ovenden, and Nigel Smith, *A radical's books: the library catalogue of Samuel Jeake of Rye, 1623–90* (Woodbridge: Boydell & Brewer, 1999), pp. 282–3; *Bibliotheca Furliana* (Rotterdam, 1714), p. 157.

[54] Thomas Edwards, 'Preface', *The third part of Gangraena* (London, 1646); Samuel Rutherford, *Christ dying and drawing sinners to himself* (London, 1647), pp. 342–348.

[55] Edwards, 'Preface', *The third part of Gangraena*.

[56] See, for instance, John Saltmarsh, *Free grace, or the flowings of Christs blood free to sinners* (London, 1646).

[57] Benjamin Bourne, *The description and confutation of mysticall Antichrist the Familists* (London, 1646), p. 108.

suggestion that the sanctified Christian cannot sin, but also troubling were the related themes of deification, celestial flesh, and a kind of pantheistic monism, not to mention the anti-historical interpretation of Scripture. At the heart of the spiritualists' doctrine of free grace was the mystery of an epistemic authority, inward experience, that was not only superior to the written revelation but incomprehensible to the outsider. Rutherford found repugnant the claim in the *Bright starre* that 'all meanes, ordinance, light, understanding, willing, thinking are annihilated and nothinged, and that the beleever beholds God without meanes in this life and so we have no more to doe with the word or to grow in grace and knowledge'.[58]

Mystical theology undoubtedly stimulated radical preaching. The 1653 edition of John Everard's *Gospel-treasures opened*, containing some of his translations as well as his sermons, contains an 'Approbation' by the radical Independent ministers Thomas Brooks and Matthew Barker, together with the imprimatur of another influential London Independent, Joseph Caryl.[59] They expressed their hope that the open-minded reader would 'finde thine heart in the Book, and the Book in thine heart'.[60] Brooks and Barker both preached experimental religion before parliament and the London elite between 1647 and 1651; Barker, less of a firebrand and less influenced by Stoic virtue ethics than Brooks, was also more obviously a proponent of mystical theology. In two sermons for the lord mayor and aldermen of London and the House of Commons, published by Everard's biographer Rapha Harford, Barker promoted the doctrines of Everard and 'the Mysticall Divines'. He set out an account of mystical ascent whereby God acts upon the soul in two stages of 'Illumination' and 'mortification', to raise the soul into a 'Deiforme state'.[61] Barker insisted that objectified knowledge of God was impossible; God could not be known except through inward illumination. The heart of the Christian is 'a Book ingraven with the ingravings of God, & the Epistle of Jesus Christ, written not with ink, but the Spirit of the living God'. Without the Spirit, in 'the flesh', God is 'incomprehensible, and inconceivable'.[62] Barker's emphasis on the Spirit's role in opening up knowledge of God, otherwise obscure to the shadowed intellect, might simply read as Reformed epistemology; but his account of this illumination as an ascent to 'deiformity' clearly owes more to mystical than to Calvinist theology. Barker derived his mystical thought not only from Everard but also from a Jesuit commentary on Dionysius, the Flemish theologian

---

[58] Rutherford, *A survey of the spirituall Antichrist opening the secrets of familisme and antinomianisme in the antichristian doctrine of John Saltmarsh and Will. Del* (London, 1648), p. 38.

[59] See Tom Webster, *Godly clergy in early Stuart England: the Caroline Puritan movement, c. 1620–1643* (Cambridge: Cambridge University Press, 2003), p. 260.

[60] John Everard, *Some Gospel-treasures opened* (London, 1653), §C2v.

[61] Matthew Barker, *A Christian standing & moving upon the true foundation* (London, 1648), pp. 16, 21.

[62] Matthew Barker, *Jesus Christ, the great wonder* (London, 1651), §A2v, p. 16.

Balthasar Cordier's 'Ad Mysticam Theologiam S. Dionysii Areopagitae'.[63] Though not one of the leading lights in the London preaching scene, Barker was sufficiently respected to be called upon to preach before the Commons on fast days and on 5 November 1652.[64]

The circle around James Nayler, in which female prophets were so esteemed, seems to have developed a notion that a tradition of mystics and prophets pointed in the direction of the fuller revelation realized in the Quaker movement. This was given its clearest expression in the writings of Robert Rich, mostly retrospectively after the Restoration. In 1657, Rich published a series of prophetic memoranda which had been sent to the Houses of Parliament at the time of the high-profile trial of James Nayler, in collaboration with George Fox and others,. These letters condemned the persecutors of Christ within his prophets. Fox suggested that, just as in the Gospel, it was 'the strength which was ordained for the Babes and Sucklings' which had 'set the Priests and Rulers on rage against Christ'.[65] Rich, however, was no 'holy pauper'. He was a wealthy merchant with colonial property, ridiculed as the 'mad merchant' for his emotional (and potentially blasphemous) ministrations to the mutilated and beaten Nayler, singing and weeping at Nayler's feet, stroking his hair, and licking his wounds.[66] In 1666, Rich recollected 'the Spirits, of certain Friends to the Bridegroom, who longed to see this day of the Son in Man... appearing as he doth now in many, face to face, as bone of their bone, and flesh of their flesh'.[67] Along with 'dear Saltmarsh, honest Erbury, Doomesday Sedgwick' (all radical army preachers), Rich's list included Sir Henry Vane, Hendrik Niclaes, Jacob Boehme, 'the whole Family of Love', George Withers, and curiously, two men advanced in years but still alive in 1666, John Amos Comenius and 'Brave Mr Hobbs'.[68] Rich had enjoyed a rich diet of mystical theology, linking the radical theologians of the revolutionary period with the historical mystical tradition:

> I have read the *Imitation of Christ*, writ by Thomas of Kempis. Also Cardinal Cusanus, his first, second and third Rule of Perfection, and his Idiot; with others of the like Divine Nature, all tending to a Holy Life, by virtue of Christ's Holy Spirit in us, the only way to Life and Salvation. Allelujah. I have also read many Divine Works writ by H.N. Jacob Behm, John Saltmarsh, Dr Everard, William

---

[63] Barker, *A Christian standing*, p. 21; Barker, *Jesus Christ, the great wonder*, epigraph on title page, p. 19. Cordier's essay was published with his *Opera S. Dionysii Areopagitae cum scholiis S. Maximi* (Antwerp, 1634).

[64] See entry for 28 Oct. 1652, in *Journal of the House of Commons, vol. 7: 1651-1660* (London, 1802), p. 198.

[65] Robert Rich, *Copies of some few of the papers given into the House of Parliament in the time of James Naylers trial* (s.l., 1657), p. 6.

[66] Thomas Burton, '27 December 1656', *Diary of Thomas Burton Esq, vol. 1: July 1653-April 1657*, ed. John Towill Rutt (London, 1828), p. 266.

[67] Robert Rich, *Love without dissimulation* (London, 1666), p. 6.

[68] Rich, *Love without dissimulation*, p. 6.

Sedgwick, William Erbery, Dr Gill, Dr Taylor, with others that were inspired of God, and spake of the second Coming of Christ in the Sanctified, and of that blessed Day which should attend his Appearance. Allelujah.[69]

By contrast, when the scholarly Scots converts to Quakerism, Robert Barclay and George Keith associated Quaker thought with mystical divinity, they boasted of an affinity with Plato, Plotinus, Origen, and the Cappadocian fathers, as well as the medieval mystics: Tauler, the *Theologia germanica*.[70] They did not mention Erbery, Saltmarsh, and Everard in the same breath as the ancient and medieval masters. Nonetheless, the mystics of the English Revolution lived long in Quaker memory. Ambrose Rigge, in an appeal to the Bristol Friends to 'remembrance how it was with them at the beginning', published in 1700, recalled the preachers of the 'New Jerusalem' who anticipated the truth of the light within: 'I shall write down some of these Men's names that use to hear in those Days, as Walter Cradock, William Arberey, Joshua Sprig, Thomas Brooks, John Webster, Dr. Everard, Peter Sterer, William Dell, John Saltmarsh, Morgan Floyd'.[71] With the exception of Everard (who died in 1641), these were all ministers associated with the radical elements in the New Model Army.

The most voracious consumers of contemporary mystical and visionary texts included avid readers of Jacob Boehme in the Bradfield Rectory circle around John Pordage. Boehme was in many ways an ultimate 'holy fool': the illuminated shoemaker, supposedly inspired by nothing more than a trinitarian combination of the Holy Spirit, Paracelsus, and Valentine Weigel. In his circle of English admirers, women were also held in high regard as prophetic agents and preachers. In John Pordage's *Theologia mystica*, published posthumously (by the prophetess Jane Lead) in 1683, he adopted a 'manic style', similar to that employed by Abiezer Coppe, in defence of immediate revelations and visions. This was a posture of folly, to confound the worldly wise. Pordage admitted that he was not himself innocent of worldly wisdom:

> I am not against humane learning, I have known what it is; but I would not have it set above the Spirit of God; nor the teachings of the Spirit to truckle under it: For God has said, *He will destroy the wisdom of the Wise*, and he will make himself known to babes, and such who in a childlike Innocency wait for the teaching of the most high, and *bring to nothing the understanding of the prudent*. The wisdom of this World is indeed but folly at the best.[72]

---

[69] Robert Rich, *The epistles of Mr Robert Rich to the seven churches* (s.l., 1680), p. 107.

[70] George Keith, *Divine immediate revelation and inspiration, continued in the true church. Second part* (London, 1685), pp. 45–6.

[71] Ambrose Rigge, *A tender exhortation to Friends at Bristol, to bring to remembrance how it was with them in the beginning* (London, 1700), pp. 12–13.

[72] John Pordage, *Theologia mystica, or, the mystic divinitie of the aeternal invisibles* (London, 1683), §H4r–v.

An intriguing manuscript miscellany in the Sloane collection at the British Library contains various materials associated with the Pordage circle. It includes a lease for the Baptist minister Thomas Lamb dated 1647, and, among other 'theological treatises' (mostly Behmenist in character), there are fragments of Jane Lead's 'Visions & revelations' or prophetic diary, dated November 1676; and a translation of a 1641 vision of Hans Engelbrecht, another humble lay prophet of the Thirty Years' War. It also contains a unique early modern translation into English of the 'Life of Saint Mary the Aegiptian'.[73] This seventeenth-century translation of a seventh-century account of a fifth-century desert mystic, traditionally attributed to Sophronius, is undated, but can be speculatively linked to the Pordage circle by the contents of the wider miscellany. Mary of Egypt was occasionally cited by early Stuart authors (both Catholic and Protestant) as an exemplar of early Christian female piety, but the details of her strange 'life' were obscure in vernacular texts.[74] A teenage prostitute turned penitent, Mary is said to have encountered the 'singular holie monke called Zozimus' during his Lenten peregrinations in the Egyptian wilderness. The description of her naked appearance is startling: 'it was a humane creature, but stranglie disguised, the haires as white as snowe, and long down to the foote and all the bodie so parched with ye sunne that it was as black as a coale: this creature being aware of him fledde very fast from him'. Mary had supernatural knowledge of Zozimus, and he 'understood there by yt she was illuminated by god'; he fell upon the ground and 'asked her benedictions'.[75]

The narrative recounts the conversion and subsequent temptations of Mary as she wandered in the wilderness, assaulted by 'sensuall appetites', the 'flames of unlawfull lust' and 'tentations of fornication... wch of all others were most grievous, violent and frequent'.[76] Having overcome these urges through extraordinary feats of prayer and self-denial, inspired by visions of the Blessed Virgin, Mary performed miracles, and was endowed with extraordinary untutored knowledge:

> when Zozimus heard her speake ye words of scripture, hee asked her whether she had reade it: no (quoth she) besides yourselfe I never saw man nor beast since I came hither, and to learning I was never sett, neither have I heard anie other either reade it, or sing it, but ye word of God wch is ever livinge giveth instruction unto all.[77]

---

[73] 'The Life of Saint Mary the Aegiptian', British Library, Sloane MS 2569, fols. 46r-54. The immediate source for the translation is unclear; it references the medieval edition Nicephorus Callistus, and probably derives from a medieval Latin edition; it does not seem to be connected to the contemporary French edition published in the *Vies des pères* by Arnauld D'Andilly in 1653, later translated into English in 1726. On the attribution of the fragments to Jane Lead, see my 'Manuscript divinity in the manuscript writings of Jane Lead and Ann Bathurst', in Ariel Hessayon, ed., *Jane Lead and her transnational legacy* (London: Palgrave Macmillan, 2016), pp. 173-6.

[74] See, for instance, Thomas Heywoode, *Gynaikeion: or, nine bookes of various history* (London, 1624), p. 273.

[75] 'Life of Saint Mary', fols. 46r-v.   [76] 'Life of Saint Mary', fols. 50v-51.

[77] 'Life of Saint Mary', fol. 51v.

It is a hagiographical text with themes so jarring for a Reformed audience in seventeenth-century England that it is scarcely surprising the 'Life' was not published. Mary of Egypt became, instead, another reference point for Restoration attacks on enthusiasm and popery. Henry Foulis, for instance, ridiculed the papists for their 'senceless signs of Sanctity', and for commending 'Mary of Egypt, for going stark-naked'.[78] The existence of the translation in manuscript form, alongside more contemporary reports of visions experienced by lay women and men, illustrates both its appeal and its difficulty as a text. Its account of a 'holie woman...endued wth the spirit of prophesie', at the feet of whom a learned monk fell prostrate, would always have savoured of Roman superstition, but it would take on additional dimensions in the wake of the Revolution and its petticoat prophets. By contrast, for those who looked (not for the first time in Christian history) to female visionaries as bright innocent lanterns of the Holy Spirit, in an age of discredited and domineering clergy, of worldly theologians embroiled in fruitless controversy, the naked wild-woman full of miraculous knowledge represented an unimpeachable demonstration of divine presence and power.

Experiential Knowledge

The mystical theology of the revolutionary radicals was allied to, but distinct from, Roman Catholic mysticism. In their 'realized eschatology'—that is, the conviction that they were living in the new age of Christ's coming—its advocates were prophets as much as contemplatives. A repeated theme of the radical prophets of the Revolution was that knowledge of God, and especially the understanding of the mysteries in Scripture, had been hidden 'under Babylon', and that it was now breaking forth in unexpected and disruptive ways to humiliate and discredit the old ways of knowing. Women would be key agents of the new dispensation of knowledge. One of the earliest women to herald the dawning of new revelations, in her characteristically enigmatic prose, was Lady Eleanor Davies. In a message to parliament in 1643, Davies anticipated 'a full expression of our Lords coming to be revealed to a woman; That secret disclosed'. She compared the disclosure of this secret to the appearance of Christ to Mary Magdalen after his resurrection, asking:

> Wherefore then not to be revealed to us, before others in such case: and as soon to his handmaids as his menservants; the spirit of God to be poured on them, and so now, as well as then, when she had the first happy sight of him, after his rising.

---

[78] Henry Foulis, *The history of Romish treasons and usurpations* (London, 1671), p. 19.

The revelation of Christ's coming in the Spirit would reveal for the first time the meaning of the Scriptures, the understanding of which had been 'buried in another Language'.[79] God's book had not yet 'come of age'; it was 'under custody of Metaphors and Figures' until the time when the true referents of those metaphors or figures would be fully known.[80] Mary Cary also envisioned the opening of the sealed book of Scripture in her *Word in season* (1647), in which she commented that:

> if it were so in the Apostles times, that through imperfection in knowledge there were circumstantiall errors amongst the Saints, then it is no wonder if there be many more now, there having been such an universall darknes spread over the world by the midnight of Poperie that hath been in the world.[81]

In the new dispensation, 'we all expect the breakings forth of truth more & more'.[82] The prophet Thomas Tany looked forward to an era in which understanding would cause 'contests and disputes to cease', and 'man restored from darkness to light'. For Tany, this would be a mystical 'unvailing' of 'the vailed truth that lies hid and buryed by mans invention', which God was 'bringing forth in man; for ye shall all be taught of me saith the Lord'. He very specifically included women in his vision of the expansion of knowledge and understanding of the concealed truths: 'men and women' will 'discern and know the mystery of the sealed book, which is the Scripture or word of God, as you call it'.[83] In his defence of women's speaking, the Quaker Richard Farnworth argued that for the conventionally learned, the Holy Spirit 'is invisible and incomprehensible', and 'the Scriptures are a mystery', but female prophets were given access to the mysteries, just as 'the Spirit of the Lord was made manifest through the female kind, as women in former ages'.[84] Farnworth rejoiced that 'now the Key of *David* is found again, and it is turn'd about freely to unfold the Mystery, that hath been hid, and revealeth the Mystery both to Sons and Daughters'.[85]

The question of the authority of women as messengers of a new revelation of Christ was entangled in the debates about the nature of knowledge about God, and the role of university learning. The challenge of radical mysticism in the English Revolution was, among other things, a challenge to traditional ways of knowing.

---

[79] Eleanor Davies, *The star to the wise, 1643 to the high court of Parliament* (London, 1643), pp. 12–13.
[80] Eleanor Davies, *The bill of excommunication for abolishing henceforth the Sabbath* (London, 1649), p. 4.
[81] Cary, *A world in season*, p. 8.   [82] Cary, *A world in season*, p. 8.
[83] Thomas Tany, *Theauraujohn his Theous on apokolipikal: or, Gods light declared in mysteries* (London, 1651), pp. 31–2. On the mystical, alchemical, and Kabbalistic influences on Tany, see Ariel Hessayon, *'Gold tried in the fire': The prophet Theauraujohn Tany and the English Revolution* (Aldershot: Ashgate, 2007).
[84] Richard Farnworth, *A woman forbidden to speak in the church* (London, 1654), §A1v–A2r.
[85] Farnworth, *A woman forbidden*, pp. 5–6.

Scholarly theology came to be seen as alienated from, if not antithetical to, true understanding of the Christian mystery. Walter Cradock is said to have complained about those who 'think all divinity and the mystery of Christ and the Gospel is bound up in Schoolmen and Common-place-books', and behaved as though 'the Mystery of Christ and the Gospel could be carryed from Oxford into the country in a clog-bag'.[86] It is clear, as Nicholas McDowell has demonstrated, that many of those who taught radical theology and heralded an age of 'Illiterate Mechanick' preachers, were themselves deeply learned university-educated men (among them John Pordage, John Saltmarsh, William Erbery, William Dell, and Abiezer Coppe).[87] This does not, however, render their challenge to the universities, and especially to what they regarded as discredited forms of divinity, less powerful. The pulpits of men like Dell and Erbery—at the heart of the universities of Oxford and Cambridge—brought them into a direct confrontation with the traditional seats of scholarship. They could speak against the universities, from the heart of their experience of humane learning. Several of these male spiritualists were, as this book seeks to illustrate more fully, supporters of women as preachers and ministers, and this was entirely congruent with their epistemological radicalism. It is also important to situate these thinkers within a cultural moment involving not only radical English prophets and tub-preachers, but also Catholic ingénues and their confessors; not to mention Lutheran lay visionaries like Jacob Boehme, the cobbler of Görlitz. It was a moment for vernacular prophets and mystics to answer the clamour for certain knowledge and demonstrations of divine truth. There is clear evidence that some of the revolutionary prophets, both male and female, drew from mystical influences, and shared a common language of affective, participatory knowledge of God through mystical communion.

John Dury's reformism contained a strongly mystical as well as a millenarian element. Dury's career as a Westminster divine and reformer during the civil wars placed him in an influential position. He preached before the House of Commons in November 1646, setting out his vision of a universal reform of the universities:

> for the education of the sonnes of the Prophets... with the soundnes and purity of spirituall learning, that they may speak the true language of Canaan, and that the gibberidge of Scholastical Divinity (which is nothing else but the language of corrupt humane reason...) May be banished out of their society.

This transformation of education would lead to the 'building up of the spirituall Jerusalem in the souls of all men, both young and old', and the overthrowing of the

---

[86] Henry Pinnell, *Nil novi: this years fruit, from the last years root* (London, 1654), pp. 24–5.
[87] Nicholas McDowell, *The English radical imagination: culture, religion, and Revolution, 1640-1660* (Oxford: Oxford University Press, 2003), esp. pp. 1–21.

'mystical Babylon'.[88] It has been observed that Dury failed to include women in his scheme for the 'Advancement of Universal Learning', and he certainly cannot be considered radical on the status of women. Although he was employed for a time in the 1640s at the Hague as chaplain to Mary Stuart, and envisaged schooling for girls, Dury explicitly excluded women from the organization and execution of the plans he set forth in 1649–50.[89] Education for girls would enable women 'to become good and careful houswiues, loving towards their husbands and their children when God shall call them to be married; and understanding in all thing belonging to the care of a Family'.[90] Dury's relations with particular women, however—notably the woman who would become his wife in 1645, Dorothy Moore—indicate that he became more open to the involvement of women in active Christian service. In a letter dated 1644 to Katherine Jones, Lady Ranelagh, when he was courting Moore, he admitted to having held conventionally misogynistic assumptions about 'the silly weakenes & want of Capacity which doth appear in most of the feamale kinde'. More recently, however, he had come to the generous conclusion 'that God hath not deprived that parte of mankinde of Eminent Graces, with strength of parte & abillityes to doe him spirituall service & to be more heelpefull in some things towards the advancement of the kingdome of his sonn then even men themselues'.[91] Dury was in fact surrounded by influential and erudite women: the queens of Bohemia and Sweden; the scientist, Lady Ranelagh; as well as the Hebrew scholar, Dorothy Moore; the Dutch scholarly prodigy, Anna Maria van Schurman; possibly also the educationalist, Bathsua Makin. Such were the attainments of these high-ranking women that Carol Pal has characterized them as the 'Republic of Women'.[92] This exposure to, and sympathy for, learned women perhaps led Dury to suggest that 'such [girls] as may be found capable of Tongues and Sciences (to perfect them in Graces and the knowledge of Christ for all is to be referred to him above the ordinary sort) are not to be neglected; but assisted towards the improvement of their intellectuall abilities'.[93]

While Dury continued to value scholarly endeavour, even in women, more radical versions of visionary mysticism encouraged a view of affective knowledge as higher, if not opposed to, speculative or notional knowledge of divinity. This distinction was clearly gendered in early modern minds. Robert Greville,

---

[88] John Dury, *A sermon preached before the honourable House of Commons, Novemb. 16 1645* (London, 1646), pp. 48–9.

[89] Hilda Smith, *All men and both sexes: gender, politics, and the false universal in England, 1640–1832* (University Park: Pennsylvania University Press, 2002), p. 50–1.

[90] John Dury, *The reformed school* (London, 1649), p. 20.

[91] Dury to Lady Ranelagh, 'Rotterdam this 4 December 1644', Sheffield University Library, Hartlib Papers, 3/2/92A–B.

[92] Carol Pal, *Republic of women: rethinking the republic of letters* (Cambridge: Cambridge University Press, 2012).

[93] Dury, *The reformed school*, p. 20.

Lord Brooke, a noted enthusiast for mystical literature, reflected on the greater capacity of women for affective piety. Despite his printed disavowals of Familist and antinomian heresy, Lord Brooke's circle, as Ariel Hessayon has demonstrated, included several 'godly clergy' with nonconformist associations and mystical inclinations. It likely included Abiezer Coppe, but also Samuel Fisher (a Baptist who would turn Quaker apologist in the 1650s), Henry Vane, and Peter Sterry, his chaplain.[94] In *The nature of truth, its union and unity with the soul* (1643), Greville suggested that women would outnumber the men among the saints, and suggested that their affections enlarged their understanding of divine love manifest in Christ:

> of the Chorus of Saints, the greatest number will bee found amongst the feminine sexe, because these are most naturally capable of affection, and so most apt to make knowledge reall. It is true, I confesse, these affections misguided, led them first into transgression; but these same affections after, carried them first to the grave, then to the sight of a Saviour, gave them the enwombing of Christ, who (in some sense) might have entertained our nature in another way (if he had so pleased;) and these affections will one day raise many of them into the sweet embraces of everlasting joy.[95]

Greville hinted here at the reversal of Eve's transgression in the 'Second Eve', the Virgin Mary, whose sex Christ dignified by using female flesh as the means by which he assumed human nature. Women's weakness, their affectivity, was also their redeeming strength, and potentially granted them more intimate access to knowledge of a loving God. Further on, Greville affirmed that 'all knowledge lieth in the affection'.[96] A former fellow of King's College Cambridge, Christopher Goad, became a notable radical defender of women's preaching, within the framework of a mystical antithesis between 'heart-knowledge' and 'head-knowledge'. Goad had been chaplain to the first Lord Saye and Sele, William Fiennes, who came under the influence of Robert Greville in the 1630s. He may also have acted as a chaplain to the Earl of Holland, Henry Rich, who harboured the mystical preacher and translator John Everard as his chaplain from 1634.[97] Among the mystics and radicals in this network, Goad was the most public advocate of women as ministers and divines. Goad contrasted 'notional' knowledge, derived from an external source, with 'feeling' knowledge which is immediate

---

[94] Ariel Hessayon, 'The making of Abiezer Coppe', *Journal of Ecclesiastical History* 62:1 (2011), pp. 38–58; see also David Como, *Blown by the Spirit: Puritanism and the emergence of an antinomian underground in pre-Civil-War England* (Stanford: Stanford University Press, 2004), pp. 402–3.

[95] Robert Greville (Lord Brooke), *The nature of truth, its union and unity with the soul which is one in its essence* (London, 1641), pp. 68–9.

[96] Greville, *The nature of truth*, p. 80.

[97] On Goad and his patrons, see Andrew Barclay, *Electing Cromwell: the making of a politician* (London and New York: Routledge, 2016), pp. 72–3; on Henry Rich's mystical and antinomian tendencies, see Como, *Blown by the Spirit*, pp. 44–5, 65–6.

and inward: 'A discovery by the spirit is not a notional discovery, as when a man or a letter shall come and tell us: but such a discovery of sin and hell as makes us feel it'.[98]

> That the Lord Jesus and his power is in all Saints as well as in Ministers. The Apostles Spirit joynes with them when they are gathered together. The whole Church, men and women, the simplest as well as the wisest, the weakest as well as the strongest, with the power of the Lord Jesus...It is the Spirit that makes Ministers: and those Ministers that are made by the Spirit, do minister the Spirit. And that is ministring the Gospel when we Minister the Spirit.[99]

The ministry of women represented a new dispensation of divine knowledge, whereby 'the wise of the world shall be laid by; silly and weak women shall be instructed, babes and sucklings shall be fill'd with strength, and the mysteries of the Kingdom shall be hidden from the wise'.[100]

A later edition of John Everard's works in 1657 included a new recommendation, by John Webster, formerly an army chaplain, physician, and, most notoriously, educational reformer behind a proposal to dismantle and reform the structures of university learning in the early 1650s. Webster's mysticism was not derived only from Everard: he attributed his own conversion to an encounter with the northern mystical network known as the 'Grindletonians' during his curacy at Kildwick-in-Craven in Yorkshire, from 1632. The parish had previously been the centre of the activities of the mystical preacher Roger Brereley, under whose influence radical (perhaps Familist) ideas about union with the indwelling Christ, the futility of ordinances, and the perfection of the saints, spread in the region. Although it was some way east of the actual town of Grindleton, Kildwick was close enough for Webster as curate to preach there on occasion 'out of good will' but not for profit.[101] The parish neighboured John Lambert's estate in the Craven district, and Webster would later appeal to Lambert for patronage. Webster also had strong Paracelsian interests, and owned books by Jacob Boehme.[102] He recommended *Some Gospel-treasures opened* as a 'precious Book', 'having myself found so much sweetnesse in it'.[103] Inspired by a confluence of mystical inspirations and currents, Webster was set on a path of 'unknowing' more explicitly iconoclastic than that of Everard. In several treatises, he made a stark contrast between 'that which is acquired, and that which is infused': the 'Humane Learning...that is or

---

[98] Christopher Goad, *Refreshing drops, and scorching vials, severally distributed to their proper subjects* (London, 1653), p. 83.
[99] Goad, *Refreshing drops*, p. 64.   [100] Goad, *Refreshing drops*, p. 88.
[101] Quoted in Farr, *John Lambert*, p. 174.
[102] On Webster's Paracelsianism, see Charles Webster, *From Paracelsus to Newton: magic and the making of modern science* (Cambridge: Cambridge University Press, 1982), pp. 96–8. On his book catalogue, see Hessayon, *Gold tried in the fire*, p. 303.
[103] In John Everard, *The Gospel treasury opened* (London, 1657), §b7r.

many be acquired by Natural power, capacity and industry', and 'evidential and experimental knowledge, which men partake of, by the sending in, inflowing and indwelling of the Spirit of Christ'.[104] For Webster, this vast gulf entailed an absolute separation of spheres between spiritual and temporal power, between grace and nature. He embarked upon a sustained attack on the whole system of ordination and a far-reaching call for the withdrawal of the civil magistrate from Christ's kingdom. The only support that religion should have from the magistrate was 'negative and permissive', and, 'whatsoever a mans opinion or way of worship be', he should be protected and defended.[105] This was not, of course, a new or isolated view: it was anticipated in the tolerationist principles of the New England separatist Roger Williams, and of men like John Saltmarsh and William Dell.[106] Webster was, however, distinctive in his insistence not only upon the implications of toleration for a national clergy, but also for a separation of epistemological spheres which would leave academic theology adrift. He was at the centre of a debate over the legitimacy of ordination in 1653, along with the Independent mystics William Erbery and John Cardell, and found himself not unreasonably accused of 'knocking down Learning'.[107] He insisted that he was not opposed to all forms of learning, but rather 'I am for the setting up of that divine Teaching, & learning of the Spirit of God, that the Schools do call infusive; for we have not received the Spirit of the World, but the Spirit which is of God'.[108]

The revolutionary agenda proposed by Webster was developed more fully in his *Academiarum examen* of 1654, which proposed to improve on the study of the arts and mathematical and natural sciences (literally a Copernican, but also a Baconian revolution), and sweep away all forms of scholarly theology, which he characterized in Erasmian terms as a 'confused *Chaos*, of needless, frivolous, fruitless, triviall, vain, curious, impertinent, knotty, ungodly, irreligious, thorny, and hel-hatch't disputes, altercations, doubts, questions and endless janglings, multiplied and spawned forth even to monstrosity and nauseousness'.[109] Theology was but a clanging cymbal if it 'were not spoken in, and from the eternal word, which is the love-essence, or essence of love'.[110] Webster's conviction that 'none but the Spirit of Christ is the true Doctor' was richly informed by his reading in mystical and occult texts, not least Nicholas of Cusa, whom he called upon as one of the 'Cloud of Witnesses against the supine negligence of the Schools' along with

---

[104] John Webster, *The saints guide, or, Christ the rule, and rules of saints* (London, 1653), p. 1.
[105] Webster, *The saints guide*, p. 37.
[106] See John Coffey, 'Puritanism and liberty revisited: the case for toleration in the English Revolution', *The Historical Journal* 41:4 (1998), pp. 961–85.
[107] Charles Webster, *The picture of Mercurius Politicus* (London, 1653), p. 8.
[108] Webster, *The picture of Mercurius Politicus*, p. 8.
[109] Charles Webster, *Academiarum examen: or, the examination of academies* (London, 1654), p. 15.
[110] Webster, *Academiarum examen*, p. 27.

Paracelsus and Jacob Boehme.[111] Webster embraced the teachings of the inspired cobbler of Görlitz. He learned at Boehme's feet about the original 'Angelical and Paradisical language', 'that ineffable word that was with God, and lay wrapped up in the bosome of eternal essence', expressed in a primordial, harmonious music before all things. It was out of this 'central Abysse of unity' that 'numerous and various seminall natures' sprang forth, 'all speaking one language in expressing significantly in that mystical Idiom'.[112]

Webster's radical challenge to the universities is well known, and he is also remembered as the author of *Metallographica: or, a history of metals* (1671), later owned and pored over by Isaac Newton, which demonstrated Webster's prowess as a student of the natural world.[113] Moreover, he famously participated in a landmark debate on the nature of witchcraft, contributing his own half-sceptical account in *The displaying of witchcraft* (1677). Webster's openness to the ministry of women, at least during the revolutionary period, has received less attention. In one of his earliest publications, *The saints guide* (1654), Webster devoted some time to examining the practice of laying on of hands in the New Testament, particularly in Acts 8, as part of his argument against the special ordination of men as ministers. He argued that the 'manifesting of [the] visible Power' of the Holy Ghost, in prophesying and speaking in tongues, came about at the same time as the baptism of all believers, 'both men and women'. It was at baptism that the apostles 'layd they their hands on them, and they received the Holy Ghost: and these were both men and women, and not all Ministers, unless every Believer be one'.[114] Elsewhere, he made it absolutely clear (quoting the egalitarian Galatians 3.28) that he did include all believers as ministers of the Gospel, as common 'partakers of the same heavenly calling, and anointed with that spirit that teacheth all things, and leadeth into all truth; where there is neither Jew nor Greek, bond nor free, male nor female, but are all one in Christ Jesus'.[115] Perhaps most notably, in *The judgement set, and the bookes opened* (1654), Webster appears to have been one of the first to offer an allegorical interpretation of Paul's prohibitions on women speaking in the church, with references to 1 Corinthians 11 and 14, and 1 Timothy 2. This interpretation was developed fully in the same year, 1654, by the Quaker Richard Farnworth, and it was frequently cited in the later 1650s in Quaker apologies for women's speaking.[116] In Webster's account, the 'woman' prohibited from speaking in the church was the 'Weaknesse or Womanishnese of

---

[111] Webster, *Academiarum examen*, pp. 5, 11, 12, 52, 55. See also Webster, *The picture of Mercurius Politicus*, p. 8.
[112] Webster, *Academiarum examen*, pp. 27–8.
[113] See Webster, *From Paracelsus to Newton*, p. 71. [114] Webster, *The saints guide*, pp. 17–18.
[115] Webster, *The saints guide*, §A3r.
[116] Farnworth, *A woman forbidden*. See also Elaine Hobby, 'Handmaids of the Lord and mothers in Israel: early vindications of Quaker women's prophecy', in Thomas Corns and David Loewenstein eds., *The emergence of early Quaker writing: dissenting literature in seventeeth-century England* (London: Frank Cass, 1995), pp. 93–5.

man', found in his 'pride, insolency, or vain-boasting'; in this sense, 'All the men in the world, be they of what parts, learning, strength, or excellencie can be named, are but WOMEN in this respect'.[117] The parallels with Farnworth's more famous (and explicit) defence, with its assertion that 'the Woman or wisdom of the Flesh is forbidden to speak in the Church', are clear.[118]

As in the case of the Quakers, this openness to more flexible, mystical understandings of the New Testament could lead to practical as well as theoretical progress on the status of women in the churches, among some of the radicalized former university men. William Bridge, once a fellow at Emmanuel College in Cambridge and another Westminster Assembly divine, reportedly appointed two mature sisters, Alice Burgesse and Jhoanne Ames, as deaconesses or 'widows' at his gathered congregation at Yarmouth in June 1650. The year previously, he 'did abundantly prove their helpfulness and needfulness from 1 Tim. v. and Rom. xvi'.[119] This appointment was an unusual event in these fellowships at the time, though women dominated the congregations.[120] In his published sermons, Bridge was a free-grace preacher, and railed against 'notional' knowledge of Christ. For Bridge, the 'In-being of Christ in the soul, is not a meer fansie, a meer notion; but carries with it the greatest reallity in the world'. Experience of Christ's love would transform the mind; "Tis a Real *Christ*, not a Notional *Christ*' that would do this.[121] In another sermon in 1649, the same year that he publicly commended his two godly widows, Bridge meditated on the Canaanite woman of Matthew 15.21–8, as an exemplar of faith. This was the woman who approached Jesus to help her demon-ravaged daughter, but was ignored and insulted as a Canaanite outsider: 'It is not meet to take the children's bread, and cast it to dogs'. Bridge drew inspiration from the woman's spirited reply ('Truth, Lord: yet the dogs eat of the crumbs which fall from their masters' table'). He observed:

> All this is said by a Woman. Women usually are not of that boldness, but more easily dash'd out of countenance. Faith rises above our Nature, and above our natural disposition. Faith had gotten into this womans heart, and she forgets her own disposition, she comes like any Man, with boldness upon Jesus Christ, follows him, and will never let him alone. Faith rises above our own Dispositions, and above our Natures.[122]

---

[117] John Webster, *The judgement set, and the bookes opened* (London, 1654), p. 84.
[118] Webster, *The judgement set*, p. 2.
[119] See John Browne, *History of Congregationalism and memorials of the churches in Norfolk and Suffolk* (New York: Cornell University Press, 1924), p. 227.
[120] See Joel Halcomb, "Godly order and the trumpet of defiance: the politics of Congregational church life during the English Revolution" in Michael Davies, Anne Dunan-Page, and Joel Halcomb, eds., *Church life: pastors, congregations, and the experience of dissent in seventeenth-century England* (Oxford: Oxford University Press, 2019), p. 31.
[121] William Bridge, *The works of William Bridge, sometime fellow of Emmanuel Colledge in Cambridge* (London, 1649), §A2v, p. 112.
[122] Bridge, *The works of William Bridge*, p. 197.

The very shamelessness of the woman, her ability to transcend her habitual diffidence and meet Jesus with boldness, is presented as an illustration of the transformative power of grace. Bridge celebrates the woman's forgetfulness of the 'natural disposition' of her sex, in the strength of her love and belief in Christ's love.

In the quest for the reformation of knowledge, William Dell was a particularly interesting and influential commentator, not as an independent scholar, or even fellow of a college, but as master of Gonville and Caius, Cambridge, between 1649 and 1660. Dell's career illustrates just how far radical theological networks penetrated the revolutionary regime: he presided at the wedding of Henry Ireton to Bridget Cromwell in 1646.[123] His attack on theology in the universities, published in its most radical form as *The stumbling stone* in 1653, certainly pulled no punches. The university, he argued, was no place for the encounter with the Holy Spirit of God, the true source of knowledge of divinity. The schools should be dedicated only to secular fields of knowledge. Real divinity was the business of the ordinary Christian:

> how grievously are the Worldly wise, and deep learned ones (as they esteem themselves) offended? that Gods Spirit alone should be a sufficient Unction for the Ministry of the New Testament, and that God should on purpose lay aside the Wise and Prudent men, and choose babes, and out of their mouth ordain his great strength to set up Christs Kingdom in the world, and to destroy Antichrists? Yea this Doctrine will chiefly offend the University.[124]

The work of theologians, exegetes and philologists of Scripture, was inimical to the essential truth of the incarnation in the Gospel: the living presence of Christ come to reside not in the historical text bound up in strange languages, but in human hearts. Dell went on, warming to his theme: what use was there for philosophy, or arts and sciences, in the 'Ministry of the New Testament'? What need was there for the Gospel, of 'Scarlet, and Tippets', or 'Hoods and Caps, &c'? 'No need at all', was Dell's conclusion, for 'it is one of the grossest errors that ever reigned under Antichrists Kingdom, to affirm that Universities are the fountain of the Ministers of the Gospel'.[125] The tone of Dell's polemic was not just forceful, it was downright menacing.

> [S]hall then your Masters, Plato, Aristotle, Pythagoras, &c. wretched Heathens, who with all their wisdom knew not Christ, but are dead and damned, many

---

[123] Blair Worden suggests, however, that Dell's tenure in the Cambridge mastership was not exactly celebrated by Cromwell himself. See Blair Worden, *God's instruments: political conduct in the England of Oliver Cromwell* (Oxford: Oxford University Press, 2012), p. 154.
[124] William Dell, *The stumbling-stone* (London, 1653), p. 26.
[125] Dell, *The stumbling-stone*, pp. 26–7.

hundred years ago be able to deliver you? Or shall Thomas, and Scotus, and other Schoolmen with their cold, vain, and Antichristian Divinity help you?...No certainly; but if you continue in your bitter Emnity against the true and spiritual Word and Gospel of Christ, Christ lives and reignes to bring you down wonderfully, and to make your Name a shame and a Curse to the whole true Church of God.[126]

Dell's fury was clearly aimed at the opponents of radical prophets of the new kingdom. He set against the 'worldly wise' of the universities,

the poor People of God, that small handful of believers that are amongst you, whom you despise in your hearts, and reckon but as the filth and off-scouring of the place, even they shall see your downfall, your sons and daughters shall prophesie. There needs nothing to the Ministry of the New Testament but only Gods pouring our his Spirit.[127]

In his appeal to the promise of Joel 2.28, that sons and daughters would prophesy and the Spirit would be 'poured out' on all flesh, Dell gave an indication that he envisaged female as well as male ministers of the New Testament. The implications of this radical critique of head-knowledge in the universities were spelled out by others. Among the Fifth Monarchists and other radical groups, there evolved a genre of spiritual autobiography, featuring the narratives of the saints, known as 'experiences'. These were testimonies of divine knowledge attained through the vicissitudes of life, and through discoveries in the heart. This kind of knowledge was directly opposed to 'head-learning'. Bernard Capp argued on the basis of Fifth Monarchist congregation lists that 'women easily outnumbered men' in the movement, and the 'experiences' are often those of women.[128] These testimonies to divine grace certainly included formulaic content (much biblical allusion and paraphrase, for example), and the narrative structures were somewhat controlled, but they also allowed for the intrusion of individual biographical elements and human perspectives, not least female perspectives, which shaped the interpretation of Christ's work in the soul and in the world. The *Spirituall experiences, of sundry beleevers* (1653), collected by Vavasor Powell, for instance, contained many testimonies from women saints. One 'M.K.', who described her life as 'a comicall Tragedy, or a tragical Comedy', wrote eloquently about her spiritual formation, starting with the homework assignments set by her mother, including the study of a portion of Scripture and Erasmus respectively each day from the age of 7. M.K.'s spiritual development was shaped

---

[126] Dell, *The stumbling-stone*, p. 30.   [127] Dell, *The stumbling-stone*, pp. 24–5.
[128] Bernard Capp, *The Fifth Monarchy men: a study in seventeenth-century English millenarianism* (London: Faber, 1972), p. 82.

by highly gendered experiences: first the loss of her mother, and the necessity of stepping into a responsible and visible role as woman of the house; then her father's death, for which she blamed herself (she had taken too much 'joyfull pride' in her role as her 'fathers right hand'). Once married, she experienced violent and even murderous fantasies about one of her husband's friends, who tempted her spouse to drink and to spend his time idly. She then fell prey to temptations to adultery. All of this drove her to a state of spiritual dejection, from which she was delivered by a vision of Christ 'nailed upon the Crosse for mee, wounded, buffeted, stript, and spit upon for me; dead, buryed, rose againe, ascended into Heaven, and sitting on the right hand of his Father, and my God, making intercession for mee; which gives me assurance of my Gods everlasting and unchangeable love'.[129] Another woman, 'L.P.', recalled having been in a black depression while pregnant in the early 1630s, and having experienced a merciful word from God about the 'innocency of the childe', which 'became a meanes to stay my hand from laying violence upon my selfe'.[130] In due course L.P. herself became convinced of everlasting grace, and experienced daily 'communion with Christ'.[131]

These female 'experiences' in Powell's collection were largely conventional accounts of conviction and a breakthrough into the knowledge of divine grace, but they illustrate the role of human events and vicissitudes in forming understanding. A more radical account of the role of female-centred experience in awakening spiritual understanding can be found in another Fifth Monarchist work of 1653, John Rogers' *Ohel or Beth-shemesh*. Among the Fifth Monarchists, Rogers was most clearly influenced by mystical texts, including Benet of Canfield's *A bright starre*, in the Giles Randall edition of 1646. He found in this Capuchin mystic's account of spiritual communion a compelling account of the saints' transformation:

> Blessed Saints! that are swallowed up in such an annihilation and Enochian life, Gen. 5.24. when self is turned out of doors, and Christ all in all, and the love of God alone looked upon; when a man reflects not on himselfe [as Giles Randal sayes in his Bright Star, ch. 14.] but all on God in free-grace.[132]

As Nicholas McDowell has argued, 'Rogers believed that all the conversion experiences of his gathered church in Dublin that he collected in 1653 exemplified the process of progressive illumination through "annihilation" of reason and the will outlined by the Catholic mystic Benet of Canfield'.[133]

---

[129] Vavasor Powell, 'Experiences of M.K.', *Spirituall experiences, of sundry beleevers held forth by them at severall solemne meetings* (London, 1653), pp. 160–1, 164–5, 188–9.
[130] Vavasor Powell, 'Experiences of L.P.', *Spirituall experiences*, pp. 228–31.
[131] Powell, *Spirituall experiences*, p. 233.
[132] John Rogers, *Ohel or Beth-shemesh: a tabernacle of the sun* (London, 1653), p. 382.
[133] Nicholas McDowell, 'The beauty of holiness and the poetics of antinomianism: Richard Crashaw, John Saltmarsh and the language of religious radicalism in the 1640s' in Ariel Hessayon and David Finnegan eds., *Varieties of seventeenth- and early eighteenth-century English radicalism in context* (Farnham: Ashgate: 2011), p. 46.

Rogers' *Ohel or Beth-shemesh* is an extraordinary text, containing a discourse on women's equality: a declaration 'That in the Church all the Members, even Sisters as well as Brothers, have a right to all Church-affairs; and may not onely implicitely but explicitely vote and offer or object, &c'.[134] Rogers insisted that the distinction to be made in the churches was not 'to be a difference of Sexes, ages, or relations'—not in fact a distinction between persons at all, but rather between 'the precious and the vile, the clean and the unclean'. In his remarkably powerful challenge to the congregations in Dublin which 'would rob sisters of their just rights and priviledges', Rogers set out to 'prove their liberty'.[135] The usual biblical supports were cited: Joel 2.28, demonstrating the 'liberty of the Saints', both sons and daughters, in the last days. Rogers mentioned both Luther's and Calvin's commentaries in support of his conclusion that the Spirit would be bestowed most especially on 'the Servants, and upon the hand-maides'.[136] He also cited 1 Corinthians 1, in which Paul contrasted worldly wisdom with God's election of 'the weak ones, and the despised ones, and the poore mean base ones'. A host of authorities—from Beza and Melanchthon to Gregory Nazianzen and John Chrysostom—is brought in to support his claim that church affairs should be conducted 'without respect of persons'.[137] Bernard of Clairvaux is made to speak in favour of women's 'spirituall liberty and Christian equality in the Church', for his saying that 'Christ turn'd Eva to Ave', redeeming the transgression of Eve through the agency of Mary.[138] One of the arguments Rogers made in defence of godly women's contributions to the church was their 'strong affection to the truth', or 'women surpassing men for piety and judgement'; affection was a stronger quality in women than in men, who are like 'sturdy steel and iron, hard to work upon'.[139] The link between affection and knowledge of truth is made firmly here, and Rogers mentioned a series of biblical women who illustrate the point: among them Priscilla, who surpassed Apollos 'for knowledge', and Mary Magdalen who 'outran, and outreached all the twelve Disciples in her diligence to seek out Christ: to whom Christ first discovered himself after his resurrection, and bid her declare it to his Disciples; she was the first Preacher of Christs resurrection'.[140] While Rogers' apology is undoubtedly erudite in its references, the purpose of his text was to illustrate how God was opening up knowledge in a way that would confound 'the wisdome of the world', by working 'through the contrariest means'.[141]

The defence of women's equality in the churches set forth by Rogers comes at the conclusion of a torrent of 'women's experiences': testimonies concerning revelations of grace to a host of female saints in the gathered congregation at

---

[134] Rogers, *Ohel or Beth-shemesh*, p. 463.
[135] Rogers, *Ohel or Beth-shemesh*, p. 464.
[136] Rogers, *Ohel or Beth-shemesh*, p. 464.
[137] Rogers, *Ohel or Beth-shemesh*, p. 467.
[138] Rogers, *Ohel or Beth-shemesh*, p. 472.
[139] Rogers, *Ohel or Beth-shemesh*, pp. 473–5.
[140] Rogers, *Ohel or Beth-shemesh*, p. 474.
[141] Rogers, *Ohel or Beth-shemesh*, p. 47.

Dublin. These include the testimony of Elizabeth Avery, the prophetess who had published her interpretation of Scripture prophecies in 1647. As noted above, Avery was herself the daughter of a theologian, the distinguished Puritan scholar Robert Parker, whose work *De politeia ecclesiastica Christi* (1616) would be a defining statement of congregational ecclesiology. Parker had also written anti-popish polemics against ceremonies, and an exposition of the Book of Revelation published in 1650. Parker was so important for early Stuart separatism that Cotton Mather described him as 'in some sort the father of all the non-conformists in our age'.[142] His daughter, to the annoyance of her brother Thomas, took it upon herself to interpret Scripture, and to do so by claiming direct revelation, rather than consciously adopting a scholarly approach. Elizabeth Avery began the story of her spiritual experiences in *Ohel and Beth-shemesh* with a conversion as a young child, when she felt an inner conviction while she was playing on a Sabbath day. She went on to tell the affecting story of the illness of three of her children, 'and one childe above all, a most sweet childe, and one, that I least thought of them all would have died'. When the beloved child died, she 'went to the Garden to wail and moan' and was 'left in an horror, as if I were in Hell'.[143] Despite finding some fleeting spiritual comforts, Avery continued to suffer misfortune and spiritual affliction (including the loss of a beloved minister, and abandonment by her friends), until she experienced an ecstatic transport in which 'Christ was manifested to my spirit'. It was at this point, she claimed, that she experienced the comfort of the knowledge of divine grace.

> In the times of the Wars in England, I was brought out of Egypt into the Wilderness. O! I was much refreshed by the Lord two or three years, and was much contented, and had his teachings within me, yea, and (many times) without his outward instruments; for I had his Spirit, his voice speaking within me, and God alone was with me, and no strange god.[144]

From this point on, Avery could not tolerate any outward preaching, particularly the external testimony of male ministers. Superficially, for a short time she retained a residue of her former diffidence, 'having mens persons in admiration, and thus God suffered me for a while to go after them'. This old habit led her to forget 'now how God had taught me within', and took her to Oxford, where she witnessed 'disputes between Master Kiffith and others, very hot' (perhaps William Kiffin, the Baptist preacher), but 'saw nothing of God there, and was

---

[142] Cotton Mather, *Magnalia Christi Americana, or, the ecclesiastical history of New England* (Hartford: Silas Andrus, 1820), book III p. 433.
[143] John Rogers, 'A fuller testimony as it was taken from Elizabeth Avery', *Ohel or Beth-shemesh*, p. 403.
[144] Rogers, 'A fuller testimony', p. 404.

troubled at it, and could not after that hear him or others'. Interestingly, it was John Lambert who encouraged Elizabeth Avery to hear William Erbery preach in Oxford.[145] Perhaps influenced by Erbery's mysticism, with its radical message of the 'bewildernessed' saints, Avery absented herself from sermons and ordinances altogether, finding that in a public gathering, she 'was so tormented that I could not bear it; for I could not joyn with them, nor hear, nor pray'. She would take herself off to a garden to mourn in a sort of self-imposed exile, or wilderness, until she rediscovered the understanding of 'Christ in me'.[146] This narrative of alienation from Reformed preaching, followed by a transforming mystical revelation of Christ within, consistently featured in the women's 'experiences'.

While some content of the testimonies seems indistinguishable from the language and assumptions of Puritan self-writing (suicidal despair in agonies of conscience; catharsis in an outpouring of grace), on closer inspection the experiences clearly reflect a mystical epistemology of the Spirit's inner witness, and show that classical Puritan preaching served only to drive these female auditors to despair. They echo Mary Penington's 'experiences' of Puritan Independency in the early 1640s, before the advent of (and her conversion to) the Quaker movement: she and her young husband 'saw death there, and that it was not that our souls sought'.[147] In Rogers' anthology, the 'experiences' mount up, of women alienated or inwardly tormented by Puritan teachings about sin and damnation, then brought to consolation either by Rogers' own mystical preaching, by that of another mystically inclined minister, or by their own experiences of union with Christ. Following the encounter with free-grace teaching, Ruth Emerson found herself 'wrapped in' Jesus Christ and moved to 'resign myself up' to him; Tabitha Kelsall was alienated by the Particular Baptist Paul Hobson's ultra-Calvinistic teachings, and 'withdrew from Ordinances' until she encountered grace and true 'communion' in Christ.[148] Dorothy Emett was 'much cast down' by the Calvinist preaching of John Owen, and 'could have no rest within me', until she heard a sermon at Cork on Romans 9, 'the Spirit witnesseth with our spirits, that we are the sons of God', since which time she had known 'a full assurance of Gods love to me in Christ'.[149] The men's experiences are just as affective and mystical in their tone. Captain John Spilman, for instance, confessed how the preaching of none other than William Bridge, at the Yarmouth church where women were deaconesses, had 'touched me to the heart', and he discovered 'some sweet enjoyments of Jesus Christ' and came to 'love Christ, in all, and all that was Christs'.[150]

---

[145] Rogers, 'A fuller testimony', p. 404.   [146] Rogers, 'A fuller testimony', pp. 404–5.
[147] Mary Penington, 'A brief account of some of my exercise from childhood', in David Booy, ed., *Autobiographical writings by early Quaker women* (Aldershot: Ashgate, 2004), p. 82. See also Alec Ryrie, *Protestants: the radicals who made the modern world* (London: HarperCollins), pp. 129–30.
[148] Rogers, 'A fuller testimony', pp. 411, 414 (1–2).   [149] Rogers, 'A fuller testimony', p. 412.
[150] Rogers, 'A fuller testimony', pp. 4–5 (415–16).

John Rogers' own testimony is emotive, recounting the terror of hell instilled into him by a firebrand preacher in his youth, and his years of poverty in Cambridge as a young sizar when he was forced to eat leather and 'old quills and pens' from the dunghill. These humbling experiences set him against 'the glory and great ones of the world', and gave him an affinity with the poor saints.[151] All of these testimonies, many of the women's before the men's, preface the chapter by Rogers on women's greater affection for and knowledge of Christ, and his proposal that they should enjoy equal rights with men in the congregations. They served to illustrate and support his argument for the abolition of distinctions between persons. Rogers was, inevitably, taken to task by a Presbyterian commentator: in this instance, the Anglo-Irish minister Zachary Crofton, who interpreted Rogers' teaching as tending towards the conclusion that 'the distinction of Sexes' in society and the church was 'Antichristian'. Rogers promoted a religion which overturned 'Male-sovereignty' and 'Female-subjection, so that people once Christianized, must no more know any difference of Sexes'.[152] Crofton's account of Rogers' 'position for womens power', of course, makes rather a different, rather more favourable, impression on many twenty-first-century readers than it would have made on the Presbyterian contemporaries hostile to Rogers and his female-affirming mystical theology.[153]

This chapter has sought to situate a tendency in the radical levelling mysticism of the 1640s to affirm female testimony and preaching within the context of a wider challenge to academic or scholastic ways of knowing, and claims to religious authority. Where the confrontation with traditional orthodoxy and clericalism can be found, there is almost always at least the hint of reformism on women's participation: not only in John Rogers' thought, but in that of Webster, Dell, Vane, Bridge, Goad, and Dury. That confrontation was also clearly the frame within which female prophets and mystics made their public interventions. The radicals' dramatic and comprehensive disavowal of the former order was continuous with their apocalyptic account of discontinuity. Their focus on truth as love rather than as doctrinal orthodoxy—or on the 'real Christ' rather than the 'notional Christ'—deprived the educated clerics of exclusive rights when it came to the pulpit and presses, and gave significance and dignity to the spirituality of the unlearned. It is obviously important to acknowledge the argument that such ideas merely entrenched the association of women with soft, experiential knowledge, and did nothing to enable their participation in learning. It is also to be observed, however, that the challenge of the seventeenth-century radicals anticipated in at least one

---

[151] Rogers, 'A fuller testimony', pp. 419–35.
[152] Zachary Crofton, *Bethshemesh clouded* (London, 1652), pp. 190, 195. See also Crawford Gribben, *God's Irishmen: theological debates in Cromwellian Ireland* (Oxford: Oxford University Press, 2007), pp. 153–4.
[153] Crofton, *Bethshemesh clouded*, p. 190.

key respect the challenge of feminist epistemology. Quite apart from questioning the reservation of learning to a limited power-holding elite, they shared in some sense the notion that lived experience—not least that of women—can inform understanding. Most trenchantly, the radicals rejected an 'objectified' God, a notional Christ external to oneself, constructed out of abstract philosophical concepts and the languages and narratives of antiquity.

4
Grace and Sin

Free-grace teachings swept across the London city parishes, and beyond, in the 1630s and 1640s. It is not, of course, as though no Protestant had heard of 'free grace' before the radical London preachers of that period took up the theme. The distinctive aspects of the controversies around grace in the pre-revolutionary and revolutionary contexts included the polarizing political context, the heightened apocalyptic expectation of a break rather than continuity with previous dispensations or covenants, and the interaction with heterodox mysticism. From the 1630s, alongside the conventional Reformed themes of justification by faith, perseverance in grace, and union with Christ, more subversive claims about the perfection of the saints were surfacing, influenced by Familist mysticism. David Como has shown definitively that the new preaching of free grace in London pulpits in the 1630s fed into the radical theology of the revolutionary period, and in significant respects represented a kind of mutation of or dialectic within Puritanism.[1] It is true, of course, that the most radical antinomians rejected one of the foundational marks of Puritan ecclesiology, the exercise of moral discipline, and opposed the Pharisaism and hypocrisy they perceived in mainstream Puritanism. Nonetheless, they continued to operate broadly within 'the cultural landscape of early Stuart puritanism'.[2] Como also, however, illustrates how this radical milieu of antinomian preaching and belief drew on Familist influences. It is clear that by the 1640s, Familist and mystical ideas about deification and perfection were publicly held in antinomian circles. There is a certain instability about these interacting streams, as the more affective tendencies in Calvinist spirituality sometimes merged into mysticism and radical spiritualism. The interaction between mainstream Reformed ideas about grace and union with Christ, and radical spiritualist teachings, illustrates the kernel of truth in Alec Ryrie's assertion that 'Protestant radicalism is simply Protestant orthodoxy with the guard-rails removed', though it also suggests that there is more at play than Reformed theology unguarded.[3] This chapter examines the implications, for female audiences and advocates, of the new wave of free-grace spirituality, with doctrinal guard-rails removed.

---

[1] David Como, *Blown by the Spirit: Puritanism and the emergence of an antinomian underground in pre-Civil-War England* (Stanford: Stanford University Press, 2004).
[2] Como, *Blown by the Spirit*, p. 29.
[3] Alec Ryrie, 'Scripture, the Spirit and the meaning of radicalism in the English Revolution', in Bridget Heal and Anorthe Kremers (eds), *Radicalism and dissent in the world of Protestant reform* (Göttingen: Vandenhoeck & Ruprecht, 2017), p. 117.

Free Grace

Hostile contemporaries reported that antinomian doctrines had a distinctive appeal to women, and there seems to have been some basis for this claim. Most famously, Anne Hutchinson was a vocal proponent of 'antinomian' theology in the New England controversy, but a host of other women were inspired to publish or prophesy on the theme, especially in the later 1640s and 1650s.[4] Of course, the association between defiant women and free-grace doctrine was a gift to heresiographers, who could readily insinuate that these teachings led to licentiousness and dissolution. The affinity among women for the more radical positions on free grace has not been fully examined, except through the lenses of commentators like Thomas Edwards, and this chapter section takes a fresh look at the theological narratives and imagery which seem most to have moved women to embrace and preach such doctrines. The first theme I consider is that of mystical marriage, and the vision of Christ as a spiritual lover, sweeping in to liberate the soul from the abusive first husband, the Law. This powerful imagery of the soul as an enslaved woman, dramatically emancipated by a divine lover from the tyranny of sin and the threat of legal punishment, permeates the writings of some of the most active female visionaries and their patrons. It was not merely a therapeutic but a transformative doctrine, awakening in women such fresh, affective meanings in the Scriptures that they felt compelled to communicate them. Christ as spiritual husband has been a perennial theme of Christian spirituality, with biblical as well as patristic roots, but in the context of radical notions about union with Christ, the matrimonial analogy became itself something susceptible to radicalized interpretation.[5] The radicals' full-blooded conception of total union of the saints with Christ, and Christian liberty transcending all legal observances and traditions offered the potential for reconsidering human relationships, including women's status. A second theme which clearly resonated with a female audience is that of the merciful Christ as mother, nursing the soul as a helpless babe, showing towards his creatures a depth of compassion and unconditional love which surpassed that of a human mother. This metaphor was explored in light of radical free-grace theology, by two thinkers who supported women's ministry (one of them a woman herself, Anna Trapnel), and seems to have emerged organically from meditation on the proximity of Christ to the believer in the union of faith: a closeness conveyed more naturally by the image of a mother than by that of a father.

In 1648, Samuel Rutherford identified John Saltmarsh and William Dell as the two army preachers most prominently responsible for disseminating antinomian

---

[4] Como, *Blown by the Spirit*, pp. 51–2.
[5] On the theme of mystical marriage in early modern Reformed culture and politics, see Elizabeth Clarke's rich study, *Politics, religion and the Song of Songs in seventeenth-century England* (Basingstoke: Palgrave Macmillan, 2011), especially ch. 5 on the theme in women's writing.

doctrine.[6] Saltmarsh was notoriously associated with female activists, including the women at Brasted in Kent who were allegedly not only allowed to preach, but 'break Bread also', an apparent reference to the administration of the Lord's Supper.[7] Among other errors, Rutherford accused Saltmarsh of teaching that 'all men and women shall preach the Gospel without studying'.[8] Saltmarsh's preaching dripped with the myrrh of mystical marriage imagery. In his *Free grace, or, the flowings of Christs blood free to sinners* (1646), Saltmarsh characterized the Law as a domineering spiritual husband, troubling the soul with 'accusings or condemnations of it'. Saltmarsh criticized those preachers who held out the threat of judgement under the Law, in order to bring souls to a state of 'humiliation, and contrition, and confession' in the misguided expectation that this would bring them to conversion.[9] For Saltmarsh, the breakthrough could never come by the threat of punishment, which inspired fear but not love. It could only take place when the spirit knows that 'they are not now under the Law, but under Grace; and the Law hath no more dominion over them, and they are dead unto that Husband, and they are now upon a new foundation, Jesus Christ himself being the chief corner-stone'.[10] The contrast between subjection and servitude under the Law (or under sin, the knowledge of which is the same thing as the Law), and freedom in Christ, is essentially Pauline, and certainly evocative of Luther and mainstream Reformation soteriology. What was distinctive in Saltmarsh and the other 'antinomian' preachers was the radical (and strongly gendered) account of spiritual union with Christ.

It was acknowledged by antinomian preachers that the union they envisaged between Christ and the soul surpassed the marriage union in ordinary life. John Eaton, sometimes described as the father of antinomian preaching, wanted his audience to go beyond the 'similitude' of the union 'between ordinary husband and wife' in their understanding of mystical marriage. He quoted a French martyr to the effect that 'the Christian man is made one with Christ, flesh of his flesh, and bone of his bone'; Eaton concluded that 'the union betwist Christ and every child of God, is more close and entire, than between husband and wife'.[11] This was echoed in the preaching of Walter Cradock, one of the most popular free-grace preachers in the 1640s, who urged his listeners (male and female) to consider themselves 'a son, a daughter of God, one in Christ, married to Christ, bone of his bone, and flesh of his flesh'.[12] For Saltmarsh too, the mystical marriage enjoyed by

---

[6] Samuel Rutherford, *A survey of the spirituall antichrist opening the secrets of familisme and antinomianisme in the antichristian doctrine of John Saltmarsh and Will. Del* (London, 1648).

[7] Thomas Edwards, *Gangraena* (London, 1646), p. 89. See also Ann Hughes, *Gangraena and the struggle for the English Revolution* (Oxford: Oxford University Press, 2004), pp. 113, 200–1.

[8] Rutherford, *A survey of the spirituall antichrist*, p. 215.

[9] John Saltmarsh, *Free grace, or the flowings of Christs blood free to sinners* (London, 1646), p. 41.

[10] Saltmarsh, *Free grace*, p. 45.

[11] John Eaton, *The honey-combe of free justification by Christ alone* (London, 1642), p. 432.

[12] Walter Cradock, *Divine drops distilled from the fountain of Holy Scripture* (London, 1649), p. 177.

the liberated and reconciled Christian was nothing less than full communion with the Godhead:

> Now God and the soul thus reconciled, are in a full enjoyment of each other, as the husband and the spouse, the father and the son; there is no parting rights and propriety; God hath not any thing in Christ, in Heaven, or Earth, but it is theirs: all things are yours, and you are Christs, and Christ is Gods, and every thing of theirs is his.[13]

Here Saltmarsh reversed the law of coverture—the principle, supposedly introduced by Norman rule, that a married woman's property became that of her husband—in his account of the marriage between Christ and the soul. Instead, all of the husband's property and status, no less than the whole of heaven and earth, are shared equally with the spouse. There is more than the hint of a reference to property law and the rights of married women in Saltmarsh's meditation on free grace. Of course, the implication of this for some radical theologians was that the spouse's own identity was subsumed by that of the husband. John Webster, the spiritualist schoolmaster and educational reformer, expanded on the theme of the liberty of the saints as the spouse of Christ, but ultimately compared the soul's union to Christ as that of 'a good wife... not ashamed to be as nothing in the presence of her Husband'; he went on, 'let her be nothing, so He may be all: for she acknowledges that she is only rich in her Husbands riches, and wise in his wisdom, and strong in his strength'.[14] Nonetheless, the more positive idea of the wife's participation in the freedoms and rights of the husband came through strongly in certain women's writings. For example, the Fifth Monarchist prophet Mary Cary, in her *Little horns doom and downfall* (1651) which interpreted Daniel 7 in light of recent political events, made the point emphatically that the spouse becomes co-owner with Christ of all he possesses:

> The truth is, that which is given to the head, is given to the members, that which is given to the Husband, the wife must partake of: for there is nothing that he possesses, which she hath not a right unto. And the Saints of Christ are the members of Christ, they are the Lambs wife: and having given himselfe unto them, he will not with-hold any thing that is his from them; but when all the Kingdomes, and Dominions under the whole heaven are given to him, they shall possesse them with him.[15]

Cary's prophecy was dedicated to three prominent wives: the Lady Bridget Cromwell, Lady Elizabeth Ireton, and Lady Margaret Role. These women, like

---

[13] Cradock, *Divine drops*, p. 171.
[14] John Webster, *The judgement set, and the bookes opened* (London, 1654), p. 85.
[15] Mary Cary, *The little horns doom & downfall* (London, 1651), p. 54.

'transplendent stars' in the firmament, had been honoured by God 'among the many pious, precious, prudent, and sage Matrons, and holy women, with which this Common-wealth is adorned; as with so many precious jewels, and choice gemmes', and Cary encouraged them to use their status to defend and maintain the truths she herself set out.[16]

In their account of free grace, preachers made much of the image of the 'bond-woman' as the type of Christians living under the law, against the Christian under grace as 'free-woman'. The theme is taken of course from the stories of Hagar and Sarah, the servant and the wife of Abraham, whose typological status (along with that of their respective offspring, Ishmael and Isaac) was long-standing. In Galatians 4, Paul set up the allegorical contrast between the slave woman as the mother of a generation bound under the law of Sinai, and Sarah, the free wife of the Abrahamic covenant who gave birth to the children of the promise. The allegory, with its central theme of liberation, took on fresh significance in radical theology. The spiritualist schoolmaster John Webster used the offspring of Sarah and Hagar as images of opposing religious impulses. The bond woman's children are driven by 'an outward compulsory cause': by 'fear or hope' of hell or heaven, taking up the 'strictest forms of worship'—'washings and dippings and conformity to Fellowships'—very zealously, and observing ordinances to the letter, but failing to realize that they are under a 'miserable delusion' and living in a hell of their own making.[17] By contrast, the children of the freewoman are inspired to worship from an 'inward Principle', the 'Principle of Freedom', and the 'power of love', which is a 'Heavenly Principle of mercy, pitty, and loving kindnesse, and bowels of mercy'.[18] Walter Cradock, whose preaching at All Hallows the Great in London inspired many female auditors, sought to cultivate that principle of freedom in his congregation:

> Therefore see the language that God puts into our mouthes when he sends us to preach; he sends us not to hire *servants:* for that Parable is to another end; we are not sent to get *Gally-slaves* to the Oares, or a *Beare* to the stake: but he sends us to wooe you as *spouses,* to marrie you to Christ; and in wooing there must not be *harsh* dealing; and when a man hath wooed and got a wife she must be *kindly* used, and not *harshly*; she hath much freedome, otherwise than when she was a *servant*, and a *drudge*. So, we come not as to servants, you shall be wives of Jesus Christ, you shall have liberty, and Christ, &c all in him shall be yours.[19]

Freedom and marriage are here joined, and Cradock explicitly distanced from the idea of the free wife the associations of domestic work, drudgery, and servitude.

---

[16] Cary, *The little horns doom*, §§A3v, A5v. [17] Webster, *The judgement set*, p. 173.
[18] Webster, *The judgement set*, p. 173.
[19] Walter Cradock, *Gospel-libertie in the extensions limitations of it* (London, 1648), p. 28.

William Bridge, the Congregationalist preacher who appointed women as deaconesses in 1650, took the analogy in a different direction and, in his meditation on the union of Christ with the believer's soul, imagined a scenario in which a man married his servant: 'whilst she was his maid, she was not so bold, nor could expect so much from him: when she becomes the Wife, then she is more bold, and can expect more, because now she is nearer'.[20] If marriage provided an analogy for mystical union, then the soul's union with Christ also provided an ideal type of marriage (as well as other kinds of Christian fellowship), with all the implications for human relationships which that entailed.

Walter Cradock and John Saltmarsh were also public supporters of Sarah Wight, the child prophet who gave spiritual advice and comfort to a succession of visitors, from the bed where she lay fasting and meditating. Wight proclaimed the release of the bondslave: 'Where the Spirit of God is, there is libertie; he sets the soul at liberty, that was in bondage; for I was in bondage'.[21] Wight's ostentatious infirmity, as she lay 'weak and spent' from lack of sustenance, seems to have been as performative as it was real, a dramatized symbol of her emptiness as a vessel of grace.[22] Nonetheless, the outward, physical weakness and confinement were in stark contrast to her strength and freedom as a spiritual director. Her speech was quick and articulate. It was remarked on that while formerly she had been 'slow in her speech', after her liberative spiritual breakthrough, she 'now hath such freedom; speaking as with a new tongue'.[23] In his prefatory epistle to Henry Jessey's transcription of her 'conferences' with visitors, Saltmarsh was struck by the difference between Wight's account of her 'Legall' and her 'Gospel condition'. Under Law, she was 'in bondage, in blackness, and darkness, and tempest'; under grace, she was filled with 'the voice of joy and gladnesse', and 'discoveries' of God's love. Sarah's inspirations were, for Saltmarsh, a clear sign of the advent of a new dispensation of grace, a 'New Covenant' in which 'his people shall be more and more revealed'. Saltmarsh compared 'such precious manifestations of the Lord' to a river of living water, running down 'from the Throne of Grace,... though it flow in the vallies, in the poore, low, and humble Christians'.[24] Jessey compared Wight to the Samaritan woman at the well, and the resurrected Dorcas, as female witnesses to the Gospel of grace.[25] One visitor was struck by the fact that people of all sorts came from far away to hear her speak; Wight herself responded, 'The Queen of Sheba came far to heare this Wisedom of Solomon; but behold, a greater then Solomon is here: Christ himself, to work a New Creation in the soul'.[26]

---

[20] William Bridge, *The works of William Bridge, sometime fellow of Emmanuel Colledge in Cambridge* (London, 1649), p. 85.
[21] Henry Jessey, *The exceeding riches of grace advanced by the Spirit of grace, in an empty nothing creature, viz. Mistress Sarah Wight* (London, 1647), p. 115.
[22] Jessey, *The exceeding riches of grace*, p. 76.   [23] Jessey, *The exceeding riches of grace*, p. 88.
[24] 'Mr Saltmarsh his Letter', in Jessey, *The exceeding riches of grace*, §a2v.
[25] Jessey, *The exceeding riches of grace*, §a1r.   [26] Jessey, *The exceeding riches of grace*, p. 126.

This remark naturally enough provoked some controversy, and the distinction between Christ and his instrument was more or less dissolved.

Sarah Wight was eloquent on the subject of 'free grace', and many of those who sought her counsel were women in a state of despair about their sin. One 'afflicted woman' came to her so depressed, beset by haunting visions of her damnation (complete with the stench of brimstone), her reported expressions were heartbreakingly abrupt and dejected. On faith in Christ as Saviour, she simply commented 'Its not for me'. In response to Sarah's evocations of divine mercy and kindness, she said, 'God hath forsaken me'.[27] Wight herself had experienced a rather frightening self-destructive crisis, in which, as she recalled, 'I abus'd my body...I beat my head oft against the wall; and took flesh in my teeth'.[28] She was tortured in her soul by what she called her 'Terrors', which caused her as a 15-year-old child to dream of death's oblivion, and to fantasize of feeding her own body to the dogs at the doghouse at Moorfields.[29] In the midst of her terrors, she ceased to eat, consuming only a little water and small beer. Clearly, there is much here to interest a child psychologist. Within her own frame of reference, however, this was a spiritual crisis; though it was her body she instinctively punished to silence the inner demons. What lay at the heart of her terror was the thought of her sin, and the horror of alienation from God. The miraculous transformation effected in her heart, turning her from despair to the deepest comfort, is the whisper of Christ speaking to her in a vision, at about 10 o'clock at night, the whisper of a lover:

> Thou art mine, my desire is towards thee. I will heal thy backslidings; I love thee freely, I forgive all thy sins for my Names sake; as though they had never been committed. Come and see, how I have loved thee! How I have ever loved thee! Behold and admire this love of mine. Fathom this sea of my love if thee canst, which drownes the multitude of thy sins: and see how I have ever loved thee from eternity, with an endlesse, boundlesse, and everlasting love: the number of thy sins, and multitude of thy transgressions against me, shall never be able to seperate the union that I have made between thee & me.[30]

Wight's converting experience of free grace was framed in terms of union and mystical marriage. In April 1647, she had an insight into the 'open fountaine' of God's love, and described the love of Christ for the sinful soul in terms redolent of the Old Testament prophets: he is married to a harlot with many lovers.[31] Rather than using this imagery as the basis for a jeremiad against the sin of the nation or of individuals, Sarah Wight presented this as a comforting and hopeful prospect.

---

[27] Jessey, *The exceeding riches of grace*, pp. 78, 83.
[28] Jessey, *The exceeding riches of grace*, p. 115.
[29] Jessey, *The exceeding riches of grace*, p. 130.
[30] Jessey, *The exceeding riches of grace*, p. 134.
[31] Jessey, *The exceeding riches of grace*, p. 17.

As her contemporary Mary Cary put it, for all the soul's transgressions under the Law, she is Christ's 'beloved Wife' to whom he, '[a]s a tender Husband unbosomes himself'.[32]

One of the visitors to Sarah Wight's bedside was one 'Hanna Trapnel', then a young woman with none of the notoriety she would later acquire as the most prominent of the Fifth Monarchist female prophets. Her experiences paralleled those of Sarah Wight in many aspects. After her mother's distressing death in around 1645, she wrestled with a tormented conscience, and contemplated suicide. From 1647 onwards, she became inspired by visions and prophetic foresight; culminating in a short period from the end of 1653 when she entered a trance and uttered doggerel verse *ex tempore* from her bed. Subsequently, following her arrest and brief imprisonment at Bridewell, she was an itinerant preacher across Wales and the West Country.[33] The essence of her own conversion to the vocation of a prophetess and preacher was her experience of 'free grace', which first came to her in January 1642 at All Hallows the Great, where she heard a sermon by the antinomian preacher John Simpson.[34] This was very much the milieu of Sarah Wight, who also attended sermons by Simpson, and was visited by Cradock, then lecturer at All Hallows the Great and associate of Simpson from 1643 to 1646. As in the case of Wight, Trapnel's conviction of the truth of free grace was hard-won: 'Oh what a knotty piece was I for the great Jehovah to work upon!', she recalled.

> I could not believe; though many that cryed down free grace as a doctrine of liberty to sin, I found no doctrine so striking at my sins as it, and though some would tell me I had found out an easie way to heaven now, to go to heaven in believing, but I found it a hard way, yea, impossible, for I could not believe till the day of Gods power.[35]

Trapnel's insight was identical in its outlines to that of Wight: she perceived an outpouring of comfort for the soul in despair, the eternal abundance of grace, and the impossibility of alienating God: 'there is free grace enough, an ocean, to swallow up, not my sins onely, but many more, a fountain open for all manner of sins ... you cannot out-sin mercy, your sins are finite, but grace is infinite'.[36] The boundlessness and universality of grace was the defining concern of the female free-grace preachers, and the theme chimes with the universalism espoused by several of their contemporaries. For all her preoccupation with political events, Anna Trapnel's writing could be close in style and content to that of late-medieval

---

[32] Mary Cary, *The resurrection of the witnesses and Englands fall from (the mystical Babylon) Rome* (London, 1648), p. 11.
[33] See Stevie Davies, 'Anna Trapnel (*fl.* 1640–1660)' in David Cannadine, ed. *Oxford dictionary of national biography* (Oxford: Oxford University Press, 2004).
[34] Anna Trapnel, *A legacy for saints* (London, 1654), p. 8. [35] Trapnel, *A legacy*, p. 6.
[36] Trapnel, *A legacy*, p. 7.

mystical writers, though she gave no indication of having encountered this literature. The theme of mystical marriage pervaded her verse and prose, and involved not only an ecstatic experience of union with Christ, but also communion with fellow saints. Her soul was first 'enamoured with Christ', and in this enraptured state 'Christ sweetned every creature to me, oh how sweet was the feasts of love, that my soul was made partaker of in every creature!'[37] It was this swelling love, overflowing into her relationships with others, which drove Trapnel to speak publicly: 'I could not keep love in, it would flame forth into a declaration, I must now tell Saints what I had now received'.[38] This affective knowledge of free grace caused Trapnel to see the Scriptures in a new light, and to open them up to those around her. An elderly aunt of hers, a 'very godly woman', wept to see her niece so aflame with love. Trapnel mentioned this to show how she enlivened spiritual affections in others, as a way of justifying her public interventions: 'this year in which I was new-born, I shall (the Lord helping me) give forth some few of those discoveries, which whole volumes cannot contain; Let free grace have all the glory'.[39]

While mystical marriage was a conventional Reformed theme in the teaching of free grace, that of Jesus as mother was not. It would not be until 1670 that a new, Catholic edition in English of Julian of Norwich's *Revelations* would be available in print. This was the fifteenth-century text most notable among mystical writings for its identification of Jesus (as well as the 'deep Wisdom of the Trinity') with a nursing mother, 'in whom we be endlesly born'.[40] Some similar imagery can also be found in the devotional works of Anselm of Canterbury; it seems equally unlikely that Trapnel would have encountered it there. Occasionally, early modern authors would compare sacramental communion to a child at the mother's breast.[41] A contemporary analogy was sometimes made between a weaning mother, who embitters the breast with wormwood or mustard, and God's use of temporal afflictions to 'wean' the Christian off earthly comforts.[42] Some free-grace theologians opened up the possibilities for assigning maternal qualities to the second person of the Trinity. Anne Yemans, whose anti-legal meditation on divine love was published in 1648 by Giles Calvert, wrote of the maternal intensity of Christ's love, which 'passeth the love of women to their children, yea the greatest love that they can bear to them'.[43] An anonymous tract on 'the incomparable free

---

[37] Trapnel, *A legacy*, p. 9.   [38] Trapnel, *A legacy*, p. 9.   [39] Trapnel, *A legacy*, p. 12.

[40] Julian of Norwich, *XVI revelations of divine love shewed to a devout servant of our Lord called Mother Juliana* (London, 1670), pp. 149, 151.

[41] See, for instance, Richard Gove, *The communicants guide* (London, 1654), pp. 61–2.

[42] *The work of affliction opened in a sermon, preached at the funeral of Mrs Elizabeth Harvey* (London, 1658), p. 10; Richard Gove, *Pious thoughts vented in pithy ejaculations* (London, 1658), p. 38. Gove appears to have taken a very lively interest in observing the habits of suckling infants at their mother's breast as a source of inspiration for his writings.

[43] Anne Yemans, *Crooked pathes made straight: or, the wayes of God made knowne to lost sinners, or bewildered saints* (London, 1648), p. 150.

grace of Christ' published in 1650 described Christ's offering of himself to the sinner in these terms: 'Christ will hold the child whiles it doth cry, till it sucke and be stilled'; elsewhere, 'when he suckles us, he gives the milke of the breasts of consolation freely himselfe'.[44] Others described the new-born saints as coming forth from Christ's 'womb'. Henry Vane developed this theme, musing on 'this mystical dispensation' (of the new reign of Christ in the saints) in which 'the second Person in the Trinity is the author and Minister, from beginning to ending, forming and bringing forth the first Rule of it in Christ, as he makes him the *first-born of every creature*, the Mother of all living, and womb unto the whole first creation'.[45] Trapnel's vision of the maternal Jesus, quite remarkable among early modern meditations on Christ, may have owed something to Sarah Wight, to whose bedside Trapnel had made that pilgrimage in the 1640s.[46] In a letter published in 1656, Wight, another woman deeply spiritually influenced by her mother, characterized the soul's 'parents' as 'God our Father, and Wisdom our Mother, which is Christ'.[47]

Her emerging appreciation of maternal qualities in Christ seems to have coincided with Trapnel's grieving for her own mother, clearly a profound spiritual influence on the young Anna. In her discovery of the operations of grace after this bereavement, Trapnel found that 'great was his care for me, no tender mother like to Jesus'. She reports that 'the Saints told me when I mourned for the loss of my tender mother, that Christ would be more tender, and would be all to me in the loss of earthly comforts; and he was more to me then they told me, he was double Comfort'.[48] Further on in her reflection following the loss of her mother, Trapnel affirmed that Christ has a dual identity: 'Christ may be said to be both the Mother and the Childe: now as a young childe naturally for certain, is at the first in the womb of his mother, so the children of God spiritually, are said to be in Christ'.[49] The consideration of Christ's intimate relation to the saints, both as mother and child, was not simply to be a source of their spiritual consolation, for Trapnel. It was also the source of their authorization, as she developed her theme of union in the same passage: 'God chusing such foolish, weak, base, despised men and women, to be an habitation for himself and Christ, who is one in him, to dwel in, and to walk in them, and to take up their abode in them'.[50] There was reciprocally a dual identity for the humble saints: the saint as mother was the place of God's dwelling, just as the saint as child dwelled within the divine mother. In her *Discourses*, the voluminous transcription of her ecstatic verse, which was printed but not widely disseminated (and consequently less well known to

---

[44] Anon., *A most glorious representation of the incomparable free grace of Christ* (London, 1650), pp. 6, 15.
[45] Henry Vane, *The retired mans meditations, or, the mysterie and power of godlines* (London, 1655), p. 6.
[46] See Jessey, *The exceeding riches of grace*, §a1r.
[47] Wight, *A wonderful pleasant and profitable letter*, p. 67. The image of Christ as feminine Wisdom hints at an association with the Sophia doctrines of the Behmenist circles.
[48] Trapnel, *A Legacy*, p. 13.   [49] Trapnel, *A Legacy*, p. 13.   [50] Trapnel, *A Legacy*, p. 13.

scholars, now held in Oxford's Bodleian Library), Trapnel went further in her meditation on Jesus as mother. Christ was a lactating mother, his/her 'breasts are full of milk', and s/he shows great compassion to the infant who cannot easily suckle:

> O he is ready with his fingers
> To keep the nipple in mouth...
> His finger brings the nipple so fine,
> Unto the little sucklings mouth.[51]

The theme here is the merciful communication of divine grace, and the imagery of a nursing mother is quite startlingly anatomical, but it evokes rather effectively the unconditional self-giving of the mother to the helpless infant. Trapnel seemed to have been familiar with the challenges and demands of the nursing mother, though she herself was unmarried and (we assume) childless at the time of writing.

The most sympathetic companion to Anna Trapnel's maternal mysticism, in the context of dynamic free-grace preaching in the period of the English Revolution, is to be found in Robert Prier's *Looking-glass for a proud Pharisee* (1648). Prier was an Independent activist in the parish of St Michael Bassishaw, one of the city churches seething with radical elements. He refused to pay tithe in 1645–6, and promoted lay preaching.[52] The theme of Prier's *Looking-glass* was that of 'the ministry and a gift of the Grace of Christ, given unto men of all sorts, as well to unlearned men as to learned men'. He also explicitly included women in the true ministry: 'most men and women have the truth of God in respect of mens persons, as a Bishop, or a great learned Doctor'.[53] Within the framework of free-grace doctrine, Prier proclaimed 'the liberty of the subjects of the Kingdom of Christ', both 'men & women', to preach and teach divinity.[54] He scorned the former ordinances of the episcopal church, which, among other insults to lay people, 'made fools of women, in causing them to come covered with white vails through the streets, to be churched'.[55] Prier's outrage at the humiliation of women under the old order was matched by his advocacy of their freedom to publish the Gospel under the 'new birth' of Christ's rule. Only the sinner made new by free grace, whether male or female, could truly 'magnifie free grace'. Indeed, the first example Prier gave of a biblical witness to divine grace was Mary Magdalen, in her anointing of Christ's feet with her tears.[56] Throughout his treatise, Prier consistently used inclusive references to 'man or woman' in discussion of the saints (or,

---

[51] Anna Trapnel, *Poetical discourses (1657–8)*, Bodleian Library S. 1. 42. Th, pp. 84–5.
[52] See Keith Lindley, *Popular politics and religion in civil war London* (Brookfield, VT: Scolar Press, 1997), pp. 85, 297.
[53] Robert Prier, *Looking-glass for a proud Pharisee* (London, 1648), §§a2v–a3r.
[54] Prier, *Looking-glass*, p. 63.   [55] Prier, *Looking-glass*, p. 65.
[56] Prier, *Looking-glass*, p. 59.

indeed, the Pharisees). This was another distinctive feature of some free-grace writing of the Revolution, including that of Saltmarsh.

It is striking, then, that the closest parallel to Trapnel's meditation on Jesus as mother can be found within this wider discourse on the universal liberty of true Christians to preach the Gospel of grace. It hardly needs to be said that the significance of the maternal analogy lies in Christ as the agent of regeneration. The new birth, more fully discussed in Chapter 1, 'Incarnation', was one of the defining themes of radical theology, and certainly dominated all contemporary teachings on free grace, whether conventionally Calvinist or spiritualist. It hardly takes a feminist's leap of imagination to arrive at the identification of Christ with a mother, on the basis of the New Testament metaphor of the second birth, though it has only occasionally been explored in Christian spirituality before the twentieth century. The use of maternal imagery to describe—even define—Christ's work of regeneration appears to be far more explicit and thorough-going in the thought of these two radical, and notably lay, theologians than in other English Protestant writings of the period. Prier wrote extensively on Christ's motherhood, characterizing him (after Psalm 110.3) as 'the womb of the morning', incubating the saints for their heavenly birth. He concluded, '[a]nd thus Christ may be said to be a Mother, as the Prophet and the Apostle doth allude unto, and Christ himself do confirm'.[57] As in Trapnel, Prier's understanding of Jesus as mother lent itself to a pastoral application as well as having significance for the doctrinal framework for sanctification, or rebirth. He wrote:

> Now these new-born children do not hang upon the brests of the creature, or any created forms, no nor upon ordinances onely, but even upon the brests of God alone; and through Christ they milk out their divine consolations, and therewith they are abundantly satisfied. A true believer is as neer unto Christ, as a natural childe is unto his mother. Christ as a Father or a Mother, is more indulgent unto his children, then any earthly mother can be.[58]

The maternal imagery brings God very close: closer, arguably than the image of a father. Walter Cradock, alluding to the paternal language of Romans 8.15, sought to explain the relationship of affection between God and Christian, without which there could be no true faith: 'if thou call on God with *feare*; and canst not cry *abba, abba*, that is as much as *daddie, daddie*, as our babes use to say, if thou doe not come so high, thou art *spoiled*, and *undone*'.[59]

---

[57] Prier, *Looking-glass*, p. 302. The biblical passages to which Prier refers are 2 Corinthians 5.17, 'If any man be in Christ, he is a new creature'; Isaiah 43.19, 'And it shall spring forth'; John 3.3–7, 'And be born again'.
[58] Prier, *Looking-glass*, p. 303.
[59] Walter Cradock, *Glad tydings from Heaven, to the worst of sinners* (London, 1648), p. 43.

For Prier and Trapnel, the picture of a gracious 'daddie' was not sufficiently intimate. Prier expanded on his theme with the fond, familiar language of a mother's affection: 'Christ as mother doth bear his children upon his sides, and as a mother doth bear with the weaknesses and infirmities of children, and doth dandle them upon his knees, and as a mother, doth comfort his sick children and bemoan himself over them'.[60] The male pronouns are a little jarring to modern readers (though certainly not as jarring as female pronouns would be to a seventeenth-century reader), but it seems evident that for Prier, as for Trapnel, the maternal metaphor was more fitting and illuminating as a way of conveying the boundlessness of Christ's free grace than the paternal metaphor could be. Indeed, Prier suggested that those contemporary Pharisees who claimed to know God as Father knew him not as the God of love but as the object of fear, like the Jews.[61] Prier shared Trapnel's account of Christ's dual identity as mother and child, placing the Christian in the position of both infant and parent: 'as Christ was said to be the Mother, and proved, so Christ may be said to be the childe, the spiritual childe that is born, or is to be born in men and women, that come to be true Christians'.[62] Again, the double analogy was an outworking of Prier's doctrine of 'Free-grace', a way of picturing union with Christ.

The Mystery of Iniquity

When Valerie Saiving defined 'feminine' sinfulness as the tendency towards self-annihilation in 1960, she addressed a twentieth-century model of female domesticity and passivity; a culturally specific diagnosis of 'the human situation' (though one which resonated beyond that particular historical moment).[63] Gendered ideas of sinfulness, especially structural sin, tend to adjust to context. The Revolution helped to reorient conceptions of the nature of sin, and women were active participants in this reorientation. Sarah Wight and other free-grace theologians came to the conclusion, echoing Augustine and the leading Reformation thinker (themselves inspired by John 16) that sin was unbelief. As she put it, '[t]he great sin Christ dyed for, is unbeliefe'.[64] Unbelief was the enemy of love and union; but God himself acted to 'soften hard and unbeleeving hearts'; he had 'brought such as were aliens and enemies, to be neer in himselfe'.[65] The implication of conceiving of sin in this way was that it squarely targeted those 'unbelievers' who rejected the

---

[60] Prier, *Looking-glass*, p. 304.   [61] Prier, *Looking-glass*, p. 2.
[62] Prier, *Looking-glass*, p. 305.
[63] I am grateful to Taylor & Francis, to the editors of *Prose Studies*, and to Thomas Corns and Ann Hughes for granting permission to reproduce here my essay '"The evil masculine powers": gender in the thought of Gerrard Winstanley', in Thomas Corns and Ann Hughes, eds., *Gerrard Winstanley: theology, rhetoric, politics*, a special edition of *Prose Studies* 36:1 (2014), pp. 52–62. Valerie Saiving, 'The human situation: a feminine view', Journal of Religion 40 (1960), pp. 100–12.
[64] Jessey, *The exceeding riches of grace*, p. 73.   [65] Jessey, *The exceeding riches of grace*, p. 51.

spirit of God speaking in his handmaids. Anna Trapnel made this connection explicit: the great sin of the powers that be was their denunciation of the witness of the Spirit in Christ's sons and daughters. Trapnel saw herself as the 'poor handmaid' sent 'into the Pallace' to convict the Protector and his government of 'their transgression' against the Holy Spirit.[66] For Elizabeth Avery, too, writing somewhat earlier in 1647 under a different sort of 'persecuting' regime, 'none are damned, but for the sin of unbelief'; and the sin of unbelief was most fully embodied in the persecution and 'cruel usage' of the simple saints, both female and male.[67]

The association of the ruling powers, especially a persecuting church, with the essence of sinful faithlessness had some pedigree. There had been much discussion in English Reformation polemic of the 'mystery of iniquity' of 2 Thessalonians 2.7, widely taken as a reference to the church of Rome. Amid the conflict of the 1640s, the 'mystery of iniquity' quickly became reconceived by radical reformers as a tyrannical spirit, the oppressive violence of a persecuting regime, whether Presbyterian or popish. William Dell designated the persecuting spirit 'the very mystery, of the mystery of iniquity among us, and the very head of Antichrist which is yet to be broken'. It was born of the ultimate sin of unbelief, the 'not regarding the promise of the Father, or the pouring out of the Spirit by the Son'.[68] In this part of the chapter, I suggest that this 'mystery of iniquity' became strongly gendered in the thought of at least one important radical theologian, Gerrard Winstanley. The revolutionary message of Gerrard Winstanley contained at its heart a confrontation with and rejection of traditional patriarchalism, which he called 'masculine powers' or 'kingly rule'. While some commentators have characterized as essentially 'patriarchal' his programme for the reformation of magistracy, I argue that Winstanley sought to reimagine masculinity, in such a way that it became divorced from the ruling instinct (identified with Adam, or the flesh), and associated instead with the humility of Christ in whom the masculine and the feminine were brought into harmony. Although apparently enigmatic and ambiguous in the values he assigned to the genders, Winstanley's ideas assumed a coherence in view of the complex relationship between gendered metaphor and sexual differences in his thought.

The Diggers enumerated the humiliations and sufferings inflicted on four of their number at George-Hill on 11th June 1649, recalling that they had been set upon not only by the ringleaders of the mob on horseback, William Starr and John Taylor, but also by

---

[66] Jessey, *The exceeding riches of grace*, p. 70.

[67] Elizabeth Avery, *Scripture-prophecies opened: which are to be accomplished in these last times, which do attend the second coming of Christ* (London, 1647), pp. 15, 23.

[68] William Dell, *Power from on high, or, the power of the Holy Ghost dispersed through the whole body of Christ* (London, 1645), pp. 7–8.

some men in womens apparell on foot, with every one a staffe or club, and as soon as they came to the diggers, would not speak like men, but like bruit beasts that have no understanding, they fell furiously upon them, beating and striking those foure naked men, beating them to the ground, breaking their heads, and sore bruising their bodies, whereof one is so sore bruised, that it is feared he will not escape with life.[69]

The detail about the clothing of the assailants was considered sufficiently significant that it was repeated later in the account, and in another report produced in *A New-yeer's gift*.[70] As David Cressy has noted, 'Men dressed as women sometimes during enclosure riots or other public disorders, linking social protest to traditions of festive inversion'; possibly to disguise their identity, but also, perhaps, as a gesture of contempt.[71] In the Diggers' defence, the adoption of a false, female appearance by the savage mob stood as a powerful contrast to the 'naked' and innocent victims: 'love suffers under thy hypocrisie'.[72] The affront caused by the cross-dressing mob was probably not caused by any shock at gender transgression, but rather by outrage at the scornful dishonesty that it implied. As in the popular Protestant critique of popery, and the radicals' apprehension of all ecclesiastical power, tyranny went hand in hand with hypocrisy, fraud, and illusion. Nonetheless, there was a hint in this brutal little episode of a concern, organic to Winstanley's thought (especially early on), about the corrupting misappropriation of gendered characteristics. It has been said that he was ambiguous in assigning 'morally positive and negative values to the feminine',[73] as well as to the masculine, and it is true that gendered categories were sometimes applied enigmatically. But they were not confused, and should be regarded as absolutely central to his thinking. Although ultimately undeveloped, Winstanley's discussion of gender relations (both metaphorical and literal) pointed in a direction that was as interesting, and potentially as radical, as anything conceived in the seventeenth century.

The status of women as a sex 'is never', as Elaine Hobby has observed, 'given focused attention' in the Digger pamphlets; and Winstanley's editors have observed that his writings were 'ambiguous about women: the patriarchal vision of *The law of freedom* is qualified by his sensitivity to the drawbacks of a "ranterish" unchastity for women, and by his insistence in 1649 that Christ

---

[69] *A declaration of the bloody and unchristian acting of William Star, and John Taylor in Walton, with divers men in womens apparell, in opposition to those that dig upon George-hill in Surrey* (London, 1650), pp. 1–2.
[70] Anon., *A New-yeers gift for the parliament and armie* (London, 1650), p. 44.
[71] David Cressy, *Travesties and transgressions in Tudor and Stuart England: tales of discord and dissension* (Oxford and New York: Oxford University Press, 2000), p. 109.
[72] *A declaration*, p. 5.
[73] B.J. Gibbons, *Gender in mystical and occult thought: Behmenism and its development in England* (Cambridge: Cambridge University Press, 1997), p. 130.

was rising in daughters and in sons'.[74] Certainly, Digger writings often struck a remarkable inclusive note: and perhaps the pithiest expression of their doctrine of universal human dignity was the statement, frequently repeated, that 'every particular man and woman is a perfect creation, or a world of him, or her self'.[75] A politicized notion that the macrocosm of the created world was contained, perfectly, within each individual whether male or female, grounded a high view indeed of the dignity of the individual and as such had the capacity to underpin a far-reaching reforming agenda. At times, however, Winstanley's anthropology as well as his practical programme for social renovation followed conventional patterns. In *The new law of righteousnes*, published in the revolutionary year 1649, Winstanley remarked on 'the state of the world' as he saw it:

> That in times past and times present, the branches of man-kind have acted like the beast or swine; And though they have called one another, men and women, yet they have been but the shadows of men and women. As the Moone is the shadow of the Sun, in regard they have been led by the powers of the curse in flesh, which is the *Feminine* part; not by the power of the righteous Spirit which is Christ, the *Masculine* power.[76]

The standard Aristotelian and Augustinian association of the feminine with flesh and the masculine with spirit and/or reason in this passage perhaps deflects attention away from what is the more fundamental point. Men and women alike had been corrupted by the 'powers of the curse', becoming like shadows of their true selves, acting 'like the beast or swine'. If, some months later, the bestial mob which persecuted the Diggers would take on women's clothing, their abandonment of a masculine for a feminine appearance might be construed as a symbolic reenactment of the Fall, of humankind's deviation from the rule of Christ to the rule of the flesh.

Nonetheless, the relationship between gendered metaphor and physical sex was complex and indirect. Another, rather startling, application of the analogy appeared in Winstanley's letter to the visionary Lady Eleanor Davies dated December 1650, in which he complained of her exploitation and non-payment of workers. In the autumn of that year, Winstanley and several companions had

---

[74] Elaine Hobby, 'Winstanley, women and the family', in Andrew Bradstock, ed., *Winstanley and the Diggers 1649-1999* (London: Frank Cass & Co., 2000), p. 65; Thomas Corns, Ann Hughes, and David Loewenstein, eds., 'Introduction', *The complete works of Gerrard Winstanley* (Oxford: Oxford University Press, 2009), vol. 1, p. 25.

[75] Gerrard Winstanley, *The saints paradice or, the Fathers teaching the only satisfaction to waiting souls* (London, 1648), p. 76; William Everard et al., *The true Levellers standard advanced* (London, 1649), p. 6; Gerrard Winstanley, *The new law of righteousnes* (London, 1649), p. 7.

[76] Winstanley, *The new law*, pp. 3-4.

been working on Lady Eleanor's land at Pirton in Hertfordshire.[77] His tone was confrontational and lacked any hint of deference; he rejected rather scornfully her claim to be inhabited by the spirit of the king and High Priest Melchizedek, and played on her adoption of male personae. 'Surely you have lost the breeches', he writes, 'w[hi]ch is indeed true Reason the strength of A man':

> And this shall be your marke that you have lost the breeches yo[u]r Reason: by the inward boyling vexacon of yo[u]r spirit upon the hearing hereof though you may moderate yo[u]r wordes before others; yett you shall feele the power of inward distemper rule as a king in you: & that inward power shall chaine you up in darknes, tell Reason, w[hi]ch you have trampled under foott, come to set you fre.[78]

Lady Eleanor, whose visionary identities were often borrowed from male biblical prophets (not only Melchizedek, but also Daniel), was said to have lost her breeches—undoubtedly a symbol of the masculine powers of Reason—in the way that a cuckolded or henpecked husband might.[79] What usurped the rule of reason in her was an 'inward distemper', despotic as a tyrant king, keeping her captive in bitterness and 'vexacon' of spirit.

As well as being disengaged from physical sexual difference in Winstanley's treatment, the contrast between masculine reason and feminine flesh was also not as absolute nor as morally straightforward as these references suggest. T. Wilson Haynes has even suggested that, for Winstanley, it was rather the 'masculine side of human nature' that 'corrupts the feminine and holds it in bondage'.[80] The basis for this conclusion is a single work, one of Winstanley's earliest publications, *The saints paradice* (1648). In it, he prescribed a spiritualist, experimental pathway to the recovery of the lost order and true knowledge of God (to whom he famously gave the new name, 'Reason'). Uniquely, he also linked the corruption of humanity to the domination of 'the masculine powers that rule the soul': namely, 'envy, hypocrisie, pride, anger, self-seeking, subtilty, and such like'.[81] Where the writings of contemporary Platonists like Henry More followed the ancients in describing the masculine powers and faculties in the soul as the nobler, more rational part, Winstanley characterized them in no uncertain terms as 'evil'.[82] In his

---

[77] See John Gurney, *Brave community: the Digger movement in the English Revolution* (Manchester: Manchester University Press, 2007), pp. 210–11.
[78] 'Letter to Lady Eleanor Douglas', reproduced in Corns, Hughes, and Loewenstein, *The complete works*, vol. 2, p. 425.
[79] See Esther Cope, ed., 'Introduction', *Prophetic writings of Lady Eleanor Davies* (Oxford: Oxford University Press, 1995), pp. xi–xxiii.
[80] T. Wilson Hayes, *Winstanley the Digger: a literary analysis of radical ideas in the English Revolution* (Harvard: Harvard University Press, 1979), p. 69.
[81] Winstanley, *The saints paradice*, pp. 72–3.
[82] See, for example, Henry More, *Conjectura cabbalistica* (London, 1653), pp. 40, 67–8.

commentary on John 3.19, 'the light has come into the world, and men loved darkness rather than light, because their deeds were evil', Winstanley offered the following interpretation:

> But men love darkness rather then light; men here spoken of, are the evill masculine powers of created man in his poysoned estate, as man pride, man covetousness, man hypocrisie, man self-love, and King imagination, that rules over all, and in all these; and this, or these, is the wicked man, spoken of in scripture; these I say, are called men, because they rule over the created flesh, which is the feminine part, and leads it captive in unrighteousness, and will not suffer it to obey the King of righteousness, which is called conscience likewise in the creation, man.[83]

The feminine flesh here seemed morally neutral; it was the masculine spiritual powers, the violent instincts and temptations of self-love and imagination, which usurped the gentle promptings of conscience. Men and women without distinction were subject to these impulses but, Winstanley noted encouragingly, 'No man or woman needs to be trobled at this, for let every man cleanse himself of these wicked masculine powers that rule in him, and there will speedily be a harmony of love in the great creation, even among all creatures'.[84]

It was only in *The saints paradice* that Winstanley characterized the selfishness of humankind as masculine, but the critique of a militant model of masculinity echoed elsewhere, in his writings on the evils of war, feudalism, and oppressive government (bearing in mind Christopher Hill's point that Winstanley was by no means an 'absolute pacifist').[85] The dominion of men over women was, as Hobby notes, implicitly linked to the 'kingly power' that rose up in humanity and destroyed the perfect primordial 'equality of love', creating conflict and hierarchy.[86] As he put it in *A New-yeers gift* (1650):

> Well, you see how Covetousnesse would have all the Earth to himself, though he let it lie waste: he stirs up Divisions among men, and makes parties fight against parties; and all is but for this, Who shall enjoy the Earth, and live in honour and case and rule over others: and the stronger party always rules over the weaker party.[87]

The 'weaker party', oppressed by the kingly rule, was represented perhaps most obviously by abused women. In a telling and pointed little anecdote, Winstanley

---

[83] More, *Conjectura cabbalistica*, pp. 75-6.   [84] More, *Conjectura cabbalistica*, p. 77.
[85] Christopher Hill, ed., '*The law of freedom' and other writings* (Cambridge: Cambridge University Press, 1973), p. 41.
[86] Hobby, 'Winstanley, women and the family', pp. 65-6.
[87] Anon., *A New-yeers gift for the parliament and armie* (London, 1650), p. 35.

manifested his distaste for partisanship which was destructive of compassion, and illustrated his sympathy for the weaker, 'feminine' party:

> the Kingly power swims in fulness, and laughs at the others miserie; as a poor Cavalier Gentlewoman presented a Paper to the Generall in my sight, who looked upon the woman with a tender countenance; but a brisk little man and two or three more Colonels puld back the Paper not suffering the Generall to receive it, and laught at the woman who answered them again, I thought said she, you had not sate in the seat of the scornfull; this was done in *Whitehall* upon the 12. of December 1649.[88]

The strongly apocalyptic hope articulated by Winstanley was that the 'masculine' spirit of covetousness, pride, partisanship, division, and war would be replaced by a 'spirit of Love, Patience, Humility, and Righteousnesse', bringing 'mankind into a moderate, meeke, Loving, and seasonable condition: It is the restoring spirit, teaching all men to doe as they would be done by'. He went on: 'This is the spirit of poverty, that hath been a servant in the world a long time, but now is appearing and rising up to draw all men after him'.[89] The second birth of Christ, in the hearts and bodies of the saints, would be manifest through this spiritual poverty; elsewhere called 'this plaine heartednesse without envie or guile' or 'Virgine-state of Mankinde' (the perfect image of the divine) in which 'the Sonne of righteousnesse will arise, and take the man into union with himselfe; he rules as King, and Mankinde, the living soule is freely subject with delight'.[90] It seems that here lies the key to the apparent inconsistency in Winstanley's use of the metaphor of masculinity. Human appropriations of masculine or kingly power, in the strongholds of political, ecclesiastical, economic, and intellectual authority, were usurpations of the true head, Christ. In a revolution, even an inversion of the worldly order, the ultimate human in whom all authority resided revealed himself to be the spirit and source of love and humility. 'Masculinity' was not what we thought it was. The lamb wrestled triumphantly with the dragon; innocence struggled against violence. Male and female alike must fight against the 'evill masculine powers' which, like idols in the heart, took the place of Christ's rule.

The symbolism of the Fall, as we have seen, naturally provided the framework for this analysis of the essential sinfulness in human nature. Although this was before all else a spiritual diagnosis of the human condition, it clearly had the far-reaching social and political implications for which Winstanley is better known. Whereas *The saints paradice* employed the terminology of 'masculine powers',

---

[88] Anon., *A New-yeers gift*, p. 41.
[89] Gerrard Winstanley, *An humble request to the ministers of both universities, and to all lawyers* (London, 1650), p. 5.
[90] Gerrard Winstanley, *Fire in the bush* (London, 1650), pp. 50–1.

The new law of righteousnes fixed on the mythological figure of Adam as its primary metaphor for the tyrannizing self. Winstanley's radical rejection of worldly hierarchies, as corrupting by their very nature, was stated nowhere as baldly as in the following passage:

> *Adam* appears first in every man and woman; but he sits down in the chair of Magistracy, in some above others; for though this climbing power of self-love be in all, yet it rises not to its height in all; but every one that gets an authority into his hands, tyrannizes over others; as many husbands, parents, masters, magistrates, that lives after the flesh, doe carry themselves like oppressing Lords over such as are under them; not knowing that their wives, children, servants, subjects are their fellow creatures, and hath an equall priviledge to share with them in the blessing of liberty.[91]

The fact that husbands together with magistrates were held accountable for behaving like 'oppressing Lords' over their wives suggests that Winstanley was not oblivious to the analogy (or symbiosis) between political and domestic tyranny. He showed a sensitivity to the possibility of abuse and oppression in the household which went beyond the common sensibilities of most seventeenth-century Protestant commentators on marriage, and this was certainly linked to his critique of Adamite masculinity.

It is often said that Winstanley's proposals for reform, especially in his last and perhaps most famous work, *The law of freedom*, 'supported a traditional, patriarchal family structure',[92] upholding the correspondence between the father of a family and magisterial rule: as in his assertions that 'the Father...is the first link of the chain [of] Magistracy', and that 'from the Father in a Family was the first rise of Magisterial Government'.[93] However, Su Fang Ng has very reasonably called attention to the anti-elitist thrust of Winstanley's supposed 'patriarchalism', and remarks that he 'should not be conflated with conservative patriarchalists like Filmer'.[94] For Winstanley, the magisterial office of the patriarch, in society or the family, was authorized 'by joynt consent, and not otherwise'; it was a nurturing,

---

[91] Winstanley, *The new law*, p. 5.
[92] Mark Stephen Jendrysik, *Explaining the English Revolution: Hobbes and his contemporaries* (Lanham, MD: Lexington Books, 2002), pp. 41–2; see also, for instance, Mary Murray, *The law of the father? Patriarchy in the transition from feudalism to capitalism* (London and New York: Routledge, 1995), p. 91; Gordon Schochet, *The authoritarian family and political attitudes in seventeenth-century England: patriarchalism in political thought* (New Brunswick, NJ: Transaction, 1988), pp. 161–3; Amy Boesky, *Founding fictions: utopias in early modern England* (Athens, GA: University of Georgia Press, 1996), p. 107.
[93] Gerrard Winstanley, *The law of freedom in a platform: or, true magistracy restor'd* (London, 1652), pp. 33–4.
[94] Su Fang Ng, *Literature and the politics of the family in seventeenth-century England* (Cambridge: Cambridge University Press, 2007), p. 108.

peaceable role, designed to protect the 'weakest'.[95] Significantly, it was never suggested that the father should discipline or govern the mother. Indeed, the draconian penalties he proposed for those who 'do force or abuse women in folly, pleading Community', or who 'lie with a woman forcibly' committing 'robbery of a womans bodily Freedom', and the reciprocal enjoyment and consent he envisaged for men and women in marriage suggests a benign variety of patriarchalism indeed.[96] Winstanley clearly emphasized the aggressive male over the treacherous female offence.

Notwithstanding this distinctive hostility to sexual exploitation by men, it is true that the figure of Adam, the symbol of a tyrannous and covetous spirit, stood for the masculine powers in both male and female. The lapse into 'pride and envy, lifting up himself above others, and seeking revenge upon all that crosses his selfish honours'; into 'hypocrisie, subtilty, lying imagination, self-love'; this was 'the first Adam, lying, ruling and dwelling within man-kinde. And this is he within every man and woman, which makes whole man-kinde, being a prisoner to him, to wander after the beast, which is no other but self'.[97] As Hobby suggests, 'Digger writings are free from the practice of blaming women for the Fall, and from insisting on their consequent subordination'.[98] Eve does make an appearance, in the role of the 'imagination' arising from the 'covetous power' of Adam; 'these two, Covetousnesse and Imagination, the man and the woman of sin, or Adam, and his Eve, or Ivie, does beget fruit or children, like both Father and Mother; as pride, and envy, hypocrisie, crueltie, and all unclean lusts pleasing the flesh'.[99] These figurative accounts of the Fall were precisely not historical, of course: 'herein you may see, how the publique Preachers have cheated the whole world, by telling us of a single man, called Adam, that kiled us al by eating a single fruit, called an Apple'.[100] But despite his denial that a single, historical man named Adam existed in the literal sense, Winstanley's anthropology depended on a vision of the original singularity or unity of humankind, male and female. Here he hinted at the primordial androgyny of created humanity, in the sense that the Behmenists would later expound it, although this was never fully developed or explicitly stated. He did, however, suggest that 'every man and woman in the world...are but branches of the first man; and then put them all together into one lumpe, and they make up still, but the first man perfect'.[101] The first man, Adam, and the second man, Christ, united both sexes as one flesh, in one common humanity.

It was entirely in keeping with such a vision that the rising of Christ's spirit, previously kept in servitude, was made manifest in both sexes, and the Digger

---

[95] Winstanley, *The law of freedom*, pp. 34, 39–40, 50.
[96] Winstanley, *The law of freedom*, pp. 16, 24, 88.
[97] Winstanley, *The new law*, pp. 5–6.
[98] Hobby, 'Winstanley, women and the family', p. 67.
[99] Hobby, 'Winstanley, women and the family', p. 65.
[100] Hobby, 'Winstanley, women and the family', p. 65.
[101] Gerrard Winstanley, *Truth lifting up its head above scandals* (London, 1649), pp. 22–3.

pamphlets were insistently inclusive in accepting the witnesses of the new dispensation (perhaps reflected in the Diggers' willingness to work for Lady Eleanor Davies). Winstanley's apocalyptic language was capacious: the 'light and wisdome of the Spirit of Truth... shall rise up out of the Sea of mankinde likewise, appearing in sonnes and daughters of righteousnesse, in the latter days'.[102] Christ 'is now rising in Husbandmen, Shepherds, Fishermen', and in order to 'discover his appearance in sonnes and daughters, in a fuller measure, the poore despised ones shall be honoured first in the worke'; it was through such as these that 'the imaginary learned Scholars [who] by their studies have defiled the Scriptures of old' would be exposed as frauds.[103] This 'second witness' of Christ 'is not to be restrained to Magistrates, Ministers, particular men or women; but to all the body, consisting of learned, unlearned, poor and rich, men and women, in whom the spirit of the Son dwells'.[104] The 'mysterie of God' was to be unveiled before 'every man and Woman', for: '*Gods* works are not like mens, he doth not alwaies take the wise, the learned, the rich of the world to manifest himself in, and through them to others, but he chuseth the despised, the unlearned, the poor, the nothings of the world'.[105] Just as the 'Scriptures of the Bible were written by the experimentall hand of Shepherds, Husbandmen, Fishermen, and such inferiour men of the world', so the new revelation would be received experimentally by the humble, 'the true Penmen in whom the Spirit dwells'.[106] Winstanley placed 'experiences' in the foreground (sometimes he wrote of illuminations received himself while in ecstasy), for this was the time in which 'every son and daughter' was called to 'declare their particular experiences, when the Spirit doth rise up in them, and manifests himself to them'.[107]

Not only would men and women alike testify to the new manifestation, but they would themselves be incarnate with it. Just as God inhabited the human flesh of Jesus of Nazareth, so also ultimately 'he will dwell in the whole Creation, that is, every man and woman without exception, as he did dwell in that one branch, Jesus Christ, who is the pledge, or first fruits'.[108] These rather startling claims about the intimacy between Christ himself and the saints were explained in terms even of physical identification:

> Every declaration of Christ in the Scriptures, shal be seen and known in the clear experience of every sonne and daughter (when this mystery is finished) for Christ, who indeed is the anointing, shall fill all, and all shall be the fulnesse of

---

[102] Winstanley, *Fire in the bush*, p. 33.   [103] Winstanley, *Fire in the bush*, pp. 41–2.
[104] Gerrard Winstanley, *The breaking of the day of God* (London, 1649), p. 22.
[105] Gerrard Winstanley, *The mysterie of God* (London, 1649), 'To my beloved Countrey-men'.
[106] Winstanley, *Fire in the bush*, pp. 40–1.
[107] Winstanley, *The new law*, p. 10. The title page of *The saints paradice* advertises its contents, 'Wherein Many Experiences Are Recorded'; for, 'The inward testimony is the souls strength'.
[108] Winstanley, *The new law*, p. 7.

the anointing: So that whatsoever a condition a man is in, it is one or other condition that the childe Jesus was in, growing upwards towards man-hood; there is child hood, youth and old age in the anointing.[109]

Christ would 'spread himself in multiplicities of bodies, making them all of one heart and one mind'.[110] The universal reach of this new dispensation would extend not only to humankind, but 'all other creatures, of all kinde according to their severall degrees, shall be filled with this one spirit'.[111] Such early appearances of Christ represented, according to Winstanley, the sixth dispensation in salvation history, before the perfect seventh age of the final resurrection.[112] Dispensational teachings about the manifestation of Christ in the saints can be found in the sermons of army preachers, especially William Erbery, and in the apocalyptic theology of spiritualists variously labelled 'Ranter', 'Quaker', 'Fifth Monarchist': Richard Coppin, Robert Rich, Henry Vane. In the *New law of righteousnes*, Winstanley's excitement at the transformations through which he was living was palpable, and he proclaimed the advent of a new king and a new law (indulging in a wordplay on 'David' and 'divide'):

> This new Law of righteousnesse and peace, which is rising up, is *David* your King, which you have been seeking a long time, and now shall find him coming again the second time in the personall appearance of sons and daughters; he will be a true *Davider* indeed, between flesh and spirit, between bondage and libertie, between oppressours and the oppressed; he is and will be the righteous Judge; he will lead your captivitie captive, and set you down in peace.[113]

The opposition that mattered was that of flesh and spirit, between a state of bondage and a state of freedom; not between male and female.

The repeated and careful pairing of 'sons and daughters', 'male and female', 'men and women' (which we see also in the preachers of free grace), drove home the point that this second coming was a universal 'ministration of Christ', which recognized no distinction of persons. Any 'man or woman is able to make a Sermon, because they can speak by experience of the light and power of Christ within them'.[114] It was not just legitimate but essential that individuals of all sexes should come forward to teach one another with their own insights and illuminations:

> when I look into that record of experimentall testimony, and finde a sutable agreement betweene them, and the feeling of light within my own soule, now my

---

[109] Winstanley, *The new law*, p. 16. [110] Winstanley, *The new law*, p. 38.
[111] Winstanley, *The new law*, p. 20. [112] Winstanley, *The new law*, p. 8.
[113] Winstanley, *The new law*, 'To the twelve tribes of Israel'.
[114] Winstanley, *The new law*, pp. 76–7.

joy is fulfilled. And every man and woman may declare what they have received, and so become preachers one to another... For the Scriptures doth but declare the sending down of the spirit and how he shall rule in the earth in the latter dayes: but they doe not declare every particular measure and beame of the spirits ruling, for this the sons and daughters are to declare, by their particular experiences, as they are drawn up.[115]

By means of this exchange, the particular would become one with the universal, and the scattered lights of the saints would be joined together in one bright radiance. The time had come for such experiences to supersede the old writings, 'the books in your Universitie, that tels yon what hath been formerly'; instead, the scholars are enjoined to 'read in your own book your heart', like 'these single hearted ones [who] are made to look into themselves, wherein they can read the work of the whole Creation, and see that History seated within themselves; they can see the mystery of Righteousnesse, and are acquainted every one according to his measure'.[116]

It may seem that this jubilant disavowal of old forms of learning, in favour of a wholly democratic way of knowing focused on pure experience, might be liberating not only for female readers but also for those excluded from the traditional elite institutions. Phyllis Mack has pointed out that the enfranchisement of women and men as prophets was not, of course, an emancipation or empowerment in a secular sense: the goal was self-transcendence, renunciation of the self and worldly honour.[117] For Winstanley, in order to feel Christ's rising in the heart and the consummating but dissolving experience of 'communion with the whole globe',[118] it was necessary 'to be silent and draw back, and set the spreading power of Righteousnesse and wisdom in the chair': 'And now the Son delivers up the Kingdom unto the Father; And he that is the spreading power, not one single person, become all in all in every person; that is, the one King of Righteousnesse in every one'.[119] Even while testimony and mutual preaching may be valuable for a time, the new harmony enjoyed by all of creation would ensure that 'mens words shal grow fewer and fewer', quietening the clamour of controversy and propaganda in favour of the visible fruits of righteousness.[120] Silence would be the

---

[115] Winstanley, *Truth lifting up its head*, pp. 42–3.
[116] Winstanley, *The new law*, pp. 78–9. This internalization of the history of Scripture and of Christ sounds suspiciously Familist; though Ariel Hessayon has recently sought to temper the enthusiasm of historians seeking to situate Winstanley and other radicals (as contemporary heresiographers did) within the Familist tradition. See Hessayon, 'Gerrard Winstanley: general Baptist', in David Finnegan and Ariel Hessayon, eds., *Varieties of seventeenth- and early eighteenth-century English radicalism* (Farnham: Ashgate, 2011), pp. 90–3.
[117] See Phyllis Mack, *Visionary women: ecstatic prophecy in seventeenth-century England* (Berkeley: University of Berkeley Press, 1992), pp. 127–64.
[118] Winstanley, *The saints paradice*, 'To my beloved friends'.
[119] Winstanley, *The new law*, p. 11.   [120] Winstanley, *The new law*, pp. 71–2.

'forerunner of pure language', the recovery of an original common speech.[121] As well as being broadly mystical in orientation, however, Winstanley's thought was intensely and rigorously practical. The theme of ultimate resignation was one that required 'every one to wait' rather than to 'take their neighbors goods by violence', but renunciation was required above all by those governed by their own covetousness in positions of power.[122] Then, the 'universall law of equity' would rise up

> in every man and woman, then none shall lay claim to any creature, and say, *This is mine, and that is yours, This is my work, that is yours*; but every one shall put to their hands to till the earth, and bring up cattle, and the blessing of the earth shall be common to all.[123]

I have argued that an incipient critique of traditional patriarchalism, variously expressed in terms of 'masculine powers' or 'kingly rule', lay at the heart of Winstanley's reformism. He was not as ambiguous or as inconsistent on this point as he might appear, and while the language of benign paternalism in *The law of freedom* might be problematic for modern feminists, it was an essential pathway for Winstanley to the *reconstruction* and reconception of fatherhood and of masculinity and, ultimately, of magistracy. There was, of course, no radically reforming agenda for women in society outlined in detail in the Digger tracts. This should not, however, blind us to the rich possibilities of the universalizing political anthropology expounded in these texts. The opposition which structured his thought, framing the Revolution envisaged, stood between the first man (comprehending both male and female), that is Adam: the 'selfish power',[124] the flesh; and the second man (also comprehending both male and female), Christ: the spirit of universal love. Driving forward and underpinning the political doctrine of communalism is an apocalyptic Christology, the expectation that this second man, Christ would 'dwel and rule in the flesh of his Saints'.[125] The final communion of the saints, indwelt and consumed by Christ, would dissolve the distinction between persons and, it is implied, the sexes. Winstanley described the 'Men that are wholly taken up into God', as well as primitive humanity in its first creation as having the nature of the 'Angels' of heaven: traditionally, of course, angels are sexless.[126] In his own time and place, Winstanley observed the descent of Zion and the prospect of the consummation to come:

the spreading of this one spirit in every sonne and daughter, and the lifting up the earth to be a common treasury, wil make Jerusalem a praise in the whole earth.[127]

---

[121] Winstanley, *The new law*, p. 93. [122] Winstanley, *The new law*, p. 38.
[123] Winstanley, *The new law*, p. 39. [124] Winstanley, *The new law*, p. 4.
[125] Winstanley, *The breaking of the day of God*, p. 38.
[126] Winstanley, *The saints paradice*, pp. 66-7. [127] Winstanley, *The new law*, p. 39.

5
Song

This chapter considers the significance of singing as a form of prophetic utterance, and especially women's song, in radical theology. Inspired singing, as Nigel Smith has shown, frequently accompanied radical theology and 'sectarian' practice.[1] The evidence suggests that (certainly among the Fifth Monarchist congregations) *extempore* singing was practised alongside the composition of new hymns, attesting to the relationship between individual mystical experience and communal expressions of worship in these communities. Hymn singing was an ordinance of the new Jerusalem; and congregational singing became so well established that it helped positively to foster the development of hymnody in a later generation. Importantly, women were centrally and prominently involved in the prophetic act of singing the songs of Sion. Spiritual singing was considered a manifestation of the new birth, like the Magnificat: the proclamation of the living Christ incarnate in the saints, and heaven's condescension to earth. With Mary, female prophets played a particular role as singing heralds of the kingdom of Christ, breaking forth within all humanity.

Phyllis Mack has suggested that singing in female visionaries was a more acceptable form of expression for women than reasoned argument; it was appropriately passive, or imbecilic. As she comments, 'a woman who interrupted a parliamentary meeting by babbling or singing, her eyes glazed, would probably seem less of an anomaly than one who tried to appear as a concerned citizen or minister engaging in public theological debates or rational biblical exegesis'.[2] Mack is, as ever, an astute commentator and touches on the ambiguous, derived status of the authority claimed by the visionary. An observer of Anna Trapnel's singing trances in 1654 was sceptical about the prophetic status of her psalms, because 'in the things she utters (whether in verse or prose) it's onely what she hath been conversant in before, and had the knowledge of'. In other words, she seemed to use her reason or 'strength of parts'.[3] The true mark of

---

[1] Nigel Smith, *Literature and Revolution in England, 1640–1660* (New Haven and London: Yale University Press, 1994), pp. 260–76.
[2] Phyllis Mack, *Visionary women: ecstatic prophecy in seventeenth-century England* (Berkeley: University of Berkeley Press, 1992), pp. 107–8.
[3] Letter from B.T., in Bodleian Library, Rawlinson MS A.21, p. 325. See also Erica Longfellow, *Women and religious writing in early modern England* (Cambridge: Cambridge University Press, 2004), p. 149.

authenticity in the inspired singers was the suspension of all rational faculties. Nonetheless, another dimension of meaning to the singing prophetess should be taken in to account. She was the herald of revolutionary change, not only in the world around her, but in herself: the site of the living temple, where the songs of Sion could be sung anew. The radical pamphleteer Anne Yemans wrote of the singing gift in terms of the advent of Christ's mystical presence in the saints, to destroy 'Babylon in us': 'As there are new manifestations of God in us: so there will be new songs of joy and rejoycing in the Lord'.[4]

Songs of Sion

The prophetic status of new songs and 'new psalms' in the context of radical theology reflects parallel developments in the European radical reformations. As is well known, a hymn-writing tradition developed among the Swiss Brethren and later the Mennonites, with the great hymnal known as the *Ausbund* (1564; expanded in 1583) becoming a defining, foundational text of the Anabaptist churches. The hymns were the defiant refrains of sufferers for the true faith. Sebastian Franck's contribution to this collection indicated that these were not simply anthems of confessional identity or martyr tributes, but also manifested the gifts of the Holy Spirit to a new generation. Women were established contributors to the hymn-writing tradition in North German and Dutch Anabaptism; two hymnbooks entirely composed by individual women were published by Dutch Anabaptist printers in 1592 and 1607.[5]

Among the spiritual Anabaptists, singing held a particular significance for David Joris, the Dutch glass-painter, notorious heretic, and eventual spiritual father to many Anabaptists dismayed by the fall of Münster in the 1530s. His prophetic role as the 'third David', the instrument of revelation in the third, spiritual epoch, was marked by the composition of psalms for a new dispensation. In the years prior to 1533, the year appointed by Melchior Hoffmann for the return of Christ in judgement, Joris's songs are intensely apocalyptic in tone: 'For God is our fire / Why should we grieve: / It is the last year / It shall not endure forever'.[6] His later hymns herald the dawn of a new spiritual age by means of a Dutch messiah and a vernacular tongue more holy and immediate than Hebrew, Greek, or Latin: 'Now people will taste the spiritual gifts / which are given to us in

---

[4] Anne Yeman, *Crooked pathes made straight: or, the wayes of God made knowne to lost sinners, or bewildered saints* (London, 1648), pp. 233–4.

[5] See C. Arnold Snyder and Linda Huebert Hecht, eds., *Profiles of Anabaptist women: sixteenth-century reforming pioneers* (Waterloo, Ontario: Wilfrid Laurier University Press, 1996), p. 254.

[6] See Gary K. Waite, *David Joris and Dutch Anabaptism, 1524–1543* (Waterloo, Ontario: Wilfred Laurier, 1990), p. 59.

Dutch words, / for the Spirit of the Lord rests here in the North'.[7] This emphasis on the living gifts of the Spirit led Joris, like some other Anabaptists, to experience anxiety about the promiscuity of singing in mixed congregations. His anonymous biographer noted that his new songs were written for the use of those only who had 'a true, sincere, and willing heart', for 'it vexed him that everyone sang the spiritual songs with a fleshy, impenitent heart, which did not seem proper to him'.[8] Inner holiness, a spiritual purification marked not so much by abstention from worldly pleasures as by love of God was the necessary precondition for the heart: those who are 'eunuchs inside, but not in the external flesh' are those who 'alone will sing the new song'.[9]

It was frequently claimed by seventeenth-century English heresiographers that David Joris or 'David George' was the founder of the Family of Love, and all its antichristian offshoots in the English spiritual sects.[10] Although the claim had no basis, it has been shown that Hendrik Niclaes and his followers were shaped by post-Münsterite spiritual Anabaptism.[11] Numerous cultural and theological resemblances illustrate the relationship, beyond nicodemism and the expectation of universal spiritual reformation: prophetic songs were part of Familist culture, and the Family of Love may also have thought, like Joris, in terms of three dispensations in salvation history, corresponding to the persons of the Trinity and to revelation in Law, Gospel, and Spirit. Niclaes himself was another hymn-writer, and some of his 'Psalmes and songes' were translated into English, circulating in manuscript and clandestine print.[12] The Familist psalms were loose paraphrases of the biblical psalms of lament. Niclaes called them his 'Mourning-songes',[13] and they documented his agonies of spiritual oppression, described in his *Epistles* (printed in English translation in 1575).[14]

There is a clear spiritual progression through Niclaes's psalms, and a mystical climax at which they turn from lament to thanksgiving, when sin is overcome and perfection achieved: 'Clapp then with your handes, and stampe then with your feete. / Make then your Songes of myrth at Syon: singe then alleluya in all the littell streets of Jerusalem. / No synnes shall willdernes you eny more / . . . / You shall all

---

[7] 'Appendix I: Joris's hymns on the Dutch language', Gary K. Waite ed., *The Anabaptist writings of David Joris* (Waterloo, Ontario: Herald Press, 1994), p. 291; see also Piet Visser, 'Under the sign of Thau: the Bible and the Dutch radical Reformation', in Mathijs Lamberigts and A.A. Den Hollander, eds., *Lay Bibles in Europe 1450–1800* (Leuven: Leuven University Press, 2006), pp. 103–4.

[8] 'The anonymous biography of Joris', in Waite, *The Anabaptist writings*, p. 52.

[9] 'The response to Hans Eisenburg, 1537', in Waite, *The Anabaptist writings*, pp. 172–3.

[10] See, for instance, Robert Baillie, *Anabaptism, the true fountaine of independency, Brownisme, antinomy, familisme* (London, 1647), pp. 13–16, 99–102.

[11] Niclaes's first printer had also worked for David Joris, and it was later reported that Joris had had dealings with Melchiorites living in Amsterdam. See Alastair Hamilton, ed., *Cronica. Ordo Sacerdotis. Acta HN. Three texts on the Family of Love* (Leiden: Brill, 1988), p. xii.

[12] 'Psalmes and songs given to Hendrik Niclaes', in Lambeth Palace Library, MS 869; see also Hendrik Niclaes, *Cantica certen of the songes of HN* (Cologne, 1575).

[13] Lambeth Palace Library, MS 869, fol. 15r.

[14] Hendrik Niclaes, *The principall epistles of H.N.* (London, 1575), p. 86.

knowe the Lorde yor God'.[15] This was the widely reported consummation of union with God—the 'Godding'—when 'Yee that are one with God abyde / Make nowe delight in this Tyde / For see heere is Emanuell / Godes paradice'.[16] The apocalyptic tone of the psalms—including predictions of the 'horrible destruction of all the ungodlie', 'the Ende of the wicked-worlde'—is perhaps surprising, given the reputation of the Familists for quietism. The 'day of the love' that marks the turning point in the hymn was presented as an inward, not a historic or political event, though it would not take a great leap to reconceive it as such.[17] A key difference between Niclaes's psalms and biblical psalms was the absence of an external foe. His struggles were all with internal enemies: sin and the temptations of Satan. Strikingly, the psalms, with all their biblical allusions, gave way to a series of 'Songes brought forth through H.N.', or 'Songes after the time'.[18] These were clearly new compositions, and it seems to have been these hymns, rather than the 'mourning-Songes', that were intended to be sung corporately, as they were set to named ballad tunes and translated into rhyming verse.[19] It is difficult to know how widely the songs were used, if at all. Marsh suggests that a 'laud booke' confiscated in a raid of the house of the Familist glover John Bourne might have contained H.N.'s psalms.[20] Recent research has emphasized the significance of Familism as an influence on English radical theology in the 1630s and 1640s, and these songs may form part of the background to the emergence of English 'songs of Sion' in the revolutionary period.

The significance of new songs in the Revolution should also be considered in the context of Puritan, and especially radical Puritan, queasiness about set forms. The Presbyterian *Directory of publique worship* of 1645 condemned the practice of 'reading all the prayers, which very greatly increased the burden of it' and kept the people in ignorance and idolatry, and insisted that ministers 'ought... to speak from their hearts'.[21] This priority upon inward experience was echoed in the short guidelines about psalm singing, which stipulated that 'the chief care must be to sing with understanding, and with grace in the heart, making melody unto the Lord'.[22] Some defenders of set prayers tried to argue that the repetition of metrical psalms was just as 'stinted' a form of worship as liturgical prayer.[23] The head of an inquiry into separation and emigration in the 1630s, John Ball, remarked that:

---

[15] Niclaes, *The principall epistles of HN*, fols. 49v-50r.   [16] 'Psalmes and songs', fols. 67r, 63v.
[17] 'Psalmes and songs', fols. 67r, 63v.   [18] 'Psalmes and songs', fols. 50v-70v.
[19] The tunes are as yet unidentified; Christopher Marsh has suggested they may have a Dutch provenance. Christopher Marsh, *The Family of Love in English society 1550-1630* (Cambridge: Cambridge University Press, 1994), p. 93.
[20] Marsh, *The Family of Love*, p. 21.
[21] *The directory of publique worship* (London, 1645), p. 2.
[22] *The directory of publique worship*, p. 64.
[23] On the use of this argument by apologists for a formal liturgy, see Geoffrey Nuttall, *The Holy Spirit in Puritan faith and experience* (Chicago: University of Chicago Press, 1992), p. 73.

> As the one must be done with the heart and spirit, so the other: As in the one the words are devised by men and prescribed by others, so in singing of psalmes: If the one be the invention of man, a strange prayer, the similitude of a prayer; the other is an invention of man, a strange psalme, the similitude of a psalme.[24]

Ball sought to illustrate the contradictions in the practices of those who withdrew from participation in parish worship, concluding: 'I have not read, that the singing of psalmes in a prescript form devised by others is unlawfull'.[25] These very scruples about metrical psalmody that appeared to him so self-evidently absurd were well established among certain English separatists, and appeared to have gained currency with the New Englanders. That pioneer of apocalyptic Puritan separatism, Henry Barrow, seems to have identified 'stinted psalmes' with the corrupt liturgy of the Church of England, a relic of Old Testament ceremonialism: 'inseperably ioyned & used to those scriptures, in that Temple and ministerie... now utterly abrogate'.[26] The radical Puritan and founding English Baptist John Smyth separated from Henry Ainsworth's Amsterdam congregation on the basis of its liturgical formality, including the use of set psalms. He rejected what he called 'book-worship' or the 'ministration of the lettre', because the earliest churches after Pentecost 'did use no bookes in tyme of spiritual worship but prayed, prophesyed, & sang Psalmes meerely out of their harts'.[27] The New Testament, he argued, taught that 'a man must have a Psalme, have doctryne, that is in his hart, whence he must produce it by the manifestation of the Spirit'.[28] Was not the use of 'meter, Rithme & tune' to regulate congregational singing, he asked, a way of 'quenching the Spirit?'[29]

By the 1640s, in a post-Laudian mood, the ordinance of psalm singing was a contentious subject among those engaged in the quest for spiritual worship, not least the religious leaders in the New England colonies. The preface to the famous Bay Psalm Book or *The whole booke of psalmes* (1640), the first book published in New England, outlines the controversy over the 'heavenly ordinance' of psalm singing:

> The singing of Psalmes, though it breath forth nothing but holy harmony, and melody: yet such is the subtilty of the enemie, and the enmity of our nature against the Lord, & his wayes, that our hearts can finde matter of discord in this harmony, and crotchets of division in this holy melody.—for—There have been

---

[24] John Ball, *A friendly triall of the grounds tending to separation* (London, 1640), p. 54. On the inquiry, see Polly Ha, *English Presbyterianism, 1590–1640* (Stanford: Stanford University Press, 2011), p. 116.

[25] Ball, *A friendly triall*, p. 55.

[26] Henry Barrow, *A brief discoverie of the false church* (Dort, 1590), pp. 76, 68.

[27] John Smyth, *The differences of the churches of the seperation* (Middelburg, 1608), p. 6.

[28] Smyth, *The differences of the churches*, p. 20.

[29] Smyth, *The differences of the churches*, p. 20.

three questions especially stirring concerning singing. First, what psalmes are to be sung in churches? whether Davids and other scripture psalmes, or the psalmes invented by the gifts of godly men in every age of the church. Secondly, if scripture psalmes, whether in their owne words, or in such meter as english poetry is wont to run in? Thirdly, by whom are they to be sung? whether by the whole churches together with their voices? or by one man singing alone and the rest joyning in silence, & in the close saying amen.[30]

The editors explicitly prohibited the introduction of 'extemporary psalmes' by the minister like 'conceived prayers', finding no biblical warrant for such a practice: the psalms were such timeless and comprehensive expressions of the human condition that 'by this the Lord seemeth to stoppe all mens mouths and mindes ordinarily to compile or sing any other psalmes (under colour that the ocasions and conditions of the Church are new)'.[31] But at the time that church order was being reviewed in England by the Westminster Assembly, these questions rose to the surface. In 1644, the Independent Nathanael Homes reproduced the preface to *The whole booke of psalmes* in his defence of psalm singing, *Gospel musick*.[32] John Cotton, a contributor to the New England psalter, devoted a treatise to defending the 'Gospel Ordinance' of psalm singing in 1646. He complained about the 'Anti-psalmists, who doe not acknowledge any singing at all with the voice in the New Testament, but onely spirituall songs of joy and comfort of the heart in the word of Christ'.[33] At a conference in Boston reported in 1646, John Cotton argued against the use of 'stinted forms of prayer or praise' in public worship. He was asked directly: 'What is a Psalme?', and responded that a true psalm was 'a rehearsal of those speciall mercies and particular experiences that the Lord hath done for a believer'; just as prayer must be spiritual and an individual's particular offering, so sung praise must be spiritual, a subjective response to the 'special mercies' of God.[34]

There were already some voices calling for the displacement of David's psalms with newly composed songs. A committee of the Westminster Assembly assessed the relative merits of rival new versions of the metrical psalms by Francis Rous and William Barton in 1645, commending Rous's version to the House of Lords on 14 November.[35] The *Moderate Intelligencer* reported immediately:

---

[30] 'Preface', *The whole booke of psalmes* (Cambridge, MA, 1640), §A2.
[31] *The whole booke of psalmes*, §A4.
[32] Nathanael Homes, *Gospel musick* (London, 1644), pp. 19, 25–6.
[33] John Cotton, *A Conference Mr John Cotton held at Boston with the elders of New-England* (London, 1646), pp. 6–8, p. 2.
[34] Cotton, *A Conference Mr John Cotton held*, pp. 6–8.
[35] Entry for 14 Nov., *Journal of the House of Lords* 7 (1645), pp. 701–5. However, the Lords preferred William Barton's translation. See J.R. Watson, *The English hymn: a critical and historical study* (Oxford: Oxford University Press, 1997), p. 104.

> A Message this day about the Psalmes, from the Assembly, they approve Master Rowse's Translation: Psalmes, Hymnes and Spirituall Songs are excellent things to praise God by, but some think that those that comprehend our own deliverences and mercies, and speak to our own particular condition, as those made by Luther, did to the businesse of those times, would do well also.[36]

In *Gangraena* (1646), Thomas Edwards complained that 'sectaries' (or radicals) across the country were 'taking away the old used in all Reformed Churches, and substituting new; taking away singing of Psalms, and pleading for hymns of their own making' as one of their key aims.[37] He reported that they were arguing that 'all singing of Psalmes, as *Davids*, or any other holy songs of Scripture, is unlawfull, and not to be joyned with'. Instead, 'That the singing which Christians should use, is that of Hymns and spirituall songs, framed by themselves, composed by their own gifts, and that upon speciall occasions, as deliverances, &c. sung in the Congregation by one of the Assembly, all the rest being silent'.[38] It had become the practice in certain parish churches where sectaries had been placed as ministers, that they would not allow the singing of Psalms, or, 'in places where they cannot prevaile to shut out singing of Psalmes, they in a contemptuous manner clap on their hats, in the time of singing of Psalms, and having been pull'd off, put them on again; yea in prayer also many of them keep on hats'.[39] This gesture of irreverence anticipated the Quakers' defiant hat wearing; an indication of the spiritualist radicals' refusal to bow to Scripture itself over the living inspiration of the Spirit. Edwards was also worried that 'some of our Independents having fancies in Musick singing, taking great delight in that way, they have pleaded for and brought into the Church Hymnes and Musick'.[40] To illustrate his concerns, he published a sample of a hymn 'which some of the Antinomians do sing at their meetings instead of DAVIDS Psalms'. One of the verses reads, 'All sin we finde is out of minde, / the Saints are made divine / First in the love of God above / in glory they do shine'.[41] This is rather crude antinomian doctrine, and there are interesting variations in an almost identical hymn reprinted anonymously as a broadsheet after the Restoration, in 1664 and 1684, with the title *Certain meditations upon justification by faith alone*. This version has a different, and rather less controversial first line, 'All things Behind, are out of Mind', which may reflect circumspection on account of the censors, or suggest that Edwards had a hand in sensationalizing a relatively innocuous text.[42]

---

[36] Entry for Friday, 14 Nov., *Moderate intelligencer* (London, 1645), p. 200.
[37] Thomas Edwards, *The first and second part of Gangraena* (London, 1646), pp. 44–5.
[38] Edwards, *The first and second part*, p. 27.   [39] Edwards, *The first and second part*, pp. 56–7.
[40] Thomas Edwards, *The third part of Gangraena* (London, 1646), p. 14.
[41] Edwards, *The third part*, pp. 11–12.
[42] Anon., *Certain meditations upon justification by faith alone* (London, 1664; second edn, 1684).

There is supporting evidence that the spiritual sects were substituting new songs for the old psalms. Among the first free hymns sung congregationally were those adopted by Morgan Llwyd's congregation at Wrexham from the early 1640s, where psalm singing in mixed congregations had been prohibited.[43] One such hymn characterized the 'Welsh saints' as lamenting Israelites and prophesied the 'great Ecclypse' approaching at the day of doom.[44] The impulse to compose new songs appropriate to the age paralleled the production of political ballads and military propaganda in song.[45] A cluster of 'spiritual songs' written for the use of soldiers in battle appeared during the mid-1640s, such as William Starbucke's 'Spirituall song of comfort' printed in 'the yeere wherein Antichrist is falling', namely 1643, and a hymn extolling God's works through Fairfax and Essex.[46] A broadsheet 'Song of Syon' was published in 1642 by a person calling themselves 'A citizen of Syon'.[47] These songs are thick with scriptural allusion—but composite paraphrases rather than loose translations.[48] Military anthems, psalms, and hymns did not fall into neat discrete categories: the psalm translator William Barton's collection of hymns compounded from scripture, *Hallelujah*, appeared in 1652 to celebrate Commonwealth victories at Dunbar and Worcester. In his preface, Barton announced that his hymns were

> published for the use of those who used to praise the Lord with the words of *David* the sweet Singer of *Israel*, and in the words of *Asaph, Heman, Moses*, and other holy men of God, who spake as they were directed by the Spirit of God. And they properly serve for the use of those who can *now* sing the Songs of *Sion* in their own Land, and in their own language, together with the Song of *Moses* and of the Lamb, And who can indeed Rejoyce now in this *great Salvation*, and *serve* the present Providence of God in their generation; who can sing with the Spirit, and who can sing with understanding also... Who can sing unto the Lord with the voyce of a *Psalm*.[49]

---

[43] Nuttall, *The Holy Spirit*, p. 73. The celebrated preacher Philip Henry recorded the agonies of conscience he suffered over leading Llwyd's congregation in singing a conventional psalm in July 1657, when preaching at Iscoyd Chapel, but felt vindicated when 'the lord came in with power' during the rendition of Psalm 90. 'July 3 1657', in M.H. Lee, ed., *Diaries and letters of Philip Henry... 1631–1696* (London: Kegan Paul and Co., 1882), p. 55.

[44] Morgan Llwyd, 'The Summer', in T.E. Ellis and J.H. Davies, eds., *Gweithau Morgan Llwyd* (Bangor and Liverpool, 1899), vol. 1, pp. 23–4; cited in Smith, *Literature and Revolution*, pp. 268–72.

[45] See Angela McShane, *Political broadside ballads of seventeenth-century England: a critical bibliography* (London: Pickering & Chatto, 2011).

[46] William Starbucke, *A spirituall song of comfort* (London, 1643); 'R.P.', *Berachah, or, Englands memento to thankefulnesse, being an hymne or spirituall song setting forth the praises of God* (London, 1646).

[47] Anon., *A song of Syon of the beauty of Bethell, the glory of Gods own house*, 'By a citizen of Syon' (London, 1642).

[48] Sacred poems by Milton and Waller were set to music by the 'cavalier songwriter' Henry Lawes in 1645. John Milton, *Poems of Mr John Milton, both English and Latin, compos'd at several times* (London, 1645). See Ian Spink, *Henry Lawes: Cavalier songwriter* (Oxford: Oxford University Press, 2000).

[49] William Barton, *Hallelujah, or certain hymns, composed out of Scripture, to celebrate some special and publick occasions* (London, 1652), 'To the reader'.

The old Reformation concern for the intelligibility of sung worship now took on a fresh significance: the new psalmists spoke in the pure vernacular of experience.

The more militant visionaries proclaiming the inauguration of Christ's new birth and rule in the saints, known as the Fifth Monarchists, composed new songs somewhat liturgically, as one of the new ordinances of the dawning dispensation. The theatre of contemporary national events, not merely the inward chamber of the heart, was the site of Christ's coming. On 8th October 1650, 'Three hymnes, or certain excellent new Psalmes' by the millenarian preachers John Goodwin, Vavasor Powell, and John Appletree were performed by their composers at congregations in London, to mark a day of thanksgiving for 'the total routing of the Scots Army in Musleborough-field, by his Excellency the L. Gen. Cromwell'.[50] Goodwin's hymn began, 'Repair, make ready, oh ye Saints / Jehovah is come down... / Into your mouths a Song he has put'. Powell celebrated the victories against the Scots as signs of Christ's newly established kingdom: 'The Pope, the Priest, the Anti-Christ / The Kings do quake for fear, / For Christ into his Throne doth come / His glory doth appear'.[51] In 1651, Goodwin published two more hymns or 'spirituall songs' for the appointed day of thanksgiving for the Battle of Worcester, using as an epigraph the ubiquitous words of Revelation 14.3: 'And they sung as it were a new song before his throne'.[52] A hymn by Vavasor Powell, apparently performed at Christ Church Newgate in December 1653 (shortly after Cromwell was sworn in as lord protector) captured the revolutionary tenor of Fifth Monarchist beliefs that Christ's 'Saints shall reign with him on earth / And great ones then shall bow'.[53] Christopher Feake allegedly ridiculed the singing of Psalms before his congregation at Newgate, keeping his hat on and scoffing at what he called the 'howling' in church.[54] Instead, 'Mr Feake doth exhort them, and stir them up to sing that new song of the Lambe, they now being upon mount *Sion*', and to 'make new songs' to the tunes of psalms.[55] A hymn of his has survived in manuscript, rejoicing that the 'oppressed saints' would soon 'raigne... as Kings', and that the 'the high & mighty states' would be made 'Poore and distressed againe'.[56] The Fifth

---

[50] John Goodwin, Vavasor Powell, and John Appletree, *Three hymnes, or certain excellent new psalmes* (London, 1650).

[51] Goodwin, Powell, and Appletree, *Three hymnes*, pp. 2, 7.

[52] John Goodwin, *Two hyms, or spiritual songs* (London, 1651), pp. 1–3.

[53] See Alexander Griffith, *Strena Vavasoriensis: a new yeares gift for the Welch itinerants* (London, 1654), p. 24. This was probably the same meeting at which Powell and Feake were reported to have denounced Cromwell as the 'dissembleingst perjured villaine in the world', leading to their arrest. See *A collection of the state papers of John Thurloe* (London, 1742), vol. 1, p. 641.

[54] Feake excluded psalm singing in his second parish at All Saints, Hertford, in 1646-7, inspired by the dissolution of set prayers. See Bernard Capp, *The Fifth Monarchy men: a study in seventeenth-century English millenarianism* (London: Faber, 1972), p. 52.

[55] 'J.N.', *Proh tempora! Proh Mores! or an unfained caveat to all true Protestants, not in any case to touch any of these three serpents* (London, 1654), p. 6.

[56] 'Mr Feakes Hymne: August ye 11: 1653 Christ Church', British Library, Thomason MS E. 710; see also Capp, *The Fifth Monarchy men*, pp. 67–8.

Monarchists' activities were closely monitored by Cromwell's agents. Among John Thurloe's state papers, there is a report dated May 1655 about the activities of John Roger's meeting at St Thomas the Apostle. It includes reference to the singing of a hymn, 'composed for the occasion; which the people sung very affectionately. It began thus: Come, glorious king of Zion, come to defend thy cause against all earthly powers, and to work deliverance for thy captives; and much to that purpose'.[57] So well established was hymn singing among the Fifth Monarchists that in 1659, a satirist imagined the congregation at Hugh Peter's funeral singing, from a suitably absurd-sounding hymnal, 'the two first staves of the tenth hymn of Larners twelve Songs of Sion, to the tune of The Knave of Clubs'.[58]

For others, the advent of 'new song' in the 1640s marked the end of all outward ordinances—not merely of the ceremonial law or popish rule. In September 1647, Thomas Collier preached a sermon at Putney announcing a new creation, the 'Kingdom of Heaven in the Saints'.[59] In common with other spiritual millenarians, he declared this inward apocalypse to be the 'great & hidden mysterie of the Gospell'.[60] Although, by the standards of the army chaplains who preached at Putney, Collier was politically moderate, his sermon triumphantly announced the rule of Christ in his saints and the ending of all ordinances of the former dispensation.[61] The new heavens and the new earth, he rejoiced, would bring forth 'perpetual singing of new songs of praise unto the Lord', to celebrate 'the fall of Babylon, which is effected as well within us, as without us'.[62] Whether or not Collier's song was purely spiritual or audible was left ambiguous, but he clearly regarded this as a defining prophetic event, distinguishing the old Babylonian captivity from the dawning new Jerusalem in the hearts of the saints. He wrote:

> it is called a new song, in opposition to the old, carnall, and formall singings of the world; it is such a song, that none can learn, but those who are redeemed from the earth...when once souls are delivered from this earth; as they shall in this new heaven, then they can sing new songs, and not till then.[63]

The conviction that the Revolution had introduced a new age of singing was especially characteristic of the army radicals.

Captain Thomas Butler, soon to be a militia commissioner for Oxfordshire, published an intriguing book entitled *The little Bible of the man*, printed by Giles

---

[57] *A collection of the state papers*, vol. 3, pp. 480–98.
[58] *Peter's patern newly revived* (London, 1659), p. 3. Larner was William Larner, a Leveller activist.
[59] Thomas Collier, *A discovery of the new creation* (London, 1647), §A2r.
[60] Collier, *A discovery*, p. 9.
[61] On Collier's preaching ministry, see Anne Laurence, *Parliamentary army chaplains, 1642–1651*, Royal Historical Society Studies in History (Woodbridge: Boydell Press, 1992), pp. 50–2.
[62] Collier, *A discovery*, pp. 21–2. [63] Collier, *A discovery*, pp. 22–3.

Calvert, in 1649.[64] This mystical commentary on various books of the Bible taught an essentially Familist doctrine, that the meaning of the Scriptures was not to be found through an understanding of ancient history or philology, but in the inner life and spiritual experience. A significant section was devoted to 'The book of Psalms opened in man', in which Butler lamented that 'There is no singing in the strange Land, till we come to the Lord himself',

> But the songs are heard neither in Egypt, nor in Babylon, nor in the Wilderness, but in Canaan; here we hang up our hearts and mourn, but in the strange Land are we more strangers... But when we shall absent from the body, and be present with the Lord, and not live by faith only, but by sight; when we shall not read of him, nor hear of him only, but when we shall see him face to face, then shall our joy be full, then we shall sing the song of Zion.[65]

Any singing without the spirit is 'but howling and no singing; but where its filled and enlarged with love'. Following the Apostle's injunction to sing in Ephesians 5.19 and Colossians 3.16, Butler distinguished between three genres of song which marked three stages of mystical ascent: psalms, hymns, and, the highest form, spiritual songs. 'The Psalms are doctrines', he wrote, 'mutually mixt with Praises, the Hymns thanksgivings purely, and the Songs the ravishments of love: Psalms are the tastes we have of him, the Hymns are longings after him, but the Song is the full possession of him'.[66]

The 'eternal song', according to Butler, was brought forth by sufferings, and he explicitly identified the song with regeneration and the indwelling presence of Christ: 'this is the man-child that shall be born after all'.[67] Helpfully, he reproduced samples of all three genres:

A Psalm.

> The Lord, the Lord, th'eternal God,
> who lives and reigns to make us glad;
> Our Psalm, our Hymns, our spirits songs,
> our melodies in him alone.
> We are his Organs and his Harps,
> he tunes and plays upon our hearts.
> He sings and makes most pleasant noise,
> filling us full of mirth and joys.

---

[64] On 3 Apr. 1650, the Council of State approved 'Capt. Thomas Butler to be added to the Militia Commissioners for county Oxon'. See Mary Anne Everett Green, ed., *Calendar of state papers domestic: interregnum, 1650* (London, 1876), pp. 72–135.
[65] Thomas Butler, *The little Bible of the man* (London, 1649), pp. 106–7.
[66] Butler, *The little Bible*, p. 100.   [67] Butler, *The little Bible*, pp. 102–3.

A Hymn.

> O Glory, glory, to the Lord,
> his Name be blessed all abroad;
> Our life, mirth, love and joys,
> lives and lies in his glories.

A spiritual Song.

> O Holy, holy,
> God on high,
> Eternally,
> Our melody,
> Above the sky,
> Never to dye,
> But thus to cry,
> Glory, Glory,
> To God on high,
> Eternally,
> Happy, happy.[68]

The progression from metered octave and quatrain, with rhyming couplets, to free verse (a paraphrase of the song of the seraphim in the vision of God enthroned in Isaiah 6, and the angelic song in Revelation 4.8), paralleled the journey of the soul from third-person, abstract statements of God's merits to a personal response of thanksgiving, and then to exaltation in celestial union with or 'full possession' of Christ.

The distinctive apocalyptic mysticism of the Revolution, shared with radical Reformation traditions, is key to understanding the prophetic status of singing in radical theology. The network of mystical Seekers which linked London radicals with communities in the Thames Valley region, among them Abiezer Coppe, Thomasina Pendarves, Giles Calvert, and John Pordage's household, identified song with mystical union, and indeed with divine utterance itself.[69] These were, importantly, all communities which recognized and welcomed the particular role to be played by women in opening up divine revelation. Abiezer Coppe, in *Some sweet sips of some spirituall wine* (1649), wrote of spiritual singing as a sign of the consummation of union with Christ: 'then the Lord will take you up into himself, and say, Live in me, dwell in me, walk with me... and you will sing an Hebrew

---

[68] Butler, *The little Bible*, pp. 109–10.
[69] On the network linking Pendarves, Coppe, and Pordage, see Manfred Brod, 'Doctrinal deviance in Abingdon: Thomasina Pendarves as her circle', *Baptist Quarterly* 41 (2005), pp. 92–102.

Song, one of the Songs of Sion; the Lords Song, when you are lifted up, out of a strange Land'. It would be an indication that the false self had finally been extinguished: 'when you are non-entities, walk with God and are not, because the Lord hath took you, then (I say) you will sing one of the songs of Sion, an Hebrew Song'.[70] Coppe associated his 'new song' with the song of Mary, as he shared mystically in her experience of incubating the divine presence: 'The Babe springs in my inmost wombe, leapes for joy thee, and then I sing, and never but then, O Lord my song! To me a childe is borne, a son is given, who lives in me, O Immanuel! O living Lord!'[71] Coppe's epistle concluded with a short, formless prophetic verse: 'Thy Kingdom is come / to some / their joy: / But to other doome / It is come / they cry'.[72] The Ranters' mysticism involved ritual gestures of inversion, signalling the advent of spiritual liberty and disruption to the old order, especially the ordinances of the old ecclesiastical order. According to a hostile commentator, a Ranter group which met at the sign of the 'David and Harp' in Moor Lane in November 1650 was 'heard to sing blasphemous songs in the tune of *Davids* Psalms', and later on, 'vile and filthy' drinking songs accompanied by an organist, also set to psalm tunes.[73] This rowdy singing was (apparently) accompanied by other licentious acts: parodies of the Eucharist, smoking, and drinking (see Figure 4). If the report can be believed, the choice of the David and Harp as the venue for the Ranters' revels was possibly symbolic; an indication that their new ordinances had superseded the old. Under the open heaven, the historic psalms of the old covenant were as meaningless and profane as bawdy ballads. The Ranter circle was later identified not only with the old Family of Love, but also with a newer sect known as the Sweet Singers of Israel, who were said to 'Drink, Swear and Smoak, Sing obscene Songs in Psalm-Tunes; and Divine ones, in Ballad-Tunes'; and 'drink Ale and puff *Tobacco* to excess in their very religious Assemblies'.[74] Another witness reported that they 'are merry in the Lord and sing songs'.[75] The astrologer and court physician John Partridge suggested that 'Abiezer Coppe was a Preacher among the Sweet Singers', and that in the 1650s he had enlisted Partridge's rival astrologer John Gadbury as one of the 'sweet Singers of Israel, a sort of profuse debauched Atheists'.[76]

In almost every corner of radical religion in the English Revolution, new songs of experience were sung. As was so often the case in radical thought, the literal and

[70] Abiezer Coppe, *Some sweet sips of some spirituall wine* (London, 1649), pp. 34–35. The reference to 'when you...walk with God, and are not' is to Enoch in Genesis 5.24, said to have been assumed without experiencing physical death.

[71] Coppe, *Some sweet sips*, p. 50.   [72] Coppe, *Some sweet sips*, p. 61.

[73] See John Reading, *The Ranters ranting* (London, 1650), pp. 1–2, 4; see also J.F. McGregor, 'The Ranters, 1649–60', University of Oxford, unpublished B.Litt Thesis (1969), p. 88.

[74] Anon., *The Sweet-Singers of Israel, or, the Family of Love* (London, 1678), p. 4; John Turner, *A sermon preached before Sr Patience Ward* (London, 1683), p. 67.

[75] Testimony of William Sambick in Parliamentary Archives, HL/PO/JO/10/1/359, no. 241, fol. 62r.

[76] John Partridge, *Detectio geniturarum* (London, 1691), p. 301; John Partridge, *A short answer to a malicious pamphlet called, A reply written by John Gadbury* (London, 1680). p. 2.

Figure 4 Detail of title page to Anon., *The Quakers dream* (London, 1655), an illustration originally used to depict Ranters revelling naked and singing new songs.

the metaphorical were collapsed, and 'song' could refer to both an outward expression and the inward disposition of the soul. Gerrard Winstanley addressed the 'despised Sons and Daughters of Zion' in a letter dated May 1648, exhorting them to learn 'three Songs, which God hath taught us, and will have us to sing in experience continually': 'The first is, fear (or rather love) God, and give glory to him. The second is, Babylon is faln, is faln, that great City Babylon is faln. And the third is Haleluja: for the Lord God omnipotent reigns'.[77] As in the case of Coppe and the Ranters, for many radicals, singing prophetically in experience was not merely silent or inward, but an outward expression with musical form. William Erbery in *The grand oppressor, or the terror of tithes* (1652), distinguished between the psalms of three different dispensations. The Hebrew Psalms 'under the Law', were 'in ryme and meter... in tune and melody', and sung by the multitude.[78] The 'Gospel Psalme' was a different thing, an utterance of praise: a psalm 'was a special gift of the spirit whereby some one filled with the Spirit and word of Christ did speak the praises of God with exceeding joy and full of Glory... but to sing in the

---

[77] Gerrard Winstanley, 'To the despised Sons and Daughters of Zion', *The breaking of the day of God* (London, 1649), dated 20 May 1648.
[78] William Erbery, *The grand oppressor, or the terror of tithes* (London, 1652), p. 25.

Gospel language is no more then to speak'.[79] Erbery seemed here to imply not, of course, that there was no singing in the churches, but that Gospel singing was no different in essence from preaching or glorifying God in spoken words. He noted (with a reference to the gradual exclusion of women from liturgical singing) that 'women were forbid to speak in the Church, much lesse to sing'.[80] In the age of the new dispensation, however, there would be an opening of divine music distinct from all that had gone before. Those 'who had a full discovery of God in them, were as the voice of Harpers harping with their Harps'; this was no longer a time for indiscriminate singing of 'Davids Psalms, the Churches songs' by the mixed congregations. It was a time for a new song: 'those who sing the song of the Lambe, have not Davids harp, but the Harpes of God, the joy of the Holy Spirit unspeakable and full of Glory'.[81]

When Erbery died in 1654, an admirer composed two new songs for 'the experimental Christian', to be set to the tunes of military ballads, which announced the renewal of the world as God revealed himself to be all in all. The first, 'Some brief Touches on the twelfth Chapter of the Revelation' was to be set to the famous and rousing royalist tune of 'When the King enjoys his own'.[82] The original lyrics designed to accompany the tune contained expressions of despair at the sight of the 'cobweb-hangings on the wall' at Whitehall, and hoped for the restoration of 'rich perfume' and 'princely train' with the return of the rightful king. The new lyrics, by contrast, were intensely apocalyptic in tone: 'The greatest Dragons tyranny, / Which cometh from the evil eye: / His Hydra's heads with crowns and horns, / May be the cheats in finest Forms; / In which we mounted hie'.[83] The second 'spiritual Song', to be set to the tune of 'Sound a charge', struck a powerfully antinomian and antiformalist note, insisting that churches should submit to the principles of love and liberty. Its effect was somewhat like that of Thomas Butler's mystical song, with repetitive ballad-like phrases. 'To him that's all, yet one', the author wrote,

>Sing with joy, sing with joy;
>Our God he is alone;
>Sing with joy.
>'Tis he blots out all sin;
>In him we joy and sing,

---

[79] Erbery, *The grand oppressor*, p. 25.

[80] Even in Reformation England, congregational psalm singing including women had been controversial, on account of the apostolic prohibition on women's speaking. See Micheline White, 'Protestant women's writing and congregational psalm singing: from the song of the exiled "Handmaid" (1555) to the countess of Pembroke's Psalmes (1599)', *Sidney Journal* 23:1–2 (2005), pp. 61–82.

[81] White, 'Protestant women's writing, pp. 25–6.

[82] 'J.L.', *A small mite, in memory of the late deceased (yet still living, and never to be forgotten) Mr William Erbery* (London, 1654), pp. 7–14.

[83] 'J.L.', *A small mite*, p. 7.

Cause we are one with him:
'Tis tidings glad we bring.
Sing with joy, sing with joy.[84]

The message of a new incarnation of Christ, prophesied by Collier, Butler, and Erbery, was taken up by a number of early Quakers, who believed that they represented the fulfilment of prophecy as the mystical new creation, the 'Church of the First-born', bearing Christ in their own bodies. A witness claimed that when James Nayler rode through the suburbs of Bristol in October 1656, he was accompanied by a group of six women and men singing ceaselessly, 'sometimes with such a buzzing mel-ODIOUS noyse that he could not understand what it was'.[85] In his testimony, as it was reported in the hostile London press, Nayler confirmed that his entourage 'sang praises to the Lord, such songs as the Lord put into their hearts'.[86] When asked, 'Wherefore didst thou and the rest sing before him, *Holy, holy, holy, Lord God of* Israel?', Nayler's follower Timothy Wedlock simply affirmed: 'I do own the Songs of *Sion*'.[87] While it is obviously problematic to use contemporary reports as evidence of the beliefs of Nayler's circle, they do seem plausible in light of other sources authored by the members of that group themselves, and in view of the Quakers' attitude to singing. These include a new song written by Nayler, his 'psalm of thanksgiving to God for his mercies' published in 1659.[88]

It is well known that the Quakers more generally excluded the congregational use of scripture psalmody, permitting only spontaneous 'singing with the Spirit'.[89] An early Quaker manuscript 'Concerning Singing, &c' vehemently opposed 'Hopkins & Sternhould's poetry who hath put David's prayers & prophecies...into Rhime & meeter with an addition of their own innovation & Lies'.[90] Mary Penington recalled how, in the early 1640s before she found her spiritual home among the Quakers, she and her first husband

> tore out of our Bibles the common prayer, the form of prayer, and also the singing psalms, as being the inventions of vain poets...We found that the songs of praise must spring from the same source as prayers did; so we could not use any one's songs or prayers.[91]

---

[84] 'J.L.', *A small mite*, p. 10. On the popularity of 'Sound a charge', see Angela McShane, 'Recruiting citizens for soldiers in seventeenth-century English ballads', *Journal of Early Modern History* 15 (2011), p. 121.

[85] Anon., *The grand impostor examined, or, The life, tryal and examination of James Nayler the seduced and seducing Quaker: with the manner of his riding into Bristol* (London, 1656), p. 2.

[86] Anon., *The grand impostor*, p. 5.   [87] Anon., *The grand impostor*, p. 31.

[88] James Nayler, *A psalm of thanksgiving to God for his mercies* (London, 1659).

[89] See Kenneth Carroll, 'Singing in the Spirit in early Quakerism', *Quaker History* 73 (1984), pp. 1–13.

[90] See Carroll, 'Singing in the Spirit', p. 3.

[91] Mary Penington, 'A brief account of some of my exercise from childhood', in David Booy, ed., *Autobiographical writings by early Quaker women* (Aldershot: Ashgate, 2004), p. 81.

Writing in 1654, Christopher Atkinson and George Whitehead also observed that liturgical psalmody made 'a Custome of other mens conditions, as to get them into rime and meeter and give them forth unto a company of blind people', causing 'poor, ignorant people [to] sing lies to the Lord' by singing experience that was not their own. To sing a metrical psalm was to perform the dead letter and silence the language of Christ, creating 'a custome like a stage play on *Davids* conditions'. The songs of the true church 'are everlasting': those who know the eternal Word 'can sing a new song... the song of redemption, and the song of *Moses*, and of the Lamb, which no man can learn, but they that are redeemed from the earth, and they that have the new name'. Interestingly, the Quakers also argued that witless psalm singing 'doest bring a Comparison of the songs of drunkards', and made 'ballades and songs' out of the experiences of the psalmist.[92]

Psalmists for the New Jerusalem

It was recognized by several contemporaries that there were notable precedents in the Hebrew scriptures for women's proclamation of God's word in song. John Arrowsmith, a leading Presbyterian theologian who served as master of St John's and Trinity College, Cambridge, at different points in the 1640s and 1650s, observed that 'women were wont to beare a part' in what he called the 'Eucharisticall Songs' of the people of Israel.[93] He mentioned Miriam's triumphal singing at Pharaoh's defeat in Exodus 15; the victory song of Deborah in Judges 5; and the townswomen who came to greet King Saul with singing and dancing in 1 Samuel 18. Arrowsmith acknowledged women's gifting, but in part to head off an increasingly troubling interpretation of Psalm 68.11:

> as if it allowed women to preach; because the word there rendred Preachers according to the old translation, *God gave the word, and great was the company of Preachers*, is a word of the feminine gender. Whereas the true meaning of Gods giving the word is his affording matter of joy and glad tydings in the course of his providence; and the Preachers spoken of are nothing else but the company of women that published the same in their songs.[94]

The Baptist minister Edward Drapes, from the Glasshouse church in London, identified the singing charism given to Miriam and Deborah with their status as 'prophetesses' (a status he was prepared to grant to women in the church, unlike

---

[92] Christopher Atkinson and George Whitehead, *Davids enemies discovered, who of him make SONGS, but without the Spirit and without understanding* (London, 1654), pp. 6–8.
[93] John Arrowsmith, *Englands Eben-ezer* (London, 1645), p. 17.
[94] Arrowsmith, *Englands Eben-ezer*, pp. 17–18.

that of preacher).[95] The affinity between women and the new singing dispensation deserves fuller consideration. The biblical examples of female prophetic singing (including not only the Old Testament prophetesses, but also the Virgin Mary) naturally lent authority and strength to the claims of women seeking to establish a prophetic voice through song. If women's preaching could easily be opposed on the basis of scriptural testimony, it was more difficult to exclude prophetic singing, in defence of which distinguished evidence of women's participation could be cited. Beyond this, however, it should be recognized that for some radical women operating in a context of dispensational apocalypticism, the biblical precedents were valuable primarily as an *anticipation* of the fuller realization of divine gifts in their own age. The female hymns of the Revolution were not merely pious devotions—far from it. In many cases, they radically asserted the apocalyptic fulfilment of women's commission to preach in the latter days.

Nowhere is this conviction expressed more forcefully than in Lady Eleanor Davies' prophetic publications. In February 1646, while Charles I was still trying to negotiate with parliament over church government, Eleanor Davies was confident that the age of English monarchy was over. In a 'new Psalm or Song', to be sung 'To the tune of the Magnificat', she addressed the authorities at Westminster, reflecting on the humiliations of her time as a 'woful prisoner' at Bedlam in 1637-8, following the scandal at Lichfield cathedral. Davies described her experiences at Bedlam as a mystical ordeal parallel to that of the Virgin Mary in childbirth. Her squalid room, with curtains and bedding riddled with holes eaten by rodent companions, was 'Bethlems Manger'; the 'Throne' of Christ the King was being made manifest to and in her.[96] The song communicated her conviction that the Holy Ghost had revealed, through Scripture and present events, 'New writ witnessed and Old', that 'the end' had come: 'When as Twenty four from Normand Race sprung, / cast their Crowns down, / Times hourglasse (as 'twere) run'. She calculated that there had been twenty-four successors to the English throne since the Conquest (a questionable figure), and concluded that England had reached the twenty-fourth 'hour' of the monarchy's day. A new day ('Moonday') was dawning, and heaven was opening, as indicated by the epigraph she took from the Vulgate's rendering of Revelation 4.1: 'Post haec vidi, & ecce ostium apertum in Caelo' (in the King James translation, 'After this I looked, and behold, a door was opened in heaven').[97] Eternity was opening up, and there would be no more 'tyrant time', people would 'worship no Throne but his alone, / besides whom King nor Priests is none'.[98] Lady Eleanor's song was a

---

[95] Edward Drapes, *Gospel-glory proclaimed before the sonnes of man* (London, 1648), p. 150.
[96] Eleanor Davies, *The gatehouse salutation from the Lady Eleanor. Revelat. cap. 4.* (London, 1646), p. 4.
[97] Davies, *The gatehouse salutation*, pp. 4, 6.   [98] Davies, *The gatehouse salutation*, p. 5.

prophecy of the liberation of the church, and of souls, from oppressive persecution and tyrannical power:

> Away with former fashions old and past:
> New Lights appear, new Song record at last;
> he that is otherwise
> at his peril,
> as he that righteous is, be he so still.
> So Gates and Prison Doors be no more shut,
> The King of Glory comes, your souls lift up.[99]

Davies expressed very clearly her apocalyptic vision of profound discontinuity between 'former fashions old and past', and the coming age of 'New Lights' and 'new Song'; the 'former things are passed away', as in Revelation 21.4. In her other writings, Davies frequently called her prophecy 'The New Song'; she addressed a Song about Babylon, to 'Sion most beloved'.[100] This coming out of Babylon was linked to the advent of women prophets:

> Former things are come to passe, and new things I declare unto you; no age so weake, nor sex excusing; when the Lord shall send and will put his words in their Mouth. He powreth out his Spirit upon his hand-maidens; the rich are sent emptie away, even so Father for it seemed good in thy sight.[101]

This prophetic gifting of women 'is as it were a new Song to be sung before the everlasting Throne, a salutation for Strangers and the Brethren'.[102]

The implications of this discontinuity for gender relations were suggested by the mystics of the Thames Valley, in the role assigned to women in the singing of the 'new song'. In his remarkable miscellany *Some sweet sips*, marked by his curious perfomative mania, Abiezer Coppe included the 'epistles' which passed between him and Thomasina Pendarves. His commentary on Pendarves' prophetic letter is heralded as: 'One of the Songs of Sion, sung immediatly, occasioned mediatly by a Prophesie and Vision of one of the Lords Handmaids, and Youngmen, Mrs T.P., and expressed by her in an Epistle'. It seems that for Coppe, visionary prose was itself a kind of 'song'. In her letter to Coppe, Thomasina Pendarves had written that 'though we are weaker vessels, women, &c. yet strength shall abound, and we shall mount up with wings as Eagles, we shall walke, and not be weary, run, and not faint, When the Man-Child Jesus is brought

---

[99] Davies, *The gatehouse salutation*, pp. 6–7.
[100] Eleanor Davies, *Amend, amend, Gods kingdome is at hand, amen, amen, the proclamation* (London, 1643), §§A1r, A3r.
[101] Eleanor Davies, *A warning to the dragon and all his angels* (London, 1646), §Aiijv.
[102] Davies, *A warning*, §Aiijv.

forth In Us'.[103] Even this somewhat mild protestation of a woman's infirmity was refused by Coppe: 'Deare friend, why doest in thy letter say, [what though we be weaker Vessels, women? &c.] I know that Male and Female are all one in Christ, and they are all one to me. I had as live heare a daughter as a sonne prophesie'.[104] Instead, Coppe exhorted his female friend: 'Sing oh Daughter, the Lord Sings In Thee'.[105] In the time of Christ's coming, it would be the end of 'slavery, and sore servitude'—they were coming in to a 'large land, a land of large (not carnall or licentious; but pure and spiritual) Liberty, when we are there, then are we free indeed'.[106] Coppe's song of Sion was a declaration of homecoming to the land of the free, for all living in love—but perhaps especially for women, given special liberty to prophesy in their new discovery of union with God. He enjoined Pendarves to break forth into new songs like Deborah, Mother in Israel:

Awake Lute, awake Harpe, awake Deborah, awake, it is a song, a song; a song of love: one of the songs of Sion, the Lords song. I am not in a strange land now, though in a strange posture, almost besides my self—in the Lord—Do I now walk with God, ... Hath God took me? O it is good to be here. Shall we build here a tabernacle? Not three, but one—one for thee, for thee, for thee, O God, my God, my song![107]

Abiezer Coppe was connected to John Pordage through the Abingdon prophetesses with whom he interacted, Elizabeth Poole and Thomasina Pendarves, and it is striking that at Bradfield Rectory, spontaneous singing by women was one of the prophetic exercises in the household.[108] In Pordage's own account of his hearing before the Berkshire Commissioners in 1654, where he stood accused of blasphemous teachings, he recalled that 'Goodwife *Pocock*' (a member of the Bradfield circle) 'singeth the highest hymns very sweetly, that she knoweth not a word when she beings, but is taken with a burning about her heart, and when she hath done, she cannot repeat a word of it, if it were to gain the world'.[109] Significantly, Pordage's wife Mary was, like Pendarves, given the new name of 'Deborah' (Figure 5), denoting her identification with the great prophetess and songstress of Israel.

The most prominent, notorious, and prolific female psalmist of the Revolution was the Fifth Monarchist visionary Anna Trapnel, who famously experienced trances during which she sang spontaneously in sublime doggerel. Her 'psalms of latter time', as she called them, were both mystical and intensely political,

---

[103] 'Extract of an Epistle sent to A.C. from Mrs T.P.', in Coppe, *Some sweet sips*, p. 40.
[104] Coppe, *Some sweet sips*, p. 46.   [105] Coppe, *Some sweet sips*, p. 53.
[106] Coppe, *Some sweet sips*, p. 51.   [107] Coppe, *Some sweet sips*, pp. 48–9.
[108] See Brod, 'Doctrinal deviance in Abingdon'.
[109] John Pordage, *Innocencie appearing through the dark mists of pretended guilt* (London, 1655), p. 16.

Figure 5 'Debora', in Pierre Le Moyne, *The gallery of heroick women* (London, 1652).

containing explicit attacks on the Protectorate. They also contained repeated assertions of the instrumental role to be played by women in confronting and dismantling the old order. In February 1654, Marchamont Nedham reported to the Protector that among the Fifth Monarchists at All Hallows the Great, Trapnel was 'much visited' by disciples, stirring up 'a world of mischief in London, and would do in the country' with the printing of 'her discourses and hymns, which are desperate against your person, family, children, friends, and the government' or else with a personal tour 'all over England, to proclaim them *vivâ voce*'.[110] She was duly arrested in Cornwall in March 1654.[111] Trapnel regarded her *extempore* songs as the defining sign of the coming kingdom, fulfilling the prophecy of Revelation 15 about the 'latter singing state'. Much of the 990-page transcript of her prophetic verse held at the Bodleian Library is concerned with the apocalyptic significance of her psalms, as women's songs, themselves.[112] At times she conflated the work of the spirit, overturning worldly powers and religious authorities, with the utterance of the psalm, accessible to the meanest sort. An example of this comes in a psalm dated November 1657, as Trapnel awaited the overturning of worldly powers and installation of a godly kingdom. Trapnel was the 'poor instrument' of divine prophecy, abused by apostates, and declared 'Against Cromwell & his Souldiers' that:

> The Psalm must come to all sorts, and
> Plain ordinary words it doth speak,
> To pluck down all that they do think
> To be so fine and compleat.
> ...O the Psalm it must break all this down,
> It must unto such go,
> It is from the true pillar that
> Strikes down the inward Foe.[113]

The personified psalm itself was to act, to break down strongholds of humane learning and unjust structures, cutting through with 'plain ordinary words'.

As well as being an agent of social levelling, Trapnel's psalm was a distinctively 'female Song', given by the Lord 'unto his handmaids' as a gesture of his favour. Merry Wiesner has argued of post-Reformation Europe that '[f]emale hymn writing became even more common in the seventeenth century when the language of hymns shifted from aggressive and martial to more emotional and pious'.[114] Trapnel the psalmist looked in both directions, adopting both a militant levelling stance, and, at times, an affective and mystical tone. She expected vindication by divine authority: 'O Lamb, wilt thou own what comes from females, / What the Spirit by them doth yield? / I that I will, saith the Lamb, for / That Song enters the

---

[110] 7 Feb. 1654, *Calendar of state papers domestic: interregnum*, vol. 66: 1653–4 (London, 1879), pp. 381–426.
[111] See Stevie Davies, 'Trapnel, Anna (fl. 1642–1660), self-styled prophet', in *Oxford dictionary of national biography*, online edition, 23 Sep. 2004.
[112] Anna Trapnel, *Poetical discourses (1657–8)*, Bodleian Library S. 1. 42. Th., p. 12.
[113] Trapnel, *Poetical discourses*, pp. 59–60.
[114] Merry Wiesner, 'Women's response to the Reformation', in R. Po-chia Hsia, ed., *The German people and the Reformation* (New York: Cornell University Press, 1988), p. 163.

field'. Just as 'Deborah sung over Sisera' and Miriam rejoiced with a song of victory, so Trapnel was the singing prophet of the new Israel's triumph over its enemies. As Sharon Achinstein has put it, 'women's hymns and songs were gendered "sound-tracks" for radical action'.[115] As Trapnel prophesied,

> ... for certain God will,
> He will deliver this day
> *Israel* from their enemy
> In a wonderous manner and way.
> For by a woman shall this thing
> For certain be brought to pass:
> It is a woman that God will
> Give this victory so high.[116]

Trapnel herself recalled that it was 'while I was singing praises to the Lord for his love to me, [that] the justices sent their constable to fetch me' in 1654, and she was subsequently declared a witch.[117]

This choice of women or 'poor things' and 'low words' was, on the face of it, an ambivalent honour: in their lowliness they exalted God, while learned men and hireling priests raised up themselves. Yet women were 'choice instruments' for the very reason that they had been downtrodden and marginalized, and their role in restoring the heavenly kingdom enhanced the miracle. Trapnel also developed the theme of the privilege of the poor and oppressed, in such a way that she suggested that God had a special love and esteem for these, to whom he had entrusted his revelation.

> Thou hast a respect very great
> To the poor, mean and low;
> And therefore thou revealest thy self
> To them, and lets them know
> Thy hidden secret mysteries,
> That are hid from prudent men:
> O such thou dost preserve, and dost
> Make known thy self to them.
> That doth make choice of poor and low
> To live in thy presence and sight!
> Thou magnifies thy self, O Lord,

---

[115] Sharon Achinstein, *Literature and dissent in Milton's England* (Cambridge: Cambridge University Press, 2003), p. 215.
[116] Trapnel, *Poetical discourses*, pp. 68–9, 212–13, 929.
[117] Anna Trapnel, *Anna Trapnel's report and plea, or, a narrative of her journey into Cornwall* (London, 1654).

> In discovering thy heart,
> And to the foolish ones thou dost
> Much of thy mind impart.
> Thou hidest from the wise and learned
> And from the prudent men
> What thou revealest unto babes,
> What thou makest known to them.[118]

Women partook in a special way in this privilege given to the poor, and Trapnel did not consider herself unique in her vocation. She was a 'handmaid to the handmaids' to whom God showed his favour. 'O thus you see that the Lord doth / Love the female indeed', she sang, 'Jesus Christ hath a regardful eye / Unto his handmaids too': Trapnel lists the elect women in the Scriptures given a leading or vital role in salvation history as a sign of God's special love or kindness to women.[119] 'God did love his Sarah dear', for instance; and 'The Lord he loved his Hannah'. Above all, he favoured Deborah, the psalm singer:

> He delighted in *Deborah*,
> And unto her did give
> That strength and courage, so as she
> Caus'd *Israel* to live.
> She as it were did new life convey,
> So much in her was seen
> Of a spirit of true Prophecie,
> When she dwelt by the Palm-trees green:...
> ...The Lord he lov'd his Deborah,
> And caused her for to sing
> A very pretious Psalm of what
> He at that time did bring.
> He at that time brought to pass by her,
> For chosen Israel,
> For Deborah among hand-Maids
> Did very much excel.[120]

Whether or not Trapnel regarded herself as the new Deborah, she did not consider her 'strange dispensation' of singing to be anomalous among her fellow handmaids, or to be in conflict with the biblical record.[121] Among the Fifth

---

[118] Trapnel, *Poetical discourses*, p. 811.   [119] Trapnel, *Poetical discourses*, p. 931.
[120] Trapnel, *Poetical discourses*, pp. 929.
[121] A 'strange dispensation' is the characterization given in the letter from B.T., in Bodleian Library, Rawlinson MS A.21, p. 325.

Monarchists, Mary Cary prophesied in verse; there were also singing visionaries in the Baptist congregations with whom Fifth Monarchists were so closely associated.

Another gifted female singer of the 1650s was the Baptist prophetess Katherine Sutton, whose prayers for spiritual anointing were rewarded in February 1655, when during a walk she 'was indued with the gift of singing, in such a way and manner as I had not been acquainted with before'.[122] She implored her readers not to despise her gift, 'because it is the Spirits working in the weaker vessel; for Christ did not reject the woman though weak, ignorant, and sinful'. Indeed, far from rejecting women, he bestowed on them special honours (Sutton shared her gifts especially with other young women), as was demonstrated in the example of Mary Magdalen, who had 'first knowledge of the resurrection', a sign of the reversal of Eve's transgression:

> Christ finished the work of his father, to take care of the weakest of his stock, that as the woman was first in the transgression, she might have first knowledge of the resurrection, the gift of the well of watter, which springs up unto everlasting life: and this guift God is pleased to give it unto women as well as unto men.[123]

Sutton was anxious to assert that her song was miraculous and spontaneous, assuring her readers that 'these are not studied things, but are given in immediately'.[124] When Hanserd Knollys wrote his preface to her *Experiences* in 1663, he commended her as a prophetess, and affirmed that psalms, like prayers, should be *extempore* utterances. Knollys reported that 'I have known some other Godly and gracious Christians...who have this gift of Singing: and I my self have some experience of this kinde of Anoynting of the Spirit of praise'. To sceptics, he insisted that 'some few poor gracious humble soules have good Experience, that there is sometimes a measure of the holy Spirit powred upon them, where by they are so filled with the Spirit, that they break forth into singing'. This was an anticipation of the time 'when the Redeemed of the Lord shall return and come with singing to Zion'.[125] Sutton's spiritual singing, and Knollys's defence of it, chimed with the anti-formalist objections to 'stinted' singing and prayers made by other radical psalmists. Knollys wrote:

> Now as to take a book and read a prayer out of it, or to say a prayer without the Book, is not to pray in the Spirit, so to read a Psalme in a Book, and sing it, or to

---

[122] Katherine Sutton, *A Christian womans experiences of the glorious working of Gods free grace* (London, 1663), pp. 12–13. On spontaneous spiritual singing in Baptist worship, see Matthew Stanton, *Liturgy and identity: London Baptists and the hymn-singing controversy* (Oxford: Centre for Baptist Studies, 2022).
[123] Sutton, *A Christian womans experiences*, p. 40.
[124] Sutton, *A Christian womans experiences*, p. 44.
[125] Sutton, *A Christian womans experiences*, p. 44.

sing the same Psalme without the Book is not to sing in the Spirit: If the singing of Psalmes be a part of Gods worship (as doubtless it is) then it ought to be performed by assistance of the spirit, for the true worshippers ought to worship God in spirit and truth.[126]

Knollys insisted that 'The holy Spirit can dictate the Matter, yea and words of praise and singing, as well as the matter and words of prayer'.[127] This opposition between in-the-spirit and spiritless worship corresponded to a wider antithesis between grace and law, freedom and tyranny, which, in some more radical accounts, had great significance for women's ministry.

This liberative narrative emerges powerfully in the *True account of the great tryals and cruel sufferings* of two Quaker missionaries, Katharine Evans and Sarah Cheevers, including their letters, writings, and experiences while imprisoned by the Maltese Inquisition for preaching in the late 1650s, concludes with a series of 'victorious Hymns and Songs, and Praises, all in Verse; The same sprung from the Seed of Life, its perfect Righteousness'.[128] The first song is a prophecy of judgement on Antichrist and the hard-hearted, who persecute 'his little ones', but others proclaim the descent of the New Jerusalem, the advent of 'perfect Love and Unity', and the opening of the gates of heaven so 'That all may come / I'th free-born Son, / (Th'Light) to dwell in your Land'.[129] Their own testimonies and newly composed hymns are introduced by a remarkable prefatory epistle by Daniel Baker, who offers a coherent but undoubtedly radical apology for women's ministry in terms of the Christian's progression from Law to Grace. Corresponding to Quaker thought more widely, the 'seed' is Christ within; Baker appears to make a gendered distinction between the seed in men and women: it is 'in the Male Christ, in the Female, the quickening Spirit, the Lord from Heaven', but these are in effect identical concepts. 'Christ in the male, the same in the female, where He is risen and manifest as King, Priest, and Prophet'.[130] Where the seed is the guiding principle, women 'are not under the Law, which saith, the woman is not to usurp authority over the man'. Under the freedom of 'Grace and Truth', those in whom 'the Man-Child, the holy Child Jesus', is 'begotten of God in the female, as well as in the male', are no longer subject to the law which stipulates that 'Woman is to be under obedience'.[131] Baker observed that women are enjoined to 'learn in silence, and to ask her Husband at home'. But what, he asked, 'if she have a disorderly drunken Husband (and not Christ the Man, the

---

[126] Hanserd Knollys, preface to the 'Courteous Reader', in Sutton, *A Christian womans experiences*, §*2r–v.
[127] Knollys, preface to the 'Courteous Reader', §*2v.
[128] Daniel Baker and Katharine Evans, *A true account of the great tryals and cruel sufferings undergone by those two faithful servants* (London, 1663), p. 88.
[129] Baker and Evans, *A true account*, pp. 90, 101.   [130] Baker and Evans, *A true account*, §A5r.
[131] Baker and Evans, *A true account*, §§A4v, A5v.

true Husband, the true Lord) how can he teach her'?[132] Evans and Cheevers notably both travelled to Malta under their own steam, without their respective husbands and children, to whom they wrote warm letters. These masterless women spent their time in prison like Paul and Silas, the apostolic missionaries whose miraculous escape is recorded in Acts 16, preaching, praying, and singing hymns. At one point, at Easter 1662, they fasted from bread and water for three days, when their captors were feasting on meat, and stripped down to their petticoats. Eventually, they broke their fast, and sang a new hymn to the bridegroom, 'A Sion Song of Glory bright'.[133]

The significance of new songs in the period of the English Revolution not only as 'battle hymns of the republic', but as prophetic texts, has been set out by several literary scholars and historians.[134] In this chapter, I have sought to contribute to an understanding of these experimental forms, by illustrating the extent to which they were symbolic markers of a new dispensation, a new age of direct experience of and full communion with the divine. This conception of inspired singing as an apocalyptic sign took its cue not only from prophetic scripture and apocalyptic interpretations of the psalms, but also, it seems likely, from traditions in Familism and spiritual anabaptism. Women, it is argued, played a critical proclamatory role as singing instruments of the Spirit. Their prophetic song signalled that the new age was not only one in which females would be endowed with authority of speech, but also one in which the alienated and oppressed would be liberated and repatriated to Sion, brought to a spiritual homecoming in mystical union and the full freedom of the experience of grace.

---

[132] Baker and Evans, *A true account*, §A5v.   [133] Baker and Evans, *A true account*, pp. 228–32.
[134] See Smith, *Literature and Revolution*, p. 260; Achinstein, *Literature and dissent*, pp. 214–17.

6
Church

This chapter examines the gendered dimensions of the confrontation between mystical radicals and ecclesiastical institutions in the English Revolution. It explores how the radicals' disruptive understanding of Christian communion, the anthropology which supported that understanding, and their abandonment of clerical hierarchy contributed to an environment hospitable to female participation. This was the wholesale repudiation of a spiritual system in which male ministers had privileged access to the sacred at every level, even in the Reformed churches. Male clergy had the monopoly over the celebration and distribution of the sacraments; over preaching; over the interpretation of Scripture (through their possession of biblical languages); over the governance of the church. The mystical radicals, in their challenge to the professional ministry and to the instrumentality of authorized sacraments, and in their advocacy of lay, uneducated, and female preachers, took significant steps in disturbing patriarchal institutions. The female prophets described their departure from the ordinances of the mainstream churches in terms of coming 'out of the wilderness', a spiritual homecoming. I also consider afresh the influence on this anti-confessionalism in the English Revolution of two sixteenth-century radical traditions: the Family of Love and Paracelsianism. Both movements had deeply spiritualist ecclesiologies, and irenic or quietistic tendencies in other European settings. In an environment of revolutionary aspirations and apocalyptic hopes, the gendered language and themes of Familist and Paracelsian spiritualism took on a harder, more confrontational and separatist, edge.

Out of the Wilderness

Themes of exile and estrangement shaped early modern spirituality (both Catholic and Protestant) from the questing early years of the Reformations, through generations afflicted by violent conflict, exclusion, and martyrdom. Identification with the displaced people of Israel—wandering in the wilderness, or grieving in Babylon—ran deep, especially in the Reformed churches and among radical separatists. In mystical reform movements, motifs of wilderness and exile spoke to a powerful sense of alienation from the confessional politics of the magisterial churches in the sixteenth and seventeenth centuries. Reformers on both sides of the confessional divide, as various as Andreas Osiander, Jean de

Labadie, and Bartolomé de Carranza, would discover that the line between the pursuit of spiritual renewal within the churches and the experience of exclusion for mystical heresy was easily crossed. As spirituality itself became more rigidly confessionalized, in important cases (such as that of Labadie, traced so evocatively by de Certeau), the experience of marginalization led to an effort to extract the spirit of Christianity, the mystical heart of true, timeless, universal Christian religion, from specific institutional frameworks in which it was subordinated to worldly agendas and powers.

A distinctive sensibility, strongly mystical in character, surfaced in the expressions of spiritual alienation and displacement sent forth in print by army preachers and spiritualist radicals during the wars in the three kingdoms of the British Isles, and their aftermath. This was not always simply a complaint about the persecuting national church and the abuse of consciences, a political case for toleration, although the protest against spiritual oppression was certainly present and clearly articulated. This chapter identifies in radical texts a lament for divine absence, the divestment of God's spiritual presence from the institutions and teachings of Christendom in general; and a triumphal proclamation of communion in the Spirit, in the corporate body of the saints: what some radicals called the 'church of the first-born'.[1] I explore how the language and imagery of these texts drew from Paracelsian and Familist influences, illustrating how ideas subversive of the confessional institutions, which were quietistic and irenical in one environment, could inspire revolutionary impulses—including radical thinking about women and gender—in another. The responses of female and female-affirming radicals to the ecclesiastical crisis of the period tended to include a vision of Christ returning to his spiritual temple, in the flesh of the saints, both male and female. A spiritual ecclesiology together with this eschatological narrative provided essential context for women's participation, and for the mystical spirituality which sustained radical dissent. This account of the translation of the Gospel-church to a higher state of spiritual union, and of a mystical homecoming from Babylon, or from wandering in the wilderness, chimed with the prophet's sense of alienation from a hierarchical structure with a learned male clergy at its helm. The radical mystics understood 'mystical Babylon', and Antichrist, primarily as spiritual states within each soul, though this did not exclude the diagnosis of Babylonish and anti-Christian diseases in the established institutions and legal demands of the churches: indeed, internal and external Babylon were profoundly interlinked. In

---

[1] See, for instance, Robert Bacon, *Christ mighty in himself & members revealed* (London, 1646), p. 160; Thomas Collier, *A general epistle to the universal church of the first born* (London, 1649); Ambrose Rigge, *To the whole flock of God everywhere, the church of the first born* (London, 1660). On the use of the phrase as a reference to the 'universall assembly' of the mystical church, see also Ariel Hessayon, 'Abiezer Coppe and the Ranters', in Laura Lunger Knoppers, ed., *The Oxford handbook of literature and the English Revolution* (Oxford: Oxford University Press, 2012), p. 364. The phrase 'church of the first-born' would also be used routinely self-referentially by the Quakers, including James Nayler and Robert Rich.

certain biographical instances, such as those of Pinnell, Sedgwick, or indeed John Everard (a Puritan firebrand in the 1620s before his interest in mystical theology developed), a mystical ecclesiology represented the outworking of impulses shared with the separatist wing of Puritanism.[2] Coming 'out of Babylon' initiated the process of examining the legitimacy and spirituality of all ordinances.

Assessments of the role of radical spiritualism and mystical theology in early modern religious change have sometimes revealed an underlying, seductively nostalgic narrative of the loss of Christian community and cohesion. Ernst Troeltsch characterized mysticism or 'spiritualism' after the Reformation as a 'social type' of religion, not quite either ecclesiastical or sectarian but in an unstable relation to both forms of organization. Although personally attracted to the non-dogmatic quality of 'spiritual religion', Troeltsch wrote that it 'tends to sweep away the historical element altogether', becoming 'non-historical, formless, and purely individualistic'.[3] Troeltsch's critical judgement of the mystical type was that it was essentially parasitical: it 'creates no community, since it possesses neither the sense of solidarity nor the faith in authority which this requires nor the no less necessary fanaticism and desire for uniformity. It lives on and in communities which have been brought into existence by other, ruder energies'.[4] It was a narrative that captured the imagination of scholars writing, in the later twentieth century. Steven Ozment's 1973 study of mystical dissent in the Reformation, while in some respects celebratory, nonetheless concluded that its legacy was 'not only tolerance of diversity but also rejection of bureaucracy, not only the integrity of the individual but also the depersonalization of social institutions, not only a firm sense of self but also scorn for imperfect community'. For Ozment, 'It is not too much to say that in [mystical] dissent the seeds of social disintegration are as prominent as those of individual liberation'.[5] He argued that the roots of this social disintegration lay in an unexpected 'liaison' between late-medieval nominalism and mystical theology. Both led to scepticism, not only about the power of natural reason to apprehend God, but also about the use of established earthly instruments, the basic building blocks of Christian community, as the means by which God revealed himself and wrought salvation in the world. The hierarchical, propertied, political church, involved in the secular world in all

---

[2] See Richard Thomas Bell, 'The minister, the millenarian, and the madman: the Puritan lives of William Sedgwick, ca. 1609-1664', *Huntington Library Quarterly* 81:1 (2018), pp. 29-61.
[3] Ernst Troeltsch, *The social teaching of the Christian churches*, trans. O. Wyon, 2 vols. (London: George Allen & Unwin, Ltd, 1931), pp. 743, 83.
[4] Troeltsch, *The social teaching*, p. 796. See Johannes Zachhuber, 'Mysticism as a social type of Christianity? Ernst Troeltsch's interpretation in its historical and systematic context', in Louise Nelstrop and Simon Podmore, eds., *Exploring lost dimensions in Christian mysticism: opening to the mystical* (Farnham: Ashgate, 2013), pp. 69-84.
[5] Steven Ozment, *Mysticism and dissent: religious ideology and social protest in the sixteenth century* (New Haven, CT: Yale University Press, 1973), p. 247.

its aspects, was from this perspective antithetical to divine power and wisdom. Ozment explained,

> In the late Middle Ages one did not have to be a learned theologian to know that God had spoken more authoritatively through persecuted prophets, ragged ascetics, and even a braying ass than through the religious authorities who lay claim to his truth. He was a God who dwelt more intimately among those who deny the world in body and in spirit than among those who attempt to run it from the pulpit and by the sword.[6]

'Holy fools' made their incursions upon the ground—authority and revelation—traditionally possessed by the ecclesiastical institution. This 'raw material for dissent' in late-medieval thought was, for Ozment, realized in the anti-intellectual and anti-institutional strain of Reformation spiritualism.[7] The spiritualist challenge represented a form of iconoclasm which did not simply deface the trinkets of the old order—the dumb statues and icons masquerading as sacred objects—but challenged the very framework holding together traditional Christian society, exposing 'the penultimate character' of its institutions.[8]

These judgements on mystical dissent as fundamentally anti-social, a disintegrating force, tend to overlook the inequalities and burdens imposed by traditional society, as well as the powerful calls for solidarity and justice which surfaced within the mystical challenge. It is telling that one of Ozment's other major works was a celebratory account of the Reformation family and especially Protestant fatherhood; reformed social institutions seen very differently by feminist historians, notably Lyndal Roper.[9] If mystical religion pulled at the threads of social, ecclesiastical, and ideological uniformity (however desirable or genuinely integrative such uniformity might be), more positively it provided a channel for intellectual challenge and symbolic disruption. The critique of traditional authority mounted by apocalyptic mysticism could be vigorous, and well placed, even while its offering by way of substitute was a vision of the 'golden city', an ideal heavenly community in which all were equal. As Ozment concluded,

> For our dissenters final authority lay in principle with the individual, the invisible, the ethically ideal, the perfect community—things no earthly society could ever be. When the values and goals of mystical theology were gathered into

---

[6] Ozment, *Mysticism and dissent*, p. 2; see also Steven Ozment, 'Mysticism, nominalism, and dissent', in Charles Trinkaus and Heiko Oberman, eds., *The pursuit of holiness in the late Middle Ages and Renaissance* (Leiden: Brill, 1973), pp. 67–92.
[7] Ozment, *Mysticism and dissent*, p. 247.   [8] Ozment, *Mysticism and dissent*, p. 246.
[9] Steven Ozment, *When fathers ruled: family life in Reformation Europe* (Cambridge, MA: Harvard University Press, 1983); Lyndal Roper, *The holy household: women and morals in Reformation Augsburg* (Oxford: Clarendon Press, 1989).

the arsenal of dissent, the institutional links with truth were severely weakened, if not severed altogether. A *translatio imperii* from institutional to anthropological structures, from official to experiential criteria, from traditional to ethical norms of authority was undertaken.... History failed the test of eternity. Were not princes ravenous predators, government the Devil, learned scholars sophists, priests mindless lackeys, the masses slaves of Bacchus, the written word a fleeting shadow, the traditional rite an affront to God, temporal things the excrement of stars?[10]

Such idealistic challenges should not be too easily dismissed as failing the test of social and political utility. They would, of course, provide the utopian foundation for many programmes for social and political renewal—including feminist reformism—in later generations. The language of the 'new Jerusalem' would characterize the prospect of practical transformations to society well into the twentieth century, not least in the English political sphere. One of Ozment's more powerful insights in *Mysticism and dissent*, an insight I regard as vital for understanding the evolutions and trajectories of spiritualist nonconformity in seventeenth-century England, is that the distinction between quietistic dissent (or 'nicodemism') on the one hand, and sectarian separation or even violent resistance on the other was not absolute. Both withdrawal and confrontation reflected a fundamental resituating of authority. As Ozment put it eloquently: 'quietism Is no less negative a judgment on established power than violent revolution. Mystical salvation is the discovery of the final power and authority of the Self within one's own self'.[11]

The post-Reformation movement best known for its nicodemism was, of course, the Family of Love, the network which shared a strongly allegorical, spiritualized reading of the Scriptures and a spirituality of deification: the 'Godding' and 'Christing' of believers, or their transformation into the essence of divinity. A recent article by David Como examines the evidence provided to the Laudian regime by Giles Creech, a cutler, of a Familist network operating in late 1630s London. Como's reconstruction of this network and its wider associations offers intriguing indications of connections which help to account for the penetration of these ideas and their public articulation in the 1640s. Among those identified as leading Familists were the mystical preacher, John Everard, and Henry Faldo, brother-in-law of John Pordage.[12] Although this evidence does not demonstrate definitively that radical circles were influenced by Familism as early

---

[10] Ozment, *Mysticism and dissent*, p. 247.   [11] Ozment, *Mysticism and dissent*, p. 12.
[12] See David Como, 'The Family of Love and the making of English Revolutionary religion: the confession and "conversions" of Giles Creech', *Journal of Medieval and Early Modern Studies* 48:3 (2018), pp. 553–98; see also Ariel Hessayon, 'Pordage, John (bap. 1607, d. 1681, religious leader and physician', in David Cannadine, ed., *Oxford dictionary of national biography* (Oxford: Oxford University Press, 2004).

as the 1630s, it certainly points in that direction, and supports other, later indications of influence: not least the printing of works by Hendrik Niclaes by Giles Calvert, and the presence of distinctive Familist themes in radical theology.

An important motif for Familism was that of the spiritual wilderness, in which the true church of Christ was desolate and displaced, after the 'woman in the wilderness' of Revelation 12. The verb 'Wilderness' or 'Bewilderness' seems to be a distinctively Familist term, used by the translator of Niclaes's 'The glasse of righteousnes', which described the 'Wildernessed' state of the Old Testament patriarchs as they awaited the spiritual tabernacle of Christ.[13] It was also adopted by the translator of Hiël in his 'Declaration of the revelation of John', an anonymous manuscript translation dating from the 1650s, where he writes that 'the Love of God (as I said) keepeth herself secret and hidden in the wildernessed heart of the humanitie'.[14] Translations of Niclaes in print contrasted the wilderness of the carnal world with the heavenly kingdom of peace.[15] Implicitly and explicitly, the imagery of the wilderness pointed towards an eschatological hope: the homecoming. The writings of Niclaes and others were full of apocalyptic longing, for the time when 'God shall at his tyme; accomplish it all in the last dayes'.[16] 'Christian ceremonies', wrote Niclaes, in a prophecy republished by Giles Calvert in 1649, 'were not the everlasting commandment of God'; they were meant as gateways, to usher in a new 'ministration', the 'service of love now in the last time'.[17] The evidence of religious conflict was that 'the former Christian ceremonies after the Letter, do bring in controversie', and they would pass away in the age in which Christ would return to his spiritual tabernacle, the heart.[18] In the meantime, the wilderness signified the alienation and disorientation of the human spirit, under institutional churches or 'ministrations' from which God had withdrawn his sacred presence. These 'ceremonies of the Law' would be overtaken by the knowledge of 'the Grace of God, come unto Us, now in the last time, according to the Promises' (Figure 6).[19]

The Familist belief in a new 'ministration' or 'service of the love' was identified by an earlier generation of scholars (chiefly A.L. Morton and, following him, Christopher Hill), with the 'Everlasting Gospel', a teaching which influenced

---

[13] H.N., 'The glasse of righteousnes', Bodleian Library, Rawlinson MS C. 544, §A2v. Interestingly, it is a term also employed by John Pordage's most prominent female associate, the prophetess Jane Lead, *Ascent to the mount of vision* (London, 1699), p. 38, to describe the natural earth before the spiritual renewal of all things.

[14] Hiël, 'Declaration of the revelation of John', Cambridge University Library, Additional MS 2806, p. 133.

[15] See Hendrik Niclaes, *A publishing of the peace upon earth* (Cologne, 1574), pp. 4–5; and Hendrik Niclaes, *Terra Pacis: a true testification of the spiritual land of peace* (London, 1649), references throughout.

[16] H.N., 'The glasse of righteousnesse', §B1r.

[17] Hendrik Niclaes, *The prophecy of the spirit of love set forth by H.N.* (London, 1649), pp. 244–5.

[18] Niclaes, *The prophecy of the spirit*, p. 246.   [19] Niclaes, *The prophecy of the spirit*, pp. 255, 35.

Figure 6 God and man, in Hendrik Niclaes, *A figure of the true and spiritual tabernacle* (London, 1655), p. 109.

many radical thinkers in the 1640s.[20] This was the idea that a new dispensation in salvation history was being instituted: conceived by some as a third age of the

---

[20] See A.L. Morton, *The everlasting Gospel: a study in the sources of William Blake* (London: Lawrence and Wishart, 1958); Christopher Hill, *The experience of defeat: Milton and some contemporaries* (London and New York: Verso, 1984).

Spirit, after the ages of Law and Gospel, in a Trinitarian scheme which bore more than a passing resemblance to the eschatology of the twelfth-century Cistercian abbot, Joachim of Fiore. There are indications that this Familist sensibility flowed in with the free-grace teachings and mystical currents of the Revolution, as a sense of apocalyptic fulfilment gave rise to the belief that the church was coming out of the wilderness. Christians were coming out of the 'ministration' of the Law associated with the Father, into the 'Service of the Love' associated with the Holy Spirit. The radical preacher John Saltmarsh wrote evocatively in 1647 in the language of Isaiah 13.21, of God's abandonment of the 'present ministration':

> [W]hen the line of Gods season was run out to its point and extremity, that he would no longer stay there, nor have his glory inhabit in such or such a ministration, then that ministration became but a place of desolation, a solitary place for the Satyrs to dwell in, and the screech Owle to sing in, that is for the Spirit of Apostacy and of Antichrist or iniquity to possesse and act in.[21]

William Erbery, who had been condemned with Saltmarsh for heresy by Sion College in December 1644 (alongside John Milton and the Socinian John Biddle, among others), similarly wrote of a wilderness state in which Christians were alienated from divine life.[22] As he wrote in 1652, the 'scattered Saints, are weeping and full of sorrow, in their bewildernessed state'; they 'cannot sing one of the songs of Zion, they being in a strange land, not in the life of God alone, but living still in Babylon, in flesh and self, in which they feel themselves imbondaged'.[23]

As Morton and Hill suggested, the apocalyptic dimension in Familism appears to have contributed to the radical disavowal of ordinances by the mystical sects. Laments about the wilderness state under the old ordinances are everywhere echoed in the radical religious literature of the period, but nowhere more loudly than in John Rogers' 1653 work *Ohel or Beth-shemesh* (with its lengthy defence of women's ministry). Rogers observed that 'hitherto hath many a sad soule sate and sign'd, yea and the Church in the Wildernesse too bewayl'd with Mary, weeping, Joh. 20.13. Oh! They have taken away my Lord, and I know not where they have laid him'.[24] He urged his readers to escape 'out of Babylon, flye into Sion, into the Fellowship and Church-Way of the Gospel, wherein Christ is King'.[25] The wilderness state had been endured since the fourth century, when the church lost its 'primitive face':

---

[21] John Saltmarsh, *Sparkles of glory* (London, 1647), pp. 74–5.

[22] See Richard L. Greaves, *Glimpses of glory: John Bunyan and English dissent* (Stanford: Stanford University Press, 2002), p. 23.

[23] William Erbery, *A call to the churches; or, a packet of letters to the Pastors of Wales, presented to the baptized teachers there* (London, 1652), p. 17.

[24] John Rogers, *Ohel or Beth-shemesh: a tabernacle for the sun* (London, 1653), p. 16.

[25] Rogers, *Ohel or Beth-shemesh*, p. 17.

the Church was now cloathed with enough of outward beauty; riches, greatnesse, and ornaments, were in abundance, which bewitched many from the Truth, and which proved the most irresistible temptations that could be, to corrupt Magistrates, Ministers, People, Ordinances, and all her worship... and to bewildernesse her.[26]

Again, 'bewildernesse' is the verb (a distinctively Familist word, I suggest, found nowhere outside Familist and radical texts) used for the corruption of the primitive church. On the basis of Thomas Brightman's intepretation of Revelation 11–12, Rogers suggested that the 'Discipline of the Church should begin to be restored unto her primitive face and fairness' around 1643 years after Christ:

about which time her Deliverance and Freedome came running in, and the Congregationall Churches got upon their feete, and began to look forth as the morning, Cant. 6.10 though many black Clouds and Mists were cast upon them some ten yeares agoe, to grieve them... But Master Brightmans judgement is, to have it begin one thousand six hunded and fifty... in which yeares he fore-told the true Discipline of the Church should begin to be restored unto her primitive face and fairnesse.[27]

The time of the church's 'deliverance' from the wilderness was therefore now. What would this restored, primitive discipline look like? Rogers contrasted the wilderness—a place neglected, barren, disorientating, dangerous, deprived, oppressive—with the 'Eden' of God's promise, the enclosed and fruitful garden where Christ and the saints enjoy 'a communion of love'.[28]

The mystical radicals of the Revolution shared this narrative of the heart's repatriation from an alienated state, as Christ was spiritually manifest in little 'temples' or 'tabernacles'; not as counterparts to the institutional church, but in a mystical communion superseding ecclesiastical structures. Such a vision resonated with the female prophets who published with Giles Calvert in the period after 1646, for whom it contained a liberative significance and a strong imperative to tolerate diversity and dissent. The period in which a number of female prophets published for the first time, 1647–8, was a time of intense debate about toleration and the role of the magistrate in safeguarding the orthodox church. Rhetoric against clerical tyranny had been escalating in the 1640s to a high pitch. The radical pamphleteer Michael Quintyne, a public advocate of religious toleration and the removal of the secular power or 'Caesar' from ecclesiastical affairs since 1641, wrote in 1645 of the oppression of the magisterial church 'under a spirituall Aegypt and Babylon, the great cathedrall State that compels all high and lowe, rich

[26] Rogers, *Ohel or Beth-shemesh*, p. 21.
[27] Rogers, *Ohel or Beth-shemesh*, p. 20.
[28] Rogers, *Ohel or Beth-shemesh*, p. 42.

and poore, bond and free, to be subject or to perish, by deprivation of humane rights'. Violence was done to consciences 'under guilded conformitie and uniformitie with forced hypocrisie in a way of Religion'.[29] In common with other mystical radicals, not least Winstanley, Quintyne thought in terms of a correlation between 'the Mystery of Iniquitie' (meaning violence or tyranny) in the 'personall or particular; and the publique or politicall part'. The overcoming of both spiritual and political wellsprings of Antichrist 'helps to gain and preserve the welfare of man in generall'.[30] It is striking that for Quintyne, an undeservedly little-known commentator on state-church relations, ecclesiastical tyranny was framed as anti-*human*, not just anti-Christian, sin.

By 1647, this polemical stance was adopted by the Independents against the Presbyterians, the new magisterial reformers in town. Anti-clerical language was used even by the most irenical of Independents, such as Walter Cradock, who inveighed against those ministers who 'take all power into their owne hands; and to leave the people, and call them the laity, the drosse, the vulgar, to leave them as vassalls, and slaves, and to call themselves, the Clergie, and the Church, and the like'.[31] William Erbery, writing after the regicide but looking back on the events of the late 1640s, suggested that the three types of secular government—monarchy, aristocracy, and democracy—were paralleled in three types of church government: the

> Prelatick Church was Monarchicall, all were ruled by one, by an Arch-Bishop, the Kingly Power or Prerogative fell by that: The Presbyterian Church is an Aristocracy, the Elders or chief of these govern as 'twere in a Parliament... The Independent, or baptized Churches (both as one) are a pure Democracy, for not the ruling men, or Ministers, but all the Members, have equall power.[32]

The rise of Independency, or congregationalism, and religious toleration would correspond to the ascendancy of democracy. For Erbery, this development also mapped onto a progression in English preaching from 'low and legall' doctrines, namely classical Puritanism (represented by, among others, William Perkins and Nicholas Byfield); to 'the Doctrine of free Grace' (taught by Richard Sibbes and Tobias Crisp, placed interestingly alongside each other by Erbery); to 'the letter of Scripture, and the flesh of Christ', or the external, historical Christ (in John Goodwin); to the discovery of 'Christ in the Spirit', the 'holy of holiest', by the army preachers: Dell, Sedgwick, Sterry, Sprigg.[33] There was a direct relationship,

---

[29] Michael Quintyne, *A short discovery of the mystery of iniquitie* (London, 1645), p. 6.
[30] Quintyne, *A short discovery*, p. 6.
[31] Walter Cradock, *Glad tydings from heaven, to the worst of sinners* (London, 1648), pp. 30–1.
[32] William Erbery, *The grand oppressor, or the terror of tithes* (London, 1652), pp. 23–4.
[33] Erbery, *The grand oppressor*, pp. 31–2.

for Erbery, between the levelling spiritual doctrine of mystical union, and the collapse of patriarchal institutions in church and state.

Radical women were among the early advocates of toleration in the public sphere. Katherine Chidley wrote her *Justification of the Independent churches*, a partial defence of toleration, in 1641, in an all-out attack on the writings on church government by the heresy-hating Presbyterian Thomas Edwards. Chidley described ecclesiastical canon law as 'the Discipline of Antichrist', to be cast off at 'the bright comming of Christs Kingdome (into the hearts of men)'.[34] She suggested that the New Testament ordinances had become 'apostate' under the magisterial churches, to be recovered by later generations 'when God should by his Spirit direct them to know the same'.[35] The supremacy and freedom of the Holy Spirit over the church was central to this justification. It was the call of the Holy Ghost, not the will of church officials, that authorized ministers, Chidley's case for toleration was limited to Independent congregations which 'performe Christs publike worship', and she did not envisage religious freedom as expansively as did some women writing at a time of possibility after the abolition of the episcopacy.[36] Mary Cary published for the first time in 1647, with the intent to 'condemn that Antichristian principle in Popery, to injoyn all to beleeve as the Church beleeves'; and deny that 'the Civill Magistrate by any power or force... should go about to suppress' those in error.[37] Elizabeth Avery, a member of John Rogers' Dublin congregation by 1652, set out a similarly apocalyptic critique of persecution in her exegesis of the book of Daniel in 1647. The spirit of 'Babylon and Antichrist is over all states which govern by an Arbitrary power', and all worship 'that comprehends all'.[38] The Babylonian church (whether episcopal or Presbyterian) 'slays the people of God with the sword of the heart', by her 'vile reproaches' and 'cruel hatred': this was a spiritual tyranny, over souls, not merely restrictive of personal freedoms.[39] She alluded obliquely to 'violence done unto the Saints' in the spring of 1647; apparently a reference to the Presbyterian reaction against Independency and its close ally in the cause of toleration, army radicalism.[40] This was not exactly a pacific vision of freedom of conscience, however: Avery prophesied that the saints will endeavour 'by force and might, to heal Babel'.[41] Anne Yemans, writing in 1648, adopted a more irenical tone and implicitly supported toleration, insisting that God was not in the possession of one particular party, but that each group or opinion within the church had its own share of the truth. She urged her readers,

---

[34] Katherine Chidley, *The justification of the independent churches of Christ* (London, 1641), §*2r.
[35] Chidley, *The justification*, p. 5.   [36] Chidley, *The justification*, p. 20.
[37] Mary Cary, *A word in season to the kingdom of England* (London, 1647), pp. 9–10.
[38] Elizabeth Avery, *Scripture-prophecies opened: which are to be accomplished in these last times, which do attend the second coming of Christ* (London, 1647), p. 2.
[39] Avery, *Scripture-prophecies opened*, p. 4.   [40] Avery, *Scripture-prophecies opened*, p. 15.
[41] Avery, *Scripture-prophecies opened*, p. 9.

bee not troubled, because thou seest many several opinions in the world, for God is not limited to any one of them; for God hath, and will reveal his whole mind to his Church: but every particular one knows but in part, and opinions are but the shels: let us not strive for them.[42]

Spiritual Antichrist, for Yemans, 'doth tyrannize over us all, some in one way, and some in another', and it is this tyrannical spirit which 'causeth us to despise and undervalue one another, for that which is of God is loving and kind to all'.[43] Yemans' pluralist ethic chimes with that of Anna Trapnel, who sang in one of her prophetic trances about the free-ranging, inclusionary spirit of God, who 'takes all the parts of Christ, / He takes the whole body', unlike the clergy and scholars who 'are so fastned to one part, / That the whole they cannot take in'.[44]

In Avery's account, the true, spiritual church had been 'brought into the wildernesse' for a season, like the woman clothed with the sun after delivering her child, but a 'glorious state of the Church...shall follow'. Yemans described the 'spirituall wildernesse that Christ brings his Saints into, before hee giveth them a full possession of Canaan, that is, that glorious inheritance, which is Christ'. Somewhat in contrast to Avery and Cary, who identified Babylon and mystical Antichrist with Rome and ecclesiastical hierarchy, Yemans tended more to spiritualize and internalize the dominion of Antichrist, in sympathy with Familist ideas. For Yemans, 'The church of God hath been in the wildernesse ever since Anti-christ began to reigne: and Anti-christ is that which is like Christ, yet opposeth Christ, and it began in the Apostles dayes'.[45] The wilderness condition is cold and comfortless, but an essential, purgatorial spiritual process; rather like the mystics' dark night of the soul:

> A wildernesse is a barren place; he will strippe us of all our excellent things, so far as it is not purely of himselfe; hee will come with the North-winde, and nip, and deaden, and blast all our most excellent performances, that wee shall have nothing to trust to, but see our selves in a barren condition like a wilderness.[46]

Similarly, Mary Cary wrote in 1648 of the church as having been 'driven into the wildernesse: that is, into a desolate, bewildred, barren, and sad condition'. It was impossible 'for the Church to be in any other then a wildernesse condition, untill the ruine of the Beast, and the fall of Babylon'.[47] Elizabeth Avery was dismissive of

---

[42] Anne Yemans, *Crooked pathes made straight: or, the wayes of God made knowne to lost sinners, or bewildered saints* (London, 1648), p. 183.
[43] Yemans, *Crooked pathes made straigh*, p. 186.
[44] Anna Trapnel, *Poetical discourses* (1657–8), Bodleian Library S. 1. 42. Th, p. 786.
[45] Yemans, *Crooked pathes made straight*, p. 187.
[46] Yemans, *Crooked pathes made straight*, p. 187.
[47] Mary Cary, *The resurrection of the witnesses and Englands fall from (the mystical Babylon) Rome* (London, 1648), pp. 56–7.

those who, like the people of Israel, thought 'that it is best for them to continue still in Babylon; especially those who do not onely live under the Ordinances, but in them, in abundance of sensible consolation'.[48] On the other hand, the wilderness was identified as a place of temporary spiritual refuge for the saints: 'that place of safety in which the spiritual man doth reside, which is God himself, who does manifest his presence most unto his Saints in their desolate and disconsolate condition'.[49] Her definition of the empire of Babylon was quite comprehensive: 'Babylon and Antichrist is over all States which govern by an Arbitrary power, and over all Churches, whether National or others, and all Worship'.[50] Babylon was virtually synonymous with the institutional church: even that which is 'most agreeable to the letter of the Word'; rather startlingly, she affirmed that 'Babylon is in the purest worship'.[51] There was, however, a specific instantiation of the rule of Babylon: it 'doth more mystically appear to be in this present State and Church of England'.[52] Mary Cary was more precise about the ways in which the kingdom of England, which had of course 'cast of the Popes supremacy' long before the 1640s, remained part of the mystical Babylon: it continued to 'enslave, and vassalize the Saints', and 'exercise authority over the consciences of Saints'.[53]

Avery, Cary, and Yemans adopted in essence the structure of Familist eschatology. Their account of a new divine manifestation shared many features with that of William Erbery, as well as Familist writings. Avery came to the conclusion that the great crisis in which she and others found herself was not only caused by the apostasy of the 'National Church of England', which had 'no rule from the Word for what they practise', but the empire of Babylon in all the churches which recognized the authority of the outward letter, while denying that of the living temples of Christ. Only in the individual saints could Babylon or Antichrist be overcome, and the saints come into 'their own Country' from the wilderness, for Christ was not manifest in the external forms of the churches. Souls would be in a state of exile 'till God is manifested in the flesh of the Saints, as he was in the Humanity of Christ'.[54] As Mary Cary explained in *The resurrection of the witnesses*, the temple was a 'figure' of the living church in the Saints of God: 'as God was in a speciall manner present in that Temple, so he is in a speciall manner present in his people'.[55] Yemans likewise described the saints as Christ's 'spirituall building', and defined the heavenly Jerusalem, the church as bride, as 'the Spirit of God in all the children of God, that is this body, the Church'.[56] For Avery, this time of the rising of Christ in his spiritual tabernacle was unfolding: 'now the Lord is come into the temple in many of the Saints, though we have a being as yet in

---

[48] Avery, *Scripture-prophecies opened*, p. 18.
[49] Avery, *Scripture-prophecies opened*, p. 6.
[50] Avery, *Scripture-prophecies opened*, p. 2.
[51] Avery, *Scripture-prophecies opened*, p. 2.
[52] Avery, *Scripture-prophecies opened*, p. 3.
[53] Cary, *The resurrection of the witnesses*, p. 96.
[54] Avery, *Scripture-prophecies opened*, pp. 2, 8.
[55] Cary, *The resurrection of the witnesses*, p. 35.
[56] Cary, *The resurrection of the witnesses*, p. 214.

Babylon, amongst the dens of lions, and the mountains of the leopards'.[57] Her claims about the status of the saints remain remarkable:

> There is more excellency in the Saints then in the truth... They are the temples of the living God, the sons and daughters of God Almighty, who do partake of the same nature, union, love and glory as Christ our Saviour, our Head and Elder Brother... I do not speak here of Truth as God is said to be Truth; nor dare I speak of it as Christ is called the Word of God... But I speak of Truth as it is held forth by the ministery of man in Babylon, which appeareth most glorious unto the carnal sense, being held forth by men of learning and parts, which shall fall in the fall of Babylon.[58]

Women and men were equally participants in the saints' deification. Anne Yemans wrote of the dissolution of distinction between persons among the saints, by God's 'infusing of the fulnesse of himselfe into them, working effectually in them... those that are the weakest members In this spirituall body, the Church, hath as much honour with God, as the highest members, and are as glorious'.[59] This corresponds to the popular preacher Thomas Collier's levelling doctrine of the church: 'the Kingdom of Christ, his Church, although gathered in many bodies, yet it is but one body, and every body hath the same power, the same priviledges, so that it ought to be a body compacted together'.[60] Avery described herself as the 'instrument' of God 'to whom I acknowledge all'; but this characterization as a mere passive 'instrument' rather downplays the total identification with the divine which she asserted for herself and other saints, male and female. Mary Cary affirmed that the saints 'in whom God in a speciall manner dwells' are, like the temple of the first covenant, 'the means whereby knowledge is dispensed, and instruction is received: for it is the Saints that are as lights in the World'. All the saints, wrote Cary, were prophets and gifted to prophesy, as 'an habitation of God through the spirit'.[61] As Jesus rises 'higher and higher, in his other dispensations', so 'he will more and more pour out his Spirit upon his people... upon Saints, learned and unlearned, male and female, old and young'.[62]

The 'homecoming' eschatology of these female prophets was, by the very nature of the claims they were making, intimately felt. It involved a shift in perspective from apprehending an 'objectified', and male-imaged, God by means of the church's external ordinances, to acknowledging the manifestation or habitation of God within themselves, which appears in some cases to have been spiritually (or psychologically) transformative. Quaker women in the next generation would take

---

[57] Avery, *Scripture-prophecies opened*, p. 5.   [58] Avery, *Scripture-prophecies opened*, p. 11.
[59] Yemans, *Crooked pathes made straight*, pp. 136–7.
[60] Thomas Collier, *The titles of the severall pieces* (London, 1647), p. 228.
[61] Cary, *The resurrection of the witnesses*, p. 37.
[62] Mary Cary, *The little horns doom & downfall* (London, 1651), p. 282.

up the same themes with passion. In 1659, Sarah Blackborow, anticipating the 'immortal Birth' of the 'Babe of glory' in human hearts, wrote:

> And truly sadness often possesses my heart when I behold the World in the alienation, out from the power and pure life, driven from the presence of the living God, into the earthly nature and carnal mind, there labouring and seeking, professing, getting into Church-fellowships, and all acting in that which adulterates from God, both Priest and people.[63]

This alienation would be overcome when all people 'know again the kingdom of God in them, and that near them, and not a far off from them'.[64] Margaret Abbott also addressed those 'alienated from the Lord', who were bound to the 'customs, and traditions, and the Worldly Worships' of the churches and sects, but failed to turn to 'Christ within them'.[65] In a characteristically lively jeremiad delivered to the city of London (and its suburbs), Ester Biddle testified to having been 'alienated from God, and a stranger to his life' until she found the city of God within herself: 'The Lord is risen in Sion'.[66] The divine presence had been with her 'in a vast howling wilderness, in a strange Land, and amongst strange people, who have not truly worshipped the God of heaven and earth'.[67] Now the day of the Lord had come, 'whose Reign is begun upon the earth, and whose Tabernacle is with men, whose dwelling and abiding is with the sons and daughters of men'.[68]

The Tabernacle of the Sun

Alongside apocalyptic Familism, which provided an important framework for spiritualist anti-confessionalism in the English Revolution, the influence of Paracelsus—and his disciples—should also be considered. The radical spiritualism with which Paracelsus, though never openly dissenting, is associated appeared to offer an alternative pathway through and out of religious conflict and competing ecclesiastical paradigms. In one notable case in seventeenth-century Europe, a secular ruler sought to promote Paracelsian mysticism as an antidote to confessional contention. The central German principality of Anhalt was in the 1580s and 1590s beset by controversies over the introduction of Reformed iconoclasm

---

[63] Sarah Blackborow, *Herein is held forth the gift and good-will of God to the world* (London, 1659), p. 2.
[64] Blackborow, *Herein is held forth*, p. 3
[65] Margaret Abbott, *A testimony against the false teachers of this generation* (London, 1659), pp. 1–2, 4.
[66] Ester Biddle, *A warning from the Lord God of life and power, unto thee the city of London, and to the suburbs round about thee* (London, 1660), pp. 7, 12.
[67] Biddle, *A warning from the Lord*, p. 18.   [68] Biddle, *A warning from the Lord*, p. 14.

and changes in ceremonial practice.[69] The region was at the centre of the divided confessional landscape in the Holy Roman Empire, neighbouring Saxony but also Brandenburg, which would turn Calvinist in 1613. In 1611, a clandestine printing press was established by Prince August of Anhalt-Plötzkau, one of the Anhalt territories formed in 1603, to disseminate works by Paracelsus and his disciple, Valentin Weigel, throughout the German-speaking world. These texts promoted a non- (or even anti-)confessional form of Christianity elevating spiritual experience over ceremonial observance or dogmatic propositions. As Carlos Gilly has observed, certain influential German Paracelsians—especially followers of Weigel—not only sought to transcend 'the confessional confines of the existing churches, but also rejected and combatted the churches, pronouncing them to belong to "external Christendom"'.[70] Anticipating the Quaker challenge to institutional religion and radical strains of Pietism, they disavowed 'churches of stone', ceremonies, and observances.[71] These texts would illuminate 'the errors and mistakes of the Papists, Lutherans, Calvinists'.[72] Although the activities of August of Anhalt's secret press were abortive, he sponsored the wide distribution of a varied corpus of spiritualist and mystical texts (both of the Reformation and late-medieval periods) by the publishers Lucas Jennis and Johann Francke from Frankfurt and Magdeburg respectively, recommended for the use of those seeking an education in the *Schule des Heiligen Geistes*, or school of the Holy Spirit.[73]

It is more difficult to track the reception of Paracelsian spiritualism in seventeenth-century England than it is to trace medical or alchemical Paracelsianism, but there are indications of significant influence on some of the leading radical mystics, dating from at least the 1630s.[74] The affinities with the anti- (or perhaps trans-)confessional religion promoted by the Anhalt regime are intriguing, and suggest a parallel effort to overcome partisan religious politics. John Everard's mystical translations corresponded closely to the output of the Paracelsian presses: Tauler, the *Theologia germanica*, Sebastian Franck.[75] Giles Randall and Giles Calvert carried on the work of Everard in the 1640s and 1650s, publishing mystical

---

[69] See Joseph Herl, *Worship wars in early Lutheranism: choir, congregation and three centuries of conflict* (Oxford: Oxford University Press, 2004), pp. 110–11; Bridget Heal, *A magnificent faith: art and identity in Lutheran Germany* (Oxford: Oxford University Press, 2017), esp. pp. 68–70.

[70] Carlos Gilly, '"*Theophrastia Sancta*"—Paracelsianism as a religion', in Ole Peter Grell, ed., *Paracelsus: the man and his reputation, his ideas and their transformation* (Leiden: Brill, 1998), pp. 177–80.

[71] Gilly, '*Theophrastia Sancta*', p. 177. [72] Gilly, '*Theophrastia Sancta*', p. 180.

[73] See Gilly, '*Theophrastia Sancta*', p. 180; also Theodor Harmsen, 'The mind's eye: images of creation and revelation in mystical theology and theosophy', in Peter Forshaw, ed., *Lux in Tenebris: the visual and the symbolic in Western esotericism* (Boston, MA: Brill, 2017), pp. 155–6.

[74] The influence of Paracelsus on English medicine and chemistry was outlined by Allen Debus in *The English Paracelsians* (New York: Franklin Watts, 1966); P.M. Rattansi's earlier article, 'Paracelsus and the Puritan Revolution', *Ambix* 11:1 (1963), pp. 24–32, while acknowledging the 'surge of interest' in Paracelsus in the 1650s, was also concerned primarily with the reception of his medical therapy.

[75] John Everard, *Some Gospel-treasures opened* (London, 1653). He also showed some knowledge of Paracelsus in his translation of *The divine pymander of Hermes Mercurius Trismegistus* (London, 1649).

and spiritualist works by Weigel, Paracelsus, Hendrik Niclaes, Jacob Boehme, as well as a wealth of contemporary anti-confessional literature. Everard's radical disciples in revolutionary England included the schoolmaster John Webster, who admired Paracelsus as 'that singular ornament of Germany'.[76] John Pordage, as we have seen, was clearly shaped by Paracelsian mariology, no doubt stimulated by interactions during his period of medical study in Leiden. Wherever there was the influence of Jacob Boehme, there were also Paracelsian elements. In particular, the idea of man as microcosm chimed with mystical claims to communion with (and apocalyptic incarnation of) the divine in the flesh of individual saints. Henry More regarded Paracelsus's theory of the microcosm as a wellspring of 'the wildest Philosophical Enthusiasmes that ever was broached by any either Christian or heathen'.[77] Woman or man as microcosm, as an organizing idea, underpinned some of the most radical political philosophy as well as theological anthropology in the Revolution, such as that of Gerrard Winstanley, famous for his assertion that 'the world is mankinde, and every particular man and woman is a perfect creation of himself, a perfect created world'.[78] The notion that the macrocosm was fully present in the microcosm, that the history and experience of the whole world was a figure of the inner life of woman or man, grounded belief in universal human dignity, and a radical critique of scandalous tyranny over individual souls.

The preeminent English Paracelsian, Robert Fludd (1574–1637), can be connected with English mystical radicals principally through the translator John Everard, with whom he had scholarly interactions from around 1626, when Everard began to show an interest in alchemy.[79] In various publications, which appeared during and after his lifetime, Fludd described the 'little world called man' in terms of a temple of the Holy Ghost, or tabernacle:

> It is apparent, then, that the incorruptible Spirit is in all things, but most abundantly (next unto the great world) in the little world called man: ... *the Holy spirit of discipline filleth the whole world.* So also, and in the very like manner, the same incorruptible spirit filleth the little world (est enim Templum Spiritus Sancti it is the Temple of the Holy Ghost) and hath put his Tabernacle in the heart of man, in which it moveth, as in this proper macrocosmicall Sunne in Systole, and Diastole, namely, by contraction and dilatation

---

[76] John Webster, *Academiarum examen: or, the examination of academies* (London, 1654), p. 70.

[77] Henry More, *Enthusiasmus triumphatus* (London, 1656), p. 46.

[78] Gerrard Winstanley, *The saints paradice or, the fathers teaching the only satisfaction to waiting souls* (London, 1648), p. 74.

[79] A letter from Everard to Sir Robert Cotton mentions an interaction with 'Doctor Floud', British Library, Cotton MS Julius C. III, fol. 173r. Everard first contacted Cotton, the manuscript collector who supplied Augustine Baker with works of medieval mysticism, in January 1624, driven by his interest in an obscure alchemical manuscript, later published by Elias Ashmole, entitled *The way to blisse* (London, 1658); British Library, Cotton MS Julius C. III, fol. 171r. See also David Como, *Blown by the Spirit: Puritanism and the emergence of an antinomian underground in pre-Civil-War England* (Stanford: Stanford University Press, 2004), p. 222.

[sic] without ceasing, and sendeth his beames of life over all the whole frame of man, to illuminate, give life, and circular motion unto his spirit.[80]

The presence of God 'in his creatures', in the microcosm just as fully as in the macrocosm of the created universe, provided 'the ground-work of Divinity', the 'true and essentiall philosophy, or *sophia*' (Figure 7). God puts his 'tabernacle in the sun' and in the 'dark cloud'; 'his Spirit is said *to* descend from heaven like a dove ... and *to* fill the earth, and to make man his temple, and to be in all things'.[81] John Rogers may also have alluded to something like this occult theology in *Ohel*

Figure 7 The cosmos, in Robert Fludd, *Utriusque cosmi maioris scilicet et minoris metaphysica* (London, 1617), p. 141.

[80] Robert Fludd, *Doctor Fludds answer unto M. Foster* (London, 1631), pp. 65–6.
[81] Robert Fludd, *Mosaicall philosophy grounded upon the essentiall truth* (London, 1659), p. 21.

or Beth-shemesh: a tabernacle for the sun (1653). The phrase 'tabernacle for the sun' is ultimately taken from Psalm 19.4-5, 'In them hath He set a tabernacle for the sun, which as a bridegroom coming out of his chamber, and rejoiceth as a strong man to run a race'. Fludd's ecclesiology was somewhat enigmatic, but he identified the 'Church of God' with 'the habitations or kingdoms of the true Sophia': namely, the living temples of 'Christ Jesus (which as he is all in all, so is he but one simple essence)... who is but one and the same in us all; for in him and by him, we are all made brethren, and coheirs with him, of eternity'.[82] Like John Pordage, the Paracelsian Fludd affirmed a generative female principle, divine Sophia, in the Godhead (the 'eternall Unity... in it self is male and female'); and this lively presence of Christ in the world, the church of living tabernacles, is identified as being one with Sophia.[83]

It is clear that by the late 1650s, when Fludd's *Mosaicall philosophy* was published, Paracelsian religion was somewhat in vogue in certain circles. Millenarian expectation of the new Jerusalem aligned with alchemical interests in the discovery of the philosopher's stone. In 1658-9, reports were circulating about Mary Cary's prophecies concerning the philosopher's stone, understood, as by John Pordage's female disciples at Bradfield, in terms of divine communion with human nature. Christ's appearance in the mystical bride, the body of the saints, would finally overturn mystical Babylon. Cary was by then known as 'Mary Rand' or, more disparagingly, 'Mary Rant'. Henry Oldenburg corresponded with Robert Boyle in September 1658, about the predictions of 'Maria Rante, foretelling, that the making of Gold shal be vulgarly knowne AD. 1661'.[84] He remarked sceptically that he was unsure

> whether the philosophers stone will become soe speedily vulgar, as Mary Rante hath prophesyed but I see many juste grounds of appreciating gold, and of raysing vulgar things to bee more truly excellent, than gold or Jewells. And of amplifying the dominion of good men over Gods works and of turning curses into blessings.[85]

Around Easter 1659, Samuel Hartlib felt compelled to engage with 'Mary Rant and her writings' after 'these holy days are over', reporting that he had 'not only now, but very often, been importuned heretofore on her behalf'.[86] Mary Cary did not make explicit reference to alchemy or magic in her published writings, though she

---

[82] Fludd, *Mosaicall philosophy*, pp. 28, 32.   [83] Fludd, *Mosaicall philosophy*, p 140.
[84] Oldenburg to Boyle, 10 Sept. 1658, in Michael Hunter, Antonio Clericuzio, and Lawrence M. Principe eds., *The correspondence of Robert Boyle*: vol 1: *1636-61* (London and New York: Routledge, 2001), p. 290.
[85] Quoted in Charles Webster, *The great instauration: science, medicine and reform, 1626-1660* (London: Duckworth, 1975), p. 12.
[86] Hartlib to Boyle, 5 Apr. 1659, in Hunter et al., *The correspondence of Robert Boyle*, p. 325.

did write censoriously about the popular appeal of astrology among 'prophane men... apt to admire Booker and Lilly'.[87] While the specific prophecy concerning the philosopher's stone has not been identified, undoubtedly her prediction was of a piece with the Fifth Monarchists' belief in the advent of Christ's reign in the saints, when base human material would be transmuted into the golden substance of Christ's presence. This would be the time when, as she wrote in August 1653, 'the saints shall be abundantly filled with the spirit, and not only men, but women shall prophesy; not only aged men but young men; not only superiors but inferiors; not only those that have University learning, but those that have it not; even servants and handmaids'.[88]

The most active promoter of Paracelsus' philosophy during the period of the Revolution was Henry Pinnell, at one time curate of the notorious antinomian minister, Tobias Crispe, in the Wiltshire parish of Brinkworth (the village of his birth), and later a parliamentarian army chaplain in the regiment of Colonel John Pickering.[89] Pinnell's *A word of prophesy, concerning the parliament, generall, and the army* published in 1648, contained clear marks of Paracelsian philosophy in his account of human nature as the 'earthly and fleshly Microcosme, or that little world, Man'.[90] In 1657, he would translate and publish *Philosophy reformed* by the Paracelsian alchemist, Oswald Croll, as well as *Three books of philosophy written to the Athenians* by Paracelsus himself.[91] (Croll was court physician and diplomat to Prince Christian I of Anhalt-Bernburg, the half-brother of August; both were caught up in the confessional disputes in the Anhalt territories.)[92] Pinnell offers a clear example of the influence of Paracelsus on the spiritualist ecclesiology of the radical mystics. Importantly, Pinnell has been identified with the 'Mr Pennill', convinced of the necessity of separation by the female activist and separatist pioneer in the city of Bristol, Dorothy Hassard. During his time as a preacher at St Leonard's church in Bristol in around 1643, the hapless Pinnell was 'severall times sett on by Mrs. Hazzard, like a Priscilla', until he joined with the gathered congregation which met in her home.[93]

Pinnell's interactions with female prophets and pioneers suggest an openness to the operations of the Holy Spirit, outside the bounds of the institutional church. In

---

[87] Mary Cary, 'To the reader. Dated the Sixth Moneth (alias August) 1653', in the second edition of *The resurrection of the witnesses* (London, 1653), §B2r.

[88] Cary, *The little horns doom*, p. 238.

[89] See David Como, *Radical parliamentarians and the English Civil War* (Oxford: Oxford University Press, 2021), p. 43; also Christopher Hill, *The collected essays of Christopher Hill* (London: Harvester Press, 1986), p. 152.

[90] Henry Pinnell, *A word of prophesy, concerning the parliament, generall, and the army* (London, 1648), §A3r.

[91] Henry Pinnell, *Philosophy reformed & improved in four profound tractates* (London, 1657).

[92] See Bruce T. Moran, 'Courts and academies', in Katharine Park and Lorraine Daston, eds., *The Cambridge history of science*, vol. 3: *Early modern science* (Cambridge: Cambridge University Press, 2003), p. 262.

[93] Pinnell, *A word of prophesy*, p. 96.

his published writings, he made reference both to his earlier associations in Bristol, among them Walter Cradock, and to his interactions with the godly in Wiltshire.[94] Even as a curate in the 1630s, he was becoming a seeker after the true church, not in the pulpits or stone buildings, but in the experiences of the saints. In his *Word of prophesy* (1648), he recalled that 'when I was under the teaching of men I got more from simple countrey people, husband-men, weavers, &c. about Brinkworth, Southwick, and those parts in Wiltshire, then ever I did, or yet have by books and preachers'.[95] (Pinnell returned to live in the village of Brinkworth after a period out of employment in the 1650s.)[96] During his time as an army chaplain, Pinnell became further radicalized, not least by hearing 'as in a wildernesse, the Voice cryed by Mr Sedgwick and Mr Saltmarsh, Forsake, and come out of these crooked and carnall wayes and paths'.[97] In his published writings, Pinnell had little to say about the ministry of women, but an anecdote included by Simon Ford in his letter to Thomas Edwards during the time of Pinnell's army service suggests that Dorothy Hassard was not the only woman to whom Pinnell had looked for guidance and inspiration. Ford had investigated a community at Poole with a radical element, which had been '*Anabaptized* into an expectation of I know not what Revelation by one *Pinell*'. In a bid to convince Ford of the authenticity of their special revelations, the group urged him to meet 'a woman (their Oracle a Supernumerary *Sybill* at least) lately delivered of a childe, whose extasies they much confided in'.[98] The unnamed woman failed to impress Ford, but she had evidently become an important figure in Pinnell's circle. Pinnell's friend John Maddocks later tried to distance the group from the 'distracted woman' in his published response to the Ford letter, while continuing to defend 'the discoveries of Gods spirit to his people'.[99]

The network linking Hassard, Pinnell, Saltmarsh, Sedgwick, and Cradock illustrates something of the fluidity of the radical milieu in the 1640s. These connections also point to receptiveness in these networks to the lights of women, among some of those coming 'out of Babylon' in the spiritualist quest for the true church. Like the weavers and husbandmen of Wiltshire, women were innocent of the great corruption and suppression of 'Pure and Spirituall Worship' by the 'Romeish Babylon': no woman had ever held one of the high ecclesiastical offices by which the English hierarchy 'did Lord it over God's Heritage'.[100]

---

[94] See Henry Pinnell, *Nil novi: this years fruit, from the last years root* (London, 1654), p. 24.
[95] Pinnell, *A word of prophesy*, p. 49.
[96] See Henry Pinnell, *Staurodidache kai stauronike: the doctrine & dominion of the crosse* (London, 1659): the location of Brinkworth is given at the end of the preface, dated 30 Dec. 1657, §C4v.
[97] Pinnell, *Staurodidache kai stauronike*, p. 4.
[98] Thomas Edwards, *Gangraena* (London, 1646), p. 84. This was the same woman, mentioned in Chapter 1, who experienced Christ's presence as a strong fragrance.
[99] John Maddocks, *Gangraenachrestum, or a plaister to alay the tumor, and prevent the spreading of a pernitious ulcer* (Oxford, 1646), pp. 20-1.
[100] Roger Hayden, ed., *The records of a church of Christ in Bristol, 1640-1687* (Bristol: Bristol Record Society, 1974), p. 82.

Women were not just ambassadors of true Reformation, but also, as visionaries, signs in the landscape of the manifestations of God outside the stone walls of decadent churches. In a more than metaphorical sense, women embodied the true, spiritual church. Back in Brinkworth in the late 1650s, Henry Pinnell translated a discourse on the cross by the Franciscan preacher of Mainz, Johann Wild ('Johannes Ferus', 1497–1554), a confessionally ambiguous figure whose sermons were suppressed by the 1590s. Wild was not unlike Pinnell's other sixteenth-century obsession, Paracelsus, in that he was a Catholic humanist with decidedly ambivalent views about the institutional churches. He also had a high view of female piety, and explored the metaphorical and historical affinities between women and the church. In his meditations on Christ's passion, Wild reflected on the prominence of faithful women in the story. Unlike the male apostles, who 'shift for themselves, and get them out of sight', the female disciples 'follow Christ even to the Cross, and stay with him even to the very death'. By this, God shows how he 'chuseth the weak things of the world to confound the mighty, 1 Cor. 1'.[101] In Pinnell's translation, Wild celebrated the women's courage:

> But they are much to be commended, that the fear neither of the *Jews*, nor of the *Romans* could hinder them from following after Christ, and that they would no more forsake him when he was dead, then when he was living. This is to take good and bad together with ones Friend. The Disciples fled, but the Womenkind stood it out, as being willing to repair and make amends for the wrong done to all mankind in Paradise. And because those holy Women did so stoutly stand it out, and tarryed to see the end of the holy Passion, they were likewise counted worthy to have the first sight of Christ after his Resurrection. They were last with Christ when he dyed, and first with him when he lived. A godly man will learn many good things from those Women, *&c*.[102]

Chief among the faithful women was the Virgin mother: more than the apostles themselves, 'Mary signifieth the Church'.[103] Catholic tradition had long established that Mary symbolizes the church, but Pinnell, in his lengthy preface to Wild's Passion meditation, went further. The women to whom mysteries were disclosed at the death and resurrection of Jesus were associated with privileged access to a higher, spiritual communion transcending the provisional worship of the visible church. Pinnell urged his readers to follow Jesus

> not only from Galilee to Jerusalem, but from Jerusalem also here below, the outward and litteral Service, and Worship, unto Mount Calvery, and from thence

---

[101] Pinnell, *Staurodidache kai stauronike*, p. 368.
[102] Pinnell, *Staurodidache kai stauronike*, p. 404.
[103] Pinnell, *Staurodidache kai stauronike*, p. 375.

to the Sepulchre; thither let us hasten with Mary Magdalen... and there let us wait; we shall have some Angelical invitation to come near.[104]

Henry Pinnell's apocalyptic vision of the church entailed a journey out of 'the outward and litteral Service' into spiritual communion. In his own *Word of prophesy*, Pinnell had envisaged the dissolution of all ecclesiastical arrangements, as all things returned to God in a final consummation of the divine purposes. This disappearance into God would parallel Christ's own ascension:

> Though in the dayes of his flesh, and after his resurrection he appeared in many forms, yet he left all and forsook them at his ascension to the Father, by his reduction and resolution into the Godhead, disappearing, and deserting all visibilities, when he delivered up the Kingdome to the Father, that God might be all in all. Now all Ministrations, Ordinances, Christ himself our life, the word of truth by which we were begotten, all return into God: this is the perfect state of Christ and in this state we are perfected with him.[105]

Pinnell's spiritual ecclesiology bore many resemblances to that of William Sedgwick, the preacher who, alongside John Saltmarsh, most influenced him during his army service. Sedgwick developed a highly gendered doctrine of the mystical church in his published collection of sermons, *Some flashes of lightnings of the sonne of man* (1648). In his eighth sermon, Sedgwick reflected on the different dependent relationships set out in 1 Corinthians 11.3 (also picking up Ephesians 5.23): God as the head of Christ; Christ as head of the church; and the husband as head of the wife. Rather than pressing a message of dominion and subordination in these relationships, Sedgwick characterized them as interdependent relations, resolving in union and equality. God kenotically empowers Christ, Christ the church, and man the woman: 'God hath given a power to Christ, over himself. And Christ hath given a power to Man over himself. As man doth give a power to the woman over himself'.[106] He was careful not to imply any subordination in the Trinity: 'The Love of the Father is so great to his Sonne, that he is for his nature equal with him; so for his love he sets him up above him. He delights to see him Honoured whom he loves, to set Him above himself'.[107] By extension, the 'Husband hath the greater glory, when he gives [honour] to the woman'. Just as the 'greatnesse of God never manifests it self more, then in coming down and being a Servant; or, his power appears most in Subjection', so 'A loving Husband gives all the power that hee hath over his Family, unto his wife'.[108]

---

[104] Pinnell, *Staurodidache kai stauronike*, §A2v. [105] Pinnell, *Nil novi*, p. 22.
[106] William Sedgwick, *Some flashes of lightnings of the sonne of man* (London, 1648), p. 159.
[107] Sedgwick, *Some flashes of lightnings*, pp. 159–60.
[108] Sedgwick, *Some flashes of lightnings*, p. 163.

Sedgwick's sermon goes on to assert the equality of humankind with God through the transforming work of the incarnation: 'we are raised to a high estate, to be one with him in power and great glory; that it may be counted no robbery to be equall with him'.[109] The equality and harmony within the Trinity, between God and humanity, and between a husband and wife are all figured in the nuptial union of Christ and the church: 'Woman is the glory of the Man: The Church is the riches of Christ. We are the glory of Christ. Christ is the glory of God'.[110]

What is most striking about Sedgwick's discussion of the church is that he implicitly abandoned something of the doctrines, fundamental to classical Christian theism, of divine impassibility (or the absence of human passions or emotions), aseity (the essential attribute of autonomy and self-existence), and perhaps even immutability. There is no evidence to suggest that Sedgwick consciously queried the attribute of divine self-existence, but his account of the relationship between Christ and the church put some considerable pressure on an image of God as wholly self-sufficient. Just as the wife and the husband have need of each other, Christ has need of the church. As he put it, 'God is poor without Christ'; 'Christ is a poor head, if he hath not his Church'; and 'Christ is alone and solitary, till he entertains the Church into fellowship with himself'.[111] Most startlingly of all: 'God is not well, or safe, til he is committed to you, in you', and 'As we are safe no where but in GOD, so GOD is safe no where but in US; as GOD is our keeper, so we are his'.[112] This idea of the deficiency of Christ outside the church was not unheard of in Reformed theology. James Ussher preached before James I in June 1624 on the high status of the church, which (echoing the Pauline statement in Ephesians 1.23) 'should be accounted the fulnesse of him that filleth all in all'. Though Christ 'in himself' was 'most absolutely and perfectly complete; yet is his Church so neerely conjoyned unto him, that he holdeth not himselfe full without it'. Indeed, if any member of the church 'remaineth yet ungathered and unknit unto this mysticall body of his, he accounteth, in the meane time, somewhat to be deficient in himselfe'.[113]

Sedgwick made a distinctive additional move, however, in linking this interdependence to gender relations. In the same way that Christ and the church have no health when divided, so man is not man without woman and cannot exist independently of her: as it is suggested in 1 Corinthians 11.11, they 'are unseperable, Man and Woman: in the Lord, they are unpartable'.[114] The final consummation of the marriage relationship is a mutual surrender of self-will and all pretence of power and domination of one over the other. As Sedgwick put it, 'though she rule over me, yet I rule, because she is my self'; and again, 'as I give

---

[109] Sedgwick, *Some flashes of lightning*, p. 166.
[110] Sedgwick, *Some flashes of lightning*, pp. 170–1.
[111] Sedgwick, *Some flashes of lightning*, p. 171.   [112] Sedgwick, *Some flashes of lightning*, p. 172.
[113] James Ussher, *A briefe declaration of the universallitie of the church of Christ* (London, 1629), p. 5.
[114] Sedgwick, *Some flashes of lightning*, p. 175.

you [the woman] my will, so I give you my power; and you cannot abuse me, because you are my self'.

> In communion, you are now the Man, and I the Woman; as I was the man, and you the woman: as I was mighty in you; and you weak in me: as I was weak in you, and you mighty in me.[115]

In a private correspondence with a younger Christian, Sedgwick assumed a feminine voice as spiritual mother: 'thou art gott into my bosome, art in my wombe as thou layest & findest the place soe fruitfull soe full of warmth & nourishment'.[116] This assumption of an hospitable, metaphorical female body is compatible with his ideas about the interchangeability of gender roles, as well as his emphasis on mutual dependency in mystical communion. Sedgwick's rejection of the ideal of masculine independence from women chimes with modern feminist objections to the philosophical assumptions underpinning traditional Western theism, especially the insistence on the absolute autonomy of a male-imaged God. Pamela Sue Anderson summarised the problem: 'the theistic God is... precisely the opposite of what would be the ego-ideal for a female subject.... God as a 'masculinist' ideal is held to possess aseity'.[117] Daphne Hampson asks the probing question, 'what kind of fears of entanglement have been projected' onto a God who is 'self-sufficient, alone, not in any way constrained, and not needing to take into account what is other than "himself"?'[118] Sedgwick's God is presented in terms wholly alien to the philosophical account of classical theism. God is not God (and man is not man) without the society of the other; he is 'poor' and 'not well', and estranged from himself. The implications for human relations, including masculine ideals, seem to have been perceived quite lucidly by Sedgwick.

Sedgwick would apply a similarly gendered interpretation to the relationship between king and parliament, and parliament and nation: he sought after reconciliation and restoration rather than division. The mutual interdependence of male and female could be used as a figure for monarch and parliament, as for Christ and the church: just as

> you are brought forth by one, and in one Spirit, so by one another, as Man and Woman; The same Spirit producing the KING out of the Parliament, and so out of the People; and the Parliament and People out of the KING; As Man is by Woman, and Woman of Man.[119]

---

[115] Sedgwick, *Some flashes of lightning*, p. 180.
[116] Undated letter 'From Wm Sedgwick', Worcester College, Oxford, Clarke MS 18, fol. 18r.
[117] Pamela Sue Anderson, *Re-visioning gender in philosophy of religion: reason, love and epistemic locatedness* (London and New York: Routledge, 2017), p. 50.
[118] Daphne Hampson, *After Christianity* (London: SCM Press, 1996), p. 125.
[119] William Sedgwick, *The leaves of the tree of life: for the healing of the nations* (London, 1648), p. 81.

This alchemical dialectic, the union and interchange of male and female principles, suggests a Paracelsian influence. This impression is deepened by the fact that Sedgwick's ideas found their way into a work emerging from the Bradfield circle around the Paracelsian physician and minister, John Pordage: Mary Pocock's *Mystery of the deity in the humanity* (1649).[120] Educated at Oxford in the 1620s, Sedgwick had once been a fairly conventional Puritan, approving of a Presbyterian settlement as the most scriptural model of church government in his fast sermon of 1643.[121] The process whereby he emerged as a prophetic mystic during his time as minister to Ely Cathedral between 1644 and 1649 is unclear, but he became notorious as 'Doomsday Sedgwick' for his predictions of the imminent end of all things.[122] In March 1647, a contemporary reported that he came to London from Ely to proclaim 'that the World will be at an end within fourteene dayes, Christ then coming to Judgment, and that Christ appeared to him in his studdy the last weeke at Ely and told him so much'. Like Eleanor Davies, he was dismissed by contemporaries and posterity (with the honourable twentieth-century exception of Christopher Hill) as being merely 'distempered in minde', a mentally disturbed soothsayer.[123] In his imaginative account of human-divine and gender relations (as well as political theology), Sedgwick was, however, a highly original and fertile theologian. As in the case of Eleanor Davies, he deserves greater recognition for his ability to see beyond the immediate doctrinal horizon.

During his mystical phase, Sedgwick's doctrine of the church was a radically spiritualized one, according to which God's kingdom and temple is established in the heart of the saints. The longed-for union of Christ with the church, exactly analogous to the union of the husband and wife, entailed, in Sedgwick's account, a fulfilment of Christ himself and a reconciliation of natures which had only been hinted at in the liturgies and ordinances of the old churches. This was not just an abstract doctrine of the church, but a lively spirituality centred on communion. From passages such as the one extracted below, it is quite possible to imagine how Sedgwick's emotive preaching would have roused his audience (male and female), awakening in them a sense of intimacy with Christ, and discovery of their true being:

> The King is in you, the King is with you, and in you in victory; triumphing in the meanest and lowest state and condition. Ye may see by the Spirit of the LORD and faith, the mighty power of God; there is with us, and in us, the fulnesse of

---

[120] 'M.P.', *The mystery of the deity in the humanity, or the mystery of God in man* (London, 1649). On the influence of Sedgwick, see Manfred Brod, 'The seeker culture of the Thames Valley', in M. Caricchio and G. Tarantino, eds., *Cromohs virtual seminars: recent historiographical trends of the British studies (17th–18th centuries)* (Cromohs: Cyber Review of Modern Historiography, 2006), §5.

[121] William Sedgwick, *Scripture a perfect rule for church government* (London, 1643).

[122] See Hill, *The experience of defeat*, pp. 97–117.

[123] C. H. Firth, ed., *The Clarke papers: selections from the papers of William Clarke* (London: Camden Society, 1891), vol. 1, p. 4.

God: all wisdome, all righteousnesse, all certainty, all good, conquering all evil, all joy, removing all sadnesse, all sinne taken away, therefore shout: turn our demands and questions into liftings up the heart and spirit, & rejoice in such acclamations as these: I have found; I am; I enjoy Kingdome, glory, life; Christ, and every thing that is good. Shout; speak out, speak aloud, in the name of the LORD, and say, Yee are the children of the living God; say, God lives in you. Let's hear it aloud, speak boldly, confidently; open your hearts largely, and say, Christ is in you: I have Him; I am with Him; He is in me; I am in Him; here He is; He dwels in me; I am His Temple; I see Him now; I see the LORD my Saviour, I have heard of Him with the hearing of the ear, but now mine eyes see Him: I have Him: I enjoy Him.[124]

In the 1650s, 'Doomesday Sedgwick' was sympathetic to the Quakers, visiting James Nayler in prison in 1656 and receiving a mention in Robert Rich's *Love without dissimulation* (1667) alongside a host of other revolutionary mystics who were in their time 'Friends to the Bridegroom': among them 'Honest Erbury', Dell, Coppe, Coppin, Webster, Saltmarsh, Randall, Pordage, and, intriguingly, a number of women, some of whom have not been identified.[125] Like Nayler, Sedgwick attracted the charge of blasphemy for allegedly asserting that 'he was God'.[126] This was in fact precisely the essence of his teaching on mystical union, as it was set out in his sermons.

The mystical revolution which united the radicals, or the reformation of the heart, started from an apprehension of the living saints (both male and female) as the body of Christ on earth, against ecclesiastical institutions, ordinances, or offices, and certainly against political forces domineering over the spiritual bride. This 'anti-formalism' has been a familiar theme in the scholarly literature on civil war radicalism; what this chapter has highlighted is the centrality of gender to the whole radical discourse on the church. Affectingly, the radical theologians portrayed Christ's appearance in the inner tabernacle as a homecoming from exile or a wilderness state. Nowhere was this narrative of coming out of alienation—linked explicitly to the arbitrary powers of a clerical elite—more powerfully articulated than in women's prophetic writings. It is manifestly the case, moreover, that radical female prophets were among the early advocates of toleration and religious pluralism. While women themselves contributed a distinctive voice to debates about the nature of the church, radical theologians more broadly quested after renewed insights into Christ's mystical relationship to his bride. Most strikingly, William Sedgwick's meditation on the

---

[124] Sedgwick, *Some flashes of lightning*, pp. 55–6.
[125] Robert Rich, *Love without dissimulation* (London, 1666), p. 6.
[126] Thomas Burton, '10 December 1656', in John Towill Rutt, ed., *Diary of Thomas Burton Esq*, vol. 1: *July 1653–April 1657*, (London, 1828), p. 104.

interdependence of bridegroom and bride carried with it implications of reciprocity and mutuality in marriage, so consistently analogous to the relation of Christ and the church in the New Testament and in Christian tradition. His remarkable teaching on this theme disrupted the established, foundational idea in Christian theism that God has no need of another.

Conclusion

Several of the older women, such as Eleanor Davies and Katherine Chidley, did not live to see the Restoration. It has been suggested that Elizabeth Avery returned to conventional observance after 1652, in the absence of John Rogers' patronage, even having a child christened in June 1653.[1] The younger visionaries, among them Anna Trapnel, Mary Cary, and Sarah Wight, disappeared from public view before or after 1660. Quaker women, of course, remained active in the public sphere, though the embattled environment for dissent and the emergence of internal mechanisms for censorship altered the nature of and context for their interventions. It has become a commonplace observation that the climate of anti-enthusiasm in the Restoration Church was strongly gendered, in part a reaction to women's public ministry in the 1640s and 1650s which seemed to illustrate so precisely the heretical, disordering nature of the forces unleashed by the Revolution.[2] Following Meric Casaubon's devastating secular characterization of a Catholic female mystic's inspirations as melancholic and delusional 'enthusiasm', radical prophecy was also susceptible, along with Catholic mysticism, to a pathological analysis. It is tempting, in view of the obscurity which descended upon the female activists of the earlier generation, to reduce the account of their legacy to this hostile climate. The reaction was complex and many-layered, helpfully targeting both Roman Catholic and radical nonconformist opposition to the restored Church, and positioning the ecclesiastical establishment as virile and rational, as well as orthodox. A polemic against popery by the Aberdeen divine John Menzies, professor of divinity at the Marischal College, established a neat identification between 'Papists and Quakers' on the basis of the authority they gave to 'Women Preachers': 'do not Papists hold Hildegardys, Katherine of Sens [Siena] and Brigit, &c. for Prophetesses?'[3] Edward Stillingfleet, royal chaplain in the 1670s and one of the most influential spokesmen for the Restoration Church settlement, made the most of the appeal to antiquity, comparing both Catholic mystical divinity and the 'pretended' revelations of the sects to the early Christian heresy of Montanism: the 'New Prophecy' movement of the second and

---

[1] Crawford Gribben, *God's Irishmen: theological debates in Cromwellian Ireland* (Oxford: Oxford University Press, 2007), pp. 172–3.
[2] See, for instance, Michael Heyd, *Be sober and reasonable: the critique of enthusiasm in the seventeenth and eighteenth centuries* (Leiden: Brill, 1995), pp. 78–88.
[3] John Menzies, *Roma Mendax, or the falshood of Romes high pretences to infallibility and antiquity evicted* (London, 1675), 21.

third centuries, which gave prominence to female visionaries. These modern Montanisms were grounded on 'a Fanatick Enthusiastical Spirit', which 'deprived men of the use of their Reason' and gave rise to 'female Enthusiasts'.[4]

The female prophets of the period of revolution were instrumentalized by Restoration propaganda, and sometimes became figures of fun more than of horror. It was in Peter Heylyn's life of Archbishop Laud, *Cyprianus anglicus* (1668), that the humiliating story can be found in which Lady Eleanor Davies, famous for her habit of anagramming, found her own name anagrammed as 'NEVER SO MAD A LADIE' by the dean of Arches in an appearance before the Court of High Commission.[5] Anna Trapnel was often mentioned in narrations of the civil wars and Interregnum, as a disruptive 'Quaking Prophetess' who maliciously stirred up discontent in the West Country with her 'delusions'.[6] The Tory astrologer John Gadbury, in an essay on prodigies published in 1660, ridiculed those who 'credit the voices and Revelations of Hannah Trapnel, and Dorcas Erbury', arguing that 'for any man to credit, or give heed to vain, idle, and addleheaded women, and to esteem their Predictions, or twarling stories, as prophecies, or oracles, is the greatest Argument of Imbecility or weakness, that can be'.[7] Thomas Comber, then a Yorkshire minister, betrayed something like admiration for Trapnel's uncanny facility for accurate predictions in his *Christianity no enthusiasm* (1678), though his point was to show that she 'exceeds both the Quakers and most of the other Pretenders' in her enthusiasm, and still failed as a prophetess. 'She was for the Reign of Jesus, destroying the fourth great Monarchy, fore-told that all the Monarchies are going down, Jesus was at hand. Among the rest, she fore-told [we must have no more Kings,] and yet she was swallowed up of the Glory of God'.[8] In a Restoration farce entitled *Mr Turbulent: or, the melanchollicks*, a box of printed texts belonging to an enthusiast included Mother Shipton's prognostications, Theaurau John Tany's prophecies, and 'Hannah Trapnel's Visions', among Quaker, Ranter, and Muggletonian writings; all fair game for satire in 1682, and laughed off as the 'idle Fancies of Lunatick Brains'.[9] Trapnel's name remained a byword for 'Enthusiastick, Hysterical Millennaries' and their delusions, for decades after the Restoration.[10]

Women's association with intellectual innocence had been, for many seventeenth-century radicals, precisely the basis for their authority as preachers

---

[4] Edward Stillingfleet, *An answer to Mr Cressy's Epistle apologetical* (London, 1675), pp. 62–3.

[5] Peter Heylyn, *Cyprianus anglicanus, or, the history of the life and death of the Most Reverend and renowned prelate William, by divine providence Archbishop of Canterbury* (London, 1668), p. 266; Eleanor Davies, *The new Jerusalem at hand* (London, 1649).

[6] James Heath, *A chronicle of the late intestine war in the three kingdoms of England, Scotland and Ireland* (London, 1676), pp. 359–60.

[7] John Gadbury, *Natura prodigiorum or, a discourse touching the nature of prodigies* (London, 1660), p. 190.

[8] Thomas Comber, *Christianity no enthusiasm* (London, 1678), p. 96.

[9] Anon., *Mr Turbulent: or, the melanchollick* (London, 1682), p. 60.

[10] See James Yonge, *Sidrophel vapulans, or, the quack-astrologer* (London, 1699), p. 38.

in a degenerate age. All positive memory of the spiritual gifts of women in the Revolution was not lost. A mystical verse entitled *An alarm to judgement* (1678), strongly apocalyptic in tone and probably Fifth Monarchist in origin, called for spiritual transformation and liberation from the body of gross flesh into 'a mistical coelestian' state (an echo of the heavenly flesh doctrine which spread through radical networks in the Revolution, examined in Chapter 1). The anonymous author recalled the ecstatic trances of 'a maid cald Hannah Trapnel' and another 'named Sarah Wite' who had experienced such transcendence.[11] Mary Pordage was remembered in the 1690s by the Philadelphian Society as the pioneer visionary of a movement of the Holy Spirit in the seventeenth century, the first in a new generation—ahead of her husband—to be blessed with 'Mystical Knowledg & Experiences' and 'a fresh Rising Gale of Extraordinary Power'.[12] Robert Smith, a depressed son of a minister from Litchfield in Hampshire, drew solace from reading the experiences of Sarah Wight in the 1680s.[13] Timothy Rogers, the son of John Rogers (whose egalitarian views are set out in Chapter 3) and a dissenting minister afflicted with bouts of depression, also found great consolation in Sarah Wight's testimony. He quoted her liberally on divine mercy: 'I have obtained mercy, that thought my time of mercy past for ever'; again, 'he has given me peace that was full of terror'.[14] Rogers, a prolific devotional writer despite the constant disruptions to his ministry resulting from his inner turmoil and hypochondria, was his father's son in that he warmly valued women's experiences and perceived great spiritual strength in women. In *The character of a good woman* (1697), he observed that women were responsible 'for the Devotion and Numerousness of our Assemblies', and that they were 'generally more serious than the men...far beyond us in the fervors of Devotion'.[15]

In the later seventeenth century, it was chiefly the Quakers who sustained the memory of the radical army chaplains. From the 1670s, Quaker women arguably experienced a greater circumscription of their activity through the formation of separate men's and women's meetings with separate agendas. Nonetheless, the movement kept alive something of the radical spirit of the charismatic preachers, and Quaker women were engaged and active in prominent and distinctive ways. New editions of works by Dell and Webster were printed by the female publisher Tace Sowle in the 1690s, and the chaplains were generally honoured as spiritual forebears.[16] William Erbery died in 1654, and while his Quaker daughter Dorcas

---

[11] Anon., *An alarm to judgement* (London, 1678), pp. 213–14.
[12] Richard Roach, 'Wt are the Philadelphians & wt is ye Ground of their Society?', in Bodleian Library, Rawlinson MS D. 833, fol. 54v.
[13] Robert Smith, *Satans temptation, and Gods preservation* (London, 1685), p. 19.
[14] Timothy Rogers, *A discourse concerning trouble of mind and the disease of melancholly* (London, 1691), p. 428.
[15] Timothy Rogers, *The character of a good woman* (London, 1697), §b2r.
[16] See William Dell, *The tryal of spirits in both teachers and hearers* (London, 1699); William Dell, *Baptismōn didachē* (London, 1697); John Webster, *The saints guide* (London, 1699).

melted into obscurity after the Nayler affair, her father would be canonized as part of Quaker prehistory. He was listed by William Penn along with John Saltmarsh, William Dell, Richard Coppin, and John Webster as authors 'of Books forrunning' Friends' experience.[17] After an astonishingly intense and influential period of activity as a free-grace preacher and writer in the mid-1640s, John Saltmarsh did not even see the regicide. His death at the end of 1647 took on a kind of mythical significance, as it followed an episode in which he had sought an audience with Fairfax and Cromwell, refusing to remove his hat in deference, on account of their imprisonment of the Levellers and abandonment of the cause of the poor. The prophetic message he took to Fairfax, that 'the Armies falling from their first principles would occasion their ruine and destruction', appeared in print alongside Restoration editions of Mother Shipton's prophecies.[18] As late as 1698, a female prophetic exegete, M. Marsin, recalled Saltmarsh's death as a witness to the coming of Christ to vindicate the poor, and reform all of humanity.[19]

The significance of the inspired women of the Revolution and their radical advocates does not inhere in their negative legacy, the environment of anti-enthusiasm in the later seventeenth century. Neither should their stories be confined to the prehistory of Quakerism, notwithstanding the importance of that movement. Anglican anti-enthusiasm planted the seeds of a counter-reaction: Catholic and non-juring as well as Quaker, and, eventually, evangelical. There was also a variety of 'anti-enthusiasm' or 'anti-superstition' among radical dissenters themselves in their confrontation with the magisterial churches, whereby irrational appeals to spiritual authority, and types of religious, political, or intellectual exclusion were interrogated. The questions which had been opened up by the revolutionary moment could not be unasked. Their theological questions were not the mad ravings of eccentrics, but had a rationality of their own which resounded for generations. Why should there be no comprehensive equality among human persons, when all were equal under God? How could a God of unconditional love also be the God who reprobates? Why were the clergy more concerned to defend their status and suppress lay preachers than they were to feed and clothe the poor? Some of these ethical and theological issues were seen differently from a perspective outside the traditional churches, by those with a lower stake in preserving received doctrines and structures, not least women. The importance of religious dissent as a critical force in English (and British) intellectual and political history after 1660 is clear, and women contributed centrally to

---

[17] 'October 1693'; see Richard S. Dunn and Mary Maples Dunn, eds., *The papers of William Penn*, vol. 3: *1685–1700* (Philadelphia: University of Pennsylvania Press, 1987), p. 378. Charles Leslie claimed that Penn 'almost copyed verbatim' from William Erbery's *The babe of glory: breaking forth in the broken flesh of the saints* (London, 1654) in his *Christian Quaker*, though the passage he points to is at most a paraphrase.

[18] Anon., *Mother Shipton's prophesies* (London, 1661, 1678), p. 7.

[19] M. Marsin, *The first book, a clear and brief explanation upon the chief points of the New Testament* (London, 1698), p. 259.

both charismatic and rationalist streams of dissent. It is impossible to isolate suffrage, socialist or democratic movements in the English-speaking world from the activism of nonconformists, whether Quaker, Methodist, Baptist, or Unitarian. As Phyllis Mack observed, 'we can trace a direct line from the earliest Quaker women leaders to the nineteenth-century movements of abolition and women's suffrage and to twentieth-century feminism and peace activism'.[20] It might also be true, of course, that the nature of radicalism in the 1640s and 1650s helped to entrench gender conservatism in the mainstream churches as an almost unconscious reflex.

There are naturally limits to the extent to which the longer term implications of the gender radicalism of the English Revolution can realistically be traced. The female prophets and their patrons were not the direct ancestors of the feminist movement, though within a defined frame of reference their critical challenge contained feminist elements. It is perhaps more rewarding to consider how the evidence of the Revolution offers insights into the relationship between theological or intellectual radicalism, disruption to cultural and political symbols, and a renewed vision of gender relations and female nature. Some of the most radical religious texts of the English Revolution bear witness to the quest for the reformation of the heart, a levelling spiritual revolution transforming understandings of God, and of human experience. God would be known experientially, through a union of the affections with essential divine love, not by notional, speculative, formal, or polemical divinity. There was, I have argued, a correspondence between the prominence of women as visionaries, and this experiential theology. For several of the most original thinkers in the radical milieu, inspired by ancient and contemporary mysticism, this quest became associated with renewed insights into gender in God and in relationships of power. Female prophets advanced a much more expansive account of divine grace, and doctrines based on universalizing principles, with implications for gender relations. They gave voice to a powerful critique of persecuting and tyrannical church institutions, so incompatible with the divine compassion with which they experienced a deep affinity, and claimed an authority as women to speak as the custodians of the higher truth of love. Radically levelling mystical doctrine was clearly allied to political or ecclesiastical levelling, as the challenge to figureheads and traditional hierarchies pointed toward the horizon of a more egalitarian world. Conversely, images of the divine feminine—whether maternal metaphors for Jesus, or the identification (only ever found in manuscript sources) of the Virgin Mary with an eternal goddess figure, holy Wisdom—surfaced in communities and networks where women's prophetic and preaching gifts were valued and fostered. A radically inclusive account of salvation and grace, standing in stark opposition to Reformed orthodoxy on

---

[20] Phyllis Mack, *Visionary women: ecstatic prophecy in seventeenth-century England* (Berkeley: University of Berkeley Press, 1992), p. 9.

election, was expressed unconventionally through feminine theological imagery and symbolism. The very autonomy of God himself was questioned within a framework of reciprocal, mutually strengthening relationships whereby Christ and church, male and female were interdependent. Reform hospitable to perspectives traditionally excluded from the institutions of knowledge and power did not come without a profound shaking of those spheres.

Bibliography

Manuscript Sources

BODLEIAN LIBRARY
Clarendon MS 30
Rawlinson MS A. 21
Rawlinson MS A. 354
Rawlinson MS A. 404
Rawlinson MS C. 266
Rawlinson MS C. 544
Rawlinson MS C. 610
Rawlinson MS D. 833
Tanner MS 67

BRITISH LIBRARY
Cotton MS Julius C. III
Harley MS 1296
Sloane MS 2569
Thomason MS E. 710

CAMBRIDGE UNIVERSITY LIBRARY
Additional MS 26
Additional MS 32
Additional MSS 2802–9

DOWNSIDE ABBEY
Baker MS 12

EDINBURGH UNIVERSITY
MS DC.4.1

EMMANUEL COLLEGE, CAMBRIDGE
MS 289
MS 294

LAMBETH PALACE LIBRARY
MS 869
MS 1559

LONDON SOCIETY OF ANTIQUARIES
MSS/0138

NATIONAL ARCHIVES
PROB 11/328/403
SP 16 [State Papers, Charles I]
SP 29 [State Papers, Charles II]

PARLIAMENTARY ARCHIVES
HL/PO/JO/10/1/359

ROYAL SOCIETY
Boyle Papers, MS 1/40/11

SHEFFIELD UNIVERSITY LIBRARY (Accessed via The Hartlib Papers, Digital Humanities Institute, www.dhi.ac.uk/hartlib/)
Hartlib Papers, 3/2/92
Hartlib Papers, 22/21

STANBROOK ABBEY
MS 5

WORCESTER COLLEGE, OXFORD
Clarke MS 18

Primary Literature

Abbott, Margaret. *A testimony against the false teachers of this generation* (London, 1659).
Ainsworth, Henry. *Annotations upon the book of Psalmes* (Amsterdam, 1617).
Allen, Richard. *An antidote against heresy* (London, 1648).
Anon. *A discoverie of six women preachers, in Middlesex, Kent, Cambridgshire, and Salisbury* (London, 1641).
Anon. *A song of Syon of the beauty of Bethell, the glory of Gods own house* (London, 1642).
Anon. *Strange and miraculous newes from Turkie* (London, 1642).
Anon. *The fulnesse of Gods love manifested* (London, 1643).
Anon. *Parliament scout communicating his intelligence to the kingdome* (London, 10 August 1643).
Anon. *Divine light, manifesting the love of God unto the whole world* (London, 1646).
Anon. *Theologia germanica*, trans. Giles Randall (London, 1648).
Anon. *A declaration of the bloody and unchristian acting of William Star, and John Taylor in Walton, with divers men in womens apparell, in opposition to those that dig upon George-hill in Surrey* (London, 1650).
Anon. *A most glorious representation of the incomparable free grace of Christ* (London, 1650).
Anon. *A New-yeers gift for the parliament and armie* (London, 1650).
Anon. *The heads and substance of a discourse; first private, and afterwards publike; held in Axbridge, in the county of Somerset, about the 6th of March, 1650. Between Iohn Smith of Badgworth, and Charls Carlile of Bitsham, &c. on the one part; and Thomas Collier of Westbury on the other* (London, 1651).

Anon. *The grand impostor examined, or, The life, tryal and examination of James Nayler the seduced and seducing Quaker: with the manner of his riding into Bristol* (London, 1656).
Anon. *The Quakers quaking: or, the most just and deserved punishment inflicted on the person of James Naylor for his most horrid blasphemies* (London, 1656).
Anon. *A true narrative of the examination, tryall and sufferings of James Nayler* (London, 1657).
Anon. *Mother Shipton's prophesies* (London, 1661, 1678).
Anon. *Certain meditations upon justification by faith alone* (London, 1664; second edn 1684).
Anon. *An alarm to judgement* (London, 1678).
Anon. *The Sweet-Singers of Israel, or, the Family of Love* (London, 1678).
Anon. *Mr Turbulent: or, the melanchollick* (London, 1682).
Arrowsmith, John. *Englands Eben-ezer* (London, 1645).
Atkinson, Christoher and George Whitehead. *Davids enemies discovered, who of him make SONGS, but without the Spirit and without understanding* (London, 1654).
Avery, Elizabeth. *Scripture-prophecies opened: which are to be accomplished in these last times, which do attend the second coming of Christ* (London, 1647).
Bacon, Robert. *Christ mighty in himself & members revealed* (London, 1646).
Baillie, Robert. *Anabaptism, the true fountaine of independency, Brownisme, antinomy, familisme* (London, 1647).
Baker, Augustine. *Sancta Sophia, or, directions for the prayer of contemplation* (Douai, 1657).
Baker, Augustine. *The life and death of Dame Gertrude More*, ed. Ben Wekking, Analecta Cartusiana, 119/19 (Salzburg: Salzburg Institut für Anglistik und Americanistik: 2002).
Baker, Daniel and Katharine Evans. *A true account of the great tryals and cruel sufferings undergone by those two faithful servants* (London, 1663).
Bakewell, Thomas. *An answer, or confutation of divers errors broached, and maintained by the seven churches of Anabaptists* (London, 1646).
Ball, John. *A friendly triall of the grounds tending to separation* (London, 1640).
Barker, Matthew. *A Christian standing & moving upon the true foundation* (London, 1648).
Barrow, Henry. *A brief discoverie of the false church* (Dort, 1590).
Barton, William. *Hallelujah, or certain hymns, composed out of Scripture, to celebrate some special and publick occasions* (London, 1652).
Bateman, Susanna. *I matter not how I appear to man* (London, 1657).
Baxter, Richard. *Reliquiæ Baxterianæ* (London, 1696).
Benet of Canfield, *A bright starre* (London, 1646).
Besse, Joseph. *A collection of the sufferings of the people called Quakers* (London, 1753).
Biddle, Ester. *A warning from the Lord God of life and power, unto thee the city of London, and to the suburbs round about thee* (London, 1660).
Blackborow, Sarah. *Herein is held forth the gift and good-will of God to the world* (London, 1659).
Boehme, Jacob. *Of Christs testaments, viz: baptisme and the supper* (London, 1652).
Boehme, Jacob. *A consolatory treatise of the four complexions* (London, 1654).
Boehme, Jacob. *Concerning the election of grace* (London, 1655).
Boehme, Jacob. *Aurora, that is, the day-spring, or dawning of the day in the orient* (London, 1656)
Boehme, Jacob. *The fifth book of the author, in three parts, the first, of the becoming man or incarnation of Jesus Christ* (London, 1659).
Booy, David, ed. *Autobiographical writings by early Quaker women* (Aldershot: Ashgate, 2004).

Bourne, Benjamin. *The description and confutation of mysticall Antichrist the Familists* (London, 1646).
Bridge, William. *The works of William Bridge, sometime fellow of Emmanuel Colledge in Cambridge* (London, 1649).
Bromley, Thomas. *The way to the sabbath of rest, or, the souls progresse in the work of regeneration* (London, 1654).
Brown, David. *The naked woman, or a rare epistle sent to Mr Peter Sterry minister at Whitehall* (London, 1652)
Burrage, Champlin. 'A true and short declaration, both of the gathering and joining together of certain persons [with John More, Dr Theodore Naudin, and Dr Peter Chamberlen]: and also of the lamentable breach and division which fell amongst them', *Transactions of the Baptist Historical Society* 2:3 (1911), 145–6.
Burroughs, Jeremiah. *An exposition of the prophesie of Hosea* (London, 1652).
Burton, Thomas. *Diary of Thomas Burton Esq*, vol. 1: *July 1653–April 1657*, ed. John Towill Rutt (London, 1828).
Butler, Thomas. *The little Bible of the man* (London, 1649).
Cary, Mary. *A word in season to the kingdom of England* (London, 1647).
Cary, Mary. *The resurrection of the witnesses and Englands fall from (the mystical Babylon) Rome* (London, 1648).
Cary, Mary. *The little horns doom & downfall* (London, 1651).
Cheesman, Christopher. *Berk-shires agents humble address to the commissioners for compounding* (London, 1651).
Chidley, Katherine. *The justification of the independent churches of Christ* (London, 1641).
Church, Henry. *Divine and Christian letters to relieve the oppressed* (London, 1636).
Clarkson, Lawrence. *The lost sheep found* (London, 1660).
Collier, Thomas. *A discovery of the new creation* (London, 1647).
Collier, Thomas. *The titles of the severall pieces* (London, 1647).
Collier, Thomas. *A general epistle to the universal church of the first born* (London, 1649).
Collier, Thomas. *The pulpit-guard routed, in its twenty strong-holds* (London, 1651).
Comber, Thomas. *Christianity no enthusiasm* (London, 1678).
Coppe, Abiezer. *Some sweet sips of some spirituall wine* (London, 1649).
Coppin, Richard. *The exaltation of all things in Christ, and of Christ in all things* (London, 1649).
Cotton, John. *A Conference Mr John Cotton held at Boston with the elders of New-England* (London, 1646).
Cradock, Walter. *Glad tydings from heaven, to the worst of sinners* (London, 1648).
Cradock, Walter. *Gospel-libertie in the extensions limitations of it* (London, 1648).
Cradock, Walter. *Divine drops distilled from the fountain of Holy Scripture* (London, 1649).
Cressy, Serenus. *Exomologesis, or, a faithfull narration of the occaision and motives of the conversion unto Catholick unity of Hugh-Paulin de Cressy* (Paris, 1653).
Crofton, Zachary. *Bethshemesh clouded* (London, 1652).
Cudworth, Ralph. *A sermon preached before the Honourable House of Commons at Westminster, March 31, 1647* (London, 1647).
Davies, Eleanor. *A warning to the dragon and all his angels* (London, 1625).
Davies, Eleanor. *Amend, amend, Gods kingdome is at hand, amen, amen, the proclamation* (London, 1643).
Davies, Eleanor. *The star to the wise, 1643 to the high court of parliament* (London, 1643).
Davies, Eleanor. *A prayer or petition for peace November 22, 1644* (n.l., 1644).
Davies, Eleanor. *The restitution of reprobates* (London, 1644).

Davies, Eleanor. *The gatehouse salutation from the Lady Eleanor* (London, 1646).
Davies, Eleanor. *Je le tiens, or, the general restitution* (London, 1646).
Davies, Eleanor. *The Lady Eleanor her appeal present this to Mr Mace the prophet of the most high, his messenger* (London, 1646).
Davies, Eleanor. *A warning to the dragon and all his angels* (London, 1646).
Davies, Eleanor. *The mystery of general redemption* (London, 1647).
Davies, Eleanor. *The writ of restitution* (London, 1648).
Davies, Eleanor. *The bill of excommunication for abolishing henceforth the Sabbath* (London, 1649).
Davies, Eleanor. *The blasphemous charge against her* (London, 1649).
Davies, Eleanor. *The new Jerusalem at hand* (London, 1649).
Davies, Eleanor. *Sions lamentation, Lord Henry Hastings, his funerals blessing, by his grandmother, the Lady Eleanor* (London, 1649).
Davies, Eleanor. *Tobits book a lesson appointed for Lent* (s.l., 1652).
Dell, William. *Power from on high, or, the power of the Holy Ghost dispersed through the whole body of Christ* (London, 1645).
Dell, William. *Right reformation: or, the reformation of the church of the New Testament, represented in Gospell-light* (London, 1646).
Dell, William. *The stumbling-stone* (London, 1653).
Dell, William. *The tryal of spirits in both teachers and hearers* (London, 1699).
Dell, William. *Baptismōn didachē* (London, 1697).
Drapes, Edward. *Gospel-glory proclaimed before the sonnes of man* (London, 1648).
Dury, John. *A sermon preached before the honourable House of Commons, Novemb. 16 1645* (London, 1646).
Dury, John. *The reformed school* (London, 1649).
Eaton, John. *The honey-combe of free justification by Christ alone* (London, 1642).
Edwards, Thomas. *Gangraena* (London, 1646).
Edwards, Thomas. *The first and second part of Gangraena* (London, 1646).
Edwards, Thomas. *The third part of Gangraena* (London, 1646).
Ellis, Humphrey. *Pseudochristus: or, a true and faithful relation of the grand impostures, horrid blasphemies, abominable practises, gross deceits; lately spread abroad in the county of Southampton* (London, 1650).
Erbery, William. *The great mystery of godlinesse* (London, 1639).
Erbery, William. *The armies defence, or, God guarding the camp of the Saints and the beloved city* (London, 1648).
Erbery, William. *A call to the churches; or, a packet of letters to the pastors of Wales, presented to the baptized teachers there* (London, 1652).
Erbery, William. *The grand oppressor, or the terror of tithes* (London, 1652).
Erbery, William. *The babe of glory: breaking forth in the broken flesh of the saints* (London, 1654).
Erbery, William. *The testimony of William Erbery, left upon record for the saints of suceeding ages* (London, 1658).
Everard, John. *The divine pymander of Hermes Mercurius Trismegistus* (London, 1649).
Everard, John. *Some Gospel-treasures opened* (London, 1653).
Everard, John. *The Gospel treasury opened* (London, 1657).
Everard, William et al. *The true Levellers standard advanced* (London, 1649).
Farnworth, Richard. *A woman forbidden to speak in the church* (London, 1654).
Firth, C.H., ed. *Selections from the papers of William Clarke*, vol. 2 (London: Camden Society, 1894).

Fludd, Robert. *Doctor Fludds answer unto M. Foster* (London, 1631).
Fludd, Robert. *Mosaicall philosophy grounded upon the essentiall truth* (London, 1659).
Foulis, Henry. *The history of Romish treasons and usurpations* (London, 1671).
Fowler, Christopher. *Daemonium meridianum: Sathan at noon* (London, 1656).
Fox, George. *A New-England-fire-brand quenched* (London, 1678).
Gadbury, John. *Natura prodigiorum or, a discourse touching the nature of prodigies* (London, 1660).
Gell, Robert. *Gell's remaines, or, select several Scriptures of the New Testament opened and explained*, ed. R. Bacon (London, 1676).
Gibbens, Nicholas. *Questions and disputations concerning the Holy Scripture* (London, 1601).
Goad, Christopher. *Refreshing drops, and scorching vials, severally distributed to their proper subjects* (London, 1653).
Goodwin, John, Vavasor Powell, and John Appletree. *Three hymnes, or certain excellent new psalmes* (London, 1650).
Goodwin, John. *Two hyms, or spiritual songs* (London, 1651).
Gove, Richard. *The communicants guide* (London, 1654).
Gove, Richard. *Pious thoughts vented in pithy ejaculations* (London, 1658).
Greville, Robert (Lord Brooke). *The nature of truth, its union and unity with the soul which is one in its essence* (London, 1641).
Griffith, Alexander. *Strena Vavasoriensis: a new yeares gift for the Welch itinerants* (London, 1654).
Harlow, Jonathan with Jonathan Barry. *Religious ministry in Bristol 1603–1689: uniformity to dissent* (Bristol: Bristol Record Society, 2017).
Hayden, Roger, ed. *The records of a church of Christ in Bristol, 1640–1687* (Bristol: Bristol Record Society, 1974).
Heath, James. *A chronicle of the late intestine war in the three kingdoms of England, Scotland and Ireland* (London, 1676).
Heylyn, Peter. *Cyprianus anglicanus, or, the history of the life and death of the most reverend and renowned prelate William, by divine providence archbishop of Canterbury* (London, 1668).
Heywoode, Thomas. *Gynaikeion: or, nine bookes of various history* (London, 1624).
Homes, Nathaniel. *Gospel musick* (London, 1644).
Howe, Obadiah. *The Universalist examined and convicted* (London, 1648).
Hunter, Michael, Antonio Clericuzio, and Lawrence M. Principe, eds. *The correspondence of Robert Boyle*, vol 1: *1636–61* (London and New York: Routledge, 2001).
Jessey, Henry. *The exceeding riches of grace advanced by the Spirit of grace, in an empty nothing creature, viz. Mistress Sarah Wight* (London, 1647).
Jones, Sarah. *To Sion's lovers being a golden egge to avoide infection* (London, 1644).
Journal of the House of Commons (London: His Majesty's Stationery Office, 1802).
Julian of Norwich, *XVI revelations of divine love shewed to a devout servant of our Lord called Mother Juliana* (London, 1670).
'J.L.', *A small mite, in memory of the late deceased (yet still living, and never to be forgotten) Mr William Erbery* (London, 1654).
'J.N.', *Proh tempora! Proh mores! or an unfained caveat to all true Protestants, not in any case to touch any of these three serpents* (London, 1654).
Keith, George. *Divine immediate revelation and inspiration, continued in the true church: second part* (London, 1685).
Knollys, Hanserd. *An exposition of the first chapter of the Song of Solomon* (London, 1656).

Lead, Jane. *Ascent to the mount of vision* (London, 1699).
Love, Christopher. *Short and plaine animadversions on some passages in Mr Dels sermon* (London, 1647).
Love, Christopher. *A cleare and necessay vindication of the principles and practices of me Christopher Love* (London, 1651).
Maddocks, John. *Gangraenachrestum, or a plaister to alay the tumor, and prevent the spreading of a pernitious ulcer* (Oxford, 1646).
Marshall, Stephen. *A sermon of the baptizing of infants preached in the Abbey-Church at Westminster* (London, 1644).
Marsin, M. *The first book, a clear and brief explanation upon the chief points of the New Testament* (London, 1698).
Mather, Cotton. *Magnalia Christi Americana, or, the ecclesiastical history of New England* (Hartford: Silas Andrus, 1820).
Menzies, John. *Roma Mendax, or the falshood of Romes high pretences to infallibility and antiquity evicted* (London, 1675).
Milton, John. *Poems of Mr John Milton, both English and Latin, compos'd at several times* (London, 1645).
More, Gertrude. *The holy practises of a devine lover, or, the sainctly ideots deuotions* (Paris, 1657).
More, Gertrude. *Spiritual exercises* (Paris, 1658).
More, Henry. *Conjectura cabbalistica* (London, 1653).
More, Henry. *Enthusiasmus triumphatus* (London, 1656).
'M.P.', *The mystery of the deity in the humanity, or the mystery of God in man* (London, 1649).
Nayler, James. *A psalm of thanksgiving to God for his mercies* (London, 1659).
Nickolls, John. *Original letters and papers of State* (London, 1747).
Niclaes, Hendrik. *A publishing of the peace upon earth* (Cologne, 1574).
Niclaes, Hendrik. *Cantica certen of the songes of H.N.* (Cologne, 1575).
Niclaes, Hendrik. *Terra pacis: a true testification of the spiritual land of peace* (London, 1649).
Niclaes, Hendrik. *The prophecy of the spirit of love set forth by H.N.* (London, 1649).
Palmer, Anthony. *The Gospel new-creature; wherein the work of the spirit is opened, in awakening the soul* (London, 1658).
Partridge, John. *A short answer to a malicious pamphlet called, a reply written by John Gadbury* (London, 1680).
Partridge, John. *Detectio geniturarum* (London, 1691).
Phoenix, Anne. *The saints legacies or, a collection of certain promises out of the Holy Scripture* (London, 1629).
Pinnell, Henry. *A word of prophesy, concerning the parliament, generall, and the army* (London, 1648).
Pinnell, Henry. *Nil novi: this years fruit, from the last years root* (London, 1654).
Pinnell, Henry. *Philosophy reformed & improved in four profound tractates* (London, 1657).
Pinnell, Henry. *Staurodidache kai stauronike: the doctrine & dominion of the crosse* (London, 1659).
Poole, Elizabeth. *An alarum of war given to the army and to their high court of justice* (London, 1649).
Pordage, John. *Innocencie appearing through the dark mists of pretended guilt* (London, 1655).
Pordage, John. *Theologia mystica, or, the mystic divinitie of the aeternal invisibles* (London, 1683).

Pounset, John. *Certaine scruples from the army: presented in a dialogue between a minister of the new moulded presbytery, and a souldier of his excellencies (formerly new-moulded, but now despised) army* (London, 1647).
Powell, Vavasor. *Spirituall experiences, of sundry beleevers held forth by them at severall solemne meetings* (London, 1653).
Prier, Robert. *Looking-glass for a proud Pharisee* (London, 1648).
Prynne, William. *A fresh discovery of some prodigious new wandring-blasing-stars & firebrands* (London, 1645).
Quintyne, Michael. *A short discovery of the mystery of iniquitie* (London, 1645).
Reading, John. *The Ranters ranting* (London, 1650).
Rich, Robert. *Copies of some few of the papers given into the House of Parliament in the time of James Naylers trial* (s.l., 1657).
Rich, Robert. *Love without dissimulation* (London, 1666).
Rich, Robert. *The epistles of Mr Robert Rich to the seven churches* (s.l., 1680).
Rigge, Ambrose. *To the whole flock of God everywhere, the church of the first born* (London, 1660).
Rigge, Ambrose. *A tender exhortation to friends at Bristol, to bring to remembrance how it was with them in the beginning* (London, 1700).
Rogers, John. *Ohel or Beth-shemesh: a tabernacle of the sun* (London, 1653).
Rogers, Timothy. *A discourse concerning trouble of mind and the disease of melancholly* (London, 1691).
Rogers, Timothy. *The character of a good woman* (London, 1697).
'R.P.', *Berachah, or, Englands memento to thankefulnesse, being an hymne or spirituall song setting forth the praises of God* (London, 1646).
Rutherford, Samuel. *Christ dying and drawing sinners to himself* (London, 1647).
Rutherford, Samuel. *A survey of the spirituall Antichrist opening the secrets of familisme and antinomianisme in the antichristian doctrine of John Saltmarsh and Will. Del* (London, 1648).
Saltmarsh, John. *Examinations, or a discovery of some dangerous positions* (London, 1643).
Saltmarsh, John. *Free grace, or the flowings of Christs blood free to sinners* (London, 1646).
Saltmarsh, John. *Some drops of the viall, powred out in a season, when it is neither night nor day* (London, 1646).
Saltmarsh, John. *Sparkles of glory* (London, 1647).
Sedgwick, William. *Scripture a perfect rule for church government* (London, 1643).
Sedgwick, William. *Some flashes of lightnings of the sonne of man* (London, 1648).
Sedgwick, William. *The leaves of the tree of life: for the healing of the nations* (London, 1648).
Sikes, George. *The life and death of Sir Henry Vane, Kt.* (London, 1662).
Slatyer, William. *The compleat Christian, and compleat armour and armoury of a Christian* (London, 1643).
Smith, Robert. *Satans temptation, and Gods preservation* (London, 1685).
Smyth, John. *The differences of the churches of the seperation* (Middelburg, 1608).
Starbucke, William. *A spirituall song of comfort* (London, 1643).
Sterry, Peter. *A discourse of the freedom of the will* (London, 1675).
Sterry, Peter. *The rise, race, and royalty of the kingdom of God in the soul of man* (London, 1683).
Stillingfleet, Edward. *An answer to Mr Cressy's epistle apologetical* (London, 1675).
Sutton, Katherine. *A Christian womans experiences of the glorious working of Gods free grace* (London, 1663).

Tany, Thomas. *Theauraujohn his Theous on apokolipikal: or, Gods light declared in mysteries* (London, 1651).
'T.C.', *A glasse for the times by which according to the Scriptures, you may clearly behold the true ministers of Christ, how farre differing from false teachers* (London, 1648).
Trapnel, Anna. *Anna Trapnel's report and plea, or, a narrative of her journey into Cornwall* (London, 1654).
Trapnel, Anna. *The cry of a stone* (London, 1654).
Trapnel, Anna. *A legacy for saints* (London, 1654).
Trapnel, Anna. *Poetical discourses (1657–8)*, Bodleian Library S. 1. 42. Th.
Trapp, John. *Commentary or exposition upon these following books of holy Scripture: Proverbs of Solomon, Ecclesiastes, the Song of Songs, Isaiah, Jeremiah, Lamentations, Ezekiel & Daniel* (London, 1660).
Ussher, James. *A briefe declaration of the universallitie of the church of Christ* (London, 1629).
Vane, Henry. *The retired mans meditations, or, the mysterie and power of godlines* (London, 1655).
Warren, Elizabeth. *The good and old way vindicated* (London, 1646).
Webster, John. *The picture of Mercurius Politicus* (London, 1653).
Webster, John. *The saints guide, or, Christ the rule, and rules of saints* (London, 1653).
Webster, John. *Academiarum examen: or, the examination of academies* (London, 1654).
Webster, John. *The judgement set, and the bookes opened* (London, 1654).
Webster, John. *Metallographica: or, a history of metals* (London, 1671).
Webster, John. *The displaying of witchcraft* (London, 1677).
Webster, John. *The saints guide*, second ed. (London, 1699).
Weeks, John. *Truths conflict with error: or, universall redemption controverted* (London, 1650).
Weyer, Matthias. *Theologiae mysticae triumque: illius viarum, purgativae, illuminativae atq; unitivae praxis viva*, trans. Johanne Spee (Amsterdam, 1658).
Weyer, Matthias. *The narrow path of divine truth described* (London, 1683).
White, Jeremy. *The restoration of all things: or, a vindication of the goodness and grace of God. To be manifested at last in the recovery of his whole creation out of their fall* (London, 1712).
Wight, Sarah. *A wonderful pleasant and profitable letter written by Mris Sarah Wight, to a friend* (London, 1656).
Winstanley, Gerrard. *The saints paradice or, the fathers teaching the only satisfaction to waiting souls* (London, 1648).
Winstanley, Gerrard. *The breaking of the day of God* (London, 1649).
Winstanley, Gerrard. *The mysterie of God* (London, 1649).
Winstanley, Gerrard. *The new law of righteousnes* (London, 1649).
Winstanley, Gerrard. *Truth lifting up its head above scandals* (London, 1649).
Winstanley, Gerrard. *Fire in the bush* (London, 1650).
Winstanley, Gerrard. *An humble request to the ministers of both universities, and to all lawyers* (London, 1650).
Winstanley, Gerrard. *The law of freedom in a platform: or, true magistracy restor'd* (London, 1652).
Yemans, Anne. *Crooked pathes made straight: or, the wayes of God made knowne to lost sinners, or bewildered saints* (London, 1648).
Yonge, James. *Sidrophel vapulans, or, the quack-astrologer* (London, 1699).

Secondary Literature

Achinstein, Sharon. *Literature and dissent in Milton's England* (Cambridge: Cambridge University Press, 2003).
Adcock, Rachel. *Baptist women's writings in Revolutionary culture* (Abingdon: Routledge, 2016).
Anderson, Elizabeth. 'Feminist epistemology: an interpretation and a defense', *Hypatia* 10:3 (1995), 50-84.
Anderson, Pamela Sue. *Re-visioning gender in philosophy of religion: reason, love and epistemic locatedness* (London and New York: Routledge, 2017).
Bailey, Richard. *New light on George Fox and early Quakerism: the making and unmaking of a God* (San Francisco: Edwin Mellen Press, 1992).
Barclay, Andrew. *Electing Cromwell: the making of a politician* (London and New York: Routledge, 2016).
Bauckham, Richard. 'Universalism: a historical survey', *Themelios* 4:2 (1978), 47-54.
Bell, Mark. *Apocalypse how? Baptist movements during the English Revolution* (Mercer University Press, 2000).
Bell, Richard Thomas. 'The minister, the millenarian, and the madman: the Puritan lives of William Sedgwick, ca. 1609-1664', *Huntington Library Quarterly* 81:1 (2018), 29-61.
Bentley Hart, David. *That all shall be saved: heaven, hell and universal salvation* (Yale, CN: Yale University Press, 2019).
Beyer, Jürgen. *Lay prophets in Lutheran Europe, 1550-1700* (Leiden: Brill, 2017).
Bingham, Matthew. *Orthodox radicals: Baptist identity in the English Revolution* (Oxford: Oxford University Press, 2019).
Boesky, Amy. *Founding fictions: utopias in early modern England* (Athens, GA: University of Georgia Press, 1996).
Bouldin, Elizabeth. *Women prophets and radical Protestantism in the Britsn Atlantic world, 1640-1730* (Cambridge: Cambridge University Press, 2015).
Bradstock, Andrew, ed. *Winstanley and the Diggers 1649-1999* (London: Frank Cass & Co., 2000).
Brod, Manfred. 'Doctinal deviance in Abingdon: Thomasine Pendarves and her circle', *Baptist Quarterly* 41 (2005), 92-102.
Brod, Manfred. 'The seeker culture of the Thames Valley', in M. Caricchio and G. Tarantino, eds., *Cromohs virtual seminars: recent historiographical trends of the British studies (17th-18th centuries)* (Cromohs: Cyber Review of Modern Historiography, 2006), 1-10.
Browne, John. *History of Congregationalism and memorials of the churches in Norfolk and Suffolk* (New York: Cornell University Press, 1924).
Cannadine, David, ed. *The Oxford dictionary of national biography* (Oxford: Oxford University Press, 2004).
Capp, Bernard. *The Fifth Monarchy men: a study in seventeenth-century English millenarianism* (London: Faber, 1972).
Capp, Bernard. *England's culture wars: Puritan Reformation and its enemies in the Interregnum, 1649-1660* (Oxford: Oxford University Press, 2012).
Carnes, Natalie. *Beauty: A theological engagement with Gregory of Nyssa* (Eugene, OR: Wipf & Stock, 2014).
Carroll, Kenneth. 'Singing in the Spirit in early Quakerism', *Quaker History* 73 (1984), 1-13.
Christ, Carol P. and Judith Plaskow, eds. *Womanspirit rising: a feminist reader on religion* (San Francisco: Harper & Row, 1979).

Clarke, Elizabeth. *Politics, religion and the Song of Songs in seventeenth-century England* (Basingstoke: Palgrave Macmillan, 2011).
Clucas, Stephen. 'Samuel Hartlib's *Ephemerides*, 1635–59, and the pursuit of scientific and philosophical manuscripts: the religious ethos of an intelligencer', *The Seventeenth Century* 6:1 (1991), 33–55.
Coakley, Sarah and Paul Gavrilyuk, eds. *The spiritual senses: perceiving God in Western Christianity* (Cambridge: Cambridge University Press, 2011).
Coffey, John. 'Puritanism and liberty revisited: the case for toleration in the English Revolution', *The Historical Journal* 41:4 (1998), 961–85.
Como, David. 'Women, prophecy and authority in early Stuart Puritanism', *Huntingdon Library Quarterly* 61:2 (1998), 203–22.
Como, David. *Blown by the Spirit: Puritanism and the emergence of an antinomian underground in pre-civil-war England* (Stanford: Stanford University Press, 2004).
Como, David. 'The Family of Love and the making of English Revolutionary religion: the confession and "conversions" of Giles Creech', *Journal of Medieval and Early Modern Studies* 48:3 (2018), 553–98.
Como, David. *Radical parliamentarians and the English Civil War* (Oxford: Oxford University Press, 2021).
Cope, Esther. *Handmaid of the Holy Spirit: Dame Davies, Eleanor. never soe mad a ladie* (Minnesota: University of Michigan Press, 1992).
Corns, Thomas and David Loewenstein, eds. *The emergence of early Quaker writing: dissenting literature in seventeeth-century England* (London: Frank Cass, 1995).
Corns, Thomas, Ann Hughes, and David Loewenstein, eds. *The complete works of Gerrard Winstanley* (Oxford: Oxford University Press, 2009).
Cornwall, Susanna. 'The kenosis of unambiguous sex in the body of Christ: intersex, theology and existing for the other', *Theology and Sexuality* 14:2 (2008), 181–99.
Crawford, Patricia. 'Historians, women and the civil war sects, 1640–1660', *Parergon* 6 (1988), 19–32.
Crawford, Patricia. *Women and religion in England, 1500–1700* (London and New York: Routledge, 1993).
Cressy, David. *Travesties and transgressions in Tudor and Stuart England: tales of discord and dissension* (Oxford and New York: Oxford University Press, 2000).
Cressy, David. *England on edge: crisis and revolution, 1640–1642* (Oxford: Oxford University Press, 2006).
Cressy, David. *Charles I and the people of England* (Oxford: Oxford University Press, 2015).
Cuming, G.J. and Derek Baker, eds. *Popular belief and practice*, Studies in church history (Cambridge: Cambridge University Press 1972).
Davies, Michael, Anne Dunan-Page, and Joel Halcomb, eds. *Church life: pastors, congregations, and the experience of dissent in seventeenth-century England* (Oxford: Oxford University Press, 2019).
Davis, J.C. *Alternative worlds imagined, 1500–1700: essays on radicalism, utopianism and reality* (London: Palgrave Macmillan, 2017).
Davis, J.C. *Fear, myth and history: the Ranters and the historians* (Cambridge: Cambridge University Press, 1986).
Debus, Allen. *The English Paracelsians* (New York: Franklin Watts, 1966).
De Certeau, Michel. *The mystic fable*, vol. 1: *the sixteenth and seventeenth centuries*, trans. Michael B. Smith (Chicago: University of Chicago Press, 1992).
Ehrman, Bart. *Heaven and hell: a history of the afterlife* (New York: Simon & Schuster, 2020).

Fang Ng, Su. *Literature and the politics of the family in seventeenth-century England* (Cambridge: Cambridge University Press, 2007).
Farr, David. *John Lambert, parliamentary soldier and Cromwellian major-general, 1619–1684* (Woodbridge: Boydell and Brewer, 2003).
Feroli, Teresa. *Political speaking justified: women prophets and the English Revolution* (Newark: University of Delaware Press, 2006).
Finnegan, David and Ariel Hessayon, eds. *Varieties of seventeenth- and early eighteenth-century English radicalism* (Farnham: Ashgate, 2011).
Font, Carme. *Women's prophetic writings in seventeenth-century Britain* (New York and London: Routledge, 2019).
Font Paz, Carme. 'The case for prophecy: politics, gender and self-representation in seventeenth-century prophetic discourses', *Revista Alicantina de Estudios Ingleses* 22 (2009), 63–78.
Forshaw, Peter, ed. *Lux in Tenebris: the visual and the symbolic in Western esotericism* (Boston, MA: Brill, 2017).
Gentles, Ian. *The New Model Army: agent of revolution* (New Haven and London: Yale University Press, 2022).
Gibbons, B.J. *Gender in mystical and occult thought: Behmenism and its development in England* (Cambridge: Cambridge University Press, 1997).
Gillespie, Katharine. *Domesticity and dissent in the seventeenth century: English women writers and the public sphere* (Cambridge: Cambridge University Press, 2004).
Gilly, Carlos. '"Theophrastia Sancta"—Paracelsianism as a religion', in Ole Peter Grell, ed., *Paracelsus: the man and his reputation, his ideas and their transformation* (Leiden: Brill, 1998), 151–85.
Gouldbourne, Ruth. *The flesh and the feminine: gender and theology in the writings of Caspar Schwenckfeld* (Milton Keynes: Paternoster, 2006).
Greaves, Richard L. *Glimpses of glory: John Bunyan and English dissent* (Stanford: Stanford University Press, 2002).
Grell, Ole Peter, ed. *Paracelsus: the man and his reputation, his ideas and their transformation* (Leiden: Brill, 1998).
Gribben, Crawford. *God's Irishmen: theological debates in Cromwellian Ireland* (Oxford: Oxford University Press, 2007).
Gurney, John. *Brave community: the Digger movement in the English Revolution* (Manchester: Manchester University Press, 2007).
Ha, Polly. *English Presbyterianism, 1590–1640* (Stanford: Stanford University Press, 2011),
Hamilton, Alastair. *The apocryphal apocalypse: the reception of the second book of Esdras (4 Ezra) from the Renaissance to the Enlightenment* (Oxford: Clarendon Press, 1999).
Hamilton, Alastair, ed. *Cronica. Ordo Sacerdotis. Acta HN. Three texts on the Family of Love* (Leiden: Brill, 1988).
Hampson, Daphne. *Theology and feminism* (Oxford: Blackwell, 1990).
Hampson, Daphne. *After Christianity* (London: SCM Press, 1996).
Heal, Bridget. *A magnificent faith: art and identity in Lutheran Germany* (Oxford: Oxford University Press, 2017).
Heal, Bridget and Anorthe Kremers, eds. *Radicalism and dissent in the world of Protestant reform* (Göttingen: Vandenhoeck & Ruprecht, 2017).
Herl, Joseph. *Worship wars in early Lutheranism: choir, congregation and three centuries of conflict* (Oxford: Oxford University Press, 2004).
Hessayon, Ariel. *'Gold tried in the fire': The prophet Theauraujohn Tany and the English Revolution* (Aldershot: Ashgate, 2007).

Hessayon, Ariel. 'The making of Abiezer Coppe', *Journal of Ecclesiastical History* 62:1 (2011), 38-58.
Hessayon, Ariel. 'Abiezer Coppe and the Ranters', in Laura Lunger Knoppers, ed., *The Oxford handbook of literature and the English Revolution* (Oxford: Oxford University Press, 2012), 346-74.
Hessayon, Ariel. 'Winstanley and Baptist thought', *Prose Studies Special Issue: Gerrard Winstanley: Theology, Rhetoric, Politics* 36 (2014), 15-31.
Hessayon, Ariel, ed. *Jane Lead and her transnational legacy* (London: Palgrave Macmillan, 2016).
Heyd, Michael. *Be sober and reasonable: the critique of enthusiasm in the seventeenth and eighteenth centuries* (Leiden: Brill, 1995).
Hill, Christopher, ed. *'The law of freedom' and other writings* (Cambridge: Cambridge University Press, 1973).
Hill, Christopher. *The experience of defeat: Milton and some contemporaries* (London and New York: Verso, 1984).
Hill, Christopher. *The world turned upside down: radical ideas during the English Revolution* (London: Penguin, 2019).
Hinds, Hilary. *God's Englishwomen: seventeenth-century radical sectarian writing and feminist criticism* (Manchester: Manchester University Press, 1996).
Hobby, Elaine. *Virtue of necessity: English women's writing 1649-1688* (London: Virago, 1988).
Holstun, James. *Ehud's dagger: class struggle in the English Revolution* (London and New York: Verso, 2000).
Hughes, Ann. *Gangraena and the struggle for the English Revolution* (Oxford: Oxford University Press, 2004).
Hughes, Ann. *Gender and the English Revolution* (Abingdon: Routledge, 2012).
Hunter, Michael, Giles Mandelbrote, Richard Ovenden, and Nigel Smith, eds. *A radical's books: the library catalogue of Samuel Jeake of Rye, 1623-90* (Woodbridge: Boydell & Brewer, 1999).
Irigaray, Luce. 'Divine women', *Sexes and genealogies* (New York: Columbia University Press, 1993), 55-72.
Jendrysik, Mark Stephen. *Explaining the English Revolution: Hobbes and his contemporaries* (Lanham, MD: Lexington Books, 2002).
Johnson, Elizabeth. *She who is: the mystery of God in feminist theological discourse* (New York: Crossroad, 1992).
Kerr, Jason. 'Elizabeth Attaway, London preacher and theologian, 1645-1646', *The Seventeenth Century* 36:5 (2021), 733-54.
Kishlansky, Mark. *The rise of the New Model Army* (Cambridge: Cambridge University Press, 1979).
Knox, Ronald. *Enthusiasm: a chapter in the history of religion* (New York: Oxford University Press, 1950).
Lake, Peter. *The box-maker's revenge: 'orthodoxy', 'heterodoxy' and the politics of the parish in early Stuart London* (Manchester: Manchester University Press, 2001).
Lamberigts, Mathijs and A.A. Den Hollander, eds. *Lay Bibles in Europe 1450-1800* (Leuven: Leuven University Press, 2006).
Lamm, Julia, ed. *The Wiley-Blackwell companion to Christian mysticism* (Oxford: Blackwell, 2017).
Laurence, Anne. *Parliamentary army chaplains, 1642-1651*, Royal Historical Society studies in history (Woodbridge: Boydell Press, 1992).

Lennon, Kathleen and Margaret Whitford, eds. *Knowing the difference: feminist perspectives in epistemology* (London and New York: Routledge, 1994).
Lindley, Keith. *Popular politics and religion in civil war London* (Brookfield, VT: Scolar Press, 1997).
Lloyd Jones, G. *The discovery of Hebrew in Tudor England: a third language* (Manchester: Manchester University Press, 1983).
Loewenstein, David. *Treacherous faith: the specter of heresy in early modern English literature and culture* (Oxford: Oxford University Press, 2013).
Longfellow, Erica. *Women and religious writing in early modern England* (Cambridge: Cambridge University Press, 2004).
Ludlow, Dorothy. 'Shaking patriarchy's foundations: sectarian women in England, 1641-1700', in Richard L. Greaves, ed., *Triumph over silence: women in Protestant history* (Westport, CN: Greenwood Press, 1985), 93-123.
MacDonald, Gregory, ed. *All shall be well: explorations in universal salvation and Christian theology, from Origen to Moltmann* (Eugene, OR: Wipf & Stock, 2011).
Mack, Phyllis. *Visionary women: ecstatic prophecy in seventeenth-century England* (Berkeley: University of Berkeley Press, 1992).
Manning, Brian, ed. *Politics, religion and the English civil war* (London: Edward Arnold, 1973).
Marsh, Christopher. *The Family of Love in English society 1550-1630* (Cambridge: Cambridge University Press, 1994).
Marsh, Christopher. '"Godlie matrons" and "loose-bodied dames": heresy and gender in the Family of Love', in David Loewenstein and John Marshall, eds., *Heresy, literature and politics in early modern English culture* (Cambridge: Cambridge University Press, 2006), 59-81.
McClymond, Michael J. *The Devil's redemption: a new history and interpretation of Christian universalism* (Grand Rapids, MI: Baker, 2018).
McDowell, Nicholas. *The English radical imagination: culture, religion, and Revolution, 1640-1660* (Oxford: OUP, 2003).
McGinn, Bernard, ed. *Meister Eckhart and the Beguine mystics: Hadewijch of Brabant, Mechthild of Magdeburg and Marguerite Porete* (New York: Bloomsbury, 1997).
McGinn, Bernard. *The varieties of vernacular mysticism (1350-1550)* (New York: Crossroad, 2012).
McGregor, J.F. 'The Ranters, 1649-60'. Unpublished B.Litt Thesis (Oxford: University of Oxford, 1969).
McRandal, Janice, ed. *Sarah Coakley and the future of systematic theology* (Minneapolis, MN: Fortress, 2018).
McShane, Angela. *Political broadside ballads of seventeenth-century England: a critical bibliography* (London: Pickering & Chatto, 2011).
McShane, Angela. 'Recruiting citizens for soldiers in seventeenth-century English ballads', *Journal of Early Modern History* 15 (2011), 105-38.
Mercedes, Anna. *Power for: feminism and Christ's self-giving* (London and New York: T & T Clark, 2011).
Michaud, Derek. *Reason turned into sense: John Smith on spiritual sensation*, Studies in philosophical theology 62 (Leuven: Peeters, 2017).
Milton, Anthony. *England's second Reformation: the battle for the Church of England* (Cambridge: Cambridge University Press, 2021).
Mortimer, Sarah. *Reason and religion in the English Revolution: the challenge of Socinianism* (Cambridge: Cambridge University Press, 2010).

Morton, A.L. *The world of the Ranters: religious radicalism in the English Revolution* (London: Lawrence and Wishart, 1970).
Murray, Mary. *The law of the father? Patriarchy in the transition from feudalism to capitalism* (London and New York: Routledge, 1995).
Nuttall, Geoffrey. *The Holy Spirit in Puritan faith and experience* (Chicago: University of Chicago Press edition, 1992).
Ostovich, Helen and Elizabeth Sauer, eds. *Reading early modern women: an anthology of texts in manuscript and print* (New York and London: Routledge, 2004).
Ozment, Steven. *Mysticism and dissent: religious ideology and social protest in the sixteenth century* (New Haven, CT: Yale University Press, 1973).
Ozment, Steven. 'Mysticism, nominalism, and dissent', in Charles Trinkaus and Heiko Oberman, eds., *The pursuit of holiness in the late Middle Ages and Renaissance* (Leiden: Brill, 1973), 67–92.
Ozment, Steven. *When fathers ruled: family life in Reformation Europe* (Cambridge, MA: Harvard University Press, 1983).
Pal, Carol. *Republic of women: rethinking the republic of letters* (Cambridge: Cambridge University Press, 2012).
Pennington, Madeleine. *Quakers, Christ, and the Enlightenment* (Oxford: Oxford University Press, 2021).
Po-chia Hsia, R., ed. *The German people and the Reformation* (New York: Cornell University Press, 1988).
Poor, Sara. 'Mechthild von Magdeburg, gender and the "unlearned tongue"', *Journal of Medieval and Early Modern Studies* 31:2 (2001), 213–50.
Poor, Sara S. and Smith, Nigel, eds. *Mysticism and reform, 1400–1750* (Notre Dame, IN: University of Notre Dame Press, 2015).
Purkiss, Diane. 'Producing the voice, consuming the body: women prophets of the seventeenth century', in Isobel Grundy and Susan Wiseman, eds., *Women, writing, history 1640–1740* (Athens, GA: University of Georgia Press, 1993), 139–58.
Purkiss, Diane. *Literature, gender, and politics during the English Civil War* (Cambridge: Cambridge University Press, 2005).
Rattansi, P.M. 'Paracelsus and the Puritan revolution', *Ambix* 11:1 (1963), pp. 24–32.
Raymond, Joad. *Milton's angels: the early modern imagination* (Oxford: Oxford University Press, 2010).
Reay, Barry. *The Quakers and the English Revolution* (New York: St Martin's Press, 1985).
Roper, Lyndal. *The holy household: women and morals in Reformation Augsburg* (Oxford: Clarendon Press, 1989).
Rublack, Ulinka. *Reformation Europe*, 2nd ed. (Cambridge: Cambridge University Press, 2017).
Ryrie, Alec. *Protestants: the radicals who made the modern world* (London: HarperCollins, 2017).
Sacks, David Harris. *The widening gate: Bristol and the Atlantic economy, 1450–1700* (Berkeley: University of California Press, 1992).
Saiving, Valerie. 'The human situation: a feminine view', *Journal of Religion* 40 (1960), 100–12.
Salters, R.B. *Jonah and Lamentations* (Sheffield: Sheffield Academic Press, 1994).
Schochet, Gordon. *The authoritarian family and political attitudes in seventeenth-century England: patriarchalism in political thought* (New Brunswick, NJ: Transaction, 1988).
Schubert, Anselm. 'Celestial sex: Paracelsus and the teaching of the "heavenly flesh" of Christ' (trans. James Stayer), *Church History and Religious Culture* 101 (2021), 194–213.

Schüssler Fiorenza, Elisabeth. *Jesus, Miriam's child, Sophia's prophet: critical issues in feminist christology* (New York: Continuum, 1995).

Scott, Tom. *Thomas Müntzer: theology and revolution in the German Reformation* (New York: St Martin's Press, 1989).

Smith, Hilda. *All men and both sexes: gender, politics, and the false universal in England, 1640-1832* (University Park: Pennsylvania University Press, 2002).

Smith, Nigel. *Perfection proclaimed: language and literature in English radical religion, 1640-60* (Oxford: Oxford University Press, 1989).

Smith, Nigel. *Literature and Revolution in England, 1640-1660* (New Haven and London: Yale University Press, 1994).

Snyder, C. Arnold and Linda Huebert Hecht, eds. *Profiles of Anabaptist women: sixteenth-century reforming pioneers* (Waterloo, Ontario: Wilfrid Laurier University Press, 1996).

Soskice, Janet. *The kindness of God: metaphor, gender and religions language* (Oxford: Oxford University Press, 2007).

Spink, Ian. *Henry Lawes: Cavalier songwriter* (Oxford: Oxford University Press, 2000).

Stanton, Matthew. *Liturgy and identity: London Baptists and the hymn-singing controversy* (Oxford: Centre for Baptist Studies, 2022).

Summit, Jennifer. *Memory's library: medieval books in early modern England* (Chicago: University of Chicago Press, 2008).

Szulakowska, Urszula. *The alchemical Virgin Mary in the religious and political context of the Renaissance* (Newcastle: Cambridge Scholars Publishing, 2017).

Temple, Liam Peter. *Mysticism in early modern England* (Woodbridge: Boydell Press, 2019).

Tolmie, Murray. 'Thomas Lambe, soapboiler, and Thomas Lambe, merchant, General Baptists', *Baptist Quarterly* 27:1 (1977), 4-13.

Toscano, Margaret and Isabel Moreira. *Hell and its afterlife: historical and contemporary perspectives* (Farnham and Burlington, VT: Ashgate, 2010).

Versluis, Arthur. *Wisdom's children: a Christian esoteric tradition* (New York: SUNY, 1999).

Waite, Gary K. *David Joris and Dutch Anabaptism, 1524-1543* (Waterloo, Ontario: Wilfred Laurier, 1990).

Waite, Gary K., ed. *The Anabaptist writings of David Joris* (Waterloo, Ontario: Herald Press, 1994).

Walker, D. P. *The decline of hell: seventeenth-century discussions of eternal torment* (Chicago: University of Chicago Press, 1964).

Ward, Graham. *Christ and culture* (Oxford: Blackwell, 2005).

Watson, J.R. *The English hymn: a critical and historical study* (Oxford: Oxford University Press, 1997).

Watt, Diane. *Secretaries of God: women prophets in late medieval and early modern England* (Cambridge: Brewer, 1997).

Webster, Charles. *The great instauration: science, medicine and reform, 1626-1660* (London: Duckworth, 1975).

Webster, Charles. *From Paracelsus to Newton: magic and the making of modern science* (Cambridge: Cambridge University Press, 1982).

Webster, Tom. *Godly clergy in early Stuart England: the Caroline Puritan movement, c. 1620-1643* (Cambridge: Cambridge University Press, 2003).

White, Micheline. 'Protestant women's writing and congregational psalm singing: from the song of the exiled "Handmaid" (1555) to the countess of Pembroke's Psalmes (1599)," *Sidney Journal* 23:1 (2005), 61-82.

Wilson Hayes, T. *Winstanley the Digger: a literary analysis of radical ideas in the English Revolution* (Harvard: Harvard University Press, 1979).

Worden, Blair. *God's instruments: political conduct in the England of Oliver Cromwell* (Oxford: Oxford University Press, 2012).

Zachhuber, Johannes.'Mysticism as a social type of Christianity? Ernst Troeltsch's interpretation in its historical and systematic context', in Louise Nelstrop and Simon Podmore, eds., *Exploring lost dimensions in Christian mysticism: opening to the mystical* (Farnham: Ashgate, 2013), 69–84.

Index

For the benefit of digital users, indexed terms that span two pages (e.g., 52–53) may, on occasion, appear on only one of those pages.

Abbott, Margaret 179
Abingdon 74–5, 157
Achinstein, Sharon 160
Adam 32–3, 36–7, 65
Ainsworth, Henry 28–9, 142
alchemy 31–2, 34–6, 39, 180–4, 190
Anabaptism 2, 57–8, 67–8, 139–40, 164, 184–5
Anderson, Pamela Sue 189
angels 29, 32–3, 36–7, 40–2, 46, 50, 57, 67–9, 103, 137, 149, 186
Anglicans 196
Anselm of Canterbury 23, 121
anti-formalism 2–5, 91–2, 162, 191
antinomianism 2, 7–8, 28n.8, 45, 46, 58–9, 91–2, 113–16, 120, 144, 152, 184
Apocrypha 66, 71, 78
apokatastasis [*see* universal salvation] 63n.46, 65, 77
Aquinas, Thomas 45, 87
Aristotle 31–2, 105–6, 128
Arminianism 59–60, 75
Arrowsmith, John 154
Ashmole, Elias 89, 181n.79
Atkinson, Christopher 154
Attaway, Mistress 10, 69–72, 77–8
August of Anhalt-Plötzkau 179–80, 184
Augustine of Hippo 45, 67–8, 125, 128
Avery, Elizabeth 10, 15–16, 19, 43–4, 73–4, 79, 108–10, 126, 175–8, 193–4

Baillie, Robert 10, 31–2, 70–1
Bakewell, Thomas 58
Baker, Augustine 81–8
Baker, Daniel 163–4
Ball, John 141–2
Ballads 140–1, 145, 149–50, 152, 154
Bampfield, Francis 74–5
Baptists (*see also* Anabaptism, infant baptism) 5, 11, 12–14, 21–2, 31–2, 40–1, 58–61, 67, 78, 99–100, 109–10, 138, 142, 154–5, 161–3
Barber, Edward 58–9
Barclay, Robert 30–1, 88, 94

Barker, Matthew 92–3
Barrow, Henry 142
Barton, William 143, 145
Bathurst, Elizabeth 77–8
Baxter, Richard 32, 50
Beguines 79–80
Belcher, John 74–7
Belcher, Mrs 74–7
Benedictine order 81–2
Benet of Canfield 89, 107
Bernard of Clairvaux 23, 108
Bible
  authority of 19–21, 62–3, 165, 177–8
  interpretation of 19, 55–6, 61–4, 68–70, 76, 78, 108, 138, 165
biblical books
  Exodus 76, 154
  Deuteronomy 68
  Psalms 28–9, 53, 83–4, 124, 138–64
  Song of Songs 45, 53, 83–4, 114
  Isaiah 23, 50–1, 57, 149, 170–2
  Ezekiel 68
  Matthew 23, 65–6, 76, 104
  Luke 23, 76
  1 Corinthians 103–4, 108, 124n.57, 187–8
  Galatians 103–4, 117
  Ephesians 148, 187–8
  1 and 2 Timothy 8–10, 103–4
  Revelation 63–4, 108–9, 146–7, 149, 152, 155–6, 159, 169–70, 173
Biddle, Ester 179
Biddle, John 15–16, 172
Boehme, Jacob 23–4, 32–5, 37–9, 46, 88–9, 93–4, 98, 101–3, 181
Behmenism 2–3, 31–3, 39, 95, 133
Blackborow, Sarah 43, 178–9
Bourne, John 140–1
Boyle, Robert 89, 183
Bradfield Rectory 34–40, 47–8, 94, 157, 183, 190
Brereley, Roger 89n.50, 101–2
Bridge, William 104–5, 110
Bristol 5–6, 13–16, 27, 94, 153, 184–5

218   INDEX

Bromley, Thomas 32, 38–9
Brooks, Thomas 92–4
Butler, Thomas 147–9, 152–3

Calvert, Giles 2–3, 15–16, 28, 30–1, 33, 43, 121, 147–50, 170, 173–4, 180–1
Calvinism 7, 55–60, 64, 92–3, 110, 113, 124, 180
Cambrai, convent at 81–3
Cambridge, University of
  Emmanuel 3n.8, 49–50, 104
  Gonville and Caius 105
Capp, Bernard 57, 74–5, 106
Carr, George 62–3
Cary, Grace 7
Cary, Mary 15–16, 23, 42, 85, 97, 116–17, 120, 161–2, 175–8, 183–4, 193
Caryl, Joseph 92
Casaubon, Meric 193
Catholicism 1–3, 19–20, 80–8, 91–2, 95–8, 107, 121–2, 165–6, 185–6, 193–4, 196–7
Celestial flesh (*see* Christology: heavenly flesh)
Channel, Elinor 18
Charles I 7, 64, 155–6
Cheevers, Sarah 163–4
Cheynell, Francis 28
Chidley, Katherine 7, 10, 15, 175, 193
children
  death of 22, 67–8, 74–5, 78
  nursing of 23, 50–1, 114, 121–5
Christ, Carol 23–4
Christina of Sweden 38–9
Church, Henry 7
Church of the First-born 37–8, 43, 153, 166–7
Church fathers (*see also* Augustine of Hippo; Gregory of Nyssa) 68–9, 94
Churches and congregations
  All Hallows the Great, Upper Thames Street 20, 117, 120, 158–9
  Bell Alley Baptist church, Coleman Street 58–9, 70
  Bell Lane Baptist church, Spitalfields 74–5
  Broadmead Baptist church, Bristol 13–15
  Christ Church, Dublin 107–9, 175
  Glasshouse Yard Baptist church, Clerkenwell 154–5
  St Andrew, Holborn 8
  St Andrew, Kildwick-in-Craven 101–2
  St Ewen, Bristol 14
  St Leonard, Bristol 184
  St Mary, Pirton 58–9
  St Michael, Bassishaw 123–4
  St Michael, Brinkworth 184–5
  St Philip, Bristol 13, 16n.61
  St Thomas the Apostle, Cheapside 146–7
Christology
  heavenly flesh 6, 26–44, 53–4, 177–8, 194–5
Clarkson, Lawrence 5–6, 15–16, 33, 56
Coleman Street 10, 58–9, 71
Collier, Thomas 12–13, 40–1, 147, 153, 178
Comber, Thomas 194
Comenius, John Amos 93
Como, David 2–3, 13, 58–9, 113, 169–70
Congregationalists 13, 15–16, 117–18, 174–5
Conway, Lady Anne 55, 77–8
Cope, Esther 61–2
Coppe, Abiezer 5, 33, 56, 94, 98, 100, 149–51, 156–7
Coppin, Richard 30–1, 56–7, 135, 191, 196
Cordier, Balthasar 92–3
Cotton, John 143
Cotton, Robert 87–8, 181n.79
Cowling, Nicholas 13, 30n.17
Cradock, Walter 5–6, 20, 94, 97–8, 115–20, 124, 174, 185
Crawford, Patricia 17
Cressy, Serenus 81–4, 86–8
Crisp, Tobias 174–5, 184
Crofton, Zachary 111
Croll, Oswald 184
Cromwell, Bridget 105
Cromwell, Oliver 27, 49, 146–7, 159, 196

Davies, Lady Eleanor 7–8, 15, 57–72, 78, 96–7, 128–9, 134, 155–6, 190, 193–4
Davies, Sir John 62–3
Deborah, judge in Israel 14, 154–7, 159–62
De Certeau, Michel 19–21, 81, 84, 166
De Labadie, Jean 165–6
Dell, William 1–3, 5–6, 91–2, 94, 98, 102, 105–7, 111, 114–15, 126, 174–5, 191, 195–6
demons 65, 104
Denne, Henry 58–60
Diggers 56, 58–9, 72, 126–8, 133–4, 137
Dionysius the Areopagite 89, 92–3
dispensational thought 2–5, 39, 41–4, 56, 96–7, 101, 118–19, 121–2, 135, 139–40, 146–7, 150–2, 154–5, 164, 169–72
Drapes, Edward 154–5
Dublin 107–9, 175
Dury, John 88–9, 98–100, 111

Eaton, John 115–16
Ecclesiology 10, 64, 82, 109, 113, 165–92
Edwards, Thomas 5–6, 10, 46, 58–61, 69–72, 78, 91–2, 114, 144, 175, 185

Elizabeth of Bohemia 62
Engelbrecht, Hans 46, 95
enthusiasm 11, 16–17, 19–20, 78, 96, 181, 193–4, 196–7
Erasmus of Rotterdam 106
Erbery, Dorcas 26–31, 35, 194
Erbery, William 5–6, 15, 27–32, 34–5, 38–44, 60, 93–4, 98, 102, 110, 135, 151–3, 172, 174–5, 177, 195–6
eschatology (*see also* dispensational thought) 73–4, 96, 135, 166–7, 169–72, 177–9
Etherington, John 89
Eucharist 2, 5, 42, 115, 150
Evans, Katharine 163–4
Eve 36–8, 65, 69, 100–1, 108, 133
Everard, John 57, 87–9, 92–4, 100–1, 166–7, 169, 180–1
Everlasting Gospel 56, 170–2

Fairfax, Sir Thomas 5, 145, 196
Familism 2–3, 30–2, 34–5, 41, 45–6, 58–9, 89, 91–2, 100–2, 113, 136, 140–1, 148, 164–7, 169–73, 176–80
Farnworth, Richard 97–8, 103–4
Feake, Christopher 85–6, 146–7
Felgenhauer, Paul 32, 46, 88
Feminist theology (*see also* Anderson, Pamela; Hampson, Daphne; Irigaray, Luce; Johnson, Elizabeth; Saiving, Valerie; Schüssler Fiorenza, Elizabeth) 23–4, 37n.64, 40–1, 42n.88, 111–12, 125, 189
Fenwick, Anne 7
Feroli, Teresa 63
Fiennes, William (Lord Saye and Sele) 100
Fifth Monarchists 4, 61, 73–5, 85, 106–7, 116, 120, 135, 138, 146–7, 157–9, 161–2, 183–4, 195
Flavel, Mrs 35–6
Fludd, Robert 181–3
Ford, Simon 46, 185
Foulis, Henry 96
Fox, George 28, 71, 93
Furly, Benjamin 30–1, 91
Franck, Sebastian 89, 139, 180–1
Franklin, William 33–4

Gadbury, John 150, 194
Gadbury, Mary 33–5
Gell, Robert 3n.8, 94
Gentles, Ian 6
Gillespie, Katherine 21–2
Goad, Christopher 100–1, 111

Goodwin, John 58–61, 146, 174
Goodwin, Thomas 5–6
Gouldbourne, Ruth 31
Great Yarmouth 104, 110
Gregory of Nyssa 51
Greville, Robert (Lord Brooke) 99–101
Grindletonians 89n.51, 101
Gustavus Adolphus 88

Hampson, Daphne 40, 189
Harriman, Anne 12–13
Hartlib, Samuel 32, 88–9, 183–4
Hastings, Henry 66–7
Hastings, Lucy 66–7
Hassard, Dorothy 5–6, 13–15, 184–6
Hassard, Matthew 14
hell 44–7, 55–8, 64–9, 71–4, 101, 109, 111, 117
Herp, Hendrik 84
heresy 10, 15–16, 34, 43, 59–60, 66, 68–70, 78–80, 89, 100, 139–40, 166, 172, 175, 193–4
Hermes Trismegistus 89
Hessayon, Ariel 30, 72, 100, 136n.118
Heylyn, Peter 63, 194
High Commission 57, 64, 194
Hill, Christopher 5, 56, 130, 170–1, 190
Hobby, Elaine 127, 130, 133
Hobson, Paul 110
Hoffmann, Melchior 31, 42, 139–40
Hutchinson, Anne 7, 114
Hughes, Ann 22
Hymns 138–64

infant baptism 67–8
Ireton, Henry 105
Irigaray, Luce 23

James I 62, 86, 188
Jeake, Samuel 91
Jessey, Henry 21, 34, 118–19
Jesuits 92–3
Joachim of Fiore 172
Johnson, Elizabeth 23, 37n.64
Jones, Sarah 29
Joris, David 139–40
Julian of Norwich 23, 55–6, 61, 82, 121

Karlstadt, Andreas Bodenstein von 80
Keith, George 94
Keith, James 48
Kelly, Abel 13
Kempis, Thomas à 88, 93

Kishlansky, Mark 6
Knollys, Hanserd 162–3
Knox, Ronald A. 16–17

Lambe, Thomas 58–60, 69–71, 77
Lambert, John 91, 101–2, 110
Laud, William 7–8, 57, 62–4, 194
Lead, Jane 48–9, 55–6, 63n.46, 77–8, 94–5, 170n.13
Levellers 5–7, 13, 15–16, 27, 57–9, 147n.58, 196
Lewin, John 30
Lichfield 7–8, 64, 155
Llwyd, Morgan 145
Love, Christopher 2
Lutherans 32, 46, 88, 98, 180
Luther, Martin 80, 108, 115, 144

Mack, Phyllis 17–18, 139, 197
Maddocks, John 185
Makin, Bathsua 99
Marsh, Christopher 18, 141
Marshall, Stephen 67
Marsin, M. 196
Mary, mother of Jesus 24, 31–2, 37–8, 66, 95, 100, 155–6, 186, 197
  Mariology 24, 31–2, 34–8, 100, 186
Mary Magdalen 20, 65, 69, 96, 108, 123–4, 162, 186–7
Mary of Egypt 95–6
maternal metaphors 23, 50–1, 57, 76, 121–5, 197–8
Mather, Cotton 109
McDowell, Nicholas 98, 107
Menzies, John 193
Milton, Anthony 2–3
Milton, John 10, 16, 37, 70, 145n.48, 172
Moore, Dorothy 99
More, Gertrude 81–5
More, Henry 129, 181
Morton, A.L. 56, 170
Muggletonians 194
Münster 139
Müntzer, Thomas 80
mystical marriage 114–22
mysticism 21, 35, 46, 50, 79–98, 101, 110–13, 123, 149–50, 167–9, 179–80, 193, 197

New Model Army 1, 5–6, 27, 94
Nayler, James 27–8, 30, 43, 93, 153, 166n.1, 191, 195–6
Nedham, Marchamont 158

New England 7, 102, 108n.141, 114, 142–3
  Boston 7, 143
Nicholas of Cusa 45, 89, 93, 102
Niclaes, Hendrik 93, 140–1, 170–1, 181
nicodemism 140, 169
Noble, Marie 8
Nominated Assembly 3, 11

Oldenberg, Henry 183
ordinances 2–3, 21, 70, 91–2, 101, 110, 117, 123–4, 138, 142–3, 146–7, 150, 165–7, 172–3, 175–9, 187, 190
Origen of Alexandria 37, 45, 47–8, 51–2, 55–7, 65, 68–9, 72, 78, 94
Osiander, Andreas 166
Owen, John 110
Oxford 20, 28, 98, 109–10, 190
Ozment, Steven 167–9

Palmer, Anthony 49
Paracelsus 24, 31–2, 34–5, 37–8, 54, 94, 102–3, 179–81, 184–6
Paracelsianism 3, 28, 30–2, 37–9, 42, 101–2, 165–7, 179–84, 190
Parker, Robert 16, 109
Parker, Thomas 109
Parliament 1–3, 11, 15, 21, 27, 57–8, 92–3, 96, 155, 189
  House of Commons 1–2, 11, 15, 92–3, 98
  House of Lords 143, 150n.76
Partridge, John 150
Pears, Iain 26
Pendarves, Thomasina 149, 156
Penington, Mary 110, 153
Pennington, Madeleine 30–1
Peter, Hugh 147
Pharisees 124
Philadelphian Society 71, 195
philosopher's stone 36, 183–4
Phoenix, Anne (*see* Fenwick, Anne)
Pinnell, Henry 5–6, 13, 46, 167, 184–8
Pirton, Hertfordshire 58, 129
Platonism 3n.8, 50–1, 78, 129–30
Pocock, Mary 36, 157, 190
Poole, Elizabeth 15, 157
Pordage, John 32–40, 46–8, 77, 94–5, 98, 149, 157, 169–70, 181–3, 190–1, 195
Pordage, Mary 36, 195
Pounset, John 11–12
Powell, Vavasor 59n.27, 61, 107, 146
Presbyterians 1–2, 8–12, 28, 31, 43, 46, 59–60, 67, 70–1, 73, 91–2, 111, 126, 141, 154, 174–5, 190

Prier, Robert 123–5
Prynne, William 6, 8–10
prophecy 3–5, 8, 11–13, 15–19, 23, 28–9, 32–3, 42–4, 48–50, 55–6, 61–6, 69–70, 85–6, 93–5, 116–17, 120, 138–40, 147, 149–59, 163–4, 169–70, 176, 183–4, 190–6
Puritanism 7, 13, 15–16, 21, 53, 57, 66, 89, 109–10, 113, 141–2, 166–7, 174, 190

Quakers 3–4, 11, 14–18, 26–31, 39–40, 43, 77–8, 88, 91–4, 97, 100, 103–4, 110, 135, 144, 151, 153–4, 163–4, 178–80, 191, 193–7
quietism 141, 165–6, 169
Quintyne, Michael 173–4

Rabbinical interpretation 53
Radical Reformation (*see also* Anabaptism; Franck, Sebastian; Joris, David; Niclaes, Hendrik; Schwenckfeld, Caspar) 21, 28, 30–2, 42, 80–1, 88–9, 113, 139–41, 149–50, 165–72, 179–81
Randall, Giles 89–91, 107, 180–1, 191
Ranters 5, 56, 127–8, 135, 150–2, 194
Reay, Barry 17
resurrection 26–7, 29, 34–7, 39, 41–2, 45–6, 52, 66, 73–4, 96, 108, 135, 162, 186–7
Rich, Henry (Earl of Holland) 100
Rich, Robert 93–4, 135, 166n.1, 191
Rigge, Ambrose 94, 166n.1
Roach, Richard 78
Rogers, John 107–12, 172–3, 175, 182–3, 193–5
Rogers, Timothy 195
Roper, Lyndal 168
Rous, Francis 143–4
Rutherford, Samuel 2, 45–6, 91–2, 114–15
Ryrie, Alec 113

Saiving, Valerie 125
Saltmarsh, John 2–3, 5–6, 16, 21–2, 40–1, 61, 91–4, 98, 102, 114–16, 118–19, 124, 172, 185–7, 191, 196
Schubert, Anselm 31
Schüssler Fiorenza, Elizabeth 8, 37n.64
Schwenckfeld, Caspar 31–2
Sedgwick, William 5–6, 34, 93–4, 167, 174–5, 185–92
seekers to 3–5, 56, 149
Shipton, Mother 194, 196

Sibbes, Richard 174
Simmonds, Martha 28
Simons, Menno 31
Smith, Nigel 56, 135n.114, 138
Smyth, John 142
Sophia and sophiology 23–4, 37–8, 122n.47, 182–3
Sophronius 95
Sowle, Tace 195
Speed, Thomas 16
spiritual senses 26, 45–54
Sprigg, Joshua 94, 174
Starbuck, William 145
Sterry, Peter 49–53, 56, 78, 100, 174
Stillingfleet, Edward 87, 193–4
Sutton, Katherine 162–3
Sweet Singers of Israel 150

Tauler, Johannes 81, 89, 94, 180
Theologia germanica 89, 91, 94, 180
Thirty Years War 46, 54, 88, 95
Tillam, Thomas 139
Thomas, Keith 6–7, 17
Thurloe, John 11, 146n.54
Trapnel, Anna 18, 23, 73, 86, 114, 120–6, 138, 157–62, 176, 194
Trinity 31–3, 38, 52, 121–2, 140, 172, 187–8
Troeltsch, Ernst 167

Unbelief 72–3, 125–6
universal salvation 15, 22, 55–78, 135, 197–8
Ussher, James 188

Vane, Sir Henry 48–50, 52–3, 93, 100, 111, 122, 135
van Schurman, Anna Maria 99
virginity 34–8, 47, 131
visions (*see* prophecy) 7, 15, 34, 39, 45, 63, 66, 94–6, 119–20, 194

Wales 38, 41n.85, 120
Walker, Susan 7
Wallenstein, Albrecht von 88
Warner, James 74–7
Warren, Elizabeth 15
Wastfield, Robert 30
Watt, Diane 61
Webster, John 5, 94, 101–4, 111, 116–17, 181, 191, 195–6
Weigel, Valentin 32, 94, 180–1
Westminster Assembly 2, 104, 143–4

Weyer, Matthias 88
White, Jeremiah 49n.123, 56, 78
Whitehead, George 154
Wight, Sarah 5, 15, 18, 21–2, 25, 34, 48, 79, 118–22, 125, 193
Wild, Johann 186
Williams, Roger 102
Wilson Haynes, T. 129

Winstanley, Gerrard 22, 48, 55–8, 72, 78, 126–37, 151, 174, 181
Worcester, Battle of 145–6
Worthington, John 88

Yeamans, William 16
Yemans, Anne 15–16, 42–3, 72–3, 121, 139, 175–8